T0323867

Work and Labor Relations in the Construction Industry

The need for a skilled, motivated and effective workforce is fundamental to the creation of the built environment across the world. Known in so many places for a tendency to informal and casual working practices, for the sometimes abusive use of migrant labor, for gendered male employment and for a neglect of the essentials of health and safety, the industry, its managers and its workforce face multiple challenges. This book brings an international lens to address those challenges, looking particularly at the diverse ways in which answers have been found to manage safe and productive employment practices and effective employment relations within the framework of client demands for timely and cost-effective project completions. While context, history and contractual frameworks may all militate against a careful attention to human resource issues, this makes them even more deserving of attention.

Work and Labor Relations in the Construction Industry aims to share understanding of best practice in the industries associated with construction and related activities, recognizing that effective work organization and good standards of employee relations will vary from one location to another. It acknowledges the real difficulties encountered by workers in parts of the developing world and the quest for improvement and awareness of some of the worst hazards and current practices. This book is both critical and analytical in approach and seeks to alert readers to the need for change. Aimed at addressing practical issues within the construction industry from a theoretical and empirical standpoint, it will be of value to those interested in the built environment, employment relations and human resource management.

Dale Belman is Professor in the School of Human Resources & Labor Relations at Michigan State University, USA.

Janet Druker is Emeritus Professor in the Business School at the University of Westminster London, UK. She is also a fellow of the Chartered Institute of Personnel and Development.

Geoffrey White is Emeritus Professor of Human Resource Management in the Business Faculty at the University of Greenwich, UK. He is also a fellow of the Chartered Institute of Personnel and Development.

Routledge Research in Employment Relations

Series editors: Rick Delbridge and Edmund Heery
Cardiff Business School, UK.

Aspects of the employment relationship are central to numerous courses at both undergraduate and postgraduate level.

Drawing from insights from industrial relations, human resource management and industrial sociology, this series provides an alternative source of research-based materials and texts, reviewing key developments in employment research.

Books published in this series are works of high academic merit, drawn from a wide range of academic studies in the social sciences.

For more information about this series, please visit:
www.routledge.com/sport/series/RRSH

Work and Labor Relations in the Construction Industry

An International Perspective

Edited by
Dale Belman,
Janet Druker, and
Geoffrey White

Routledge
Taylor & Francis Group

NEW YORK AND LONDON

First published 2021
by Routledge
52 Vanderbilt Avenue, New York, NY 10017

and by Routledge
2 Park Square, Milton Park, Abingdon, Oxon, OX14 4RN

*Routledge is an imprint of the Taylor & Francis Group, an
informa business*

Library of Congress Cataloging-in-Publication Data
Names: Belman, Dale, editor. | Druker, J. (Jan), editor. |
White, Geoff, 1949- editor.
Title: Work and labor relations in the construction industry : an
international perspective / edited by Dale Belman, Janet Druker,
and Geoffrey White.
Description: New York, NY : Routledge, 2021. |
Includes bibliographical references and index. |
Identifiers: LCCN 2020037369 (print) | LCCN 2020037370 (ebook) |
ISBN 9781138364783 (hardback) | ISBN 9780429431135 (ebook)
Subjects: LCSH: Construction industry--Personnel management. |
Construction workers--Employees. |
Construction workers--Employment. | Industrial relations.
Classification: LCC HD9715.A2 .W655 2021 (print) |
LCC HD9715.A2 (ebook) | DDC 331.7/624--dc23
LC record available at https://lccn.loc.gov/2020037369
LC ebook record available at https://lccn.loc.gov/2020037370

ISBN: 978-1-138-36478-3 (hbk)
ISBN: 978-0-367-69093-9 (pbk)
ISBN: 978-0-429-43113-5 (ebk)

Typeset in Sabon
by MPS Limited, Dehradun

Contents

List of Tables

List of Figures

Acknowledgments

We would like to thank all the authors of the chapters for their contribution to this book. Without their enthusiasm for the project and forbearance through the editing process, the work of the editors would have been much harder. We would especially like to thank Professor George Ofori for his suggestions and encouragement. We are also grateful to Pete Burgess for translation of the original text of chapter 5 and further suggestions. Many other people have contributed through their knowledge and experience and we are appreciative of the time given by those who participated in research, either through interviews or by responding to surveys. This included senior construction industry figures, managers, professionals and union officers, as well as workers on-site. Without their insights, this would have been a poorer book. We would finally like to thank Amy Wells for Zoom sessions and the editorial team at Routledge for encouraging the book proposal and the advice and support they gave over the editorial period.

About the editors

Dale Belman is Professor in the School of Human Resources and Labor Relations at Michigan State University. He conducts research on unions and labor market regulation. His book *What Does the Minimum Wage Do?* (Upjohn Institute for Employment Research 2015) reviews the last decade of research on the effect of the minimum wage on employment, hours, earnings and other outcomes. Belman has also published widely on the construction industry, truckers and trucking, public-sector employment and minimum wage and low wage work. He received his master's and doctoral degrees at the University of Wisconsin, Madison and his bachelor's degree from Bowdoin College. He is president of the Institute for Construction Economics Research (ICERES). He was also, until recently, a visiting professor at the University of Greenwich, London.

Janet Druker is Emeritus Professor of Human Resource Management at the University of Westminster Business School, where she has been based since 2011. With a PhD in Industrial Relations from the University of Warwick, her interest in the construction industry was fostered when she worked as head of research for the trade union organizing construction workers in the UK. After working in trade union education, she subsequently worked at the University of Greenwich Business School and moved on to management roles, including Head of the Business School at the University of East London, UK and Pro-Vice Chancellor at Canterbury Christ Church University UK. Current research interests include international industrial relations, reward management and corporate responsibility. During her career she has published in a range of journals, including the *British Journal of Industrial Relations, Industrial Relations Journal, Human Resource Management Journal* and *Construction Management and Economics,* and contributed to a number of books on HRM in the construction industry and reward management. She is also a fellow of the Chartered Institute of Personnel and Development.

Geoffrey White is Emeritus Professor of Human Resource Management at the University of Greenwich Business School in London, UK. He was until 2010 director of research in the Business School and is a member of the University's Centre for Research in Employment and Work (CREW). Prior to becoming an academic, Geoff worked for over 10 years for a major pay research organization, Incomes Data Services. He has written widely on work and employment issues, especially reward management, public sector pay and HRM in construction and was joint author for the first three editions of the Chartered Institute of Personnel and Development (CIPD) book, *Reward Management: Alternatives, Consequences and Contexts*. He has acted as an advisor on pay systems to the UK Low Pay Commission, The Local Government Pay Commission, the NHS Staff Council, the Hong Kong Government and the Universities and Colleges Employers Association. He was, until 2018, a Visiting Professor at Hong Kong Baptist University. He is also a fellow of the Chartered Institute of Personnel and Development.

List of Contributors

Fida Afiouni is an Associate Professor of Human Resource Management at the Olayan School of Business, American University of Beirut, Lebanon. She obtained her PhD in Human Resource Management and Industrial Relations from Paris 1 Panthéon-Sorbonne University and was the recipient of the Sharjah award for the best doctoral thesis in administrative sciences in the Arab world granted by ARADO (The Arab Administrative Development Organization). Her current research focuses on the interplay of HRM, careers and gender in the Middle East and North Africa region. She has published in the *Journal of Vocational Behavior, Human Resource Management Journal (HRMJ)* and *Business Research Quarterly*. She is an associate editor of the *International Journal of Human Resource Management* and an editorial board member on HRMJ. Fida serves as an ad-hoc consultant with the International Labour Organization (ILO) and the Office for Economic Cooperation and Development (OECD) on topics related to gender inclusive workplaces.

Divine Ahadzie, PhD, MGIOC, CMCIH (UK) works in the Centre for Settlements Studies, College of Art and Built Environment, Kwame Nkrumah University of Science and Technology, Kumasi, Ghana. He is Associate Professor and head of department. Divine has expertise in areas including project management, housing, flood risk management and informal construction skills. He researches in higher education and in civil engineering and is currently focusing on *A Model for Predicting the Performance of Project Managers in Mass House Building Projects in Ghana*.

Jens Arnholtz is an Associate Professor at the Employment Relations Research Center (FAOS), University of Copenhagen. He has a PhD in Sociology from the University of Copenhagen. His research interests are in the field of employment relations, with a special focus on cross-border labor mobility, posting of workers and Europeanization of national labor market institutions. His research has been published in journals such as the *British Journal of Industrial Relations, Work,*

Employment and Society, *European Journal of Industrial Relations* and *Economic and Industrial Democracy*. He recently published a co-edited volume entitled *Posted Work in the European Union: The Political Economy of Free Movement*.

Christian Beck is union secretary and head of the Construction Department at Industriegewerkschaft Bauen-Agrar-Umwelt (IG BAU). Born in 1985 he joined the union when he started his apprenticeship as a real estate agent. Since 2007 he was national youth secretary of the union and ran a program to build union structures in small companies. He has held his current position since 2017.

Olga Cretu is a lecturer in the Department of Management and Human Resources at Coventry University London since May 2020. She has previously taught at Westminster and Middlesex University Business Schools. She completed her PhD at Middlesex University in 2017 investigating the impact of migration, family and class on women's career strategizing across borders. Olga has worked on several research projects – *Trade Unions in Post-socialist Society: Overcoming the State Socialist Legacy?* (INTAS 2004–07); *Transition in Question: Case Studies of Labour Relations in CIS Selected Companies* (Warwick 2005–07) and *International Migration and Labour Turnover* (Padua 2010–13). Her research interests include working lives, career trajectories, migration and gender in Europe and the former Soviet Union. Her publications have featured, among others, in *Sociology*, *Studies of Transition States and Societies* and the *British Journal of Industrial Relations*.

Yaw A. Debrah (BA, MA, Simon Fraser University, Canada; PhD, Warwick University, UK; GIPM, UK) is a Professor of International Human Resource Management and International Business, Swansea University, UK. Prior to his current position he worked at Brunel University, London; Cardiff University; Nanyang Technological University, Singapore; University of Wisconsin-Madison, US and Cape Coast University, Ghana. He has been a visiting scholar at Hong Kong Baptist University; visiting professor at University of Education, Winneba, Ghana; Ghana Institute of Management and Public Administration; and China–Europe International Business School, Accra Campus. His work has appeared in many journals, including *Human Relations, Journal of Applied Psychology, Journal of Organizational Behaviour, Group and Organization Management, Tourism Management, Industrial and Corporate Change, International Journal of Human Resource Management, Journal of World Business, World Development, Journal of International Management, Asia Pacific Journal of Management* and *Thunderbird International Business Review*. Yaw is on the editorial board of *International Journal of Human Resource Management* and *African Journal of Economic and Management Studies*. He is also on the International Advisory Board of the *African Review of Economics and Finance*. His publications have been used by the IMF and the World Bank in their dealings with African governments. Yaw has a wide network of links with policy makers and practitioners in industry in Africa.

Carlos Alberto Diehl is a chemical engineer (UFRGS – Federal University of Rio Grande do Sul, 1993), with a PhD in Production Engineering from the Federal University of Santa Catarina with a sandwich doctorate from HEC Montreal in 2004. He is currently in post-doctoral studies (CNPq) in Accounting at the Universidad de Málaga, Spain. He is full professor II (EGN) of Graduate Programs in Accounting Sciences and in Industrial Engineering at the University of Vale do Rio dos Sinos (UNISINOS), leader of the research group Contest in CNPq and official guest of the Universidad Nacional de Rosario (Argentina). He is co-author of 10 books, including *Environmental Management – Incentives, Risks and Costs*; *Cost Management: An Integrated Approach between Accounting, Engineering and Administration*; *Purchase – Elements for the Negotiation Game*; *Accounting Education: Teaching and Research Topics*; *Accounting Catch-ball (Governance and Accountability in Sports Entities)*; *Corporate Governance* and *Value Creation*. He is also the editor of *Strategic Administration – Managing Organizational Competitiveness*. He has held a CNPq Productivity Scholarship (PQ) since 2012.

Christian Lyhne Ibsen is Assistant Professor at the School of Human Resources and Labor Relations at Michigan State University and Associate Professor at FAOS at the University of Copenhagen, where he also earned a PhD in Sociology in 2013. His research falls within the fields of comparative political economy, industrial relations and economic sociology. His research has focused on the development of collective bargaining systems in Northern Europe from a historical institutionalist perspective and the trends in trade union membership using Danish administrative data. His work has been published in journals such as *World Politics, Socio-Economic Review, Human Resource Management Journal, British Journal of Industrial Relations, Politics and Society, Cambridge Journal of Economics, European Sociological Review, European Journal of Industrial Relations* and *International Journal of Human Resource Management*. Christian currently serves on the editorial board of *Journal of Industrial Relations* and on the advisory board for *Global Labour Journal*.

Samar Kleib is a research assistant at the Olayan School of Business, American University of Beirut. She holds a Master's degree in Business Management and Marketing from the Lebanese University. She is a cofounder of a nanotechnology startup that got the best innovation award across the Middle East and North Africa in Stars of Science innovative reality TV show. Her research interests revolve around HRM practices in the Middle East.

Susan McGrath-Champ is Associate Professor in the Work and Organizational Studies discipline at the University of Sydney Business School, Australia. She has a PhD from Macquarie University. Her broad research interests include the geographical aspects of the world of work, employment relations and international human resource management. Susan's research portfolio includes employment, skills and training in the construction industry, the effects of competition and privatization on school teachers' working and employment conditions, organization's safety and security policies for international staff, gender pay equity and employment conditions within global production networks. She is lead editor of the pioneering *Handbook of Employment and Society: Working Space*. Her work has been published in a range of international journals and is regularly presented at national and international conferences.

Claudio Morrison is a senior research fellow at Middlesex University Business School (London UK). He previously held a British academy post-doctoral fellowship in the Sociology Department of Warwick University where he obtained his PhD. Claudio's area of expertise is comparative employment relations. His ethnographic research in the former Soviet Union focuses on industrial restructuring, workplace relations and management change. His current research includes engaged research methods as well as labor mobility, industrial relations and organizational change in post-socialist societies. His publications have featured in *Europe–Asia Studies, Post-Communist Economies*, the *British Journal of Industrial Relations, Industrial Relations* and *Work, Employment and Society*. He is the author of *A Russian Factory Enters the Market Economy* (Routledge, 2012).

George Ofori is Dean of the School of the Built Environment and Architecture at London South Bank University. He specializes in Construction Management and Economics, at the project, company and industry levels, and his main subject of research is the improvement of the capacity and capability of the construction industry, especially in developing countries. Professor Ofori was educated at the University of Science and Technology in Kumasi, Ghana, where he obtained a BSc (Building Technology in Quantity Surveying). He worked briefly in that university as a teaching assistant before traveling to the UK to study for an MSc (Building Economics and Management) degree at University College London, from where he also obtained a PhD in 1981. He was subsequently awarded a DSc degree by the University of London in 1998. Professor Ofori is a fellow of the Ghana Academy of Arts and Sciences. From 1983 to 2017 he was employed by the National University of Singapore, where he was promoted to full professor in 1999 and to head of the Department of Building for five years. He has been a consultant to many governments and international agencies on construction industry development. Amongst many publications, he was the editor of *Contemporary issues in construction in developing countries* (2012).

Russell Ormiston is an Associate Professor of economics at Allegheny College in Meadville, Pennsylvania and is president of the Institute for Construction Economic Research (ICERES). His PhD is from Michigan State University. His research addresses labor market issues in the construction industry, including the effects of prevailing wage laws and the incidence of worker misclassification. Dr Ormiston's research has appeared in *Industrial Relations, Labor Studies Journal, Journal of Labor Research* and *Work and Occupations*. He is also the lead author of a chapter on the residential construction industry in the book, 'Creating Good Jobs: An Industry-Based Approach', published by MIT Press in 2020.

Marcella Soares Piccoli, MSc, is a civil engineering graduate from the Federal University of Rio Grande do Sul (Brazil, 2011). She has practical experience in Production Engineering, with an emphasis on Quality Control and Supply Chain management and has a Master's in Production Engineering from the Federal University of Rio Grande do Sul (Brazil, 2014)/CAPES Scholarship. Currently, she is studying Production Engineering as a PhD student at the University of Vale do Rio dos Sinos (UNISINOS), conducting research on business strategy and the value chain within the construction industry. She is currently a visiting researcher at the University of Greenwich Business School. She has worked with budgeting and technical proposals for industrial and commercial construction. She worked on several complex construction projects as a senior civil engineer for over nine years, in addition to having worked on pre-construction projects, compatibility and optimization of costs with different construction alternatives. Marcella is currently participating in the Contest (Implementation and Strategic Control) research group as a PhD student at UNISINOS.

Hernán Mario Ruggirello holds a Bachelor in Sociology degree from Buenos Aires University Faculty of Social Sciences (UBA). He is currently the coordinator of social research projects in the Department of Social Research of the Unión Obrera de la Construcción de la Republica Argentina (UOCRA) in Buenos Aires, where he takes overall responsibility for the direction and coordination of research projects. He has published widely, including the following: *Technological Innovation and its Impact on Occupational Qualifications in the Construction Sector* (2018); *Labor Migration in Argentina: Migrations, Labor Informality, Social Security and Tripartite Actions* (ILO Office, Argentina, 2015); and *Child Labor and Forced Labor* (ILO, 2014).

Ekaterina Serezhkina is a senior lecturer in the Department of Sociology of the National Research University – Higher School of Economics (HSE) of Moscow (RF) where she completed her PhD in 2016. Her academic interests include sociological research methods (cross-cultural analysis, qualitative and case-study approaches), sociology of organizations and labor relations. Her current research is a comparative case study of the IT labor markets in Russia and France, focusing on workplace stress and stress management. She has published in *Sotsiologicheskie Issledovaniia* (Sociological Studies), the *Rossiiskii Zhurnal Menedzhmenta* (Russian Management Journal) and *The Journal of Social Policy Studies* (in Russian).

Issam Srour is an Associate Professor in the Department of Civil and Environmental Engineering at the American University of Beirut (AUB). His research focuses on the use of quantitative techniques and sustainability principles to solve real-world engineering and construction management problems. His work includes construction labor, information and material management. Since joining AUB, Dr Srour has led several studies focusing on construction labor management in Lebanon and more generally in the Middle East. He is an active member of the American Society of Civil Engineers (ASCE) and the Lebanese Order of Engineers. Dr Srour earned both his Master's and PhD degrees in Civil Engineering from the University of Texas at Austin. He also holds a Bachelor's degree in Civil and Environmental Engineering from the American University of Beirut.

Gerhard Syben, Dr Phil., is a former Professor of Work and Industrial Sociology at the Hochschule Bremen (Bremen University of Applied Sciences), Germany. He has written widely on the construction industry and conducted research into a range of issues, including activity profiles, competence requirements and vocational training. He owns and manages the *BAQ Forschungsinstitut* (Institute of Research on Labor, Employment and Vocational Training), conducting research on the German and European construction industries.

Alex Veen is an employment relations scholar at the University of Sydney in Australia in the discipline of Work and Organizational Studies. He completed his PhD at the University of Western Australia focusing on the industrial agreement-making choices of management across the Western Australian mining industry. He teaches employment relations and international human resource management and is currently conducting employment relations focused research on topics including the changing nature of work, the rise of the platform-based, so-called 'gig' economy and the implications for workers, management, regulators and society.

1 Introduction

Janet Druker, Geoffrey White
and Dale Belman

Why this Study?

The construction industry has a key role to play in every country in the world. It is an important employer, engaging some seven percent of workers world-wide in 2018 (International Labour Organization (ILO)) 2019: 14) of whom some 90 percent will be men (International Labour Organization 2015). It is worth $10 trillion globally (Economist 2017), and is a driver of economic development both nationally and internationally. Its importance is acknowledged by governments and international agencies as setting the framework for social and environmental infrastructure and for decent living standards. Its different subsectors, including residential construction, civil engineering (roads, highways, water plants) and industrial, mining and commercial activities, employ a wide range of skills and professions. In addition to jobs created directly, it creates work and opportunities in other sectors and across economies.

Work in the construction industry is shaped by geography and climate, economic circumstance and government policies, and social and cultural factors including human determination and achievement. The construction product is temporary and immobile, requiring new teams and new skills for each new project. It is an insecure and conflict-prone industry which makes significant demands of those who work within it. Risks are high and the challenges of the physical environment are constant. Safety procedures are at a premium.

This book sets out to document and critique the experience of work and labor relations in the construction industry from an international perspective. There have, of course, been other international studies of the construction industry (for example, Bosch and Philips 2002), but few in recent times that have at their core questions of work, employment and labor relations for the construction workforce. This book arose from discussions between the editors about the contrasting and sometimes surprising differences in labor standards in the US, in the UK and in other parts of Europe, and from there we went on to consider the very different pictures that emerge elsewhere, in particular in less-developed economies.

We were fortunate in being able to bring together an international team to pursue these issues and their work is reflected in the country chapters within this volume, each one dealing with a different national context. Each chapter is led by authors with local experience who are experts in their field.

Our perspective is international, although the book is biased in its coverage toward richer economies where conditions contrast sharply with those in the developing world (Ofori 2007). Of course, there are significant differences within, as well as between, countries – for example between the north and the south of Argentina or between the west and east coasts of the US. In every location there is a contrast between different types of construction – from infrastructure and major projects through to housing, from public works to domestic refurbishment. There is also a stark contrast in the experience of work. These contrasts extend from the type of work undertaken and the level of risk, through expectations of job security and fair treatment but also include the degree of government regulation, which may be less advanced in the least developed economies (Wells 2007). There are differences in the degree of collective bargaining regulation applied to the construction process, but also in relation to labor laws, for example concerning minimum wages, social insurance and working conditions. In addition, there are marked contrasts in the extent to which the law is implemented. Although government regulation may be well respected in some locations, in others it may be neglected or ignored, and labor inspectors may face significant challenges in application and enforcement (International Labour Organization 2017).

In spite of these contrasts, there are many similarities in the experience of construction work in the countries we consider. The workforce is mobile with each new project requiring labor, building materials and equipment to be brought to each new location. It is high risk and occupational safety and health is always of critical importance. It is volatile, with workloads and employment subject to economic fluctuation. The culture and environment reflect the male-dominated nature of the industry and, outside of south Asia, women are less likely than men to be employed in manual trades although they are winning more opportunities in professional roles (International Labour Organization 2015). There are initiatives – for example in Ghana – for women to access training opportunities. The sector is intensely local, with small firms and subcontractors often rooted in local communities having a key role to play because major contractors outsource the construction process through extensive contractual chains. Employment responsibilities are often blurred and the boundaries between employment and self-employment are frequently opaque. It is a local, but also an international, industry with major professional firms, consultants and contractors crossing national boundaries as they seek out new opportunities.

It is highly competitive and the need to win contracts brings about a pressure on contract price that shapes human relationships, driving a ruthless process of subcontracting and accompanying working conditions.

Outsourcing and subcontracting have increased significantly in most locations as principal contractors seek to minimize financial risks, so that subcontracting is ubiquitous, both within and across borders (Wells 2018). The construction sector, in line with the wider developments described by Weil (2014), has tended to fragment or to 'fissure' as major contractors seek to download risks and responsibilities. The individual worker may be engaged via an agency, paid by a payroll company and be directed on site by a sub-subcontractor who will himself be subject to the decisions of a higher-level contractor. This complicates discussion of 'employment' because so many workers are engaged casually, without necessarily being able to claim the position of 'employee' (Jorens et al. 2012). Unless the client or main contractor accepts responsibility, workers at the lower end of the contractual chain find themselves in a precarious position because fragmentation within the industry puts pressure on prices that impact significantly on the supply chain. The consequence is that workers are often engaged on an independent or self-employed basis, where they may be denied their rights as employees (International Labour Organization 2017). Trade union organization is undermined as the individual worker is isolated and the potential for solidarity is diminished. Job security is limited, often lasting only for the duration of a particular project or parcel of work. Wage rates are affected because the higher wages associated with periods of economic buoyancy are not consolidated or carried forward on future projects. Precarious employment breeds a reluctance to complain or challenge exploitative working conditions. These circumstances mitigate against effective skills training and undermine health and safety standards, which are almost invariably below the standards of other workers within the same geographical area.

Our aim here is to describe, analyze and assess the context of work in construction, to seek out practices and working arrangements that foster decent working conditions, enabling rather than disrupting the prospects for training, worker representation and decent work. It is common for academic studies to adopt a critical approach to employment relations and we empathize with this approach because employer rhetoric may disguise the underlying realities of challenging or negative work experiences. Normative approaches may seek out 'good practice' with the intention of offering a template that can be transferred or applied elsewhere but 'good practice' is sometimes hard to find within the construction sector, and our objective in this text is to seek out the circumstances through which decent work becomes possible – recognizing that this may mean different things in different locations and recognizing too that practices that work in one location are not necessarily transferable to others. The intention then is to raise questions, so that those working in or having influence within the industry, or those who are policy makers, advisers or worker representatives can review current practice with a critical and informed eye, to encourage change.

An early, seminal text concerning approaches to industrial relations outlined two very different perspectives that are relevant to our discussion (Fox 1974 cited in Kessler and Purcell 2003: 315). The term 'unitarism' is used where management decisions predominate and employees are denied the opportunity to represent their workplace interests – an approach that is recognizable in many of the accounts that follow. From this perspective, it is sometimes argued that the interests of the employer and employee coincide, because both have an interest in the success of the enterprise. However, projects in the construction sector are often short term and, because workers are mobile, they are unlikely to see employer interests as their own. In contrast, when employees are acknowledged as having separate and legitimately different interests and have the opportunity for representation within a framework that respects those interests, the term 'pluralism' is applied (Fox 1974 cited in Kessler and Purcell 2003: 315). This approach is recognizable in northern Europe, but also in Argentina where social dialog has been part of the fabric of labor relations. Within this perspective, workers will have organized themselves to create effective forms of representation to protect their interests. Employers make concessions because the power of trade unions at some point has forced them to do so.

These neat divisions were challenged by the emergence of human resource management from the 1980s, with an emphasis on co-operation, consultation and team working (Purcell and Ahlstrand 1994). It was a perspective that provided a new variant of traditional unitarism, whereby employers sought the engagement and commitment of the workforce as a means of by-passing collective organization and enhancing productivity. It had only partial and very incomplete application within the construction sector where it impacted mostly on professional and managerial employees (Loosemore et al. 2003: 304). The initial terminology, originating from Fox's work, still resonates when we consider management in the construction sector and, although it has been extended in an Australian study that highlights the importance of 'collaborative pluralism' as the basis for improvements in industrial relations practice, such collaboration is not commonplace (Bray et al. 2017).

Underlying these different perspectives is the question of power. How much power do workers have to shape workplace procedures and practices to ensure fair treatment within the workplace? Formal collective bargaining structures require employers to acknowledge and recognize the legitimate interests of workers whose interests are represented through trade unions, arrangements that provide essentially for formal regulation of wages and working conditions. A trade union presence makes fair treatment more likely, including payment for holidays and sickness. In general, it seems to be the case that the Western economies, together with Australia, are most likely to have been shaped historically in this way with trade unions having a lesser foothold and least influence in the developing economies in our study. Yet the situation is both more complex and more ambiguous than this simple outline suggests. Relationships are not static and structures that may have seemed appropriate to employers in one era may be subject to pressures that lead to change (Arnholtz et al. 2018). Our narrative reflects conflict as well as changing reference points and, whatever their history, each of the countries in this book presents an industry that is exposed to the forces of financial controls and to atomized organization. In an environment where work is outsourced through an extended subcontracting chain, work relations are fragmented, and job security minimized.

Our contributing authors for each of the country chapters were asked to outline the industry context, considering particularly the level and type of employment or labor engagement, arrangements for skills development, for health and safety and for the use that is made of migrant labor. Wherever practical and relevant, we were seeking an account of the major institutions and regulatory environment of the industry, for example the major employer and employee organizations, the relative strength of trade union membership and the machinery for determining pay and conditions. What issues arise in terms of the reproduction of labor or in terms of health and safety? What have been the major challenges that the industry has faced in terms of employment over the last 25 years? How have these challenges most effectively been addressed by governments and by industry bodies? What is the prevailing state of play? A brief outline of the content of each chapter now follows.

The Countries

In Chapter 2, Ruggirello and Druker point to the continuing importance of social dialog as a legacy of Peronist support for trade unions and regulated labor relations in Argentina. This apparently pluralist picture is both complex and incomplete because of Argentina's political history which includes periods of authoritarian government, military dictatorship and neo-liberal policies, but corporatist labor relations have survived as a component within the formal part of the sector, given active support in the 21st century by the governments of Nestor Kirchner and, subsequently, of Christina Fernandez de Kirchner and Alberto Fernandez. Political and economic volatility has had inevitable repercussions in the construction sector, impacting on employment as well as raising concerns about corruption, bribery and fraud. In spite of this, there continues to be a formal registration process for construction firms and construction workers. The registration system provides for collective bargaining, for holidays and social benefits and for a shared commitment between employers and the trade union toward training for labor market entrants and for schemes of continuing professional development. Yet the procedures are not uniformly applied. The authors highlight the segmentation that exists and point to the informality prevailing outside of the registration system. Many of those in smaller enterprises, in repair and maintenance or in domestic renovation find themselves operating informally and these workers are deprived of the benefits of registration. This includes the majority of migrant workers. The chapter highlights the importance of and the challenges to the continuing legacy of tripartite structures and social dialog.

Conflict and industrial action are widespread in Australian construction employment relations although there are marked differences, both between the various subsectors of the industry and across the different states and territories. In Chapter 3, Veen and McGrath-Champ explain the political controversies, but they also highlight the differences between the distinctive subsectors – commercial, infrastructure and residential construction and resource extraction-related construction. In residential construction self-employment is common and trade unions scarce. The industrial and commercial worlds are characterized by conflict and adversarial labor–management relations; trade unions sustain membership and an on-site union culture, whereas employers resist or seek to contain or evade union influence. Whilst there has been a trend toward outsourcing and subcontracting which has fragmented employment, the Construction, Forestry, Maritime, Mining and Energy Union, one of the most militant of Australian trade unions, has succeeded in policing employment conditions, including at the level of smaller subcontractors. Union power has been challenged by State intervention and political initiatives to constrain union activities.

Significantly, the chapter points to the 'fissured' nature of the industry as main contractors put an increasing distance between themselves and the physical process of construction, retaining overall management of the operation but relying on subcontractors – and on a more extended contractual chain – for contract delivery. The major companies have become financial and property management shells whereas workers are engaged in ever smaller units. It is a structure which mitigates against training, placing increased reliance on the use of a migrant workforce. These are recurrent themes within subsequent chapters.

The construction sector in Brazil, considered by Piccoli and Diehl (Chapter 4), is highly dependent on cheap, unskilled labor as contractors and subcontractors take advantage of workers from the countryside, who come into the larger conurbations searching for work. The political history of the country has led to the appearance of similarities with neo-corporatist arrangements in Argentina but, while the basis for formal employment is legally prescribed, there are at least as many informal workers as there are formal. Legal regulations enacted in the 1940s have been extended, providing formal workers with support in terms of conditions of work, but these laws are often by-passed because contractors seek the lowest cost solutions to labor supply at the expense of efficiency, quality and productivity. Training provision is limited and barriers to innovation and new technologies persist, because there is an absence of motivation for businesses to adapt when they can rely on unskilled and informal migrants from rural areas. Labor inspectors have played an important role in urban areas but they are too few in number to have any impact in the countryside. Given the size of the country, workers in remote locations are dependent upon the main contractors for accommodation, food and safety standards, and these issues have sparked conflict even where the workforce is not unionized. Although subcontracting is widespread, main contractors who neglect to control their subcontractors may find that they are jointly liable – for example for defaults in payment of wages. It is a provision which encourages main contractors, when hiring, to give attention to the legitimacy and financial probity of their subcontractors.

In Chapter 5, which discusses the construction industry in Germany, Syben and Beck highlight the history of social partnership in employment relationships and its continuing influence in current practice in formal collective bargaining procedures in the construction sector. They also point to the effects of change. The industry is at a crossroads, they argue, with a decline in trade union membership and national collective bargaining. Institutional interest representation, which has been characteristic of German industrial relations, has been undermined in construction, as in other areas. Fewer employers are committed to traditional arrangements, and collective agreements are less applied now than in the past. Collective bargaining has been sustained but the trade union, IG BAU, has been unable to fully resolve the difference between wages and conditions in the former East and West of Germany. The strengths of collective bargaining rest in the social funds that support holiday pay and training and these continue to be supported, although employers complain of ongoing skill shortages and difficulties in recruitment. The proportion of manual workers in the sector is declining with digitalization and, whereas formal structures in labor relations remain, their future does not appear to be guaranteed.

Ghana, a developing economy, provides a contrasting example where, as in other countries of sub-Saharan Africa, informal labor is common and labor regulation is weak. As Ahadzie, Debrah and Ofori argue in Chapter 6, while the construction industry is clearly seen by the Ghanaian government as a major force for economic development and job creation, the absence of a national agency to oversee the industry creates challenges in terms of the coordination of employment issues,

especially for skills and professional development. The construction industry is largely informal. Jobs are insecure, health and safety standards
are inadequate and formal systems of employment regulation through
trade unions and employers' bodies are relatively rare – mostly limited to
large, infrastructure projects. Trade unions face the challenge of organizing the large, informal construction workforce, mostly working on a
casual or self-employed basis. The development of construction skills is
limited by the absence of formal training programs and there is a deficit
in skills development. The authors suggest that the informal labor force
provides a neglected but potentially important sector for job creation
and skills training within the industry. The challenge is aligning the informal with the formal economy. The Ghanaian Trades Union Congress
acknowledges the importance of organizing these informal workers and
some NGOs (illustrated by three case studies in the chapter) have had
success in developing skills training programs, including bringing women
into the sector. The authors argue that an integrated, multi-stakeholder
approach to informal sector development could be developed, led by the
government.

Informality also dominates in the Middle East, a major global construction market, driven by rapid economic development in Saudi Arabia
and the Gulf States and the need for reconstruction after war and civil
conflict around the region. A major feature of the labor market has been
the movement of refugees across borders to escape conflict. In Chapter 7
Kleib, Afiouni and Srour write about the situation in the Lebanon, where
migrant workers make up the great majority of the construction workforce. Labor unions are absent from the industry and most workers find
work through family connections. The chapter draws on secondary literature and supplements this with primary research conducted among
workers on-site. The findings depict a negative picture of management
practices and working conditions, characterized by a high level of informality, an absence of policies and procedures, poor health and safety
and a lack of skills training. They also point to additional structural
challenges such as the unstable nature of the industry, the unsteady
nature of the contractual environment, the diverse nationalities of
workers on site, and the difficulty in controlling the flow of illegal foreign
workers amidst the ongoing political instability in Lebanon and the
wider region.

Informality is a core theme in the discussion of work and employment
in the Russian construction sector too. The industry has undergone
significant change over the last three decades and privatization has been
associated with an increase in the number of small and medium-sized
firms. Soviet traditions provide a backdrop to understanding current
trends because Putin's Russia sustains the appearance of regulation that
dates to an earlier era, but institutional arrangements and formal procedures in construction employment lack real substance. Informal labor

engagement has grown since 2010 and self-employment has doubled. Labor law is neglected, abuses are widespread and safety standards by-passed. State structures to govern the industry are ineffective. Membership of the main trade union has fallen and little is done to unionize the migrant workforce. Serezhkina, Morrison and Cretu (Chapter 8) outline the major changes taking place in construction work and employment and allow the viewpoint of migrant workers, who are central to urban development, to emerge. Brought into the country and into construction employment by friends or contacts, they are typically engaged through intermediaries who largely take responsibility for representing their interests. Working conditions are set informally and the workforce is segmented along ethno-national lines. The established trade unions do little to support migrant workers and Russian workers are relatively privileged within this scenario, although they too are exposed to the risks of precarious employment and occupational safety and health hazards.

In terms of employment relations, the Scandinavian countries follow the 'high road' approach of coordinated market economies. Trade union membership in the construction sector is above most other countries. Educational levels, quality and productivity are relatively high and so too are wage levels. Collective agreements between employers' organizations and labor unions are maintained, with the intention of avoiding damaging conflict and disruption to the production process. In general, employers have adopted a pluralist approach to employment relations, and the unions, for their part, have been prepared to compromise to ensure that the benefits of collective agreements and their regulatory frameworks are maintained. The chapter by Arnholz and Ibsen (Chapter 9) explains the frameworks for employment relations in the construction industries of Sweden and Denmark, and analyzes the different approaches in the two countries. Both sustain strong unions and the enforcement of collective agreements with employers. This situation has required, in the authors' words, a 'balancing act' in the relationship between capital and labor, with constant negotiation and coordination of flexibility, skill development, productivity and decent labor standards among the social partners. The result is that, in terms of value added per hour, Swedish and Danish construction is among the most productive in Europe.

In recent years, however, this harmonious picture has come under increasing strain, largely resulting from the influx of cheap migrant labor from Central and Eastern European countries following the expansion of the European Union from 2004. In particular, the European Union's neo-liberal response to dealing with the issues arising from this increased movement of labor across borders has made union organization within the construction industry more difficult. Consequently, the Swedish and Danish construction employers have adapted and pursued new strategies. Arnholz and Ibsen compare the different approaches and discuss how the specific bargaining relations in the two countries have produced these contrasting approaches, and how these differences might affect the future ability of social partners to sustain the 'high road' in the future. In their view, the Danish unions have been more successful in resisting these changes than the Swedish. Nonetheless, the authors argue that the 'high road' still exists and, following economic recovery from 2010, remains relatively robust in both countries owing to a number of factors including the continued efforts of social partners to retain a highly regulated sector, a relatively generous welfare state and high wages.

The UK, discussed in Chapter 10, provides a further example of the atomization of the construction industry, with fragmented structures accompanied by high levels of bogus self-employment, the disintegration of training and, for the mainstream section of the industry, limited trade union influence. National, multi-employer collective agreements have survived but, with notable exceptions, have little relevance to standards on site. The story is one of a conflict of interests between contractors and the workforce. In many respects it is a familiar one, but in recounting it Druker and White also point to different and contrasting standards prevailing on some major projects. Different approaches are adopted. Residential construction in the UK, for example, operates almost entirely on a self-employed basis as it does in many other countries. Self-employment and agency labor is commonplace on industrial and commercial sites too, where employment responsibilities are compounded by the prevalence of payroll companies (intermediaries for payment purposes). Yet in other parts of the UK construction industry, with clients and delivery partners who are prepared to take responsibility, a different approach is possible. These differences derive from the political sensitivity of major projects or contracts, from their sheer size and visibility, their value, their cost to the public purse and their longevity. Major contractors, who historically have demonstrated an approach that is inherently unitarist – seeking to by-pass or avoid trade unions where they can – may in particular circumstances sign up to direct employment and cooperation with trade unions, if this seems to be a contract requirement. And where they do so, they may go on to stipulate this approach in contracts with subcontractors and through the supply chain. There is variation, of course, in the detail and in the application, but commitments to training, community involvement, trade union representation, collective agreements and diversity and inclusion become the norm in such situations.

The construction industry of the US, the largest in terms of employment of the countries included in this volume, is characterized by extremes. In Chapter 11, Belman and Ormiston point to a highly institutionalized and unionized sector (known as the 'signatory sector') where labor–management cooperation (social partnership) is well developed. This part of the industry is heavily capitalized, uses advanced technologies, provides extensive training through jointly managed apprenticeship training systems and implements modern safety and health practices. Healthcare, pensions and apprenticeship training are administered collaboratively through Taft-Hartley trusts (joint labor–management trusts). Under pressure from increasingly capable non-union competition, the regulated sector has expanded the stakeholders explicitly included in cooperative agreements. Owners, governments and communities obtain valued outcomes, such as access to apprenticeship programs, assured access to a skilled labor force, and assurances that projects will not be interrupted because of labor issues, through Project Labor Agreements or Community Benefit Agreements.

In contrast, residential construction operates largely without regulatory oversight and is dominated by informal practices. Employers do not provide benefits. Some engage in wage theft through non-payment or partial payment of promised compensation, and typically do not provide safety training or equipment. Many workers are misclassified as independent contractors or paid 'off-the-books'. Payroll fraud allows employers to avoid paying the employer share of social security, unemployment insurance, workers' compensation and overtime costs and permits them to avoid the costs associated with following labor and employment laws. These practices are supported by an extensive structure of labor brokers, check cashing stores and shell companies. The spread of these practices has placed the workers' compensation systems of states such as Florida at risk. It also reduces tax payments into state and national treasuries and allows employers engaging in these practices to undercut legitimate employers. In the informal sector, employers make extensive use of undocumented workers, who are in a particularly vulnerable position and unwilling to bring complaints to government regulators.

The signatory sector in the US has been challenged by the spread of informality for the last three decades and it is coming under increasing pressure as the practices of the residential sector spread outward into light commercial, institutional and larger projects.

Formality and Informality

This is a book about disparities in work and labor relations, about segmentation of the workforce and the inter-relationship between formal working arrangements and informality at work. Over 60 percent of the world's workforce was in informal employment in 2016, and it is in developing countries, such as Ghana, that informal arrangements are most likely to be found (International Labour Organization 2019).

Informality may often seem to be associated with marginal employment or 'sweatshop' conditions, but the picture is more complex (Williams 2014). There are ambiguities and complexities in each particular context.

More formal structures emerge where terms and conditions of work are negotiated through collective bargaining between employers' associations and trade unions. They are strongest where there is employer commitment to them, particularly when main contractors take a responsibility for working conditions in the subcontracting chain. Worker protection may also be subject to government regulation. In many cases there is an interaction between the two because legislation is more likely where trade unions have influence. Collective bargaining arrangements may be recognized or consolidated through legal enactment. Formal, negotiated arrangements will typically set standards on wages, hours and working conditions, and lead to payments during holidays or for sickness. Through a recognized grading structure, they may provide a framework for labor market entry, training and career development. Collective agreements also provide for worker representation and for procedures to ensure fair treatment. They may be agreed at national level, as for example in Sweden and Denmark or in arrangements in the registered sector in the Argentinian construction industry. Characteristic of more developed economies, they represent a 'high road' in terms of labor standards and, where they exist and are observed, they provide the most effective defense of wages, working conditions and the rights of workers to representation. They also benefit employers who gain in terms of the scope for training, for improved productivity and for risk management. Government regulation may set general standards – for example, in terms of minimum wage rates – which run in parallel with collective agreements, or exist when there are no such agreements in place. Of course, regulation may also be by-passed, neglected or challenged.

Formality and informality are closely intertwined in some cases. Formal enterprises, which purport to be regulation-compliant, may neglect or be only partially observant of labor standards. There are greater or lesser degrees of compliance, but formally agreed employment conditions may be evaded as contractors seek to reduce costs and download risk, often via the services of intermediaries – agencies, subcontractors or gang-masters. In this way formal enterprises may be wholly or partially engaged in informal employment practices. In some cases, particularly in lower-paid economies, formal employment may be less common, or may be largely confined to professionals and managers with the wider construction workforce made up predominantly of casual labor. The 'low road' of the construction sector is then characterized by fragmented organizational structures, job insecurity, low training levels and poor skills development, low wages and few social supports. These problems are not confined to developing economies.

A worker in the informal sector has little protection. Engaged casually on a day basis or for the duration of a particular task or job, perhaps through an agency, he (it is almost always 'he') has no security and no income guarantee. Trade unions are often too weak and occasionally (see Chapter 8) too compliant to challenge abuse. Wages may not be paid or may not be paid in full (Chapter 7). There may be no provision for paid holidays or for sickness and informal workers are most likely to be deprived of access to social security systems. Clients, including governments and leading businesses, may be prime beneficiaries where there are savings within the construction sector, both in containing the costs of public works and in hastening the completion of projects that enable the fulfillment of policies or political promises. Yet the competitive contractual pressures exerted on subcontractors and on sub-subcontractors are to the detriment of wages and conditions of work, as well as health and safety standards, at the lower levels of the contractual chain. Labor inspectors who may be required to uphold working conditions, for example, in relation to health and safety, may be too few in number to have any real impact (Ronconi 2019: 5). Their remit is a challenging one, and they have limited capacity to monitor a mobile industry. Short-term benefits of cost-saving should be weighed against the more serious dysfunctional consequences, both for the industry and for the workforce, including the inability of the industry to re-gear to meet the challenges of training, innovation and productivity.

The Prospects for Change

At the time of writing, the industry across the globe is resuming work following the lockdowns that were consequent on the Covid-19 international pandemic. In some locations – for example, in Germany and the Nordic countries – construction activity was not fully terminated. But elsewhere the impact of closures on the construction workforce was serious. Because so many construction workers were in precarious, project-based employment, they very quickly found themselves without work. As we are writing, many construction projects are being revived, but others, particularly those at the pre-planning stage, may be shelved because the crisis in finance that is likely to follow the Covid-19 crisis will leave the construction industry in a very different position when the effects of the virus subside. What has been made abundantly clear since the pandemic broke is just how important the construction sector is to national and international prosperity.

This book was prepared before the uniquely disastrous effects of Covid-19 on health and on the economy were being felt. The research and the accounts in this book are therefore from the historic period prior to the international pandemic. The accounts are important because, while many things will change in the future, the history and experience of the industry and its ways of working will be the foundation from which other developments must be launched.

References

Arnholtz, J., Meardi, G., Oldervoll, J., 2018. Collective wage bargaining under strain in northern European construction: Resisting institutional drift. *European Journal of Industrial Relations* 24 (December 4), 341–356.

Bosch, G., Philips, P., 2002. *Building Chaos: An International Comparison of Deregulation in the Construction Industry.* Routledge, London and New York.

Bray, M., Macneil, J., Stewart, A., 2017. *Co-operation at Work: How Tribunals Can Help Transform Workplaces.* The Federation Press, Annandale, NSW.

Economist, 2017. 'Efficiency eludes the construction industry'. *The Economist:* 17.08.2017. https://www.economist.com/business/2017/08/17/efficiency-eludes-the-construction-industry (accessed 12.04.20.).

Fox, A., 1974. *Beyond Contract: Work, Power and Trust Relations.* Faber and Faber, London.

International Labour Organization, 2015. *Good Practices and Challenges in Promoting Decent Work in Construction and Infrastructure Projects: Issues Paper for Discussion at the Global Dialogue Forum on Good Practices and Challenges in Promoting Decent Work in Construction and Infrastructure Projects (Geneva, 19–20 November 2015) GDFPDWC/2015.* ILO Sectoral Policies Department, Geneva.

International Labour Organization, 2017. *Conducting Labour Inspections on Construction: A Guide for Labour Inspectors. Occupational Safety and Health Branch Labour Inspection.* ILO, Geneva.

International Labour Organization, 2019. *World Employment Social Outlook: Trends, 2019.* ILO, Geneva.

Jorens, Y., Peters, S., Houwerzijl, M., 2012. *Study on the Protection of Workers' Rights in Subcontracting Processes in the European Union: Final Study.* European Commission project DG EMPL/B2 -VC/2011/0015 Ghent University in consortium with the University of Amsterdam, Ghent.

Kessler, I Purcell, J., 2003. 'Individualism and collectivism in industrial relations' Chapter 12 In: Edwards, P. (Ed.) *Industrial Relations: Theory and Practice,* second ed. Blackwell, Oxford, 313–337.

Loosemore, M., Dainty, A., Lingard, H., 2003. *Human Resource Management in Construction Projects: Strategic and Operational Approaches.* Spon Press, London and New York.

Ofori, G., 2007. Guest editorial: construction in developing countries. *Construction Management and Economics* 25, 1–6.

Ofori, G., 2018. Construction in developing countries: need for new concepts. *Journal of Construction in Developing Countries* 23(2), 1–6.

Purcell, J., Ahlstrand, B., 1994. *Human Resource Management in the Multi-divisional Company.* Oxford University Press, Oxford.

Ronconi, L., 2019. *Enforcement of Labor Regulations in Developing Countries.*

Centro de Investigación y Acción Social (CIAS), Argentina, and IZA, World of Labor, Germany.

Weil, D., 2014. *The Fissured Workplace: Why Work Became so Bad for so Many and What Can be Done to Improve it.* Harvard University Press, Cambridge, Mass.

Wells, J., 2007. Informality in the construction sector in developing countries. *Construction Management and Economics* 25(January), 87–93.

Wells, J., 2018. Exploratory Study of Good Policies in the Protection of Construction Workers in the Middle East, *White paper.* ILO, Regional Office for Arab States, Beirut.

Williams, C., 2014. *Confronting the Shadow Economy: Evaluating Tax Compliance and Behavior Policies.* Edward Elgar, Cheltenham, UK and Northampton, MA, USA.

2 Social Dialog in the Argentinian Construction Industry

Hernán Ruggirello and Janet Druker

Introduction

In Argentina the world of work is changing. Social actors in general and trade unions and their representatives in particular are confronted with global and political change, with economic volatility and with technological innovation and new methods of production. Each of these shifts bring with them accompanying changes in employment relations. This issue assumes such importance that the International Labour Organization (ILO), as part of its centenary debates, highlighted the importance of decent work, effectively organized and managed, with safe working conditions. The ILO stresses the importance of allowing a voice to all the social actors in the labor market. In this way a permanent social dialog can be sustained, underpinning strategic alliances for more effective social, economic and cultural development. Markets should not be permitted to determine these processes of change alone, they argue, because this will assuredly lead to a widening disparities and greater inequality between rich and poor (ILO 2019). The tripartite traditions, reflected in these comments and fundamental to the operation of the ILO, have played – and continue to play – a significant part in employment relations in Argentina.

This chapter highlights the importance of the tripartite legacy and social dialog in the history of labor relations in Argentina, a country that shares certain characteristics with others in Latin America, whilst having its own distinctive history and socio-legal traditions that frame the experience of social actors in the construction sector. The first part of the chapter outlines the scale, structure and significance of the construction industry in Argentina looking at the segmentation between registered employment in construction and the informality of those outside the registration system. The second section discusses the background to labor relations in general and the institutional structures of industrial relations. The third section explains the ways in which collective bargaining is structured in the construction sector and discusses the tradition of social dialog in regulating health and safety and in facilitating access of migrants to the formal sector. We then turn to the question of training. We conclude by summarizing the segmented nature of the labor market and the implications for labor relations in the Argentinian construction sector highlighting the importance of and the challenges to the continuing legacy of social dialog.

Construction Employment in Argentina

Argentina is the third largest economy in Latin America, after Brazil and Mexico, and is an important member of Mercosur, the regional free trade pact in South America. With a population of 45 million, it has 23 geographical provinces or jurisdictions, and its employment and social conditions vary widely across the country. The capital and largest city, Buenos Aires, is an autonomous city (*ciudad autonomía*) with a population of just over 15 million.

The country is rich in natural resources, in energy and in agriculture and labor market activity is not far short of the average recorded by the Organization for Economic Cooperation and Development (OECD 2019). Yet the history of economic and financial volatility has left widespread poverty and the country had an unemployment rate of 8.9 percent at the end of 2019 (Instituto Nacional de Estadística y Censos, 2019). Over two thirds of the population work in the service sector and 22.4 percent in industry, including construction (OECD 2019). Informal employment is widespread and workers in the informal sector are deprived of access to pension and sector-based health schemes as well as to unemployment benefits. Women are under-represented in the labor market and in senior level positions in many sectors (OECD 2019: 34).

Educational attainment is above the OECD average for upper secondary education, but education at tertiary level does not perform so well and there is potential to expand vocational and technical education (OECD 2019: 51). These points are relevant to the current state of play in the construction sector and they are the factors to which we return at a later stage in this chapter.

Construction has, historically, been a leading contributor both to national and to regional prosperity in Argentina. It is of great importance, not only because of the large number of businesses and workers that are directly employed, but also because of the stimulus it provides through its demand for materials and supplies. It is labor intensive, creating and sustaining jobs – and this factor has lent it considerable significance over the years in the formulation of government and social policies intended to ensure high levels of employment.

At the same time, the industry has been vulnerable to government budget deficits, to high interest rates and to corruption charges (Raszewski 2018), factors that were especially damaging at the end of

President Macri's period in office in 2019. In February 2020, shortly after the election of the new President, Alberto Fernández, construction was showing a decline of 17.9 percent in employment compared with a year previously (Ministerio de Trabajo Empleo y Seguridad Social 2020). Corruption undermines public trust and diverts funding, typically away from projects that might benefit the public. Publicly funded construction is especially exposed both to funding cutbacks and to galloping inflation. Allegations of malpractice in the award of infrastructure projects and public works contracts have compounded these problems as public servants were alleged to have received payouts from construction firms seeking contracts (OECD 2019).

The firms and the workers in the formal sector of the construction industry are registered and the number is monitored by the Instituto de Estadística y Registrado de la Industria de la Construcción (IERIC), created in 1996. Previously this had been undertaken through the National Construction Industry Register, under the aegis of the Department of Employment and Social Security. Not all construction workers are registered and registered status carries with it substantially better terms and conditions of employment as we explain below. In response to demands for more flexibility, many large companies have concentrated on smaller and more specialized fields of work, engaging in management of the construction process but relying on outsourcing and subcontracting for specialist areas of work. This has contributed to a growth in number of small and medium-sized enterprises (SMEs) and micro-enterprises and to the significant boom in self-employment that has been experienced, putting pressure on the formal system of labor relations.

The number of registered firms and registered workers varies significantly with economic fluctuations. The industry was seriously impacted by the global financial crisis of 2008–2009. Ten years later there were fewer firms in business than in the period before 2008. There were 21,265 firms engaged in construction activity in August 2019, compared with April 2008 when there were 26,288 firms (CEIC, 2019). While President Macri was in office (2015–2019) the picture in construction was initially more stable, but the industry was affected by wider economic problems because Argentina had one of the highest rates of inflation in Latin America. Workers and small firms in the industry remain vulnerable even to modest fluctuations and, as a further economic crisis unfolded toward the end of President Macri's period in office, the industry was exposed once again to firm closures and job losses.

The level of registered employment is affected too by company failures and by employment reduction within firms. Table 2.1 highlights the year by year variations, providing figures taken from IERIC's annual survey between 2015 and 2017 and other sources from 2017 to 2019.

The figures in Table 2.1 record the number of registered workers – those who are accredited with IERIC – but construction is a diverse and

Table 2.1 Number of firms and registered employment in the private sector, construction in Argentina

Date	No. of firms	Registered employment (fourth quarter of each year)
2013	25,049	400,497
2014	23,092	397,069
2015	23,492	409,686
2016	23,160	378,147
2017	23,436	426,665
2018	21,722[*]	426,790[**]
2019	23,187[*]	378.076[**]

Source: Figures are drawn from IERIC's *Informe Anual de la Coyuntura de Construcción*, 2015 and 2017 for the period 2013–2017.

Notes
* Figures for the number of firms for 2018 and 2019 are not directly comparable with earlier years since they are drawn from CEIC (2019) Argentina Number of construction companies (Ceicdata.com/en/argentina/number-of-construction-companies).
** Figures for employment, 2018 and 2019, are drawn from the Instituto de Estadística y Registro de la Industria de la Construcción 2019.

complex sector, encompassing quite different work environments (Organización Internacional del Trabajo (OIT) 2015). The skills expected of a worker in a large, multinational company for infrastructure in the oil industry are very different from those required for housing or maintenance. Registered workers are found mostly in larger firms. As in so many other countries, it is small and medium-sized firms that predominate in Argentina, with 59 percent of workers based in firms of between one and three workers (OIT, 2015: 174), with many who are self-employed or working on their own account. There was an average of 13.8 workers per firm in 2017 (Instituto de Estadística y Registrado de la Industria de la Construcción, IERIC 2017: 45) and only around two and a half percent of workers are employed in firms of 100 or more employees (OIT 2015: 174). The employment data in Table 2.1 set out details of registered firms and workers but do not include those who are working in the informal sector, for whom equivalent information is not available. Informal workers have lower wage levels and lack the benefits of unemployment protection, contributory pensions and health insurance benefits. This group is particularly vulnerable to lay-offs and the insecurity associated with fluctuating workloads. Although IERIC and the construction workers' union (Unión Obrera de la Construcción de la República Argentina (UOCRA)) conduct site inspections and campaigns to encourage registration and penalize employers who do not comply with the requirements of the registration system, it is difficult for them to reach the informal work environments associated with smaller firms and with housing and maintenance for individual clients (OIT 2015: 166–167).

The metropolitan areas have the largest numbers of both registered construction firms and workers. The province and the city of Buenos Aires together constitute almost half (48.8 percent) of registered construction contractor and subcontractor numbers while the provinces of the region of Patagonia or the northwest are sparsely populated, with lower levels of investment and construction activity (IERIC 2017).

As in other countries, this is a predominantly male workforce but unlike some others it is a predominantly young workforce – with approximately 75 percent of workers being under the age of 45 years (Ruggirello 2011: 59). It is also a segmented workforce, divided not only by trade, but also by a hierarchy in employment terms, represented by a process of subcontracting, with work – and the risks associated with it – parceled out to different sections of the workforce, typically in ever-smaller units. There are varying levels of informality and cost pressures that bear heavily on the smaller subcontractors (OIT 2015: 185–190).

In general, Argentina has a high standard of education with a literacy level of over 98 percent. Yet in the construction sector the level of education is lower than for the population as a whole, with the majority of workers having a low-to-middle level of education. Ruggirello (2011: 55–58) shows that just under 16 percent of the registered construction workforce failed to complete primary education (up to ages 11/12 years) by comparison with an all-industry figure of 6.1 percent. Those who had completed only primary education comprised 39 percent of the total registered construction workforce. Across the workforce, in general, 21.6 percent of workers completed secondary education (up to the age of 17/18 years), whereas in the construction sector the figure was significantly lower – at 13.3 percent. When we look at the intersection between the highest level of education and the completion of courses related to the construction industry, it is clear that a higher level of general education also strengthens the likelihood of an individual successfully undertaking other types of training, in this case the possibility of going on to learn a trade or profession in the construction industry (Ruggirello 2011: 55–58).

Migrant workers contribute significantly as they do in other sectors, such as agriculture, domestic work, textile manufacture and retail, but often they are disadvantaged in terms of wages and working conditions. Migration of people from other Latin American countries into Argentina was a constant feature of the 20th century – at its height in the first half of the century and diminishing in subsequent years. The early years of the 21st century have seen a modest increase – from 4.3 percent at the time of the 2001 Census to 4.5 percent in 2011. According to the population and housing census in 2010 some 4.5 percent of the population was from outside the country. Migrants most commonly came from Paraguay and Bolivia, followed by Brazil, Chile and Peru with the qualification that Chile was diminishing in importance whereas migration from Peru was increasing.

The current pattern of migration is, however, rather different than that in the past. Whereas the late 19th and early 20th centuries were marked by inward migration from other countries, construction now is equally reliant on regional migration within Argentina – reflecting the lower levels of economic activity outside the big cities. Nonetheless, it is estimated that the migrant workforce from other Latin American countries could constitute as much as 10 percent of the construction workforce, the majority being located especially in Buenos Aires and the surrounding area and with many migrants working informally, outside of the registration system (Marmara et al. 2014). In 2015, the OIT conducted a survey of migrant workers in construction with evidence collected through fieldwork in the autonomous city of Buenos Aires (OIT 2015). The survey highlighted their insecurity, to the extent that some of them were reluctant to be interviewed, fearing that there would be repercussions in the workplace. Responses of those who did participate showed that the experience of migrants was dependent to a large extent on when they arrived – with things being more difficult in the 1990s, when regulations were more cumbersome and becoming easier after 2004. The data point to the importance of family and friends from the country of origin in opening up job opportunities and providing accommodation. Argentina is valued by these workers for the social protections it offers and for its education and health systems, which tend to be of a substantially higher standard than in the country of origin. Significantly, the survey highlighted aspirations amongst migrant construction workers to achieve formal, registered status within the industry (OIT 2015: 185). The construction industry union UOCRA, together with the industry's registration body IERIC, took positive steps to integrate and support migrant workers into the registration system – and we return to this issue at a later stage in this chapter.

To further understand the context, it is necessary to outline briefly the system of labor relations in Argentina which is dealt with in the next section.

Labor Relations in Argentina

Social dialog has been an important theme in Argentinian labor relations and, when governed by a left-leaning political party, the state has historically played a central role, providing legitimacy for trade unions and for a centralized approach to collective bargaining (Cardoso and Gíndin 2009). Etchemendy (2019) argues that this approach is characteristic of neo-corporatist relations that were typical in the tripartite arrangements that existed in Western Europe in the 1970s and 1980s. However, just as this tradition is diminishing in significance in Europe, paradoxically in

Argentina and Uruguay it survives and has been reinforced and strengthened (Etchemendy 2019).

The influence of a labor-oriented political party (Etchemendy and Collier 2007; Haider 2015; Etchemendy 2019) has been punctuated by periods of neo-liberal politics that have challenged, but not fundamentally undermined, the central role of trade unions in Argentina's economy and social order. The story is a complex one and commentators point to both authoritarian and corporatist legacies influencing the role and the priorities of Argentinian trade unions (Bensusán 2016). The history is outlined briefly below, to provide some context for understanding the importance of trade unions, collective bargaining and social dialog in the Argentinian construction industry.

Like trade unions in other Latin American countries, Argentinian unions formalized their position and established close relations with the state during the 20th century (Bensusán 2016). Collective employment relations were established during the Peronist years (1945–1965) with recognition for trade unions, both at national and at industry level (Bensusán 2016; Cardoso and Gíndin 2009). Under President Peron, trade unions achieved workplace representation, closed shop arrangements and extensive benefits systems, including healthcare (Atzeni et al. 2011). Collective bargaining was strengthened and, with the approval of the Minister of Labor, collective agreements were applied throughout an industry or sector of employment (Atzeni et al. 2011). Over time there emerged a union preference for political negotiations with the state, rather than the development of bargaining relationships with employers (Bensusán 2016). The main union confederation, the Confederación General del Trabajo (CGT) was led by Peronists from 1948, establishing a political culture that outlasted Peron and survived the subsequent military dictatorship (Cardoso and Gíndin 2009).

Despite the brutal repression by the military dictatorship (1976–1983) and subsequent periods of neo-liberal government, these structures remain broadly in place. The CGT has remained the predominant union confederation, although its compliance with the neoliberal reforms of President Carlos Menem in the early 1990s gave rise to a challenge from a new confederation from 1992, the Central de Trabajadores de Argentina (Collado 2015) and grassroots movements pointed to new forms of social and community organization (Larrabure 2018). The political initiatives of the 1990s, under the auspices of Menem, were intended to restore the power of elites and of international institutions, reducing the role of the state and privatizing public assets (Undurraga 2015). The intention was to challenge the power of trade unions. Collective bargaining was decentralized, social protection and trade union influence reduced while informal working, unemployment and subcontracting all increased (Undurraga 2015). The consequence was a growth in atypical employment, in precarious and informal working and the segmentation of the labor market (Atzeni et al. 2011).

The economic and political crisis of 2001 and the social unrest with which it was associated, led to worker mobilization and widespread protests (Atzeni and Grigera 2019). The political change that followed, with the election of President Nestor Kirchner in 2002, was associated with a new and more encouraging environment for social dialog, coupled with reduced tolerance for informal working (Cardoso and Gíndin 2009). Employers' associations were regulated by a legal code and employers continued to be organized at industry level in 'chambers' or federations (Cardoso and Gíndin 2009). The Kirchner administration sought positive relations with trade unions and, in 2004, a tripartite National Minimum Wage Council was established. At about the same time, there was a move to the left in other Latin American countries – with the election of Hugo Chavez in Venezuela and Luiz Inacio Lula de Silva in Brazil. Protests and factory occupations in Argentina provided an impetus for social change and encouraged a return to the more inclusive approach to dialog with social and labor movement organizations that had characterized the administration of Peron (Féliz 2016). The initiatives of the 1990s were put into reverse; collective bargaining was encouraged and social, 'pro-poor' policies initiated. Employment and incomes rose until 2007, although some of the employment created was in precarious jobs (Féliz 2016). Although the pace of economic growth diminished after the global financial crisis of 2008–2009, the government of Cristina Fernandez de Kirchner, elected president in 2007, continued support for social benefits and subsidies for companies that were threatening to cut jobs. The links between the trade union movement and the Justicialist (Peronist) Party were reinforced, but in 2014 there was a downturn in the economy and the peso was devalued. Real wages fell during this period of economic instability, fostering a change of government (Féliz 2016) and a further period of neo-liberalism followed under the government of President Mauricio Macri (2015–2019). Economic deterioration and hyper-inflation led to the re-emergence of the corporatist and Peronist tradition, led by the new President, Alberto Fernandez and his vice-presidential running mate, Cristina Fernandez de Kirchner. Their campaign promised a renewed period of social dialog which has been challenged subsequently by economic volatility and the global health pandemic.

In summary then, although the history of trade union organization and of collective bargaining in Argentina has not had unequivocal or continuous government support, it does not follow the trajectory of decline that has affected many other countries. Trade unions are well established, with significant resources, and collective rights remain strong. Although neo-liberal governments have challenged union power, individual employment rights have been sustained and those trade unions that are recognized, that is those whose status is acknowledged as representative within their sector, continue to have the right to bargain at industry level with the industry-wide employer associations or chambers. The position of the recognized unions is further strengthened because of their right to manage funds allocated for health and social purposes (Atzeni and Grigera 2019). Unions organize at shop floor level and grassroots activism remains significant. The system has been described as 'inclusive' (Ugarte et al. 2015) and high bargaining rates are associated with sector-wide bargaining, high coverage of collective agreements and a narrower gender pay gap than in neighboring Chile (Ugarte et al. 2015). Union influence is strengthened by the involvement of the social partners in political dialog. Although there are both authoritarian and corporatist legacies in labor relations, unions have avoided the erosion of membership and influence that has affected unions in many other parts of the world.

Yet the atypical working and precarious employment fostered by neo-liberal initiatives have left many outside the provisions of a regulated work environment. The system is one that is segmented with one estimate suggesting that almost one-third of workers are engaged outside of the formal system and unregistered for social security (Etchemendy 2019: 1429), a number that fluctuates according to economic and political circumstances. This segmentation characterizes employment and labor relations in the construction sector. This is covered in the next section.

Labor Relations in Argentinian Construction

Those trade unions that have representation rights – only one union per sector having this status – have the right to engage in collective bargaining and the right to strike. In the case of the construction sector, the Unión Obrera de la Construcción de la Republica Argentina, known as UOCRA, is recognized. Founded in 1944, UOCRA recruits industry-wide, contrasting with the trade-based approach still adopted by North American unions. UOCRA negotiates with a variety of trade bodies, including the Argentinian Construction Chamber (*Cámara Argentina de la Construcción*); the Federation of Argentinian Construction Organizations (*Federación Argentina de Entidades de la Construcción*) and the Argentinian Association of Reinforced Concrete Employers (*Asociación Argentina del Hormigón Elaborada*). The construction industry – with its fluctuating demand and mobile work locations – is not easy to organize and yet UOCRA is one of the largest trade unions in Argentina with the majority of registered workers in membership. Through its collective bargaining role and its influence via IERIC, it has a significant influence within the formal section of the construction industry.

The construction industry has a segmented labor market, with a formal and effective system of registration, coordinated through dialog between UOCRA and their employer counterparts, coexisting with a high incidence of informal working. There is a fundamental difference between the rights of registered construction workers and those who are unregistered. Workers registered with IERIC are entitled to the wages and benefits that result from collective bargaining. Pay tends to be higher and working conditions are more effectively controlled. Registration also provides the route to social benefits. Those who work informally outside the registration system are deprived of the benefits of negotiated conditions, of social security and health insurance. Given the diversity of the construction sector, informal working is most likely to be found in smaller workplaces, especially domestic and house renovation, locations that are very different from the larger and more complex sites where employers and workers will tend to be registered (OIT 2015).

The challenge of regulating working conditions and consolidating trade union organization within the construction sector is reflected throughout this volume, and in Argentina this takes a particular form that is shaped by socio-historical experience and the legacy of corporatist structures. The struggle against informality has been a cornerstone of Argentinian trade union activity in recent years and of course it is important not only that there is statutory regulation, but also that there is a system of labor inspection to ensure that regulations are observed (Ronconi 2019). Within the corporatist framework discussed above, union representatives systematically visit construction sites with the aim of monitoring the work environment, checking that the fundamental rights of construction workers are observed and seeking to ensure that workers are registered (OIT 2015). In 2004, law number 25–887 of the Labor Law created a system of labor inspections with the aim of promoting controls and reducing informal working. In general, there are likely to be fewer violations of labor law where inspection resources are committed and where there is a link between state officials and civil society organizations (such as trade unions) (Amengual 2014). This benefits workers on regulated and registered sites.

UOCRA is supported through inspections conducted by IERIC and between 2005 and 2012 they inspected 88,170 establishments covering 290,386 workers and found that almost one-third – 32.4 percent – of the workers were not registered (OIT 2015: 183). This resulted in 26,766 workers becoming registered. Clearly this is a relatively small proportion of the total and it seems that for some employers the price of non-compliance is not high. Yet the potential for inspection may itself create a measure of compliance without the intervention of an inspector, as employers recognize the price that might be paid if they were found to have been infringing regulations. Inspections are focused on larger firms – those with five or more workers (p. 182) – and are accompanied by campaigns to inform workers of their rights. The importance of IERIC's involvement is that it can impose sanctions for the firm which has engaged an unregistered worker. Sanctions can take the form of fines, and other penalties, even including site closures (OIT 2015: 96). Clearly, it is an important system, benefiting workers and supporting union membership but it is almost impossible to conduct inspections in smaller scale projects where the most disadvantaged will be located.

Two further examples of collaborative regulation can be mentioned here – first, in the field of health and safety at work and second, in the assimilation of migrant workers.

Health and Safety at Work

Health and safety at work poses significant challenges for the construction sector in Argentina, as in other countries. Failures in this area have serious consequences, from a human point of view, for workers and their families, for the businesses themselves in terms of their social and economic responsibilities and, finally, for society as a whole. A high worker mortality rate, serious injuries and poor standards in respect of occupational health, constitute problems that are addressed but not resolved within the existing framework of social dialog. Worker organizations have the potential to raise awareness and to monitor and contribute to the enforcement of health and safety standards.

In Latin America in general, and in Argentina in particular, the construction industry is composed mostly of SMEs and this currently constitutes a major barrier to implementing improvements, because smaller firms tend to operate outside of the registration system and hence are not unionized. The accident rate in these firms is much higher than in larger enterprises. SMEs have limitations in terms of their resources and technical capacity and are not always aware of standards on health and safety at work nor how to comply with them without affecting the performance of the company. There may be a lack of understanding or awareness of the risks, a lack of knowledge or resources or an absence of commitment on the part of the employer. Externally, there is a lack of the support services required to develop the activities that are essential if health and safety is to be improved. UOCRA has identified a need to develop an approach that is specifically targeted at small and medium-sized firms in the construction industry, suggesting that this should include a study of the external services used by these firms. These 'intermediary services', as they are known, comprise risk assessment or prevention services, work inspection, insurance against risks and the role of managers and representatives. Detailed research into their role could lend support to the improvement of health and safety at work in these firms.

In Córdoba, the second most populous city in Argentina after Buenos Aires, the union has played an important part, through collaboration with state labor inspectors, in challenging inadequate standards of health and safety management on site. Political campaigning by the union in the 1980s led to the creation of the 'Condiciones y Medio Ambiente del Trabajo,' the body responsible for regulation and enforcement of labor standards. The social actors cooperated in the creation of a formal consultative commission ('La Voz del Interior'), leading to liaison between safety inspectors and union officers (Amengual and Fine 2017). Labor inspection in the city failed to keep pace with the expansion of activity in the construction sector between 2004 and 2008, a period when subcontracting and the use of temporary firms was increasing (Amengual and Fine 2017). In response, UOCRA, through continued pressure and campaigning and through both formal and informal interactions between the union, the inspectorate and industry representatives, contributed to raising awareness and upholding standards on site. The threat of severe penalties for negligent employers encouraged closer attention to safety and health with infringement leading to the possibility of site closure (Amengual and Fine 2017).

The nature and the coverage of regulations on health and safety at work have subsequently been modified. Whereas in the past regulation was primarily concerned with the safety of workers in the sector, they are now more centered on occupational health and workplace risks. The emphasis has shifted from protection to risk assessment and prevention. Regulations today reflect not only collective responsibilities as far as occupational health and safety is concerned, but also the roles, rights and responsibilities of the different parties and, in particular, the areas of cooperation between employers, workers and their representatives. Yet in health at work – as in so many other areas – there is a deep divide between the formal and the informal – the regulated and those who find themselves outside of regulatory provision.

Support for Migrant Workers

As in many countries, migrant workers tend to be absorbed into the lower-paid and more precarious areas of work, which in Argentina involves work with the smaller firms and subcontractors. Migrants are often at the bottom of a subcontracting chain where parcels of work – and the risks associated with them – are subcontracted out in ever-smaller units, a process of cost-saving which feeds the hidden economy. While migrant workers may aspire to formal status, their position within the construction industry means that many remain trapped long term in the informal sector (OIT 2015).

It has been estimated that some 15 percent of migrant workers from neighboring countries may work in the construction sector (Marmara et al. 2014: 41). Research undertaken in the city of Buenos Aires (OIT 2015: 185) highlights their insecurity and points to a hierarchy depending on education, qualifications and experience. Construction provides a route into the country for many, drawing on networks of migrants, often family or friends, coming from the same country of origin, but now established in Argentina. These networks open the possibility of finding work, even without documentation, and the OIT's research describes a form of 'apprenticeship' during which the migrant goes through a process of acculturation, adjusting to local customs (OIT, 2015: 185).

It is important then, that there is an attempt to unionize and to bring migrant workers within the ambit of the formal registration system and the union campaigns vigorously to oppose xenophobia and discrimination. In principle, employees in Argentina are entitled to the minimum wage, equal pay, paid holidays, work of no more than 48 hours per week as well as entitlements to state benefits and medical cover. Yet all of these things are denied to workers in the informal sector, so that there is a divide between the formal and the informal, with workers in the informal economy accepting lower pay and worse conditions than those in the regulated sector. Union campaigns to establish rights for migrant workers include extensive training programs run throughout the country together with publication of a guide for migrant workers in construction. This provides information on the routes to regularization of the position of informal workers from Mercosur or associated countries (comprising Brazil, Bolivia, Chile, Colombia, Ecuador, Paraguay, Peru, Uruguay and Venezuela) with the aim of challenging informal working and promoting decent standards of employment (UOCRA undated, cited in OIT 2015: 94). Additionally, the union promotes the rights set out in ILO Conventions. A migrant worker without documentation can only be engaged in the informal economy and, for this reason, he or she would be unable to access social security benefits, pension rights, family allowances or social insurance (UOCRA undated). The union's aim is to facilitate worker access to social security, which is denied to those who work in the informal economy and to raise earnings levels (OIT 2015: 94).

Specifically, UOCRA supports migrants who wish to extend their legal right of residency. It supports the right of migrant workers to join the union, the right to ensure that the employer does not withhold the worker's identity documents (making it impossible for the worker to move to another employer) and the right to receive wages in full at the designated time and without deductions. Other entitlements, in line with campaigning for all workers, include the right to a contract of work, the right to a safe place of work, the right not to be physically abused, verbally threatened or subject to sexual harassment. In general, the union campaigns to ensure that employment rights are fully extended to those in the informal economy.

From the union's perspective, of course, there is a degree of self-interest in seeking to defend unregistered workers in order to protect the working conditions of registered employees, whose position is otherwise undermined by the less structured arrangements of the informal economy, but the approach overall is within the logic of a drive for regulation and for union control. It is an approach that is matched with initiatives in other areas, notably in training and it is to this issue that we now turn.

Training

UOCRA plays an important role in training both for the industry as well as for the union, with a network that, in 2020, encompassed 30 training centers, including 16 schools. The centers are a part of the public education system, attracting public funding and working closely with companies in the industry. They are in direct contact with the labor and productive communities of which they are a part so that they are able to facilitate the employability of their students. The initiatives that are taken by each of the institutions are strategically developed to relate to the social-productive conditions in the region in which they are immersed.

In general, the construction industry exhibits a low level of education, qualification and incomes and a high level of informality, especially in small establishments. Training, adapted to the socio-economic situation in each area and to labor market requirements, is intended to offset these characteristics. The union's training arm, Fundación UOCRA, responds to the educational challenge by ensuring that the training centers are open to the community within which they are located, which is to say that they are available not only for union members but also for anyone else from the community free of charge. They offer primary and secondary education for adults and provide literacy training where this is needed. Teacher training is optimized through an e-learning platform.

Craft training is offered to provide a route into employment for labor market entrants, but it also facilitates a return to work to those who are unemployed. The union works with employers to promote improvements in professional standards, through the certification of competences. Within the vocational training programs, a high priority is accorded to modular training so that training can be delivered flexibly with scope for updating or continuous development. Expectations must shift, it is argued, from the typical role of a trained worker undertaking routine and repetitive work to that of an active participant in the process of production, with the worker's activities rooted in a complex interaction between knowledge, reasoning, actions and decisions in the situations in which the work is located.

The restructuring of the technical base of the construction industry, and the innovation in materials, tools and machines used, brings multiple changes in the development of jobs, skills and the work environment. The application of information and communication technologies reduces costs and facilitates the coordination and control of operations that are geographically dispersed. It enables a wider use of pre-site manu-facturing, providing a differentiating factor in terms of material pro-duction within the process of globalization, and at the same time imposing itself as a new matrix for production, distribution and opera-tion in the global economy. The production process is more decen-tralized and more flexible, with the intention of reducing both direct and indirect costs and improving productivity. The massive growth in the number of subcontractors is an integral component of these changes. These are fragmented changes, with diverse effects within the construc-tion sector, especially when taking into account the size of the con-struction projects, the degree of formality and the particular submarket within which they are located (civil engineering, roads or industrial construction).

For the same reasons, we can see a reconfiguration of organizational structures.

The aim, from within the industry, is to respond to these challenges with public policies that provide assistance to those who need it most, through social dialog, commitment to inclusion, employment networks and, of course, training policies. The union works to ensure that early training lays the basis for continuous professional development, strengthening the provision of decent work in general and, of aspects such as health and safety at work, with incremental improvements in social protection and full compliance with labor standards.

Conclusion

To conclude, drawing both on academic and labor movement sources, this chapter has emphasized three key themes in its account of labor relations in the Argentinian construction industry.

The first theme is concerned with social dialog. Trade unions, em-ployer representatives and the state have a history of partnership which goes back to the first half of the 20th century and has evolved to shape expectations and behaviors in the labor relations sphere today. Clearly, the history of formal, regulated bargaining structures supported by the state has encountered neo-liberal challenges and there are debates about the continuity and the significance of neo-corporatist traditions. It is sometimes argued that the legacy of such structures and processes does little to support the clear articulation of a more militant class agenda (Haider 2015; Collado 2015). Yet the corporatist legacy has proved resilient and the Peronist tradition – manifest as 'Kirchnerism' in the 21st century – is, within the framework of capitalist social relations, a pro-gressive movement (Féliz 2016). Certainly, within the construction in-dustry – a sector where trade unions struggle for survival in other countries – it has enabled union workplace representation and collective bargaining, with the protection of individual rights, the promotion of health and safety standards and collectively negotiated wages and conditions applied, at least on the larger sites.

The second, related issue concerns the question of labor market segmentation. This is a theme that has been widely commented in discussions of Argentinian labor relations (Etchemendy and Collier 2007; Atzeni et al. 2011; OIT 2015) and it is one that is particularly relevant within the construction sector. The legitimacy accorded to UOCRA, the survival of national collective bargaining and the promulgation of negotiated terms and conditions of work are set within the framework of registration both for employers and for workers so that it is possible to monitor and promote activities within the 'registered' construction sector. Negotiated terms and conditions of employment are coupled with entitlements to state benefits in a way that runs counter to the experience of construction workers in many other countries. UOCRA is supported in upholding standards through the cooperation of IERIC, whose role involves checking on worker registration and combating illegal working. Together they can engage positively and shape developments both in the field of health and safety and also in training and professional development. However, outside of the registered sector the construction industry has a high incidence of informal working. This is partly because of the diversity of the sector and partly because of fluctuations in the level and in the location of product and labor demand. SMEs are most likely to be outside the registration system and home workers, as well as migrant workers in unregistered work locations, suffer from lower pay and often from poor working conditions as well as finding themselves outside of provisions for social security, health insurance and risk management. The divide between the registered system and informal working outside of it is a sharp one. Paradoxically, it reflects the benefits that result when a measure of social partnership is in place – and the drawbacks when it is absent.

The final theme, a common one within this volume, is the presence of migrant workers in the Argentinian construction industry and the treatment accorded to them. Motivated by a desire to improve their situation, they face significant hurdles, notwithstanding the agreement between Mercosur and other countries with respect to reciprocity. Migrant workers, who constitute some 10 percent of the construction workforce in Argentina, may aspire to registered status and to state benefits, but are often unable to breach the divide between registered status and informal working – with many of them remaining long term in the informal sector (Marmara et al. 2014). The response from UOCRA, in line with the approach to home workers in the informal sector, is inclusive, seeking to bring migrant workers into the registration system, a response that is intended to provide support and leaven opportunities at the same time as it offers a defense of registered workers against a weakening in the application of collectively negotiated standards.

References

Amengual, M., 2014. Pathways to enforcement: labor inspectors leveraging linkages with society in Argentina. *Industrial and Labor Relations Review* 67(1), 3–33.

Amengual, M., Fine, J., 2017. Co-enforcing labor standards: the unique contributions of state and worker organizations in Argentina and the United States. *Regulation and Governance 11*(June 2), 129–142.

Atzeni, M., Duran-Palma, F., Ghigliani, P., 2011. 'Employment relations in Chile and Argentina'. Chapter 6. In: Barry, M., Wilkinson, A. (Eds), *Research Handbook of Comparative Employment Relations*. Edward Elgar, Cheltenham, 129–152.

Atzeni, M., Grigera, J., 2019. The revival of labor movement studies in Argentina: old and lost agendas. *Work, Employment and Society 33*(5), 865–876.

Bensusán, G., 2016. Organizing workers in Argentina, Brazil, Chile and Mexico; the authoritarian-corporatist legacy and old institutional designs in a new context. *Theoretical Inquiries in Law 131*(16), 131–161.

Cardoso, A., Gíndin, J., 2009. *Industrial Relations and Collective Bargaining: Argentina, Brazil and Mexico Compared, Working Paper no 5*. Industrial and Employment Relations Department, International Labor Office, Geneva.

CEIC, 2019 *Argentina Number of Construction Companies*. Ceicdata.com/en/argentina/number-of-construction-companies (accessed 30.09.19.).

Collado, P., 2015. Social conflict in Argentina: land, water, work. *Latin American Perspectives 42*(2) March, 125–141.

Etchemendy, S., 2019. The rise of segmented neo-corporatism in South America: wage coordination in Argentina and Uruguay (2005–15). *Comparative Political Studies 52*(10), 1427–1465.

Etchemendy, S., Collier, R., 2007. Down but not out'. Union resurgence and segmented neo-corporatism in Argentina, 2003–07. *Politics and Society*, 35.

Féliz, M., 2016. Till death do us part? Kirchnerism, neo-developmentalism and the struggle for hegemony in Argentina, 2003–15. In: Schmitt, I. (Ed.), (2016) *The Three Worlds of Social Democracy: A Global View from the Heartlands to the Periphery*. Pluto Press, London, 91–106.

Haider, J., 2015. Interpreting Argentine business unionism. *Latin American Perspectives 42*(2), March 60–73.

ILO, 2019. *Centenary Declaration for the Future of Work adopted at the 108th Session of the International Labour Conference*. ILO, Geneva. 21.06.2019

Instituto de Estadística y Registrado de la Industria de la Construcción (IERIC), 2017. *Informe de Coyuntura de la Construcción: informe anual correspondiente al ano 2017*. IERIC, Buenos Aires.

Instituto Nacional de Estadística y Censos, 2019. *Indicadores de coyuntura de la actividad de la construcción. Construcción 3*(11). Ministerio de Hacienda, Buenos Aires.

Instituto Nacional de Estadística y Censos, 2019 *Trabajo e Ingresos. Cuarto Trimestre de 2019 4*(1). Ministerio de Economía, Buenos Aires.

Larrabure, M., 2018 Post-capitalist development in Latin-America's left turn: beyond Peronism and the magical state. *New Political Economy* https://doi.org/10.1080/13563467.2018.1472564 (accessed 27.02.20.).

Marmara, L., Gurrieri, J., Aruj, R., 2014 with collaboration of Gonzalez, M.E., Texido, E., Ruggirello, H., (Ed.), *Análisis Comparado de la Mano de Obra Migrante en la Construcción en la Republica Argentina, 2001–2011.* Fundación UOCRA, Buenos Aires, Buenos Aires.

Ministerio de Trabajo Empleo y Seguridad Social, 2020. *Encuesta de Indicadores Laborales Abril 2020.* Ministerio de Trabajo Empleo y Seguridad Social, Buenos Aires.

Organization for Economic Cooperation and Development (OECD), 2019. *Economic Surveys: Argentina.* OECD Publishing, Paris.

Organización Internacional del Trabajo (OIT), 2015. *Migraciones Laborales en Argentina: Protección Social, Informalidad y Heterogeneidades Sectoriales.* OIT Oficina de País de la OIT para Argentina, Buenos Aires.

Raszewski, E., 2018. Argentina could shed 40,000 construction jobs amid crisis, executives warn. *Reuters Business News.* (accessed 06.09.18.).

Ronconi, L., March, 2019. Enforcement of labor regulations in developing countries. *IZA World Labor, IZA 2019,* 1–9.

Ruggirello, H., 2011. *El Sector de la Construcción en Perspectiva: Internacionalización e Impacto en el Mercado de Trabajo.* Aulas y Andamios, Buenos Aires.

Ugarte, S., Grimshaw, D., Rubery, J., 2015. Gender wage inequality in inclusive and exclusive industrial relations systems: a comparison of Argentina and Chile. *Cambridge Journal of Economics 39,* 497–535.

Undurraga, T., 2015. Neoliberalism in Argentina and Chile: common antecedents, divergent paths. *Revista de. Sociología Política 23*(55), 11–34.

UOCRA, (undated) *Guía Informativa Para Trabajadores Migrantes.* UOCRA, Buenos Aires.

3 Evolving Employment Relations in the Australian Construction Industry

Alex Veen and Susan McGrath-Champ

Introduction

This chapter explores contemporary employment relations developments across the Australian construction industry, a sector that is increasingly recognized by both state and federal governments as critical to continued Australian prosperity. In the aftermath of the mining boom, which propelled the Australian economy through the 2008–2009 global economic recession (known in Australia as the Global Financial Crisis), the construction industry has become one of the key drivers of Australian GDP growth (Australian Bureau of Statistics (ABS) 2018a) with the industry being the country's biggest employing sector (ABS 2018b) while also having the largest number of registered businesses (ABS 2016). A large proportion of these organizations are, however, non-employing entities, highlighting the industry's fissured (Weil 2014) and sub-contracted structure (Toner 2000a). With respect to employment relations, but also economic conditions, the industry can be understood as having four distinct segments: (1) residential, (2) commercial, (3) civil and infrastructure and (4) resource extraction-related construction; as well as marked spatial differences between different states and territories (McGrath-Champ et al. 2011). The employment relations climate across the industry is fragmented and marked by a history of conflict, with different segments exhibiting their own distinct patterns of labor–management relations, shaped by levels of capital required for projects, their location, complexity and level of union involvement (Allan et al. 2010). Driven by developments in both product and labor markets in conjunction with a range of technological advances and a complex political landscape, this chapter reveals an industry that has been, and continues to be, in a constant state of flux.

The remainder of this chapter is structured as follows. First, the diverse economic performance of the various segments of the Australian construction industry is detailed. Second, the state of employment relations in the Australian industry is discussed, with sectoral differences highlighted. This is followed, third, by a brief discussion of the key employment relations stakeholders. Fourth, some regulatory developments affecting the sector are considered, including the re-enactment of the Australian Building and Construction Commission (ABCC) as well as the implications of recent changes to government procurement requirements. The implications of the fissured nature of work in the construction industry for employment relations are then addressed. Finally, the changing nature of construction work due to technological innovations and its potential implications for more best practices employment relations are discussed, leading to a concluding summary.

The Contemporary State of the Australian Construction Industry

While globally most developed economies went into recession following the Global Financial Crisis, Australia went through this period relatively unscathed due to an unprecedented demand for mineral resources by the booming Chinese economy (Downes et al. 2014). This resulted in a 'two-speed' economy that also had considerable impact on construction activities (Kearns and Lowe 2011). High levels of sectoral and geographical variation in economic activity can be found, which reflect the broader, diverse characteristics and variegated nature of the Australian construction sector. For example, during the 'boom' period, the mining states of Western Australia and Queensland were buzzing with both resource-related as well as residential construction, drawing in swathes of construction workers from other states and overseas to some of the most remote parts of the country in order to get large mines into operation and gas projects on stream. At the same time, there was a period of 'slow-speed' growth in the south-eastern states. Around 2013, when the mining boom ended somewhat abruptly following the completion of most mining-related construction and a reduction in commodity prices and investment, the northern and western resource states and territories were left in a technical recession (Greber 2017). This also negatively impacted both the residential and commercial construction segments in these states.

Tempering the economic shock of the mining downturn was a disguised form of Keynesian economic stimulus, with both State and Commonwealth governments spurring construction activity on the east coast (Jericho 2018). Record levels of government expenditure on large infrastructure projects (Wallace 2017) coupled with strong population growth and record levels of foreign investment in residential construction, constituted another boom creating employment opportunities for those workers displaced from the mining states and supporting an increasingly faltering economy (Economist 2017). In effect, the growth in residential and infrastructure construction in New South Wales (NSW) and Victoria (Vic) ensured that in the aftermath of the mining boom the

Australian economy avoided a national recession (Downes et al. 2014; Economist 2017).

The continued urban sprawl of major metropolitan areas like Melbourne (Vic) and Sydney (NSW), for instance, has required upgrades to roads, railways and other critical infrastructure (Ai Group 2015). In residential construction, changes to zoning regulation and consumer preferences have also resulted in a move away from quarter-acre residential blocks to increasing medium- to high-density residential construction development in the inner metropolitan areas. This, in turn, has provided opportunities for more innovative construction practices, such as the use of prefabrication. At the same time, there are increasing concerns about the quality of these types of residential construction projects, with experts arguing that the industry is suffering from lax building regulations and quality enforcement (O'Leary 2019). In the first half of 2019, in Sydney alone, three major apartment blocks required urgent remedial repair works (News.com.au 2019). Moreover, with echoes of the UK's Grenfell Tower disaster, the building industry in the State of Victoria has been plagued by a combustible cladding crisis, with over 600 buildings in Victoria alone identified as having high-risk cladding (Lockrey and Moore 2019). These incidents highlight that while there is increasing sophistication and use of best practice construction methods, such as Building Information Management Systems (Veen et al. 2017), at the same time the sector continues to be plagued by systematic problems involving quality, employment relations and training – with the latter two further discussed in the remainder of the chapter.

Employment Relations Landscape in Australia

The contemporary state of employment relations in the Australian construction industry is varied, with considerable differences in the industrial climate between different parts of the industry. The residential construction segment, for instance, is by and large quiescent due to the prevalence of subcontracting and high levels of self-employment, with unionism effectively extinct in this segment since the 1970s (Underhill 2002: 125). In contrast, the commercial and infrastructure segments are relatively rife with industrial conflict (McGrath-Champ and Rose Warne 2009). This segment of the industry has a reputation as an industrial hornets' nest, whereby the militancy and industrial muscle of the powerful Construction, Forestry, Maritime, Mining and Energy Union (CFMMEU) is frequently despised by management as well as conservative politicians. The considerable union power in this segment of the industry can be attributed to four critical factors (Underhill 2002). First, the delays and costs associated with industrial disruptions mean that builders are more likely to accommodate unions' demands, for example, to avoid liquidated damages. Second, the CFMMEU and its predecessor have been able to develop strong on-site union cultures, providing high levels of membership support. Third, the union has adapted itself to the more fissured nature of the industry, looking not only after members at the major construction firms but also actively policing employment conditions of the smaller subcontractors. For instance, in 2013, the Western Australia Branch of the union instigated an illegal blockage of the Perth Airport over the non-payment of wages by a subcontractor for the airport's expansion (Burrell 2016). Finally, due to the project nature of the industry and the associated relative precariousness of employment, workers develop stronger class and union identities in comparison to other industries.

To the extent that cooperation between management and unions in the industry can be found, it can be best characterized as a form adversarial pluralism (Bray et al. 2017) — although the CFMMEU's attitude in certain states like Victoria, for instance, can be framed as relatively radical whereas some managers, firms and employer associations within the industry clearly exhibit unitarist tendencies. In effect, management across the industry has mainly sought to 'contain' or 'escape' (Walton et al. 1994) existing union relationships rather than looking for avenues to foster more collaborative relationships (Bray et al. 2017). There are, however, occasional instances of collaboration, one being around mental health. Major construction firms, employer associations and unions are all supporting the 'Mates in Construction' charity – a suicide prevention initiative to enhance worker well-being in the industry. In general, however, labor–capital relations in the industry are frequently terse, strained and conflictual.

The industrial tensions in these parts of the construction sector require a historical appreciation and recognition that union militancy has been a fundamental part of pockets of the industry. In the 1980s, for example, the then Hawke Labor government pushed for the deregistration of the Builders Labourers' Federation (Ross 2004) – which was renowned for combativeness, militancy and corruption – yet also instrumental to social causes such as the 'green bans' which stopped undesirable construction development in public and social spaces (Burgmann and Burgmann 1998). The CFMMEU, its successor, has similarly frequently raised the ire of many commentators, regulators and politicians. In consequence, the employment relations climate in the Australian construction industry is heavily politicized.

Newspaper headlines from recent years suggest that the Australian construction industry continues to be hampered by high levels of industrial unrest (The Australian 2018; The Australian Financial Review 2018), with the CFMMEU frequently portrayed as a rogue union. Data on days of strike action reveal that proportionally the construction industry has a higher level of industrial disputation than other Australian industries (see Figure 3.1). In the first half of 2017, the construction sector was responsible for just over half of the strike days in Australia, with industrial activity mainly occurring in Queensland as a result of enterprise bargaining negotiations between the CFMMEU and a number

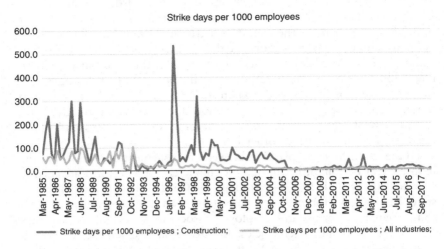

Figure 3.1 Strike days per 1,000 employees – Australia: All industry and construction industry.

of large construction firms (Nicholson et al. 2017). Despite being subjected to its own regulatory regime (discussed further below), industrial unrest is disproportionally concentrated in this industry yet, compared to the 1980s when industrial unrest in the industry was at its peak, it has significantly decreased (McGrath-Champ et al. 2011).

The Role of the State

To break the cycle of adversarial and unproductive relations that exist across segments of the industry, politicians of different persuasions have sought to intervene in the industry. A high level of state intervention is reflected by the ongoing governmental and public inquiries into the sector, such as the Cole Royal Commission established by the Howard Liberal–National coalition government in 2001, the Public Infrastructure Inquiry held by the Productivity Commission in 2014, as well as the more recent Heydon Royal Commission into trade union corruption. The initiatives by Conservative governments have been particularly marked by regulatory intervention. As Wal King (former CEO of a major construction company) explains, public scrutiny of the sector has been a regular occurrence since the latter part of the 20th century:

> [t]he commercial and industrial practices of the Australian building and construction industry have long been the subject of public scrutiny .... [It] is one of the most closely examined sectors of the Australian economy (cited in Forsyth 2007: v).

Direct as well as indirect state intervention in employment relations can be identified. Most notably, the industry is subject to a separate regulatory regime in the form of the ABCC (discussed in more detail below). Its chief purpose is to 'promote understanding and enforce compliance with Australia's workplace laws in the building and construction industry' (ABCC 2019b). At the same time, governments, through their role in setting building codes, procurement requirements for government-funded projects, licensing of trades and role in the recognition and development of trade skills, have a less direct impact on the employment relations climate in the industry. As part of the Building Code (Code for Tendering and Performance of Building Work 2016), for instance, there are new workplace relations-related requirements that the parties must comply with before they can successfully tender for Commonwealth funded construction work. If found to be in breach, there is the risk that relevant entities are 'excluded from tendering for or being awarded Commonwealth funded building work for up to one year' (ABCC 2019a). At a time of unprecedented investment by both Commonwealth and State governments in new infrastructure (Ai Group 2018) – including roads, railways, schools and hospitals – non-compliance poses a significant business risk for firms that operate within this sector. One of the requirements, for instance, is that the enterprise agreements that employers have concluded with their employees and their bargaining representatives (including unions) cannot contain any 'prohibited content' (Building Code s. 11 (3)). Effectively, the then Turnbull Liberal–National Coalition government imposed restrictions on the bargaining parties' ability to curb managerial prerogative (for instance, prohibiting the inclusion of clauses dictating redundancy requirements), restricted the role that is carved out for union officials under an agreement and circumscribed the ability of lead firms and unions to dictate standards for subcontractors throughout the supply chain. Other forms of indirect state intervention in the industry's employment relations can be found, for example, in the form of mandated apprenticeship and trainee levels for government funded projects over A\$20 million in Victoria, as part of the State government's local skill development initiative called the Victorian Major Projects Skill Guarantee (Buying for Victoria 2019).

In 2019, the re-elected federal Morrison Coalition government was seeking to introduce further workplace relations regulatory reforms, intended partly at targeting the CFMMEU and the construction sector through the Fair Work (Registered Organizations) Amendment (Ensuring Integrity) Bill 2019. The re-introduction of this previously defeated legislation, dubbed by commentators the government's 'union-busting bill', will make it easier for the government and other parties such as employers and their associations to request the deregistration of unions and their officials (Martin 2019). Potentially constraining the ability of Australian unions to represent workers, whilst also possibly in breach of Australia's commitment to the International Labour Organization's Freedom of Association provisions (Patty 2019), these laws gained increasing public prominence and acceptance following the alleged misconduct of a senior CFMMEU union official (Marin-Guzman 2019). This regulatory attempt to hamstring unions is strongly supported by all major employer associations that have a level of involvement with the construction sector, including the Master Builders Australia (2019), Ai Group (2019), the Australian Chamber of Commerce and Industry (ACCI 2019), as well as the Australian Mines and Metals Associations (AMMA 2019). This further illustrates the interventionist and anti-union sentiment that permeates conservative workplace relations politics in Australia (Cooper and Ellem 2008). Although for a while it appeared to have vanished (Cooper 2011), instead it appears to have been veiled and a resurgence has been underway under the Turnbull and Morrison Coalition governments (Forsyth 2017; Rawling and Schofield-Georgeson 2019). Given the contentious nature of employment relations in sections of the construction industry and the CFMMEU's relative strength, it is foreseeable that continued government intervention in the industry will occur.

The Rise of a Super Union

Historically the Australian construction industry has been covered by multiple unions which were organized according to crafts or trades rather than a single union representing workers across the entire industry (Burgmann and Burgmann 1998; Forsyth 2007; Macintyre and Isaac 2004). The level of union density in the industry currently sits around 11.75 percent (ABS 2018c), down from 34.1 percent in 1994 (Gilfillan and McGann 2018). Due to the legacies of Australia's award system, linked to the compulsory arbitration and conciliation system and through which minimum pay rates and conditions of employment for workers were traditionally established, unions have distinct coverage over specific trades and/or professions, or even specific geographical areas (Macintyre and Isaac 2004). In addition, most unions comprise a federally registered peak union body with associated state and territory affiliates. There are several federally registered unions with coverage over the construction industry, including the Australian Workers' Union, the Australian Manufacturing Workers' Union (AMWU), the Communications, Electrical, Electronic, Energy, Information, Postal, Plumbing and Allied Services Union of Australia (CEPU), and the above-mentioned CFMMEU. The last, notorious for its militancy, is the result of a merger between the former Construction, Forestry, Mining and Energy Union (CFMEU) and the

Maritime Union of Australia. Described by business as the 'merger from hell' (Philips 2015), these two powerful and militant organizations with a reputation for unlawful conduct merged on 27 March 2018. Considered a major threat by employers due to their combined resources, assets and ability to exercise influence over entire supply chains, there were unsuccessful attempts by both employer associations and the government to block the merger (Bray et al. 2019). AMMA, for instance, unsuccessfully appealed to the Federal Court of Australia to undo the merger (McCauley 2018).

The employer angst surrounding the CFMMEU is fuelled by its reputation, with the 2015 Heydon Royal Commission finding that its predecessor had a 'culture of disregard for the law' (Heydon 2015:138). Its organizational capacity and industrial muscle have enabled it, acting both legally, and in instances illegally, to achieve above average wage increases for members. The latest wage figures revealed that enterprise agreements in the construction sector provided workers with the highest annual wage increases, of almost six percent annually, at a time when the rest of the Australian workforce is affected by a period of stagnant wage growth (Workplace Express 2018a), characterized by maximum wages increases of around two to two and half percent, highlighting the clear economic benefits of unionization and enterprise bargaining for union members in this sector. Despite declining union density, the CFMMEU has continued to steadily increase its membership base – albeit not in line with industry expansion. It currently has around 132,708 paid-up members, up 28.8 per cent from 2003 (Gilfillan and McGann 2018).

Continued complaints by business leaders and political commentators about the CFMMEU's stronghold over the construction industry (Hannan 2018) point to the organization's engagement in continued prohibited and illegal practices, including pattern bargaining[1], engagement in unprotected industrial action, the use of secondary boycotts to pressure main contractors and the coercion of subcontractors into signing enterprise agreements (Marin-Guzman and Patrick 2018) – practices which were widely covered in the 2015 Heydon Royal Commission. The mega-union's apparent disregard for existing industrial laws has resulted in over A\$16 million dollars in penalties following cases brought forward by the ABCC and its predecessor (Workplace Express 2019b). In 2018, the Australian Competition and Consumer Commission laid criminal charges against the organization and its division in the Australian Capital Territory for engaging in anti-competitive behavior (Workplace Express 2018b). Although its industrial reputation is one aspect of the conservative camp's contempt for the CFMMEU; the other, which cannot be ignored, is its close links to the Labor party and the funding it provides to that political party (Ergas 2018). Employment relations and political context in the construction sector are tightly interwoven (Marin-Guzman 2019).

Employer Associations

Similar to the representation of workers, there are multiple employer associations advocating and lobbying on behalf of construction firms. Although the Master Builders Association (MBA) is the main peak building and construction industry association, there are other federally and state registered associations that represent firms active in building and construction, including the National Electrical Contractors Association, Ai Group, the Australian Chamber of Commerce and Industry (ACCI) and the Australian Mining and Metals Association (AMMA). Whereas under the compulsory conciliation and arbitration system, employer associations played an active role in representing member firms at the Commission, these days their role with respect to employment relations is more strategic, advocacy and policy-oriented. Some associations continue to have a 'hands-on' involvement on behalf of members, for example, through dedicated workplace relations advisory services (provided by AMMA or the Western Australian Chamber of Commerce and Industry). Additionally, the associations play a critical role in relation to training and apprenticeships, with some acting as training providers. The majority are involved in the continued formulation of state and federal training frameworks for the Technical and Further Education vocational training and education sector, which remains important for the industry's continued skill development.

Also impacting employment relations are developments in relation to workplace health and safety (WHS) regulation. In the aftermath of several deadly incidents and increasing calls for so-called 'manslaughter' laws, the MBA has been actively cautioning against the introduction of laws which could make members criminally liable for workplace safety incidents (Thornthwaite and Sheldon 2019). Associations have further been advocating a more uniform WHS approach in Australia (Thornthwaite and Sheldon 2019). Politically, associations have successfully lobbied for greater oversight of union involvement in redundancy funds (Sheldon and Thornthwaite 2015), the re-instatement of the ABCC, and introduction of the Building Code (Barry and You 2018). Associations have also been instrumental in ensuring that construction firms are able to utilize skilled migration schemes to address continued skills shortages (Toner 2000b; 2008), with some scholars arguing that the industry's increasing reliance on temporary migrants will have adverse impacts on the unions' ability to function effectively (McGrath-Champ et al. 2011), an issue to which we return below.

The Australian Building and Construction Commission

From an employment relations perspective, the Australian construction industry has been one of the key battlegrounds between the two main national political parties, Labour and the Liberal-National Coalition. Political interference in the industry is best exemplified by the introduction (Quinlan and Johnstone 2009), removal (McCrystal and Orchiston 2012) and reinstatement (Forsyth 2017) of the ABCC. As a result, the industry has been subjected to an industry-specific workplace relations regulatory environment since the early 2000s. In 2005, the Howard Coalition government – following the 2003 Royal Commission into the building and construction industry – established the ABCC as an industry-specific regulator which could address 'lawlessness on the part of building unions' (Forsyth 2016). The ABCC was provided with investigative powers greater than the police and courts (Cooper and Ellem 2008; Williams and McGarrity 2008). It was abolished by the Gillard Labour government in 2012, but reinstituted by the Turnbull Coalition government in 2016 after a double-dissolution election was held following the blockage in the Senate of the legislation enabling the reintroduction of the ABCC (Forsyth 2016; 2017).[2] This shows how far-reaching and contested this legislation and the ABCC are. The ABCC has been tasked with addressing illegal behavior on construction sites, while also seeking to foster greater productivity in the sector (ABCC 2019b). Whether it is meeting the latter objective is questionable (Allan et al. 2010) but the ABCC has actively targetted unions, with the majority of notices and proceedings brought against them (ABCC 2018). While successfully bringing procedures against unlawful union conduct, at the same time the regulator has been shrouded in controversy. For instance, in 2017 the head of the organization was forced to resign following revelations about the ABCC knowingly misrepresenting relevant workplace laws on information sheets that it distributed via its website (Baines and Smiley 2017). Queries were raised about some of the proceedings instigated, leading a senior Fair Work Commissioner to query the regulators' use of public and court resources pursuing 'a miniscule incident' of union officials meeting for tea (Workplace Express 2019a). Questions have further been raised about the increasing crackdown on the display of union insignia on workplace sites, ironically under the guise of 'freedom of association' (Marin-Guzman 2018). It is unclear how such politically contentious interventions in the sector will contribute to future productivity or foster more collaborative relations. Instead, such neo-liberal state interventions in Australian workplace relations (Cooper and Ellem 2008) appear to be meticulously planned to reduce the power and relevance of unions, seeking to sideline, preoccupy and deplete the resources of these worker organizations.

Fissuration, Subcontracting, Risk Shifting and Skills Gaps

The third section of the chapter considers the fissuration of the industry (Weil 2014) and its implications for employment relations. Subcontracting is a long-standing practice in the construction industry in Australia as in other countries. We briefly consider changes in the prevailing forms of construction subcontracting, the implications for skills and skill development and how these practices relate to some of the industry's current skill shortages and gaps.

Traditional Subcontracting

The configuration and dynamics of the construction industry in the early 21st century can be more clearly understood when contrasted to those of the late 20th century. While subcontracting is an enduring feature of the Australian construction industry, there have been major changes which have involved shifting risks and training responsibilities down the supply chain. 'Traditional' forms of subcontracting prevailed in construction and other industries such as women's garment manufacture and the film industry (Weil 2014), where production involved combining specialized activities to create diverse outcomes, that is, where the work necessitates expertise and investment in skills and equipment that may be needed only for a finite period of time. The uniqueness of the 'products' of construction mean that the know-how needed, for example, to produce an office tower is distinctly different to that for a major highway. General contractors were, historically, the lead firm taking charge of hiring, managing and coordinating subcontractors for a project. They were commonly the direct employer of so-called 'basic trades' such as carpenters, laborers and some engineers who were usually required for the full duration of projects.

Weil (2014) observed that from the 1980s major companies across the face of the construction industry (and many others) discarded their role as the direct employer of people responsible for providing the organization's products and services. In the construction industry this was accompanied by the emergence of 'construction managers' who coordinate work and are responsible for timely completion of construction within budget but do not directly employ any trades (even basic trades functions are carried out by subcontractors), with a 'project manager' responsible for the broader project. While subcontracting, as the organizational arrangement in the construction sector, may seem to be enduring (it is a new arrangement in some other industries), current forms of subcontracting are more deeply 'fissured' than earlier subcontracting.

Changing Industry Structure

By the end of the first decade of the 21st century, massive transformations within the Australian construction industry were apparent. In terms of organizational form, there was a marked 'hollowing out'– major construction companies became increasingly 'lean' reflecting the application of management principles pioneered in the manufacturing industry (McGrath-Champ et al. 2011). Main contractors distanced themselves from the physical work of construction, choosing to focus on management and coordination functions. The industry became dominated by a small number of large companies in a process of dissolution and concentration. Major companies that endured generally took on a conglomerate form and shifted to competing globally for work (McGrath-Champ et al. 2011). Foreign ownership of the industry 'majors' increased and government withdrew from direct construction activity. Main contractors extended into property development, marketing, financing and running their own property trusts, such that over the first two decades of this century, large construction companies have come to be 'as much about investment banking and risk trading as putting up buildings' (Rafferty and Toner 2019: 162; McGrath-Champ et al. 2011).

The early involvement of Australia's construction industry in real estate investment trusts along with associated influences such as financialization in the construction industry (the conversion of illiquid built assets into more liquid financial instruments) was a dominant, strategy in risk management and a source of profit by developers, major construction companies and investors (Rafferty and Toner 2019). Placing liquid construction assets in direct and intense competition for global capital against all other asset classes heightened the intensity of risk with risks shifting vertically down the contractual chain and horizontally between developer, client, financiers and head contractors. For main contractors, primarily service and financial 'shells', 'best value' is measured by the short-term mechanisms of the marketplace (McGrath-Champ et al., 2011: 1113). It is not uncommon for major construction companies, previously engaged fully and directly in construction activity, to be configured internally as sections/divisions for property development, investment management, infrastructure development and construction – with construction often one of the small(er) functions of the revamped corporate entity.

Government infrastructure became increasingly tendered out to the private sector, often through public/private partnerships. By late 2010, public sector engineering construction work had diminished from two-thirds of all private/public sector engineering construction to 40 per cent (McGrath-Champ et al., 2011). In the two decades from 1984 to 2004, the decline in the public sector workforce in Australia directly involved in construction-related activity (81 percent) massively outstripped the overall decline in the total public sector workforce (four percent) (Toner 2008).

Effects of Structural Change

One of the most profound and challenging dimensions of this structural change is the extended subcontracting arrangements occurring widely across the industry. Construction workers of most kinds, from laborers to trades and even professional and semi-professionals, have become concentrated within smaller, task-specific enterprises. The increased prominence of subcontracting has also ushered in fundamental changes in the size and structure of enterprises in the industry, shown through a massive 245 percent increase in the number of private construction establishments in the 15-year period to the early 2000s and a corresponding drop in average private construction firm size from 4.1 persons per firm in the late 1980s to 2.1 persons in 2002–2003 (ABS 2007). Construction has the largest number of businesses of any Australian industry but over 90 percent of businesses fall within the small business category. In other words, there is a high level of non-employing entities or owner operators.

By becoming finance and property management 'shells', major companies in the industry shed labor and the corresponding costs of direct employment. Through reducing 'on costs', including superannuation, long service leave, payroll tax, sick pay, holiday pay, workers' compensation and the administration costs of direct employment, main contractors are understood to 'save' around 25–30 percent. Profit margin squeeze along the supply chain limits subcontractors' capacity further down the chain to provide employment benefits dislodged by main contractors, benefits which had been established through union action and for some lengthy period accepted (if reluctantly) by employers, as reasonable entitlements. McGrath-Champ and Rose Warne (2009:1118) observed that:

> [t]he outsourcing and subcontracting arrangements that have come to define the Australian construction industry have intensified competition throughout the industry, pressured profit margins and engendered a degree of precariousness that has few parallels. This is reflected in the short operating life of many businesses and the high rate of insolvency, affecting majors and subcontractors alike.

The phenomenon of 'phoenix' companies was commented upon as early as the turn of the century by the 2002 Royal Commission into the Building and Construction Industry (RCBCI 2002), whereby an enterprise is formed for a very short period of time, maintaining revenue payments to owners but dissolved before honoring workers' statutory entitlements such as leave or long service payments, meeting insurance or tax obligations. The proprietors not uncommonly establish a 'new' business entity of similar kind once such 'liabilities' have been extinguished.

Skills Gaps

Diminished employer commitment to training and skill development has become a pervasive feature of the industry (McGrath-Champ et al. 2011) and Australia's mining industry cycles commonly intensify skills shortages in the construction industry, as noted above. With their focus shifted away from direct construction activity, the employment of skilled workers is diminished, reducing training opportunities by major companies. This has a cascading effect whereby cost and profit pressures throughout the chain of subcontracting limit subcontractors' training capacity: they are reluctant (or unable) to employ low productivity employees such as apprentices or bear the diminished productivity of a qualified employee to supervise trainees. Narrowly focused, task-orientated enterprises commonly cannot provide the scope or duration of engagement that would permit apprentice training, and for the apprenticeships that exist, wages are very low and considered insufficient. Shin and McGrath-Champ (2013) set out the effects of these arrangements within the Australian tiling sector of the construction industry.

Compounding training deficits in the private sector, the large training capacity of the government (which fed skilled workers into the wider industry) has been curtailed by government outsourcing of construction work. Non-training can be strategically motivated behavior as contractors seek to avoid investment in training to contain bottom line expenditures. The extended subcontracting chain and the repositioning of construction labor with middle and lower level subcontractors, sometimes engaged as 'self-employed' rather than as 'employees' diminishes investment in skill formation (McGrath-Champ et al., 2011: 1118). The response to the structurally driven construction skills shortage was reform of the vocational education and training system and the establishment of national training and accreditation standards in an endeavor to resolve the labor mobility problems of state-based accreditation (McGrath-Champ et al. 2011). These initiatives met with limited success and the more significant action to address skills shortages has been through Australia's migration program.

Migrants Fill Skills Gap

Migration policy during the past quarter century became more instrumental in purpose, with increased emphasis on business and skilled worker migration over the previous family reunion and humanitarian focus. This has given rise to a very significantly expanded migrant worker intake, with the construction industry reliant on meeting labor force needs by engaging migrant workers on short- or limited-term contracts to work on individual projects in particular locations. Migration involved a three-fold shift: first, a dramatic increase in the numbers of business, professional and skilled migration in the construction industry, particularly directed at addressing the shortage of professional engineers, project and site managers; second, a substantial expansion in the temporary skilled visa program and; third, a broadening of the Working Holiday Maker programme, another temporary program. Project managers and engineers are commonly recruited from countries such as the UK, South Africa, Singapore and New Zealand. The creation and expansion of the former 'Class 457' visa program was the conduit through which much of the skills shortage was offset. Under the '457' visa program temporary migrants could be recruited for up to four years. The numbers of workers under these schemes dramatically increased. Employment protections for wages, hours and so on were relatively 'light', such that workers are frequently underpaid. It appeared, furthermore, to increase employment precariousness with a tendency for employers to substitute 457 visa workers for local workers. Veen et al. (2017) note that despite the discontinuation of the 457-visa category recently to curb expedient (and often exploitative) use of temporary workers, the new subclass 482 Temporary Skill Shortage Visa program gives ample scope for construction industry employers to sponsor blue-collar migrant workers.

Employers perceive migrant workers as having a better work ethic and more enthusiasm (Wright and Clibborn 2019: 163). Unsurprisingly, construction industry employers have been active in lobbying government against periodic threats of cuts to these migration intakes. Nevertheless, there is a longstanding, research-evidenced counter current of association between migrant labor and low-quality work (Wright and Clibborn 2019) with each of worker-, employer- and State-centered accounts mapped out in terms of possible explanatory accounts.

Future of Work: Prefabrication and Robotization

The fourth section of the paper considers the future of work in the Australian construction industry. Several factors including the increasing uptake of prefabricated building materials (Veen et al. 2017), robotization (Sklar 2015), task automation (Quezada et al. 2016), as well as the uptake of building information management systems, are recasting the nature of work and employment across the industry. Based on research in the state of Victoria, but with wider relevance across the whole country, Veen et al. (2017) discern that changes, including the introduction of cross-laminated timbers and offsite construction of prefabricated building materials, are likely to impact construction industry productivity. Reports from industry participants identify a contrast between approximately five and a half to six hours of productive working time per eight-hour-day on a commercial construction site and approximately seven and half hours in manufacturing, arising from the efficiency of plant setup, making the latter potentially more cost effective. The creation and supply of pre-fabricated building materials depends on the establishment of suitable supply chain production which may or may not occur locally. Outsourcing across many other Australian industries relies particularly on Asian subcontractors and suppliers. Prefabrication opens up the opportunity for construction firms to sideline the CFMMEU – as this kind of work lies in the domain of the AMWU and avoids the need for 'collaboration' with the construction workforce.

A construction site is typically unpredictable and often a hazardous place which, at a glance, appears contrary to the highly controlled, highly predictable, factory-like circumstances in which robots can most easily be deployed. While this means that task automation and robotization constitute more innovative and adventurous futures, bolder scenarios for the construction industry foresee future possibilities with numerous jobs and tasks performed with 'smart machines' and with less traditional, manual labor (Quezada et al. 2016).

Industry informants in Australia are forecasting that key onsite roles, such as crane drivers in particular, will be redefined. 'Driverless' machines, such as those now used in advanced technology mining, are likely to become more common in construction so that cranes may be operated from a control room, with computer screens, cameras and direct communication with workers on the ground at the load and unload points (Veen et al. 2017). This recasts not just one role on a construction site but a role that has industrially been particularly powerful in the Australian construction industry. Further examples of technological innovation include Japan's heavy earth-moving machinery company, Komatsu, which pairs driverless bulldozers with drones; the adaptation of mining company Rio Tinto's danger zone, automated mining technology to the construction industry (Quezada et al. 2016); or the combined worker–robotic machine 'partnership', for example, in brick laying (Sklar 2015). These are instances of the kind of changes that could become widespread in the construction industry, if a future of innovation is embraced. An industry's culture is fundamental to shaping whether, or how quickly, such innovation occurs. Australia's aging population, including the aging of the Australian construction industry workforce, shadows that in Japan and may be a positive influence toward innovation.

Frey and Osborne (2015) observe that, just as the mechanized assembly line transformed manufacturing, allowing companies to substantially cut production costs, so sophisticated algorithms and robots with enhanced dexterity are transforming industries, including construction, that were previously impervious to factory-style production influences. This economically dominant industry which, in Australia, has an industrial relations history rife with conflict, is currently undergoing a gradual reconfiguration of work and employment practices. This will place particular demands on a training system that, in the current era, struggles to provide a sufficient flow of more traditional trades and vocational skills. A shift to higher skill and more technologically so-phisticated skill sets will require the creation of new training capacities.

Conclusion

This chapter outlined the state of the construction industry in Australia, depicting its variegation structurally and spatially, and provided a historical and contemporary landscape of employment relations. In large sections of the industry, particularly in the commercial and infrastructure segments, employment relations have been shaped by on-going, often historical, tensions between the main union, the CFMMEU and management. Subsequently, these relationships can be characterized as an arm's length form of containment (Walton et al. 1994), while management also has, at times, sought to 'escape' this relationship. Within the heavily politicized context of the industry, the regulatory actions of the state in recent years can be viewed as an elongation and (self-serving) instrument of capital in the construction industry, currently illustrated by the Morrison government through its regulatory initiatives and interventions seeking to address, curtail and diminish the influence of this militant union. While often under the guise of fostering more productive workplace relations, the extent to which either the union or employers are genuinely interested in pursuing more collaborative forms of engagement and a shift to collaborative pluralism remains to be seen (Bray et al. 2017). On one hand, employers rely heavily on the state and its apparatus to shift the balance of power and diminish the unions' influence. Similarly, although the CFMMEU has sporadically engaged in interest-based forms of bargaining (Hulme 2019), its current success in achieving wages and conditions far superior to that of other unions in current labor market conditions has been developed around an adversarial style workplace relations, which Hulme (2019) points out may be a major impediment to adopting more interest-based bargaining approaches.

The transformation of the industry over the past few decades, described in this chapter, provides insights into problematic issues accompanying the hollowing out of major construction companies and the elongation of subcontracting arrangements. In the light of prospects around future technological changes and the highly politicized nature of this economically dominant industry, which has an industrial relations history rife with conflict between the trade unions, employees and large employers, the political context in which contemporary developments are taking place needs to be carefully considered and managed since it shapes the work regimes under which the parties operate and make employment relations choices.

In April 2020, amidst the COVID-19 global pandemic, Australian construction is one industry which has been permitted by government to continue operating, despite the closure of many other industries and entire sectors as part of lockdown requirements to limit the spread of the virus. The requirement for social distancing between workers on construction sites, which slows the pace of construction activity, has been accompanied by modified regulatory provision for construction activity to occur on every day of the week instead of being limited to Monday to Saturday. How the pandemic may affect the industry in the future is also a matter for further research.

Notes

1 Pattern bargaining is a process in labor relations where a trade union gains a new and superior entitlement from one employer and then uses that agreement as a precedent to demand the same entitlement or a superior one from other employers (Edwards, 2018).

2 A 'double dissolution' is a constitutional mechanism that allows a government (which has a majority in the House of Representatives) to overcome the blocking power of the Senate. The Australian Senate is powerful and can reject a Bill (a proposed law) even if it has passed in the House of Representatives. A double dissolution 'dissolves' both Houses of Parliament – the Representatives and the Senate – in order to try to resolve an issue through an election. This can only happen when a Bill has been rejected by the Senate, or fails to pass, or passes with amendments that are not acceptable to the government, after two attempts. Derived from the Museum of Australian Democracy (https://www.moadoph.gov.au/blog/double-dissolution-what-is-it/#).

References

ABCC, 2018 *2017–18 Annual Report*. The Australian Building and Construction Commission, Canberra.

ABCC, 2019a *What is the Code?* https://www.abcc.gov.au/buildingcode/what-code (accessed 4.09.19).

ABCC, 2019b *Who are we: overview.* https://www.abcc.gov.au/about/who-we-are/overview (accessed 4.09.19).

ABS, 2007 *Forms of Employment, Australia*, Catalogue No. 6359.0 (November). Australian Bureau of Statistics, Canberra.

ABS, 2016 *8165.0 - Counts of Australian Businesses, including Entries and Exits, Jun 2011 to Jun 2015*. Australian Bureau of Statistics, Canberra.

ABS, 2018a *5204.0 - Australian System of National Accounts, 2017–18*. Australian Bureau of Statistics, Canberra.

ABS, 2018b *6291.0.55.003 - Labor Force, Australia, Detailed, Quarterly, Aug 2018*. Australian Bureau of Statistics, Canberra.

ABS, 2018c *6333.0 - 2018 Characteristics of Employment, Australia, August*. Australian Bureau of Statistics, Canberra.

ABS, 2019 *6321.0.55.001 -Industrial Disputes, Australia, June 2019*. Australian Bureau of Statistics, Canberra.

ACCI, 2019 Australian Chamber welcomes the reintroduction of the Ensuring Integrity Bill. https://www.australianchamber.com.au/news/australian-chamber-welcomes-the-reintroduction-of-the-ensuring-integrity-bill 4 07 2019, Australian Chamber of Commerce and Industry. (accessed 4.09.19).

Ai Group, 2015 *Australia's Construction Industry: Profile and Outlook.* Australian Industry Group, Sydney.

Ai Group, 2018 *Construction Outlook: November 2018.* Australian Industry Group & Australian Constructors Association, Sydney.

Ai Group, 2019 *Time for Some Sensible Amendments to Australia's Workplace Relations System.* Australian Industry Group, Sydney.

Allan, C., Dungan, A., Peetz, D., 2010 'Anomalies', damned 'anomalies' and statistics: construction industry productivity in Australia. *Journal of Industrial Relations 52* (1), 61–79.

AMMA, 2019 *Government Re-commits to Passing Ensuring Integrity Bill.* Australian Mining and Metals Association: Australian Resources & Energy Group, Melbourne.

Baines, R. and Smiley, R. 2017 ABCC boss Nigel Hadgkiss resigns over Fair Work Act breach, Labor wants Michaelia Cash to follow, *ABC News*, 13 09, https://www.abc.net.au (accessed 20.12.19).

Barry, M., You, K., 2018 Employer and employer association matters in Australia in 2017. *Journal of Industrial Relations 60* (3), 358–377.

Bray, M., Macneil, J., Spiess, L., 2019 Unions and collective bargaining in Australia in 2018. *Journal of Industrial Relations 61* (3), 357–381.

Bray, M., Macneil, J., Stewart, A., 2017 *Cooperation at Work: How Tribunals Can Help Transform Workplaces.* The Federation Press, Annandale, New South Wales.

Burgmann, M., Burgmann, V., 1998 *Green Bans, Red Union: Environmental Activism and the New South Wales Builders Laborers' Federation.* UNSW Press, Sydney.

Burrell, A., 2016 CFMEU, officials fined over Perth airport project blockade. The Australian News Limited Pty Ltd, Sydney.

Buying for Victoria, 2019 *Major Project Skills Guarantee.* https://buyingfor.vic.gov.au/major-project-skills-guarantee (accessed 20.12.19).

Cooper, R., 2011 Industrial relations in 2010: 'dead, buried and cremated'? *Journal of Industrial Relations 53* (3), 277–287.

Cooper, R., Ellem, B., 2008 The neoliberal state, trade unions and collective bargaining in Australia. *British Journal of Industrial Relations 46* (3), 532–554.

Downes, P.M., Hanslow, K., Tulip, P. 2014 *The Effect of the Mining Boom on the Australian Economy.* Reserve Bank of Australia, Sydney.

Economist, March 2017 On a chiko roll; Australia's economy, *The Economist.* The Economist Intelligence Unit N.A., Incorporated, London. 9 https://www.economist.com (accessed 20.12.19).

Edwards, S. 2018 *'Pattern bargaining in Australia'*, Fair Work Legal Advice, https://fairworklegaladvice.com.au/pattern-bargaining-in-australia/ (accessed 4.09.19).

Ergas, H. 2018 CFMEU thugs emboldened by Bill's embrace. *The Australian.* News Ltd, 2 March https://www.theaustralian.com.au (accessed 20.12.19).

Forsyth, A.J. 2007 *Workplace Relations in the Building and Construction Industry*. LexisNexis Butterworths, Chatswood, N.S.W.

Forsyth, A. 2016 Explainer: what are the ABCC and Registered Organizations bills? *The Conversation*, 15 April https://theconversation.com/ (accessed 20.12.19).

Forsyth, A.J., 2017 Industrial legislation in Australia in 2016. *Journal of Industrial Relations 59*, 323–339.

Frey, C.B., Osborne, M. 2015 *Technology at Work: The Future of Innovation and Employment*. Citi GPS, Oxford, England.

Gilfillan, G., McGann, C., 2018 *Trends in Union Membership in Australia*. Parliament of Australia: Department of Parliamentary Services, Canberra, 1–8.

Greber, J. 2017 The RBA graph that explains the downturn in WA and Queensland. *Australian Financial Review*, 9 August https://www.afr.com/ (accessed 20.12.19).

Hannan, E. 2018 ABCC 'not enough to stop the CFMEU', *The Australian, News Ltd*, 11 September https://www.theaustralian.com.au (accessed 20.12.19).

Heydon, A.C. 2015 Royal Commission into Trade Union Governance and Corruption, *Final Report*. Commonwealth of Australia, Canberra.

Hulme, C. 2019 *Better the devil you know than the devil you don't: An analysis of unions' use of interest-based bargaining in Australia*. Honours thesis submitted to The Discipline of Work and Organisational Studies. The University of Sydney, Sydney, 1–98.

Jericho, G. 2018 It's still public infrastructure projects keeping the economy afloat, *The Guardian*, The Guardian News & Media Limited, 28 June https://www.theguardian.com/au (accessed 20.12.19).

Kearns, J., Lowe, P.W. 2011 *Australia's Prosperous 2000s: Housing and the Mining Boom*. Economic Group, Reserve Bank of Australia, Sydney.

Lockrey, S. and Moore, T. 2019 Flammable cladding costs could approach billions for building owners if authorities dither, *The Conversation*, The Conversation Media Group Ltd, 6 June https://theconversation.com (accessed 20.12.19).

Macintyre, S., Isaac, J.E. 2004. *The New Province for Law and Order: 100 Years of Australian Industrial Conciliation and Arbitration*. Cambridge University Press, Cambridge, UK.

Marin-Guzman, D. 2018 CFMEU threatens Kane Constructions over ban on union flags at work sites, *Australian Financial Review*, Nine, 7 February, https://www.afr.com (accessed 20.12.19).

Marin-Guzman, D. 2019 CFMEU scandal is 'game over' for Labor faction, *The Australian Financial Review*, Nine, 20 June https://www.afr.com (accessed 20.12.19).

Marin-Guzman, D. and Patrick, A. 2018 Behind the CFMEU's Melbourne caffeine hit on Boral, *The Australian Financial Review*, Nine, 28 June https://www.afr.com (accessed 20.12.19).

Martin, S. 2019 ACTU lobbies crossbenchers to oppose Coalition's 'unfair' union-busting bill, *The Guardian*, Guardian News & Media Limited, 11 July https://www.theguardian.com/au (accessed 20.12.19).

Master Builders Australia, 2019 *Ensuring Integrity Laws A Key Step To Uphold Rule Of Law On Construction Sites*. 4 July https://www.masterbuilders.com.au/Newsroom/Ensuring-Integrity-Laws-A-Key-Step-To-Uphold-Rule (accessed 4.05.20).

McCauley, D. 2018 Employer group launches bid to decouple CFMMEU 'super union', *WAToday.com.au*. Fairfax Media Management Pty Limited Perth.

McCrystal, S., Orchiston, T. 2012 Industrial Legislation in 2011. *Journal of Industrial Relations 54* (3), 277–292.

McGrath-Champ, S., Rose Warne, S. 2009 Organizational change in Australian building and construction: rethinking a unilinear 'leaning' discourse. *Construction Management and Economics 27* (11), 1111–1128.

McGrath-Champ, S., Rose Warne, S., Rittau, Y. 2011 From one skill shortage to the next: The Australian construction industry and geographies of a global labor market . *Journal of Industrial Relations 53* (4), 467–485.

News.com.au, 2019 *Third Sydney apartment block evacuated in six months*, News Corp Australia, 10 July https://www.news.com.au (accessed 20.12. 19).

Nicholson, D., Pekarek, A., Gahan, P. 2017 Unions and collective bargaining in Australia in 2016. *Journal of Industrial Relations 59* (3), 305–322.

O'Leary, T. 2019 Australia has a new National Construction Code, but it's still not good enough, *The Conversation*, The Conversation Media Group Ltd, 9 April https://theconversation.com/ (accessed 20.12.19).

Patty, A. 2019 Australian union busting bill harmful to democracy, international trade union body says, *The Sydney Morning Herald*, Nine, 18 July http://www.smh.com.au (accessed 20.12.19).

Philips, G 2015 The union merger made in IR hell, *Australian Financial Review*, Fairfax Media, 8 December, https://www.afr.com/ (accessed 20.12.19).

Quezada, G., Bratanova, A., Boughen, N., Hajkowicz, S. 2016. *Farsight for Construction: Exploratory Scenarios for Queensland's Construction Industry to 2036*. CSIRO, Australia.

Quinlan, M., Johnstone, R. 2009 The implications of de-collectivist industrial relations laws and associated developments for worker health and safety in Australia, 1996–2007 *Journal of Industrial Relations 40* (5), 426–443.

Rafferty, M., Toner, P. 2019. Thinking like capital markets – financialisation of the Australian Construction Industry. *Construction Management and Economics 37* (3), 156–168.

Rawling, M., Schofield-Georgeson, E. 2019 Industrial legislation in Australia in 2018. *Journal of Industrial Relations 61* (3), 402–420.

RCBCI, 2002 Australia. In: Cole, T.R.H. (Ed.), *Royal Commission into the Building and Construction Industry*. Terence Rhoderic Hudson, Melbourne.

Ross, L. 2004 *Dare to Struggle, Dare To Win! Builders Laborers Fight Deregistration*. Vulgar Press, Melbourne, 1981–1994.

Sheldon, P., Thornthwaite, L. 2015 Employer and employer association matters in Australia in 2014. *Journal of Industrial Relations 57* (3), 383–400.

Shin, J., Mcgrath-Champ, S. 2013 Informal skill formation and the division of labour: the case of Korean tiling workers in Sydney. *Journal of Industrial Relations 55* (1), 80–99.

Sklar, J. 2015 Intelligent machines: robots lay three times as many bricks as construction workers, *MIT Technology Review*, (accessed 2.09.15). https://www.technologyreview.com/2015/09/02/10587/robots-lay-three-times-as-many-bricks-as-construction-workers/.

The Australian, 2018 Militant force from. pit to port, *The Australian, News Ltd*, 7 March https://www.theaustralian.com.au (accessed 20.12.19).

The Australian Financial Review, 2018 The CFMEU normalizes lawbreaking, *The Australian Financial Review*, Fairfax Media, 18 May https://www.afr.com/ (accessed 20.12.19).

Thornthwaite, L., Sheldon, P., 2019 Employer and employer association matters in Australia in 2018. *Journal of Industrial Relations 61* (3), 382–401.

Toner, P., 2000a Changes in industrial structure in the Australian construction industry: causes and implications. *Economic and Labor Relations Review 11* (2), 291–307.

Toner, P., 2000b Trade apprenticeships in the Australian construction industry. *Labor and Industry: a Journal of the Social and Economic Relations of Work 11* (2), 39–58.

Toner, P., 2008 Survival and decline of the apprenticeship system in the Australian and UK construction industries. *British Journal of Industrial Relations 46* (3), 431–438.

Underhill, E., 2002 The Australian construction industry: union control in a disorganized industry. In: Bosch, G., Philips, P. (Eds), *Building Chaos: An International Comparison of Deregulation in the Construction Industry*. Routledge, London, 114–137.

Veen, A., Teicher, J., Holland, P. 2017 Continuity or disruption? An assessment of changing work and employment in the Victorian construction industry. *Labor and Industry: A Journal of the Social and Economic Relations of Work 27* (3), 193–212.

Wallace, A. 2017 Federal Budget makes record infrastructure spend, *Spatial Source*, May 17 https://www.spatialsource.com.au/ (accessed 20.12.19).

Walton, R.E., McKersie, R.B., Cutcher-Gershenfeld, J. 1994 *Strategic Negotiations: A Theory of Change in Labor-Management Relations*. Harvard Business School Press, Boston, Mass.

Weil, D. 2014 *The Fissured Workplace: Why Work Became so Bad for So Many and What Can Be Done to Improve it*. Harvard University Press, Cambridge, Massachusetts.

Williams, G., McGarrity, N., 2008 The investigatory powers of the Australian Building and Construction Commission. *Australian Journal of Labour Law 21* (3), 244–279.

Workplace Express, 2018a Construction boom continues to propel bargained pay, *Workplace Express*, Specialist News Pty Ltd, 19 November https://www.workplaceexpress.com.au (accessed 20.12.19).

Workplace Express, 2018b Union hit with cartel charges, *Workplace Express*, Specialist News Pty Ltd, 16 August https://www.workplaceexpress.com.au (accessed 20.12.19).

Workplace Express, 2019a Costs confirmed after ABCC pursues "very miniscule incident", *Workplace Express*, Specialist News Pty Ltd, 5 March https://www.workplaceexpress.com.au (accessed 20.12.19).

Workplace Express, 2019b We didn't threaten over deal, says CFMMEU, *Workplace Express*, Specialist News Pty Ltd, 10 May https://www.workplaceexpress.com.au (accessed 20.12.19).

Wright, C.F., Clibborn, S. 2019 Migrant labour and low-quality work: a persistent relationship. *Journal of Industrial Relations* 61 (2), 157–175.

4 The Brazilian Construction Industry

Informality and Qualification in Question

Marcella Piccoli and Carlos Diehl

Introduction

Brazil is the largest country in South America both by area and by population. With more than 210 million inhabitants, it spans a vast area with a wide variation between regions in terms of development. Urban areas prosper to the disadvantage of more remote locations. As a result, there is a steady migration of people from the countryside toward the larger conurbations searching for work. Many such migrants lack education and have little knowledge or understanding of their rights in law. They often find opportunities for employment in the construction industry.

The Brazilian construction industry is a major employer. Brazil had 38,354,448 workers who were formally registered in 2017 out of a total of some 91,449,000 employed according to the Brazilian Institute of Geography and Statistics (IBGE 2017a), so it follows that the larger part of the labor force is in informal employment. Some 1.9 million workers (around five percent of those formally registered) were employed in the construction industry. Informal working in construction is common so the total number of workers employed in construction is likely to be much higher. The industry generates jobs in related areas, for example in building materials and equipment, so it is a sector of fundamental importance for the economy. Commerce is responsible for 30 percent of jobs and manufacturing for 20 percent (IBGE 2017a).

The construction industry has few qualification requirements for operatives and, as indicated above, employs many people from lower socioeconomic backgrounds. Contractors, facing tight deadlines and cost pressures, recruit untrained and inexperienced workers on an informal basis, with negative results because they have a precarious existence. There are damaging consequences for the industry too, with poor quality work resulting in inefficiency and low productivity.

Trade unions have contributed to progress through organizing workers and seeking a greater part in political representation. An important milestone in Brazilian labor history was marked in 1943 with the Consolidação Das Leis Trabalhistas (Consolidation of Labor Laws)

(CLT) laying the basis for employment rights. Under the Workers' Party in (coalition) government between 2003 and 2016, there were programs to incentivize quality and productivity in the construction industry through the creation and implementation of technological and managerial modernization mechanisms.

Given the size of the population and the history of poverty and limited access to training, government supervision and action is of great importance to protect workers and ensure that rights are sustained and, at the time of writing, unions are concerned that the situation is deteriorating. Poor employee relations in Brazil provide an impetus for workers to fight for better rights, higher wages and improved working conditions. Support, in the form of labor inspection, is hampered by the size of the country and the inadequate number of labor inspectors. Employees, who are often reliant on a single source of income for family support, may be particularly reluctant to challenge employers and those who are informally employed have little support. Since the departure of the Workers' Party from government in 2016, employers' associations and rightwing campaigners have sought to reduce labor rights and undermine the funding system for trade unions.

This chapter outlines the main characteristics of the Brazilian construction industry regarding labor recruitment, regulation and law. First, we provide an overview of the Brazilian construction industry. This is followed by an account of the history of labor relations, explaining the legislation and procedures for construction employment. This leads to a discussion of outsourcing, informality and worker rights. The focus then shifts to the limited opportunities for training, low qualifications and the implications in terms of low productivity. The discussion then turns to safety, health and the quality of working life before conclusions are drawn.

The Brazilian Construction Industry

The Brazilian construction industry is dynamic, complex and labor intensive. The workforce in the industry is mostly male, approximately 94 percent according to the latest information from the Brazilian Institute of Geography and Statistics (IBGE 2003 to 2015, cited in IBGE Instituto Brasileiro de Geografia e Estatística 2016). The construction industry is a key contributor to Brazilian Gross Domestic Product (GDP) as well as to employment in the country (Da Silva et al. 2013; Ferreira and Malliagros 1998; Rigolon and Piccinini 1997).

According to Pinehiro (2015), the construction industry is divided into two specific and distinct sectors which are classified as light and heavy civil construction. Light civil construction includes all real estate projects, such as houses, churches, commercial and similar buildings. The light construction industry is characterized by low levels of efficiency, as well as poor quality and productivity, minimal flexibility with regard to modifications, low skill levels and high labor turnover (Costa 2011; Mello and Amorim, 2009; Silveira et al. 2005). Heavy construction, on the other hand, is focused on infrastructure works that may be national in scope – for example in transport, sanitation, electricity, pipeline transportation networks and gas pipelines. Heavy construction activities are characterized by significant capital and technology, in contrast to the labor-intensive nature of the work in light construction. Investments in the sector are paramount and have positive impacts on both economic and social development (Teixeira and De Carvalho 2006).

Companies in the infrastructure segment are the largest (employing on average 42 employees), according to the IBGE which provides statistical data for the construction industry. They have the highest average monthly salary (2.9 times the minimum wage), while specialized construction services are the smallest (employing an average of 10 employees) and have the lowest average monthly salary (twice the minimum wage) (IBGE, 2017b). The construction of buildings, a segment with the highest number of total employees, records an average of 15 employees per company, who receive, on average, 2.1 times the minimum wage. Given the pressure on wages, few or no formal qualifications, poverty, low pay and an unhealthy environment, it is evident that operatives are subject to many exploitative conditions that should be a cause for concern for Brazilian society.

Historically, governments have invested in construction programs seeking economic growth (Da Silva et al. 2016; Kureski et al. 2008). One of the best-known initiatives for the development and industrialization of deprived areas in the country, the Growth Acceleration Program (*Programa de Aceleração da Construção* (PAC)) was achieved through investment in economic infrastructure (transport, energy, communications), as well as social and urban projects (housing, sanitation and mobility). It was initiated during the government of President Lula da Silva to ensure the necessary expansion of the supply of public goods and services. PAC had two stages, from 2007 to 2010, with an investment of approximately Brazilian Real (R$) 503.9 billion and, from 2011 to 2014, with an investment of approximately R$ 955 billion.

Some research has identified a degree of regional concentration in PAC investments and questioned the benefits in terms of the impact on regional inequalities in Brazil. While the investments were relevant to the whole country, it is argued that the more developed regions were the prime beneficiaries. In order to be effective in the reduction of inequality across the country, proportionately more significant investment needed to be targeted at poorer and less developed regions, to directly stimulate productive activities in those regions (Da Silva et al. 2016).

Brazil has several large construction companies that are responsible for the more significant construction projects in the country. The top five, according to the Brazilian Chamber of Construction Industry (CBIC 2019), are Odebrecht, Camargo Corrêa, Queiroz Galvão, MRV and Triunfo; and the majority of their work is focused on activities in Latin America. Some international companies have an interest in the Brazilian construction industry too. For example, Chinese companies are currently seeking opportunities to invest, such as the China Communications Construction Company (CCCC), a large Chinese infrastructure company. According to newspaper reports, the company has projects for the next ten years with investments reaching R$102 billion (Exame 2019). The main projects are ports, railways, urban development and industry. CCCC also bought 80 percent of the Brazilian company Concremat in 2016, a strategic partner to deliver projects in Brazil.

Brazilian construction is essential not only for its direct impact on the economy but also because of the activity it generates within the supply chain. The effects are felt in terms of the demand for raw materials, support services and building products, as well as through the processes of contracting, subcontracting and sub-subcontracting. The supply chain generates further demand, both on the sectors supplying inputs and within the consumer sectors (Santos et al. 2011).

The Brazilian construction industry contributed R$278 billion to Brazilian GDP in 2018. Buildings were the largest segment, with 45.5 percent of the total, an increase from just under 40 percent in 2009. Infrastructure was ranked second, with 31.1 percent (IBGE 2018), a reduction from the level sustained in 2009 (46.5 percent). The sector comprised 124,500 active companies at the end of 2018, employing approximately 1.9 million people in the formal sector distributed according to the following: 37.1 percent in building construction, 35.0 percent in specialized construction services (companies that execute parts of buildings or infrastructure works, such as the preparation of the land and the finishing works) and 27.9 percent in infrastructure works (see Table 4.1) (IBGE 2018). The figures for formal employment show a steady rise from 2007 to 2013, falling thereafter.

Despite its economic importance, the construction industry has lower productivity than other sectors due to the limited capacity and interest of small and medium-sized enterprises in improving the level of qualification and performance of employees. Investment in research and development is low, including in prefabrication techniques and technology, and there is little use of work planning systems, resulting in high rates of material waste and rework.

The productivity of construction workers between 2007 and 2012, measured in relation to formal employment, showed a decline on average of 0.4 percent per year (Martins et al. 2015), while there was growth in hiring with approximately 1,200,000 new jobs created over five years, according to the IBGE, taking the total level of formal employment to around 2.9 million (IBGE 2018). Explanations include the increase in the

Table 4.1 Brazil: construction companies, by the division of activities

Divisions, groups and activity class	Number of active companies (2017)	Number of people formally employed, 31.12 (2017)	Number of active companies (2018)	Number of people formally employed, 31.12 (2018)
Total	126,258.00	1,901,094.00	124,522.00	1,869,592.00
Construction of buildings	47,054.00	703,807.00	47,438.00	702,053.00
Infrastructure works	12,775.00	534,268.00	12,799.00	547,642.00
Specialized construction services	66,429.00	663,019.00	64,285.00	619,897.00

Source: IBGE, Diretoria de Pesquisas, Coordenação de Serviços e Comércio, Pesquisa Anual da Indústria da Construção 2017–2018.

number of active companies, the expansion of real estate credit and construction for the 2014 World Cup.

The statistics regarding productivity, however, must be viewed with caution because of the increased formalization of the workforce (those with registered documentation) between 2006 and 2009 (CBIC 2009). There may have been many informal workers (not previously registered in standard work documentation) who contributed to the product before that time but who only began to be considered within the statistical calculations during those years. In other words, a higher number of workers being counted for the same amount of output creates the appearance of lower productivity.

On the other hand, comparing the period 2012–2018, it is apparent that there was a significant reduction in the level of employment, of perhaps one million workers, which almost offsets the increase in employment in the previous five year period, providing the most recent statistic for the level of employment of 1.9 million (see Table 4.2) (IBGE 2018). These figures may mean a decrease of formal jobs in the industry, because there is a smaller number of vacancies offered in the construction industry. On the other hand, it may also represent an increase in the informality of the sector (work without registration). Employment in the construction industry varies over time according to economic circumstances but the statistical information must be treated with care.

Formal and Informal Work in Construction

The CLT (Decree no. 5,452, from May 1, 1943) sets out the rules that should be applied during the hiring process to ensure the formal status and benefit entitlement of the worker. In law, an individual worker must be formally registered. Formal work is defined as work that is formally registered or recorded on a Work and Social Security Card or *Carteira de Trabalho e Previdência Social* (CTPS). The CTPS summarizes an individual's employment record, including information on salary, employment and paid leave. The CTPS also provides evidence for social insurance and pension purposes and access for the holder to social security entitlements. Where work is informal, there is a lack of social protection, in terms of the coverage of labor legislation and social security (DIEESE 2012). Informality can occur in different ways, for example, a worker who is not registered with a CTPS card is working informally, but in some cases a firm that in general is operating legally may recruit small-scale individual entrepreneurs and illegally employed workers who work informally.

The concepts of 'formality' and 'informality' have evolved over time in Brazil within the law relating to labor relations and associated areas. Labor inspectors and prosecutors, working under the auspices of the Ministry of Labor, have the responsibility to ensure that employment

Table 4.2 Formal Employment in the Construction Industry in Brazil

Year	2007	2008	2009	2010	2011	2012
Formal employment in construction industry	1,575,883.00	1,806,258.00	2,053,443.00	2,430,119.00	2,658,643.00	2,858,180.00
Year	**2013**	**2014**	**2015**	**2016**	**2017**	**2018**
Formal employment in construction industry	2,968,136.00	2,891,141.00	2,439,997.00	2,000,884.00	1,901,094.00	1,869,592.00

Source: IBGE, Diretoria de Pesquisas, Coordenação de Serviços e Comércio, Pesquisa Anual da Indústria da Construção 2007–2018.

law is upheld (Coslovsky et al., 2017). They carry out site inspections, usually in response to complaints raised by the trade union or through the municipality. The Ministry has the right to stop work that does not meet the standards set by legislation, including situations where informal working is used or where there is a failure to comply with relevant regulations. Its role is also fundamental to the development of employment rights and to health and safety standards in the workplace. This Ministry has more recently been re-positioned so that it now works under the auspices of the Ministry of Economy, Justice and Citizenship (according to Law no. 13,844 from June 18, 2019), a change that is of significant concern, especially as it might limit the frequency and scope of work-related inspections.

In 2017 the Brazilian Council of the Construction Industry (CBIC) investigated the extent of illegal informality in the construction industry. The construction industry employs approximately two million workers through a formal contract and the CBIC research suggested that there may be another two million people who find work as part of the informal civil construction market (CBIC 2017).

In Brazil, outsourcing is more restricted than in some other countries although it is nonetheless widespread. For legal purposes, an employee is defined as someone who provides services to an employer on a regular basis, is under his employer's supervision and works for a salary. That employee should be formalized through the CTPS process. Outsourcing is permitted but it is regulated under the civil law since the assumption is that two companies are forming a contract. Under labor law, an outsourcing contractor may be jointly liable if the contracted company fails to meet its labor obligations.

Furthermore, to facilitate inspection and provide more control, the government of President Dilma Rousseff created an integrated Digital Book-keeping System of Tax Obligations (eSocial) (Decree no. 8.373 from December 11, 2014). Through this system, via an online platform, companies can communicate with the government via a 'one-stop shop' for a varied portfolio of information, including information related to employment, to social security contributions, payroll, accident-at-work communications and other notices. Electronic information simplifies the provision of information and guarantees the rights of the formal employee while simultaneously avoiding unnecessary bureaucracy for the employer and facilitating company inspections. The formality of the process ensures that documented employees, those who are formally employed, will receive their due entitlement.

The Evolution of Labor Relations in Brazil

Some historical background is needed to understand the current situation regarding labor relations in Brazil. The revolution of 1930 under

President Getúlio Vargas was a significant milestone in the history of labor. The armed movement of that time arose from industrialization as a new working class emerged to demand political participation. The resulting pressures led to challenges to the government to such an extent that it was unable to absorb public demands. Brazil was moving from a predominantly agrarian economy to an industrialized society and, in corporatist developments that paralleled the rise of Peronism in Argentina, labor laws were passed to address emerging social issues while enabling the government to create a political support base in the working class (Da Luz and Santin 2010). Vargas was responsible for the creation of the Ministry of Labor, Industry and Commerce with the intention of tackling social issues and years of struggle followed as the working class sought recognition and support within the law.

The period following 1930 is characterized by the emergence of laws to regulate labor relations. These years saw improvements to workers' rights, such as a minimum wage, a standard eight-hour working day, paid annual leave, compensation for dismissed workers, as well as medical and health assistance. The principles of plurality and union autonomy were affirmed, in addition to the recognition of collective labor agreements and the creation of labor courts. In another milestone, in 1943, the CLT brought together all existing labor legislation, creating the concept of a formal job with legal employment rights (Coslovsky et al. 2017: 80) and the institutionalization of labor relations. These years of struggle saw the emergence of trade unions as a force within Brazilian society. Under the new legislation, each trade was to be represented by a single union within a given area, funded by mandatory union contributions, paid by all formally employed workers and controlled and distributed by the government (Coslovsky et al. 2017: 81–82). The union contribution made by the employer was equivalent to one day's pay for each worker. This system of union funding also gave the government great influence over the unions.

The unions that emerged in the late 1970s and early 1980s were supported by the mobilization and widespread strikes of large proportions of the Brazilian workforce. In this period, Brazil was going through a military dictatorship and working-class action during this time contributed to the democratization of Brazilian society. Within the construction industry there were strikes, motivated by fundamental economic issues – poor quality food, inadequate accommodation, poor sanitation and bullying by security forces (Campos 2014 cited in Nowak 2018). Poor health and safety standards were also major factors in these disputes. These movements were more populist than socialist, their main weakness being the lack of support through political parties (Rodrigues 2009). Furthermore, the level of indebtedness of the country was reflected in a fall in the living standards of the population, as well as a significant increase in informality at work (Cardoso-Júnior 2001).

The 1988 Constitution contributed to progress on social rights. It introduced instruments of direct democracy, such as plebiscites, which were regulated by the National Congress in a limited way, widening the possibility of participation in politics. Other social movements emerged, calling for the decentralization of the state and for decision-making power to be closer to the population. The most significant force contributing to these movements was the Workers' Party (PT) which won power in 2002, led by President Lula Inácio, with the expectation of a decentralized system intended to favor the disadvantaged in society (Moroni 2005; Radermacher and Melleiro 2007).

The Lula government sought to engage with the trade union movement and encourage a climate of social dialogue, creating the Council for Economic and Social Development and the National Labor Forum, with the primary objective of considering social security, tax, labor and union reforms, in an attempt to build consensus on the most controversial issues. The union centers coordinated their actions, representing the workers through registered trade unions and participating in negotiations. In construction, there was a further strike wave between 2011 and 2014, associated with the Lula Government's plan for accelerated growth (PAC) (Nowak 2018). These disputes occurred on large infrastructure sites being developed in the North East of Brazil and were largely motivated by complaints similar to those in earlier strikes – poor food, inadequate accommodation, lack of medical care, low wages and absence of leave opportunities. These disputes were also largely spontaneous events and not organized by the unions. At this time, changes were made concerning the percentage of workers' salaries allocated to union contributions, through article 589 from the CLT (Decree no. 11.648, 2008).

Another significant milestone was the new agenda created according to the precepts of the International Labour Organization (ILO) in 2006. This was significant because of the tripartite nature of the ILO, bringing together representatives of workers, employers and government. President Lula signed an agreement launching the National Decent Work Agenda (*Agência Nacional do Trabalho Descente* – ANTD). The agenda supported ILO priorities in Brazil, such as the generation of more and better jobs, eradication of child labor and the strengthening of social dialogue as an instrument of democratic governance. It provided a technical cooperation program in consultation with employers' and workers' organizations that was fundamental for the improvement of workplace inspections, addressing the most extreme abuses. According to the ILO, between 1995 and 2015, 49,816 workers were rescued from a modern slavery situation at work in Brazil. Most of them were migrants who had left the countryside searching for better jobs in the main cities, attracted by false work promises (Organização Internacional do Trabalho undated). Following the intensification of inspection in urban centers, slavery was most commonly found in the construction industry.

Until recently Brazilian unions have proven relatively resilient (Coslovsky et al. 2017). Most importantly, the principle of unity as a union model prevents the existence of more than one union for one economic activity in the same territorial base. Therefore the law limits the creation of unions on a given territorial basis but allows the creation of many unions with respect to different economic activities (Cardoso and Gindin 2009). The union movement consists of hierarchical levels, encompassing confederations, federations and unions. Confederations have a national reach; federations have a state reach and unions have a city or municipal reach (Cardoso and Gindin 2009). The Confederations comprise at least three federations and are essential to political co-ordination and campaigning. In May 2007, there were 19 confederations (Cardoso and Gindin 2009), each of which consisted of at least five unions in the same sector. Currently the most important are the *Central Única dos Trabalhadores* (CUT) or 'United Central of Workers'; *Confederação Geral dos Trabalhadores* 'General Confederation of Workers'; and *Força Sindical*, 'Union Force'. The CUT defines itself as an autonomous central union committed to supporting working class in-terests and advocating freedom and autonomy in line with the Conventions of the ILO. It claims 3,806 affiliated organizations and its size and support ensure that it possesses a sense of political power. The union centers represent the interests of specific trades or sectors (CUT undated).

Unions protect workers' rights in economic, professional, social and political affairs and have the right to organize strikes to improve wages and working conditions. They also run projects aimed at improving the lives of their members, such as organizing training events on better health and safety conditions at work. Union prerogatives and duties are defined in the CLT (articles 513 and 514), as follows: To collaborate with public authorities in the development of social solidarity; to pro-mote conciliation in labor disputes; to represent the general interests of their trade or profession, or the individual interests of associates con-cerning the activity or profession carried out; conclude collective bar-gaining agreements; elect or appoint representatives of their trade or profession; and impose contributions on those eligible for membership. Furthermore, the CLT states in article 195, first amendment (law no. 6.514, on December 22, 1977), that unions are allowed to request the Ministry of Labor to carry out inspections in an establishment or sector and to investigate unhealthy or dangerous activities. Proposals to reform labor law and limit union influence have impacted union income and influence (Carbonai 2019). Union contributions are no longer manda-tory for employees, as they were in the past, so employee agreement is required for union deductions to be made. When this has been expressly authorized, employers are required to deduct the union contribution from their employees' payroll in March of each year (article 579, CLT,

Law no. 13,467 from 2017). The amount of the union contribution corresponds to the remuneration of a typical working day.

Only the most densely populated areas have seen the emergence of vibrant and effective working class activity. This is due to the evolution and regional diversity of the Brazilian economy. The state of São Paulo, for example, is the most populous federative unit in Brazil with a population of around 46 million (IBGE 2019). The São Paulo Construction Workers' Union, Sintracon (*Sindicato dos Trabalhadores da Construção Civil*) is one of the largest labor unions in Latin America. Its remit extends beyond that of a single city, representing more than 400,000 construction workers (sintracon.org.br, 2020).

The employers' associations (the word *Sindicatos* is used in Brazil for both employers' and employees' organizations) have similar prerogatives and duties as the labor unions and they are also described in the CLT and have either a state or national reach. For example, the Civil Construction Industries Union (*Sinduscon*) represents companies predominantly active in light civil construction at the state level. In contrast, heavy construction is represented by the Union of the Heavy Construction Industry (*Sinicon*), covering the entire country. They are responsible for employers' representation in agreements with the employees' unions, especially in collective bargaining. Employers' organizations represent employers' interests in labor relations and the dissemination of good practices in the industry. While it is not mandatory for employers to join employers' organizations, these associations have a significant influence and power in negotiations in the industry so that, in practice, they are likely to join.

Collective agreements are subject to annual renegotiation between employers and unions. Acting at the state level, collective agreements establish wages, setting minimum rates by trade or occupation, as well as regulating the rights and standards on health and safety for workers, including the obligations of the contractor regarding meals, snacks and personal protective equipment. Collective agreements also stipulate rules that require companies to have all the documents necessary for the hiring of both contractors and subcontractors, according to regulatory standards.

Outsourcing: Labor Standards Under Pressure

In the Brazilian construction industry, outsourcing is standard practice and construction companies subcontract many services. Outsourcing has the objective of minimizing and controlling costs – both direct and indirect – by deploying specialist subcontractors with expertise in areas where the client company lacks specialist knowledge (Cockell and Perticarrari 2010). It is argued that it has advantages, specifically that it is flexible and enables higher productivity (Druck 2016). The disadvantages for workers are that outsourcing opens the door to informality and social and employment problems result if it is not controlled (Biavaschi and Droppa 2014; Cockell and Perticarrari 2010). When under pressure, for example, in competitive contractual situations, employers often avoid using direct employment contracts to gain an advantage over competitors.

Governments have reviewed and amended laws addressing outsourcing with the intention of boosting employment and economic growth. The 1943 CLT defined outsourcing as the hiring of a specialist legal entity for a specific purpose and the subcontractor was required to employ the workers used. In recent times, this law has been reviewed and reformulated. Originally the concept of outsourcing was limited, specifying that the end activity or principal activity of the contracting company could not be outsourced but permitting outsourcing of the medium activity (temporary labor Decree no. 6,019, of January 3, 1974). Law no. 13,429 of March 31, 2017, passed under President Michel Temer, amended some aspects of this legislation, broadening the scope of outsourcing permitted. The new law allows outsourcing of all activities (end and medium) with the government claiming that companies could benefit from productivity gains.

Trades unions expressed concerns at the challenges presented by this legislation because Law no. 13,429 has the potential to undermine formal employment in the industry. It could lead to a loss of jobs for those currently formally employed, with the implication that working conditions would deteriorate. From a union perspective the results could be a destabilization of contractual arrangements, increased unemployment and the replacement of formal staff by outsourced and temporary entities (Santos 2017). Higher volatility is expected in employment contracts, with the result that career development and salary progression will be hampered (Santos 2017). Given the likelihood of outsourcing, contractors are reluctant to invest in improving skills and qualifications (Santos 2017) and the consequences of these legal amendments threaten a significant increase in worker exploitation and increase the risk of accidents at work (Druck 2016). The justification used – to boost the economy and increase employment – takes no account of the negative impact on workers. The Institute of Applied Economic Research shows in its research that, in outsourced activities, working conditions and remuneration are usually lower than those found in typical contracting activities (Campos 2018). The same research suggests that outsourcing will increase exponentially. Outsourcing is short term in perspective and in the long run leads to precarious work, with the likelihood that wages will decrease, the distribution of income will widen and this will lead to increased insecurity among workers. Union fragmentation will be another consequence when more activities are outsourced, weakening representation in both the workplace and at the political level.

Despite these union fears, the outsourcing law does offer some protection for outsourced workers. It guarantees that subcontractors' employees will have the same conditions as employees of the contracting organization, including medical care. Additionally, the main contractor will be held liable for employees' salaries should the subcontractor default – an arrangement that differs from regulations in other countries. Shared liability is an important element cited by CLT in article 455. In the event of default by the subcontractor, the employee is entitled to claim his rights from the principal contractor. This makes the outsourcing procedure imposed by contracting organizations of the utmost importance since they are obliged to consider the financial health of the subcontractor, as well as its history and performance on previous contracts. Some companies take protective measures, especially regarding the analysis of the subcontractor's business health, accessing information that can be consulted through websites using the business registration number. The main contractor may withhold a percentage of payment from the subcontractor as a guarantee that it is fulfilling obligations to its employees. The amount retained is released after the subcontractor proves compliance with the legal requirements regarding the employees (CLT Decree no. 5,452).

Informality and Worker Rights

Formal work provides indubitable benefits to the employee, for example, the legal obligation of the employer to take responsibility for the health and safety of the workforce and all the procedures that the job activity involves. The payment rules and benefits are defined through the CLT for formal workers and the act of 'signing the CLT' (that is the official employment record) is the fundamental characteristic of legal work in Brazil. The CLT also has articles that define salary values and enforce workers' rights. One of the first principles is 'autonomy' (Decree no. 5,452, article 444) according to which the contractual employment relationships can be subject to the free determination of interested parties—always provided there is no conflict with rights in labor law, with collective agreements or judicial decisions.

Due to the vast size of the country, it is only in the larger urban centers that there are active inspection systems, with inspectors focusing on the most visible enterprises. The bigger conurbations have a more significant union presence to establish, maintain and monitor workers' rights. Such support is far less common in more remote places where construction workers may be subject to 'informal contracts,' called 'word of mouth' contracts, and may not receive their most basic entitlements including food, accommodation, safety equipment or access to clean and sanitary working and living conditions (Silveira et al. 2005). Moreover, the process of inspection is time consuming, and it is often the case that a project is completed before the investigation is concluded, with the consequence that there is no penalty for the contractor or subcontractor for infringement of workers' rights. Construction companies are known to accept the risks associated with non-compliance, given the delay in, or lack of, inspection (Costa, 2011). Thus, the Ministry's performance ends up being effective only in the most notable or visible projects, typically in urban areas. Smaller scale and rural projects are unlikely to be affected and tend to escape the monitoring and inspection process.

While work is on going, employees should be subject to regular medical examinations. Maintenance of monthly timesheets is also mandatory. The certified copy of the social contract of the subcontractor should also be maintained in the place of work, to verify whether they are carrying forward the activities for which they are registered in the National Classification of Economic Activities (CNAE). The contractor and employees must fulfill the working hours as determined by the works contract and overtime working should not exceed two hours per day (when the typical working day is eight hours). The subcontractor must demonstrate full compliance with the contractual terms agreed with the main contractor. To this end, the subcontractor must deliver to the contractor, along with the invoice, the following documents (one month following the provision of services): Payroll of employees; Collection Guide and Social Security Information and GPS (Social Security Guide). In the event of default in these documents, the main contractor will be responsible for the labor and social security obligations of employees, including compliance with the Collective Labor Agreement.

In order to bypass such obligations, companies tend to avoid formal employment and take advantage of informal work arrangements. The cost of legal labor obligations, the documentation required and the contractual ties associated with it all encourage non-compliance. Abuse is facilitated by workers' lack of knowledge of their employment rights and by their desperate need for employment. Construction companies use informal contracts and, in the event of an inspection, they advise and guide their employees to deny any illegalities. The company and the contractors themselves try to transfer to the workers the responsibility of convincing the inspectors about the legality of their situation, to avoid or minimize penalties (Costa 2011). Those working in the construction industry, as well as the wider public, should be aware that such practices take place, for example in 2013 in the south and southeast of the country where public agents in occupational safety were detained (Stangler 2013).

Informal workers are deprived of benefits and may be paid below the minimum wage, with no social security payments, no pension and no health protection measures. Without a registered work permit, indicative of the formalization of the employment contract, the worker is outside the protection of the State. There is no guarantee of financial compensation in the event of disease, accidents or negligence on the part of the employer. Despite the many disadvantages, given the pressures of unemployment and retrenchment, workers often prefer to be engaged on the basis of output rather than being paid according to the minimum wage stipulated by the collective agreement (Barros and Mendes 2003). In this situation unions are ineffective and workers are fearful of losing income, leaving employers in a position of power. Also, payment by output can lead to excessive work demands, causing the exhaustion of the worker through the completion of intense activities (Singer 1999). This is a 'vicious circle' where inspections cannot be conducted properly and effectively, the worker is persuaded to work informally and the legal responsibility is removed from employers when a formal employment contract does not exist.

The rural origins of many informal workers exacerbate these problems. Unskilled migrants may find a place in civil construction through informal employment because they can be employed on basic tasks. There is no requirement for them to demonstrate possession of a recognized professional qualification and workers themselves lack knowledge and information about registration. (Cockell and Perticarrari 2010; De Oliveira and Iriart 2008; Morice 1993). Typically through internal migration, workers move from the countryside to the towns in search of work. Construction work is sometimes seen as temporary or as the last option available to them (Cockell and Perticarrari 2010). The predominance of workers with limited qualifications and low salaries demonstrates their vulnerability but also reinforces the low productivity of the sector (Costa 2011; Morice 1993).

Training and Development

While laborers qualify through experience on site, engineers and technicians must have specific documentation; for example, through graduation or schooling, as well as registration with the professional council, which represents around six percent of the total workforce. Research from 2013, published through the *Fundação Getúlio Vargas* website, explored the level of qualification in the construction industry by formal employment (Cantisani and Castelo 2015). According to the results, 68 percent of workers in the industry had attended elementary school, 28 percent had attended high school and only some five percent had a university degree (Cantisani and Castelo 2015).

The IBGE stratifies socio-occupational positions ranging from the lowest economic level to the highest (IBGE 2016). Their evidence suggests that the economic situation of the labor force in construction does not allow opportunities for career development nor for the enhancement of skills or qualifications. Construction seems to be considered an unattractive field for employment with a trend toward the 'aging' of the construction workforce (Cordeiro and Machado 2002). The industry reflects, but also reinforces, gender and racial divisions of the wider

Brazilian society. Those at the top of the industry are white and male while in the lowest paid and most vulnerable occupations there is a high proportion of people from black or mixed-race backgrounds (IBGE 2016).

Companies may have little interest in the continued qualification of the labor force since higher skills lead to better wages and ultimately a qualified worker may abandon the arduous work at the construction site. The CBIC in its research from 2017 found some crucial data about the informality of the workforce and lack of qualifications, analyzing the level of education of the informal (illegal) workers in the construction industry. According to CBIC, informal workers have no or low qualifications, poor schooling and almost no information available to them. The survey showed that 36 percent of those who work informally do not understand the significance of informal work, another 14.1 percent confuse it with self-employment and five percent believe it is self-employment. Additionally, data showed that 90 percent did not have access to structured and formal learning. The workers reported learning their skills through other workers, family members who already worked in the construction industry or learning on their own. Furthermore, some research suggest a high level of illiteracy (Cordeiro and Machado 2002).

It is important to emphasize that training and qualification at technical schools or through specialist courses for carpenters and bricklayers may be available but, due to the informality of jobs and lack of information, workers may not be able to access these opportunities. Training in the work environment may be more convenient, because of the long distances involved to reach training centers and travel restrictions due to the lack of money for transport (Cordeiro and Machado 2002). This limits the level of responsibility that they may aspire to. For instance, engineers (mechanical, electrical, or civil) must have a certificate of technical responsibility (i.e. they have a legal obligation for their work and, once qualified, they are required to sign for their work on behalf of the company). Such responsibility is not required of the large majority of the construction labor force.

Safety and Accidents at Work in the Construction Industry

The construction industry in Brazil relies on cheap labour—many workers are unqualified, living on the margins of society and willing to work in dangerous situations in order to have an income. The accident rate is high despite government, business and union efforts to improve things and the construction industry continues to be a high-risk environment (Silveira et al. 2005). Brazil was reported as having the highest number of workplace accidents globally in the 1970s and a significant number were in construction (Nowak 2018).

Across the economy, there is an average of 1.3 million accidents recorded annually, mainly due to poor working conditions and lack of compliance with safety standards. Data published by the Statistical Yearbook of Occupational Accidents (AEAT 2017) show that there were 30,025 accidents in construction in 2017, with a work accident report (Communication of Occupational Accidents, CAT) total of 112,452 formally registered accidents between 2015 and 2017. Of this number, 826 were fatal. However, there is likely to be significant under-reporting in these figures. The number of recorded accidents declined between 2015 and 2017 by 15,000. This reduction is explained by the fact that these statistics only refer to registered accidents and during this period Brazil experienced a reduction in the formality of jobs, as discussed earlier in this chapter. This reduction in formal employment may have contributed to the appearance of a decrease in accidents. Accidents resulting from informal work are not recorded by the government and therefore not accounted for in the statistics.

Furthermore, data presented in the Statistical Yearbook of Occupational Accidents exclude self-employed workers and illegal workers who, as previously discussed, are prominent within the sector. The data are inconsistent with the size of the population and the significance of the construction industry. Considering the level of informality in the sector, a much higher number of accidents would seem likely, pointing to significant under-reporting. A survey conducted in 2005 in a hospital outside the city of São Paulo analyzed medical supplies to identify construction accidents (Silveira et al. 2005). The study recorded 6,000 accidents with almost three percent being construction workers for whom there was no formal accident record (Silveira et al. 2005).

Whilst megaprojects attract international attention, they have not resulted in improvements for workers on site. The 2014 World Cup involved large movements of money and was controversial because of the scale of public investment. Severe or fatal accidents were a major concern of the workforce. During the construction of the 12 stadiums there were at least 26 strikes that stopped construction activities, of which several occurred after fatalities or serious accidents – for example, the strikes at the Maracanã stadium in 2012 and at the Corinthians Arena in 2013. Strikers' demanded improvements in working conditions, the end of arbitrary layoffs, equivalent health plans for all levels of employment and salary increases (Santos et al. 2015).

Law no. 6,514 from December 22, 1977, regulates the security and medical issues related to work. The question of safety is crucial and has led to the creation of the Internal Commission of Accident and Prevention (CIPA) through article 163 from the same law. CIPA aims to prevent work-related accidents and diseases. In each company, there are employees who have health and safety responsibilities – namely to ensure the avoidance of work-related accidents and ill health – in addition to performing the function for which they were hired. CIPA members are named '*cipeiros*' and are employees elected or appointed to represent the employees of the company for one year. CIPA membership must include both employers and employees and the total number of '*cipeiros*' varies according to the number of employees of the organization and the type of economic activity or CNAE. CNAE is a code that defines the economic productivity of a company and it may determine specific legislation to be applied to each company.

Workplace accidents should be recorded by the National Social Security Institute, through the identification of a link between the work and the accident or disease. While the situation is under investigation INSS is also responsible for the provision of financial assistance to the employee. The contracting company is obliged to inform INSS of all work accidents that occur within one working day following the occurrence, even if no stoppage of activities results, through the Communication of Occupational Accidents. This communication should be immediate, with a penalty or fine if the company does not comply with the obligations.

In short then, while those in formal employment are covered by health and safety law, the widespread informality in the construction industry heightens risks in a high-risk industry. Published data clearly understate the severity of this problem.

The Construction Industry: Challenges and Final Considerations

The construction industry is highly volatile and the level of activity is dependent on the wider economic and political climate. At the end of 2019, immediately following the election of President Jair Bolsonaro, confidence in the Brazilian construction industry was higher than at any point in the preceding five years. The Construction Confidence Index published by the Getúlio Vargas Foundation rose 1.5 points in November 2019 to 89.0 points, reaching its highest level since September 2014 (89.9 points). Another indicator which recorded an improvement was the Intention of Investments of Industry that anticipates the trend of industrial investment by measuring the dissemination of investment momentum of industrial companies. In the fourth quarter of 2018, compared to the third, it recorded an increase of 4.4 points and when compared to the same quarter in the previous year, of 1.4 points. Real estate indicators for the fourth quarter of 2019 showed a 28.3 percent increase in new developments compared to the last quarter, and an 8.4 percent increase compared to the year before (Fundação Getúlio Vargas 2019). While statistics for 2020–2021 are not yet available, it is already clear that there have been fundamental changes since 2019 and these expectations have been reversed. The Brazilian construction industry currently faces major challenges, including the global coronavirus pandemic in 2020 and its aftermath, uncertainty around the Brazilian government and regulation, and insecurity in the pipeline of orders and future contracts.

Brazil has many other problems, including high unemployment, which affect labor in the construction industry. The historical advance of labor protection through legislation has been paralleled by corporate man-euvers to avoid taxes for example. The recent revisions of labor law tend to disadvantage workers and finding a consensus between political parties remains tricky, due to the lack of formality in the industry. The 2017 outsourcing law has given construction companies the opportunity to outsource any type of work, with the consequence of increasing precarity, informality and social problems for workers.

Informality is a critical issue. Many workers are undocumented and therefore outside the scope of state support, which prevents them from accessing benefits, while simultaneously reducing government income from taxation, with negative consequences for the country's develop-ment. Most importantly, informality is associated with limited skills and a lack of qualifications and skills development, leading to poor pro-ductivity. Such realities have manifested themselves in the country over a sustained period due to a history of migration from rural areas to the cities. In this context, the unions are essential to inspect and disseminate workers' rights throughout the country.

In addition, the country still has barriers to new technologies, owing to the lack of knowledge and an absence of incentives for businesses to adapt. The introduction of best practices, including Building Information Modeling (BIM), 3D drawing tools and project management tools, will avoid rework and therefore reduce waste. The use of these technologies, however, is de-pendent on the ability of companies and individuals to accept them, develop these concepts and invest in innovation, bringing long-term benefits.

One positive development is the fact that the use of BIM will be mandatory for all architecture projects in Brazil from 2021 (Decree no. 9.983, from August 22, 2019). This is a cause for optimism, bringing knowledge as well as hope for improvements in quality and productivity. A necessary counterpoint is that qualified professionals are required to implement these technologies. Engineers and architects, as well as other construction professionals, already benefit from formal employment. In contrast, the workers on site, who represent a more significant propor-tion of the workforce, will be unable to benefit.

In conclusion, Brazil has a long way to go in managing change within the construction industry; especially in improving skill levels, training and workers' rights, change that is needed in order to tackle social and economic problems within the country. A determined drive is needed to equip the workforce with knowledge, qualifications and information, leveraging technological standards and innovations to establish strong foundations from which to build. Enhancing skill is essential to improve productivity in the industry but currently the availability of informal and cheap labor means there is little incentive for companies to invest in capital and technological change. In this context, the regulations and labor standards required to protect workers could operate as an essential driver in the construction industry's future economic and technical development.

References

AEAT, 2017. *Anuário estaístico de acidentes do trabalho.* Ministério da Fazenda, Brazilia (Federal Capital of Brazil). (accessed 8.06.20).

Barros, P.C. da R., Mendes, A.M.B. 2003 Sofrimento psíquico no trabalho e estratégias defensivas dos operários terceirizados da construção civil. *Psico-USF 8*(1), 63–70.

Biavaschi, M.B., Droppa, A. 2014. A dinâmica da regulamentação da terceirização no Brasil: As súmulas do Tribunal Superior do Trabalho, os projetos lei e as decisões do Supremo Tribunal Federal. *Revista De Ciências Sociais - Política Trabalho 2*(41), 121–145.

Campos, A.G. 2018. *Terceirização do trabalho no Brasil: novas e distintas perspectivas para o debate.* IPEA Instituto de Pesquisa Econômica Aplicada http:// repositorio.ipea.gov.br/bitstream/11058/8258/1/Terceiriza%C3%A7%C3%A3o %20do%20trabalho%20no%20Brasil_novas%20e%20distintas%20perspectivas %20para%20o%20debate.pdf (accessed 24.06.20).

Campos, P.H.P. 2014. Os empreiteiros de obras publicas e as politicas da ditadura para os trabalhadores da construção Civil. *Em Pauta 33.* https://e-publicacoes.uerj.br/ojs/index.php/revsitaempauta/article/view/13025. Cited in Nowak, J. 2018.

Cantisani, A.F. and Castelo, A.M. 2015. O perfil dos trabalhadores da construção civil. *Revista Conjuntura Da Construção*, March 2015, 10–13. http://bibliotecadigital.fgv.br/ojs/index.php/cc/article/viewFile/77299/74072 (accessed 8. 06.20).

Carbonai, D. 2019. Labor reform in Brazil, politics and *sindicatos*: notes on the general strikes of 2017. *Journal of Politics in Latin America 11*(2), 231–245.

Cardoso-Júnior, J.C. 2001. Crise e desregulação do trabalho no Brasil. *Tempo Socia 13*(2), 31–59.

Cardoso, A., Gindin, J. 2009. *Industrial Relations and Collective Bargaining: Argentina, Brazil and Mexico Compared.* International Labour Office, Geneva.

CBIC, 2009. *A produtividade da construção civil Brasileira 2009.* Câmara Brasileira da Indústria da Construção (CBIC) http://cbicdados.com.br/media/ anexos/066.pdf (accessed 10.06.20).

CBIC, 2017. 'Estudo comprova impacto da informalidade na construção civil e norteia ações da CBIC para reduzir sua incidência'. CBIC Agency 2 June 2017. Câmara Brasileira da Indústria da Construção https://cbic.org.br/estudo-comprova-impacto-da-informalidade-na-construcao-civil-e-norteia-acoes-da-cbic-para-reduzir-sua-incidencia/ (accessed 10.06.20).

CBIC, 2019. *Ranking das Maiores Construtoras no Brasil*. Câmara Brasileira da Indústria da Construção http://www.cbicdados.com.br/menu/empresas-de-construcao/maiores-empresas-de-construcao (accessed 10.06.20).

Central Única dos Trabalhadores (CUT), undated: https://www.cut.org.br/ conteudo/breve-historico (accessed 10.06.20).

Cockell, F.F., Perticarrari, D. 2010. Contratos de boca: A institucionalização da precariedade na construção civil. *Caderno CRH 23*(60), 633–653.

Cordeiro, C.C.C. and Machado, M.I.G. 2002. *O perfil do operário da indústria da construção civil de Feira de Santana: requisitos para uma qualificação profissional*. from Sitientibus, Feira de Santana: http://www2.uefs.br:8081/ sitientibus/pdf/26/o_perfil_do_operario_da_industria_da_construcao_civil.pdf (accessed 23.06.20).

Coslovsky, S., Pires, R., Bignami, R. 2017. Resilience and renewal: the enforcement of labor laws in Brazil. *Latin American Politics and Society 59*(2), 77–102.

Costa, L.R. 2011. Subcontratação e informalidade na construção civil, no Brasil e na França. *Caderno CRH 24* (62), 413–434.

Da Luz, A.F., Santin, J.R. 2010. As relações de trabalho e sua regulamentação no Brasil a partir da revolução de 1930. *História [Online] 29* (2), 268–278.

Da Silva, F.G.F., Martins, F.G.D., Rocha, C.H., Araújo, C.E.F. 2013. Investimentos em transportes terrestres causam crescimento econômico: um estudo quantitativo. *Journal of Transport Literature 7* (2), 124–145.

Da Silva, G.J.C., Martins, H.E.deP., Neder, H.D. 2016. Investimentos em infraestrutura de transportes e desigualdades regionais no Brasil: uma análise dos impactos do programa de aceleração do crescimento (PAC). *Revista de Economia Política 36* (4), 840–863.

De Oliveira, R.P., Iriart, J.A.B. 2008. Representações do trabalho entre trabalhadores informais da construção civil. *Pscicologia Em Estudo 13*(3), 437–445.

DIEESE, 2012. *A situação do trabalho no Brasil na primeira década dos anos 2000*. Departamento Intersindical de Estatística e Estudos Socioeconômicos (DIEESE), São Paulo.

Druck, G. 2016. Unrestrained outsourcing in Brazil: More precarization and health risks for workers. *Cadernos de Saúde Pública 32*(6), 1–9.

Exame, 2019. '*O tamanho do apetite Chinês no Brasil*'. Exame, 5 09 2019 https://exame.com/blog/primeiro-lugar/o-tamanho-do-apetite-chines-no-brasil/ (accessed 26.05.20).

Ferreira, P.C., Malliagros, T.G. 1998. Impactos produtivos da infra-estrutura no Brasil: 1950–1995. *Pesquisa e Planejamento Econômico 28* (2), 315–338.

Fundação Getúlio Vargas, 2019. *Sondagem da Construção. Índice de confiança na construção* https://portalibre.fgv.br/sites/default/files/2020-06/sondagem-da-construcao-fgv_press-release_abr19.pdf (accessed 25.06.20).

IBGE. Instituto Brasileiro de Geografia e Estatística, 2016. *Indicadores IBGE: Principais destaques da evolução do mercado de trabalho nas regiões metropolitanas abrangidas pela pesquisa - Recife, Salvador, Belo Horizonte, Rio de Janeiro, São Paulo e Porto Alegre, 2003–2015*. ftp://ftp.ibge.gov.br/ Trabalho_e_Rendimento/Pesquisa_Mensal_de_Emprego/Evolucao_Mercado_ Trabalho/ (accessed 22.06.20).

IBGE, 2017a. *Pesquisa Nacional por Amostra de Domicílios Contínua.* https://www.ibge.gov.br/estatisticas/sociais/trabalho/17270-pnad-continua.html?edicao=22889&t=resultados (accessed 2.06.20).

IBGE, 2017b. *Pesquisa Anual da Construção (PAIC), 2017* https://www.ibge.gov.br/estatisticas/economicas/industria/9018-pesquisa-anual-da-industria-da-construcao.html?edicao=24593&t=resultados (accessed 2.06.20).

IBGE, 2018. *Pesquisa Anual da Indústria da Construção (PAIC) 2018* https://www.ibge.gov.br/estatisticas/economicas/industria/9018-pesquisa-anual-da-industria-da-construcao.html?edicao=24593&t=resultados (accessed 2.07.20).

IBGE, 2019. https://www.ibge.gov.br/cidades-e-estados/sp.html (accessed 7.07.20).

Kureski, R., Rodrigues, R.L., Moretto, A.C., Filho, U.A.S., Hardt, L.P.A. 2008. O Macrossetor da Construção Civil na Economia Brasileira em 2004. *Ambiente Construído 8* (1), 7–19.

Martins, J.C.R., Gomes, A.C. and Rodrigues, C. 2015. *Trabalhadores da construção: perfil, expectativas e avaliação dos empresários.* Câmara Brasileira da Indústria da Construção (CBIC) (first edition). https://cbic.org.br/wpcontent/uploads/2017/11/Trabalhadores_Da_Construcao_2015.pdf (accessed 8.06.20).

Mello, L.C.B. de B., Amorim, S.R.L. de 2009. O subsetor de edificações da construção civil no Brasil: uma análise comparativa em relação à União Europeia e aos Estados Unidos. *Produção 19* (2), 388–399.

Morice, A. 1993. Une légende à revoir: l'ouvrier du bâtiment brésilien sans feu ni lieu. *Cahiers des Sciences Humaines 29* (2–3), 349–371.

Moroni, J.A. 2005. O direito à participação no governo Lula. *Saúde em debate 29* (71), 284–304. http://www.redalyc.org/articulo.oa?id=406345256006 (accessed 8.06.20).

Nowak, 2018. Mass strikes in the Brazilian Construction Sector, 2011–2014. In: Nowak, J., Dutta, M., Birke, P., (eds), *Workers' Movements and Strikes in the Twenty-first Century: A Global Perspective* Rowman & Littlefield International Ltd, London. pp. 115–131.

Organização Internacional do Trabalho, undated https://www.ilo.org/brasilia/temas/trabalho-escravo/lang--pt/index.htm (accessed 2.07.20).

Pinehiro, G.A. 2015. Indústrias da construção civil (9 March), *CBIC Câmara Brasileira da Indústria da Construção* https://cbic.org.br/industrias-da-construcao-civil/ (accessed 27.05.20).

Radermacher, R., Melleiro, W. 2007. Mudanças no cenário sindical Brasileiro sob o governo de Lula. *Nueva Sociedad 211.*

Rigolon, F.J.Z. and Piccinini, M. S. 1997. *O investimento em infra-estrutura e a retomada do crescimento econômico sustentado*, pp. 40 https://web.bndes.gov.br/bib/jspui/bitstream/1408/9654/2/Td-63%20Investimento%20em%20infra-estrutura%20e%20a%20retomada%20do%20crescimento%20economico%20sustentado._P.pdf (accessed 26.05.20).

Rodrigues, L. M. 2009. Sindicalismo e ideologias operárias: classe operária e sociedade Industrial no Brasil. In *Trabalhadores, Sindicatos e Industrializaçã* 88–119. https://static.scielo.org/scielobooks/5y76v/pdf/rodrigues-9788599662991.pdf (accessed 26.05.20).

Santos, A.M., Rossi, G.F., Toyoshima, S.H., Evangelista, W.L. 2011. Impactos comparativos do setor da construção civil sobre o emprego no Brasil: 2002-2009. *Revista de Ciências Humanas 11* (1), 24–35.

Santos, E. R. 2017, June. A nova Lei da Terceirização – Lei no 13.429/2017 – Um cheque em branco ao empresariado. *Revista Eletrônica Do Tribunal Regional Do Trabalho Da 4a Região Do Rio Grande Do Sul*, 51–59. www. editoraforum.com.br/noticias/nova-lei-da-terceirizacao-lei-no-13-4292017-um-cheque-em-branco-ao-empresariado/> (accessed 9.06.20).

Santos, O.A.J., Gaffney, C. and Ribeiro, L. C. de Q. 2015. *Brasil: os impactos da Copa do Mundo 2014 e das Olimpíadas 2016*. http://www.observatoriodasmetropoles. net/images/abook_file/livro_megaeventos_2015.pdf (accessed 8.06.20).

Silveira, C.A., Robazzi, M.L., do, C.C., Walter, E.V., Marziale, M.H.P. 2005. Acidentes de trabalho na construção civil identificados através de prontuários hospitalares. *Revista Escola de Minas 58* (1), 39–44.

Singer, P. 1999. *Globalização e desemprego: diagnóstico e alternativas* (third edition, Vol. 3). Editora Contexto. São Paulo: https://edisciplinas.usp.br/ pluginfile.php/868786/mod_resource/content/0/Paul%20Singer.%20Globaliza %C3%A7%C3%A3o%20e%20desemprego.%20Diagn%C3%B3sticos%20e %20alternativas.pdf (accessed 8.06.20).

SINTRACON, 2020. *Sindicato dos Trabalhadores da Construção São Paulo* website: https://www.sintraconsp.org.br/institucional/ (accessed 7.07.20).

Stangler, J. 2013. PF prende três pessoas por corrupção na SRTE / RS. *Jornal do Comércio* website: https://www.jornaldocomercio.com/site/noticia.php?codn= 138790%3E (accessed 5.05.20).

Teixeira, L.P., De Carvalho, F.M.A. 2006. A construção civil como instrumento do desenvolvimento da economia Brasileira. *Revista Paranaense de Desenvolvimento 1* (109), 9–26.

5 The German Construction Industry at the Crossroads[1]

Gerhard Syben and Christian Beck

Introduction

Germany has a history of social partnership between employers' associations and trade unions. National collective agreements in the construction sector are still widely applied and remain significant, not least because of their provision of social funds which support holiday pay, training and pension provision. National bargaining has, however, been weakened by the development of company level and even workplace level bargaining. Works Councils, representing workers at the workplace, have diminishing influence. This chapter outlines the changes affecting the German construction sector. First, it considers the industry context and the institutions representing worker and employer interests. It goes on, second, to explore the industry structure and the environment within which decisions are taken, looking at both the public and the private sectors. Third, it considers employment trends and then it identifies well-established training arrangements as an underpinning to high-quality labor supply. The authors conclude that the industry is at a crossroads and suggest that a continuing commitment to social partnership would provide the most effective route forward.

Context: German Construction

The German construction industry (*Baugewerbe*) embraces a wide range of activities. The term 'construction' can be confusing because it is sometimes used to refer to the construction industry as a whole, including the installation sector, as in the official classification of economic activities. But it is also sometimes used to refer to that part of construction activity carried out by small enterprises, some of which formally belong to the *Handwerk*, or small trades, sector. According to the official classification system, it comprises both the core area of building construction and civil engineering (*Bauhauptgewerbe*) together with installation and other specialist areas (*Bauausbaugewerbe*). The classic construction industry (*Bauhauptgewerbe*) includes not only buildings and civil engineering, but also demolition and works such as tiling, insulation, carpentry, scaffolding and roofing. Installation and other specialist areas include painting, heating and air conditioning, ventilation and sanitary facilities as well as electrical installation. Construction does not include architectural and engineering practices, gardening and landscaping, all of which are deemed to be in the service sector. Construction as a whole has some 2.5 million employees, 5.6 percent of all employment in Germany. (All data, unless stated otherwise, are derived from the Federal Statistical Office (Destatis) (2019)). These figures[2] were significantly higher during the construction booms of the early 1970s and the early 1990s, when the share of construction employment rose to 8.6 percent in each period, but construction remains a sector of great importance for employment in Germany.

In 2018, the total value of the output of the German construction industry stood at €350.48 billion, equivalent to 10.4 percent of GDP and 49.8 percent of gross fixed capital formation. At this point the German construction industry, as with the economy as a whole, was experiencing a phase of robust growth. Measured in terms of gross value added, the output of the construction industry proper is significantly lower than the total value of construction investment due to the high proportion of prior output from other sectors that is included in the gross total. In 2018, this figure stood at €160.45 billion, equivalent to 5.3 percent of GDP. This marks a steady decline from 8.4 percent in the 1970s and 6.8 percent in the 1990s, a common feature of mature economies. In 2018, average hourly labor productivity stood at €37 an hour (Federal Statistical Office (Destatis) 2019: 97). Up until 2005 productivity in German construction was higher than the average for the whole economy but since then has been below it.

Industrial Relations

Employees in the construction industry are represented by the industry trade union IG BAU, which also organizes in forestry, agriculture and environmental activities as well as commercial cleaning. Employees in building installation and construction engineering (sanitation, heating, air conditioning, ventilation and electrical) are organized by the metal workers' union, IG Metall.

There are two employer associations. The HDB association (*Hauptverband der Deutschen Bauindustrie*) represents larger companies and the ZDB (*Zentralverband des Deutschen Baugewerbes*) represents smaller firms. Germany has a federal constitution and consists of 16 constituent states (*Länder*) which have devolved powers in many areas, such as education and training. Both of these employer associations and IG BAU are organized at regional (*Land*) level, with these bodies sometimes covering more than one *Land*. Companies in the installation sector are organized in employer associations for their specific branch: in some instances, these operate at *Land* level or embrace more than one such region. In this respect collective bargaining in the installation sector is much more fragmented than in the building industry.

Collective agreements are concluded by IG BAU and the provisions of such agreements apply only to IG BAU members. Nonetheless, some companies grant these provisions to all their employees, irrespective of trade union membership. In such cases, non-members benefit from the efforts of the trade union, although they have no legal right to any agreed provisions. Pay settlements for the main construction industry, for roofing and scaffolding and for the painting industry are negotiated and concluded at national level. In some sectors these agreements apply directly nationwide and in others they are adopted by regional organizations and then applied to local pay scales. Although regional bodies could in theory refuse to accept a national settlement, this would be a very exceptional event. In other sectors of the industry collective agreements are negotiated and concluded only at regional level. In the main construction sector, and despite steps toward convergence in recent years, pay rates differ between West and East Germany. The construction industry is also distinctive in the existence of agreed social funds (SOKA-BAU) financed by a compulsory levy on all construction employers. This is used to finance additional holiday pay and a significant proportion of vocational training. There is also a supplementary pension financed through an employer levy with scope for additional tax-favored employee contributions. There are comparable funds for roofers, scaffolders and painters.

As with all companies in Germany, construction companies are required to be members of their respective chamber (either the Chamber of Commerce and Industry or Craft Chamber). Although certified craftworkers (*Meister*) have a two-thirds majority in the Craft Chamber, journeymen have also traditionally been represented. As a consequence, firms in the small trades/craft sector often form additional guilds (*Innungen*) that serve purely as employer associations.

Industrial relations in Germany is customarily viewed as a 'dual' system of representation, with trade unions taking on the adversarial role of negotiating with employers over economic issues, typically pay, and statutory works councils, elected by all employees, engaging at workplace level on a more cooperative basis to exercise a degree of joint regulation through information, consultation and, on some issues, mandatory codetermination. The 'ideal type' model for this system also includes industry-level collective bargaining: this not only means that the potentially conflictual engagement between trade unions and employers takes place outside the immediate workplace, but by setting wage floors for each skill level also has the wider economic effect, in theory, of regulating inter-firm competition by focusing on products and processes rather than wage costs. The inter-firm cooperation that this is designed to encourage, embodied in strong employer associations, is also the foundation for the industry-level regulation of training.

Although this model still exists in many areas of the German economy, it has been subject to considerable erosion since the 1990s. In the first instance, the challenge posed resulted from the 'posting' of workers who were brought into the country from outside Germany, working at rates that bore no relation to the German negotiated rates. The European Posting of Workers Directive (96/71/EC) required only that foreign companies bringing workers into the country should apply the regulations of their home country. In consequence a binding minimum wage was introduced in the German construction sector on January 1, 1997 (Arnholtz et al. 2018). In contrast to arrangements in other countries and in recognition of the on-going significance of collective bargaining, the German minimum wage in construction was closely tied to the collective bargaining process and was introduced as an additional lowest rung to the pay scale in the wage bargain. Henceforth, non-German companies sending workers to work in the German construction industry were required to comply with the new minimum wage (until this point foreign companies had only to apply the regulations applicable in their home country) (Möller and König 2012). The minimum wage for the main construction sector that came into force on January 1, 1997 was eight euros per hour for workers in Eastern Germany and 8.69 euros per hour in Western Germany. As from September 1, 1997, it was reduced to 7.74 euros and 8.18 euros, respectively. This minimum rate has been found to have positive effects on wage growth across the country, although the impact varied regionally with the most notable wage improvements occurring in the East (Rattenhuber 2011; Möller and König 2012). The introduction of the construction minimum wage marked a significant break with the traditional, collectively negotiated procedures of German collective bargaining. Further sectoral minima followed and, subsequently, in 2015 a statutory minimum wage was introduced nationwide.

The minimum wage has an impact on collective bargaining negotiations within the construction sector; there are concerns that the minimum rate will undermine the 'normal' collectively bargained rates. From the union perspective the aim is to maintain a certain balance between the minimum and the collectively negotiated wage rates, countering employer initiatives to play off both wages against each other. In addition, employers are constantly pursuing the collective bargaining strategy of returning to one (the lower) minimum wage. This defines the conflict-line for current negotiations.

According to the most recent study on the incidence of these core institutions, the coverage of the workforce by an industry-level collective agreement fell from 70 percent in 1996 in West Germany (56 percent in the East) to 49 percent by 2018 (35 percent in the East), with coverage in the private sector in the West down to 44 percent (Ellguth and Kohaut 2019). The effect of industry agreements is also felt more widely. In 2018, of the 73 percent of all establishments not covered by a collective agreement (many of them very small), 41 percent 'aligned' (*Orientierung*) themselves with the standards set by the industry agreement that covered their industry: these 'aligners' accounted for some 24 percent of the workforce. The percentage of firms that report such alignment has declined considerably in recent years; in 2005, the proportion stood at 77 percent (Amlinger and Bispinck 2016: 214).

Two further developments have weakened the role of industry-level bargaining, with its particular institutional effects. The first is the increase in company-level bargaining, especially in larger undertakings in East Germany: this now accounts for some 11 percent of the workforce overall. The second reflects efforts by employer associations to recruit or retain firms, in the face of declining membership, by setting up legal constructions that allow for association membership without the obligation to comply with any industry agreement the association might sign (Behrens 2013).

A more complex development in terms of its effects on industry-level bargaining is the shift in the locus of substantive negotiation from industry to workplace level through the inclusion of 'opening clauses' (*Öffnungsklauseln*) in industry agreements (Müller-Jentsch 2017). The precise mechanism through which these operate varies as between industries. Works councils may not normally negotiate on issues that are reserved for industry-level agreement, such as pay and working hours: an opening clause typically allows for some derogation of these powers, usually requiring the express agreement of the parties to the industry agreement (often for each individual instance). Such derogation can allow for a degree of workplace flexibility in implementing industry standards (such as longer reference periods for achieving agreed weekly hours) but also an outright relaxation of standards, such as cutting agreed annual special payments (13th month) for companies in economic difficulties. Trade unions and works councils might ask for the quid pro quo of retaining an operation and/or employment guarantees and commitments on investment. While this can lead to a short-term enhancement of the scope and power of works councils, such bodies lack the legal rights to resort to industrial action to support local negotiations; moreover, works council members reported that they had difficulties in adopting the role of 'collective bargaining actor' and found the experience a challenge (Amlinger and Bispinck 2016: 220).

The erosion of the incidence of the two core institutions of the German 'dual' system is strikingly illustrated in figures for the proportion of the workforce covered by both an industry-level agreement and a works council. While 41 percent of the workforce in West Germany fell into this category in 1996, by 2018 it had fallen to 26 percent. The decline in East Germany was even more striking: from 29 to 14 percent (Ellguth and Kohaut 2019: 296)

In many respects developments in industrial relations in the construction industry mirror the wider trend seen in Germany since the early 2000s, characterized by declining collective bargaining coverage, falling trade union membership and a declining incidence of coverage by works councils. Despite the challenges, and in contrast to some other sectors, the core institutions of industrial relations in construction (i.e. well-organized employers and trade unions, industry-level bargaining) appear broadly intact and available for revitalization, should circumstances permit or encourage this.

In 2018, some 62 percent of construction industry employees were covered by a collective agreement (regulating pay, pay supplements, working time and other matters) (Hans-Böckler-Stiftung 2019; Ellguth and Kohaut 2019): 64 percent in West Germany and 56 percent in the East.[3] The overwhelming majority (60 percent overall) was covered by one of the industry-level agreements: these apply to members of signatory organizations but in the case of the construction industry a number has been extended to all workplaces in the sector. This level of coverage is substantially above the average for Germany as whole and was exceeded only by financial services, energy and water and public administration.

In addition to direct coverage, the data also provide figures on the workforce coverage of those who work for employers that are not party to a collective agreement (either directly in a company-level agreement or via membership of a signatory organization) but which 'align' themselves with agreed provisions. In addition to the 64 percent figure for workforce collective bargaining coverage in construction in West Germany, firms employing a further 65 percent of employees not covered by a collective agreement aligned their provisions with agreed terms; the corresponding figure for the East in 2018 was 54 percent of the 44 percent of employees not subject to a collective agreement (Hans-Böckler-Stiftung, 2019).

The contrast between East and West Germany is less marked in construction than in some other sectors. While collective bargaining coverage in the East was 88 percent of that in the West in construction, the percentage was just 56 percent in manufacturing industry, 60 percent in agriculture and forestry and 77 percent in health and education. Looked at over time, and comparing with 2010, collective bargaining coverage in construction in the West fell by 12 percentage points from 74 percent; the recorded change in East Germany was in fact slightly positive, with a rise from 55 percent to 56 percent.

Workforce coverage by a works council is low in construction compared with other sectors, reflecting the small size of establishments, the proliferation of craft micro-enterprises and subcontracting. In 2018, just 18 percent of employees in construction were represented by a works council, compared with 41 percent for the whole economy and 65 percent in manufacturing industry.

Membership of IG BAU has fallen over the past two decades from 481,400 in 2000 to approximately 250,000 by 2018 (Deutscher Gewerkschaftsbund (DGB) 2019), with an especially steep drop in the first decade of this century. More than half of all works council members, however, were elected on union lists (IG BAU 2018).

The Changing Structure of the Industry

Fluctuations in Activity

The unification boom, which lasted from 1990 until 1994, led to a steep rise in construction investment in Germany. This was followed by a decade of crisis, with activity dropping below its 1991 level by 2005. Since then there has been a steady rise in construction investment, (with the exception of 2009 when there was a slight decline) reaching €350.48 billion by 2018. In real terms, this represents an increase of 20 percent compared with 1994, but is still below the values registered during the first half of the 1990s. Over this period, the different areas of construction activity experienced broadly the same changes, with falls across-the-board up until 2005 and a solid recovery since that year. Nevertheless, there have been some minor shifts in the balance between different areas of construction, with housing, public construction and commercial construction each responding slightly differently to the course of the economic cycle.

During the period from 2000 to 2017, buildings construction (*Hochbau*) accounted for between 84 and 86 percent of overall construction investment, with civil engineering accounting for only a small proportion of the total. Having fallen somewhat in the period running up to the end of the crisis in 2005, building construction then recovered. In this respect, civil engineering, which depends to a large extent on public contracts, is somewhat – if not greatly– more stable in response to the broader economic cycle.

The share of total construction investment accounted for by housing ranged between 56 and just short of 61 percent in recent years, with little direct discernible relationship with the economic cycle. During the decade of crisis in the 1990s and extending up to 2007, this share remained steady at some 58 percent; it then fell to 55 percent in the immediate wake of the construction crisis and began to rise once more during the economic recovery and construction boom to reach its most recent share of just under 61 percent, the highest figure since 1990. This lack of relation to the economic cycle is also highlighted by the fact that in the years following the crisis, investment in public construction was not much weaker (up 13.2 percent) and in commercial construction (up 23.3 percent) significantly stronger than housing (plus 14.6 percent).

Commercial and public construction activities have tended to mirror the course of the economic cycle more closely. Between 2000 and 2017, commercial construction accounted for 27.5–30.5 percent of overall construction investment, with the highest share recorded after 2007 in the period immediately following the protracted construction crisis. The proportion fell back once the crisis was past and also during the recent boom. Although commercial construction continued to grow during the boom, it was at a slower pace than housing construction, leading to a fall in its relative share. Public construction charted a similar course, accounting for 12–14 percent of overall construction investment. The highest share was reached during and in the wake of the construction crisis, with a declining proportion since 2010. Again, this type of construction would seem to be more stable than housing in terms of its responsiveness to the economic cycle.

Commercial Contracts

The execution of construction contracts in Germany is governed by a plethora of regulations and contextual conditions that manifest themselves in diverse ways depending, in particular, on the nature of the client.

One central initial distinction is between public and private clients. In the case of private clients, a further distinction needs to be drawn between organizations that commission construction on a regular basis, such as industrial firms, housing associations, property investors and organizations that award a building contract only very rarely, and perhaps only once.

Public bodies are required to put contracts out to tender in accordance with the provisions of the Tender and Contract Regulations for Construction Services Code – the *Vergabe- und Vertragsordnung für Bauleistungen* (VOB/A). The Code is not a legal instrument but functions de facto as such in terms of the obligation on public bodies to comply with it. It is drawn up by a standing organization made up of representatives of the public sector and the construction industry. This not only sets out a process intended to ensure fair competition but also specifies provisions that enshrine broader policy goals. For example, public bodies must divide large-scale contracts into smaller and equal-sized parts to enable small and medium-sized employers to make successful bids and to avoid large prime contractors from enjoying a built-in advantage.

The Code also imposes further constraints on the awarding of contracts by public bodies. According to Section 16d of the Code, for example, a contract may not be granted based on an offer with an unreasonably high or unreasonably low price. The Code further specifies that the contract should be awarded to the bid that appears to be the 'most economical,' 'taking into account all relevant considerations, such as quality, price, technical value, aesthetics, expediency, environmental aspects, operating and consequential costs, profitability, after-sales service and technical assistance, and completion deadlines.' And specifically: 'The lowest offer price alone shall not be decisive.'

Public bodies are often accused of behaving in a way that is completely at odds with these provisions, considering solely 'the figure at the bottom right' – that is, price – and awarding the contract to the bid with the lowest one. Such an approach is not only harmful to construction quality and employees' working conditions, but quite simply unlawful. And because of the risks that might be concealed in a successful bid made on these terms, the actual price of a building can ultimately turn out to be higher than a bid based on a more realistic assessment of costs.

One consequence of this is that public bodies require considerable resources to ensure that tendering is managed in a way that is both legally and materially compliant with the law. Officials entrusted with these tasks require both technical competence and professional experience in assessing bids together with the ability to spot hidden risks and areas where reworking and rectification could occur. Their employing organizations also need to ensure staff have sufficient time for the required checks. In other words, commissioning authorities require both a sufficient quantity and quality of appropriately qualified staff. Cuts made to commissioning departments at Federal, the *Land* and, in particular, local authority level as a result of the austerity policies of recent years mean, however, that these prerequisites are often no longer met.

A key role is also played by those bodies responsible for making the ultimate decisions and for exercising financial oversight – that is, legislatures and public audit offices. Their assessment of procurement procedures not only has considerable political influence but is also, and crucially, highly respected by the public. It is important, however, that these bodies adopt the same criteria as those imposed by the Code on the commissioning specialists employed by contracting bodies. Politicians, who have to answer to their electorates, should resist the temptation to prioritize short-term or superficial cost saving over long-term economic value. In theory, public audit bodies have the specialist skills to back such an approach but do not always enjoy the attention they merit in public discussion.

In some (but not all) *Länder*, public procurement is subject to further contract compliance provisions on employment terms and conditions.[4] These *Land*-level laws (known as *Tariftreuegesetze*) stipulate that bids may be only considered if the tenderer provides a written undertaking either to pay any required minimum wages or apply the pay rates specified in any collective agreement applicable where the services will be performed. The same obligation also applies to any subcontractors.

There are no comparable provisions in the field of private construction. Based on their long experience of project management, clients who regularly and professionally award construction contracts are usually very familiar with both the market and the range of prospective bidders, allowing them to put together a field of companies that they might wish to commission from. Private clients also frequently organize restricted tenders, in which they invite a small number of qualified contractors to submit bids. In this form of cooperation, both sides – client and contractor – have an interest in building and maintaining mutual trust as a tried-and-tested foundation for managing the risks inherent in any construction project. Empirical studies suggest this pays off economically. And construction companies report that working with highly professional clients is the key to successful cooperation in executing projects as both sides can bring the same expertise to bear, enabling a consensus to be achieved on what is needed to finish a contract, how much time it will take, and what it will cost. The execution of the contract – that is, the practice of construction – therefore leads to an ongoing review of the parties' current state of knowledge and incentivizes innovation.

One persistent concern, voiced in particular by construction companies themselves, is that under traditional procurement methods the firms that will execute building contracts, with all their expertise, are not included until very late in the process of project management, and often too late to influence decisions that might have saved time and money if made earlier. One response has been efforts to reconcile the requirements of a competitive tendering process that can drive efficiency with the advantages of the earliest feasible inclusion of bidders' skills. Nonetheless, such partnering approaches have not yet become widespread and tendering based on contracts for 'construction management' or 'management contracting' are not yet widely known in Germany.

Large construction projects commissioned by professional clients are usually carried out either by general or prime contractors (*Generalunternehmer*) or contractors that, in addition to construction, also perform project management (*Generalübernehmer*), with work on site undertaken almost exclusively by subcontractors. This also leads to the creation of chains in which the general contractor can lose sight of where responsibility lies and who is doing what and where, given the absence of any direct contractual relationship between the general contractor and subcontractor. Yet the assignment of general liability to such prime contractors has not changed much in this respect. There is also a wide variety of relationships between general contractors and subcontractors, including stable and long-term relationships, based on mutual trust, that are reaffirmed with each new episode of cooperation. Irrespective of this, the fact that large construction companies have recently tended to focus on the role of general contractor means that these either no longer employ the staff that carry out construction work or only retain a small number left over from when they previously carried out building operations directly. This situation is especially detrimental to training as it is precisely such large firms that are best placed to offer good quality training on a large scale.

Since the early 1990s, however, a new and substantial area of construction activity has emerged alongside this zone of cooperation between trusted and reliable partners. Its main feature is that it is based on labor drawn in from a range of countries and bought and sold as a commodity and subject to constantly evolving varieties of exploitation. It would not be an exaggeration to characterize this market for subcontracting as existing outside the legal framework of the German social order. Despite many efforts in terms of both new legal instruments and improved enforcement, it has only been possible to impose limited regulatory control over this sector: any new measure immediately prompts efforts to circumvent it. To take one example, both the Minimum Wage Act (2014) and the Posted Workers Act (1996), discussed above (subsequently amended several times), impose strict liability on a general contractor to ensure that their subcontractors, and the latter's subcontractors, pay the applicable minimum wage and make appropriate social insurance contributions as well as paying into industry-level social funds, such as the holiday fund (known as 'general contractor liability'). The enforcement authorities then found that, although the minimum wage was paid and properly stated on pay slips, employees were subsequently deprived of a large proportion of their pay to cover inappropriately high accommodation costs: this is just one device amongst many others.

This environment – which is typical of not all but nonetheless many construction sites – has profoundly changed the tasks of site managers. There has particularly been a collapse in the traditional relationship of trust between supervisors and skilled workers. In the past, this was characterized by long-standing personal acquaintance, with all parties aware of the strengths, weaknesses and capabilities of the other. Tasks did not need to be explained in every detail as everyone involved understood the same thing by the same term. Assigning responsibility was also very simple as the consequences of any shortcoming could swiftly be placed at the door of the person involved. In short, there was a high degree of mutual reliance. Such a relationship between management and execution is impossible if the main role of a site manager is simply to check outcomes and enforce deadlines. This is especially the case with ever longer subcontracting chains in which site managers no longer have a direct or contractual relationship with the employees carrying out a specific task (and their immediate supervisors). Site managers usually have to manage more than one construction site at a time, except on large sites, are constantly overworked and forced to perform the role of a flexible reserve that is deployed to sort out planning mistakes.

In this context, it will be interesting to see what effect the application of Building Information Modeling (BIM) might have on the work of construction supervision. This new method, which has begun to be adopted by construction companies in Germany, should allow decisions to be taken both much earlier in the construction process and more accurately than has so far been the case, eliminating the need for managers to make ad hoc decisions on matters that were either inadequately dealt with or not considered at all in the prior planning process. BIM is expected to lead to a shift in management's role to one of facilitating and controlling the execution of work tasks, leading to a decrease in management's workload and an enhancement in the quality of their work.

Those private clients that only rarely award construction contracts will usually use an architect to issue tenders and commission contractors: such clients need the specialist skills of an architect in project management and commissioning which they do not possess in-house. In addition, only certified architects have the right to sign off and submit planning drawings. One important document governing the relationship between architects and clients is the official Fee Schedule for Architects and Engineers (*Honorarordnung für Architekten und Ingenieure* or HOAI). This regulates the tasks involved in the process of developing a construction project from predesign through to detailed planning, the bringing in of specialist engineers for structural work and installation and issuing tenders and appraising bids. These tasks are carried out by an architectural practice on behalf of a client, drawing on the professional skills and experience built up possibly over many years of cooperation with clients. The professionalism of the architect is especially important for clients that lack experience in this field. It also reveals the significance of the trust between an architect and a range of construction companies – essentially those an architect is willing to recommend and those not. Nonetheless, the final decision and responsibility for issuing a contract remains with the client.

Renovation, refurbishment and modernization do not usually require planning permission and no formal application is required. Clients are generally private individuals with little or no contact with the construction industry. Clients envisaging large projects will typically seek the advice of an architect to establish the scope of the works involved and choose a builder. In most cases, however, property owners negotiate directly with the builder who carries out the work. Neighborhood networks, friends, acquaintances and colleagues also all play an important role in guiding the choices of builders, highlighting once again the importance of trust as a resource built up via relationships between builders and their clients.

Employment in Construction

During the post-unification boom, employment in the construction industry rose from 2.9 million in 1991 to 3.3 million by 1995, equivalent to
8.7 percent of the working population and the highest level seen in
Germany (note that prior to unification the former GDR and the Federal
Republic used different classification systems so comparison before these
dates is not possible). Employment then fell by almost a third in the subsequent crisis, dropping by 31.4 percent to 2.28 million. And since employment in building construction fell by nearly half during this period, it
would be reasonable to assume that the drop in the installation sector was
not quite as severe, although there are no separate figures for this segment.
Employment began to rise during the recovery in the industry that began in
2006, but the increase was comparatively sedate at just 8.6 percent for the
whole period between 2005 and 2017 with total employment rising to 2.49
million, well below the pre-crisis level. At the time of writing, only limited
data were available for 2018, a boom year in which employment was
expected to rise once again. Because of the strong growth in overall employment in this period, the construction industry's share came to no more
than 5.6 percent. In 2019 virtually all construction employers were com-
plaining of recruitment difficulties, especially for skilled trades. In the
analysis of these figures, it is clear that since the early 1990s the German
construction industry has drawn in additional workers employed by firms
located elsewhere: these are not included in German official statistics but
the presumption is that this has been on a large, if unknown, scale.

One great help in analyzing the structure of employment in construction
in Germany is the existence of a very rich information source, the so-called
'Total Survey for the Construction Industry' (*Totalerhebung für das
Baugewerbe*), compiled by the Federal Statistical Office.[5] This includes all
establishments operating in the main buildings construction industry
(*Bauhauptgewerbe*). Establishments operating in the installation sector are
included only if they regularly have at least 10 employees, excluding an
estimated 90 percent of all enterprises in the sector.

The survey allows a more detailed analysis of the effects of the construction crisis and the subsequent recovery. It should be noted, however, that the survey collects and provides data only on 'establishments'
(*Betriebe*) and not 'enterprises' (*Unternehmen*). An understanding of the
definition is important here since the meaning given to the term 'establishment' varies in German law but essentially it refers to the immediate
organizational unit for conducting a set of discrete operations (including
services). In construction, this would not necessarily be an individual site
but could be a separate department or branch belonging to a single enterprise. Consequently, companies with several separate operations
might be included multiple times.

There are some 78,000 establishments in the building construction sector (*Bauhauptgewerbe*), a figure that has remained constant over several decades despite alternating phases of crisis and recovery in the industry. As a consequence, falls in employment in the industry have led to a corresponding fall in the average size of these establishments. Whereas the average establishment had 19 employees in 1995, this had fallen to just 10 by 2005, recovering to 11 by 2017.

Establishments can be broadly assigned to one of three categories in terms of employment with broadly similar structures: small establishments with fewer than 10 employees; medium-sized establishments with between 10 and 99 employees; and large establishments with more than 100, including large units with 200 or more. The figures do not separate out establishments with more than 200 employees as the number of establishments above this level would be too small.

In establishments with more than 10 employees, only some three percent at most are proprietors and family members involved in the business. Technical and administrative staff account for 18–20 percent and supervisors 10–12 percent. Between 64 and 66 percent are manual employees, with skilled trades people more common in the larger mid-size establishments. Overall, skilled employees make up a clear majority across all establishments, regardless of size. Although skilled trades remain the largest single category of employee, first-line supervisors are significantly represented in those with at least 100 employees, especially those with at least 200, and administrative and technical white-collar staff also account for a larger proportion of the workforce in such establishments.

There are some notable differences within the category of small establishments between those that are on a micro-scale (fewer than five employees) and those with between five and nine employees. Proprietors and unpaid family members account for some 45 percent of the workforce in micro-establishments and about 10 percent in establishments with five to nine employees. Skilled employees also constitute a different proportion of the workforce depending on establishment size: this is less than a third in small establishments and around two-thirds in larger ones. Rather astonishingly, trainees account for less than two percent of the workforce in the smallest establishments and just over four percent in the larger establishments, about the same as found in establishments in all the other size categories.[6] Administrative and technical white-collar staff account for some 20 percent of the workforce in establishments with fewer than 10 employees.

This structure of employment has changed discernibly, if not fundamentally, over recent decades. Prior to the major crisis of 1995, some two-thirds of employees in the building construction sector were manual workers (63.2 percent), of which around a third were in skilled trades. By 2005, the proportion of manual workers had fallen to just under 59 percent, with an increase in the share accounted for by skilled trades compared with unskilled and semi-skilled employees. In contrast, the proportion of white-collar employees rose (although their absolute number fell during the crisis). Before the crisis, white-collar staff had accounted for 16 percent of the overall workforce but this share had risen to 20 percent by 2005. Looked at overall, this could be read as representing efforts by employers to retain skilled staff for as a long as possible. By 2017, the share of white-collar staff had nudged up to 20.4 percent: this is an aggregate figure covering both administrative/commercial and technical white-collar staff. This is unhelpful for analysis as the scale of employment of each category can imply different operational approaches. These statistics also make it impossible to compare the balance between technical staff and supervisors, both of which are active in managing construction activity but whose relative proportions reflect differing approaches and company preferences, with quite different consequences for how construction work is executed in practice.

In 2017, of the almost 54,000 people working in the industry who are self-employed as proprietors, more than 33,000 or almost two-thirds (62.3 percent) were in establishments with fewer than five employees; just over a fifth (22.4 percent) were in establishments with between five and nine employees and a tenth (10.5 percent) were in establishments with 10–19 employees. The statistics are problematic in this case too because this figure includes unpaid family members, whose numbers have not been separately identified for several years. Overall, therefore, what is clear is that more than 95 percent of the self-employed own a small establishment. Interestingly, and despite the collapse in employment in construction between 1995 and 2005, the number of proprietors and unpaid family members rose. This would be consistent with the observation that following the bankruptcy of a construction business, several of its former employees will invariably set themselves up as self-employed builders. Unfortunately, there are no detailed figures on this.

The legal status of self-employed people in Germany is not comparable to those classified as 'self-employed' in the UK, even if they do not employ anyone and there are similarities in their work situations. Self-employed people without an employee are referred to as 'solo self-employed' (*Solo-Selbstständige*) in Germany. An analysis based on data from the Total Survey found that, for the years 2009 and 2010, there were some 18,000 such 'solo self-employed' in the building construction sector in Germany. In other parts of the construction sector, the number is likely to be higher, but no data are available

Although the proportion of formally qualified white-collar employees (administrators, engineers, technicians, supervisors) in the buildings construction sector in Germany is higher in larger firms, these occupations also play a role in smaller companies. For example, the proportion of administrative and technical employees in establishments with fewer than 100 employees ranges between 17 and 20 percent, increasing significantly only in larger establishments at 23 percent in establishments between 100 and 199 employees, and 30.7 percent in establishments with more than 200 employees. Unfortunately, data are not available for any further differentiation by establishment size.

Training for Construction

The system of vocational training is a key factor in ensuring that the construction industry has ready access to skills and can recruit new entrants to the labor market and, consequently, it is highly valued. Trade union and employer representatives are unanimous in their emphasis on the importance of vocational skills both for individual companies and for the entire industry. The state also contributes and supports training through the provision of vocational schools. These vocational schools (*Berufsschulen*) provide the classroom-based component of the German 'dual system' of vocational training, in which trainees alternate between vocational schools and workplace learning. This combines practical training at the workplace and theoretical training in vocational schools, with an obligation for coordination between the two elements. Some aspects of practical training will typically be conducted at training centers that cover a number of workplaces in an area.

The formal arrangements for vocational schools vary between the *Länder*. Trainees enter this system, as a rule, straight from the first phase of their secondary education, typically between 15 and 19 years of age, depending on *Land* and this will represent the upper secondary phase for those entering traineeships. These provisions apply primarily to the so-called 'craft sector' (*Handwerk*) but also include other skills. The *Handwerk* sector is statutorily regulated by the Trade and Crafts Code (*Handwerksordnung*). This sets out the trades that are covered by the Code and regulates training and the requirements for obtaining a 'Master's certificate' that allows individuals to practice and employ others. In construction, these trades include such occupations as painting and varnishing, tiling, joinery, roofing and masonry. Craft establishments employ some five million overall, one in eight of the working population. Although the number of trainees learning construction skills is not currently at the levels seen in previous years, construction is still one of the most important fields of training in Germany, particularly for manual occupations and craft trades.

Training in construction is organized in a staged process (*Stufenausbildung Bau*), introduced in 1974, that provides for 19 skill pathways to be managed via a uniform approach. During the first year of training, trainees become familiarized not only with their own future skill but also related occupations: for the most part, this takes place either in vocational schools or the training centers noted above. In the second year, trainees are inducted into their specific area of work. On completion of this year, trainees can gain certification of their skills in building construction, civil engineering or installation (a distinction that does not entirely match the official classification of economic activities). Trainees then continue into their third year with further specialization in their chosen occupation, concluding with a further examination to obtain the status of certified journeyman (*Gesellenprüfung*).

Some trades are not dealt with in this system. These include scaffolders and roofers, installation trades (such as painting), electrical installation and construction equipment mechanics in the fields of plumbing, air conditioning, heating and ventilation and construction equipment operators.

Only an approximate figure can be calculated for the ratio of trainees to the number of skilled workers they will replace as the data from the Total Survey also include individuals engaged in retraining and on internships while figures for the number of skilled workers include individuals in occupations who received their training outside the construction industry's schemes (such as roofers or insulation engineers). Accepting these limitations, however, during the boom in 1995 construction companies employed around 567,000 skilled workers and around 80,000 trainees, yielding a ratio of seven skilled workers to each trainee: a ratio of one to nine is considered to be desirable, a benchmark comfortably exceeded during this period. By the time the construction crisis had come to an end in 2005, the number of skilled workers had fallen to 366,000 and of trainees to 35,000, giving a ratio of one to ten – a clear deterioration. Since then, in a period in which activity has remained subdued, it was initially fairly easy for firms to maintain the number of their traineeships, which remained constant at 35,000, while the number of skilled workers fell to 258,000, returning to a ratio of one to seven. By 2017, there were 32,000 trainees and 301,000 skilled workers, bringing the ratio back up to the level deemed necessary to ensure that retiring workers can be replaced.

Many companies regard running their own training scheme as essential to maintain a balanced age profile for their workforce. One major trend running counter to this, however, is that large construction companies no longer employ any workers who are directly engaged in construction activity and no longer need or have scope to offer their own training provision. Moreover, the proportion of smaller firms in the construction industry offering training is also low. The main support for training in the industry is the provision offered by mid-sized firms that often place great weight on their capacity to develop and grow their own cadre of skilled employees who develop within the employer's company culture. In general, employers continue to bemoan persistent skill shortages and managing succession in these fields. Nonetheless, companies that enjoy a good reputation in local and regional labor markets are normally able to fill all the training places they have to offer. The overall demand for training places in construction remains limited although trainees' pay in construction is one of the highest in Germany: in the West, for example, a trainee in 2019 will receive €850 a month in their first year of training rising to €1,475 by the third year.

Further training provision is also well established and well regarded in the construction industry. In the craft sector, for example, the scope to qualify as a master craftsman (*Meister*) offers attractive opportunities for promotion. Further training in the construction industry scheme to 'certified supervisor' (*Polier*) has the same effect. Both these training routes also enable individuals to engage in training as a 'construction technician' (*Bautechniker*) following completion of initial training and appropriate academic qualification, allowing them to take up roles comparable with those of qualified construction engineers.

Key Regulatory Issues

Work in construction is associated with several unique challenges. In the past, this was evident in a typical pattern of unstable employment, frequent changes of employer and periodic episodes of unemployment. As a result, employees were often unable to acquire basic entitlements, such as holidays or pensions, compromising some quite fundamental elements of employee social security.

One means of addressing these challenges was the creation, in 1949, of a number of industry-specific social funds (*Sozialkassen*), known as 'SOKA-BAU'. These are based on collective agreements and under the Collective Agreements Act (1949), which sets out a statutory system for extending collective agreements, they are extended to apply to all firms in the sector. Companies are required to pay employer contributions to these funds and to enable employees to draw on the benefits they finance. There are two main funds: the Holiday and Wage Payment Fund (ULAK) and the Supplementary Pension Fund (ZVK). Since their inception other funds have also been set up, not only for the building construction industry but also in a number of craft sectors such as painting and varnishing, roofing, stonemasonry and scaffolding.

The ULAK fund guarantees that construction workers can take an annual holiday entitlement. Employees accrue holiday on a monthly basis and this is translated into a monetary amount that the employer pays into an individual employee's account. The employer then pays the employee as usual during holiday periods and is reimbursed from the fund. This procedure ensures that construction workers will be able to take their leave entitlement, even if they change employers during the qualifying period. The ZVK, set up in 1957, provides for a collectively agreed occupational pension. In addition to their statutory pension, construction workers, including in small and micro-enterprises, will also receive an occupational pension. The system of vocational training in the industry is also financed through the social funds. All construction companies pay a certain contribution (currently 2.2 percent of the gross wage bill) into the ULAK fund; in turn, certain costs are reimbursed to those companies that train and to the trainees.

The funds are based on generally binding collective agreements negotiated by the employers and the trade union, IG BAU, in the construction industry. Although these funds have significantly contributed both to stabilizing and raising the attractiveness of the industry, the employer side has been persistent in efforts to reshape how the funds operate. One factor that attracts their criticism is the complexity of the procedures. Yet without such provision in a mobile industry, construction workers would be deprived of an important support for social benefits and the industry would be less attractive to new recruits. Understandably, the union is committed to protecting the funds and, during a ceremony to mark the 150th anniversary of the construction workers' union in 2019, Robert Feiger, General Secretary of IG BAU, highlighted that these funds were deemed 'inviolable' for the union.

The Current Situation, Problems and Perspectives

The German construction industry is at a crossroads. In industrial relations terms, up until the late 1980s the sector was notable for being rooted in a high degree of social partnership. This system has been increasingly eroded since the 1990s, a state-of-affairs manifested not only in declining collective bargaining coverage, but also in a shift to inter-firm competition based on wage costs.

The introduction of binding sector-wide agreed minimum wage rates in the mid-1990s represented a joint attempt to restore a degree of order to competition in the industry. Now, almost three decades later, this significant regulatory step has been put in doubt by employer representatives, at least in part and in the context of there being a Federal statutory minimum wage, introduced in 2015 and valued in January 2020 at €9.35 per hour. Both trade unions and employers' associations are currently struggling to develop collective bargaining solutions that can offer clear benefits to their members. However, the conflicts of interests that have become increasingly apparent over the past few decades have rendered this a truly Herculean task.

One current challenge – a legacy of the past – is finalizing the harmonization of employment terms and conditions between East and West Germany. This encompasses not only the classic issue of pay but also the payment of the '13th month' salary, the agreed supplementary pension and other matters. A number of tangible successes have been achieved in recent years but there is still a considerable way to travel and the employer side has repeatedly indicated that it has no interest in bringing this process of alignment to a swift conclusion. The rise of populist parties and related forces – especially in East Germany – highlights the significance and the importance of the social policy impact of the approach that trade unions and employer associations adopt towards collective bargaining and is a key reference point for future discussion. Certainly, a clear commitment by employers to honor collective agreements and equalize conditions between East and West would represent an obvious and very direct way to push back against anti-democratic and xenophobic forces.

The construction industry has managed quite a robust recovery from the 2008 economic crisis, evidenced, among other things, by the declining rate of insolvency and improved balance sheets, with a healthier ratio of equity to debt. An enduring complaint concerns skill shortages, which are seen as one of the greatest risks to the industry's future. The paradox is that construction companies are finding it a challenge to complete orders because of a lack of personnel. This is certainly one of the most visible consequences of cutbacks in staffing and the incessant growth in the use of subcontractors for construction work.

Working time and working time flexibility are, unsurprisingly, gaining a higher profile since, from a trade union perspective, adjustments in this area could meet the aspiration of members to reconcile the demands of work and family life. For the employers, by contrast, there is an interest in extending the scope for both flexibility and hours actually worked in the hope of making some inroads into the backlog of orders. In fact, the issue of working time goes beyond the scope of the construction industry alone. Although the labor market has been favorable from the point of view of employees in recent years, the social issue of managing work and personal life has become increasingly salient. The younger generation, particularly, is less willing to accept arduous conditions without suitable compensation and companies' ability to recruit staff has come to turn on their ability to offer an attractive working environment. Construction not only has to compete with other sectors that are based on craft skills but also with manufacturing industry, which can often offer much better conditions. The social actors in the construction industry therefore face the immediate challenge of finding a response to this situation.

These concerns are added to by the challenges of digitalization, an issue over which opinions markedly diverge, both in terms of its impact on the industry as a whole and the consequences for individual firms. It is generally accepted that digitalization will have widely differing impacts on industrial operations and on the craft sector, but there are also differing interpretations within each of these sectors as to what the appropriate response should be. And irrespective of these differences, whether digitalization proves to be a success will depend crucially on workforce skills (Syben 2018).

The fact that the construction industry can draw on the resources of collective bargaining, in the shape of the industry collective agreements and social security funds, certainly makes it well placed to respond to these challenges, for example, through collective agreements on training that complement the levy-based training system. Indeed, in the most positive scenario, the challenges and necessities of digital transformation might facilitate a renaissance of social partnership in the industry.

The current position of the construction industry – and the crossroads at which it now finds itself – might be summarized with the following questions.

Can the construction industry succeed in establishing itself as an attractive industry on an enduring basis – that is, one that is free from illegal practices and precarious forms of employment and flexible enough to meet the needs of future generations? Will it offer employees a secure income and good working conditions so that the industry can face the social challenges of the future with motivated, skilled and knowledgeable staff? Putting social partnership into practice on an everyday basis could make this possible: without it, over time the industry can be expected to slide from one crisis to the next.

Notes

1 The editors are grateful to Pete Burgess for translation of the original text and for additional content.
2 Figures are only for the former West Germany. Data for the former German Democratic Republic are not comparable. In this chapter 'West' refers to the *Länder* that made up the Federal Republic prior to 1990 and 'East' to those *Länder* that made up the former German Democratic Republic and which acceded to the West in 1990.
3 Historical data are from the Tarifarchiv of the Hans-Böckler-Foundation and are based on primary research conducted by the Federal Labor Authority's research arm, Institut für Arbeits- und Berufsforschung: for this, see Ellguth and Kohaut (2019).
4 For a map setting out where such *Land*-level provisions apply, see the presentation by the Hans-Böckler-Foundation at https://www.boeckler.de/wsi-tarifarchiv_41545.htm (accessed 18.11.19.).
5 Summary statistics (in English) can be accessed at https://www.destatis.de/EN/Themes/Economic-Sectors Enterprises/Construction/_node.html.
6 The number of trainees is ascertained differently in the Total Survey to the official training statistics and cannot therefore be compared with these.

References

Amlinger, M., Bispinck, R., 2016. Dezentralisierung der Tarifpolitik – Ergebnisse der WSI-Betriebsrätebefragung 2015. *WSI-Mitteilungen 3/2016*, 211–222.
Arnholtz, J., Meardi, G., Oldervoll, J., 2018. Collective wage bargaining under strain in northern European construction: Resisting institutional drift? *European Journal of Industrial Relations* 24(4), 341–356.
Behrens, M., 2013. Arbeitgeberverbände – auf dem Weg in den Dualismus? *WSI-Mitteilungen 7/2013*, 473–481.

DGB (Deutscher Gewerkschaftsbund), 2019. *DGB-Mitgliederzahlen* https://www.dgb.de/uber-uns/dgb-heute/mitgliederzahlen/2010 (accessed 19.11.19.).

Ellguth, P., Kohaut, S., 2019. Tarifbindung und betriebliche Interessenvertretung: Ergebnisse aus dem IAB-Betriebspanel 2018. *WSI-Mitteilungen 4/2019* (72), 290–297 https://www.boeckler.de/wsimit_2019_04_ellguth.pdf (accessed 19.11.19.).

Federal Statistical Office (Destatis), 2019. *Volkswirtschaftliche Gesamtrechnungen 2018*, Fachreihe 18, Serie 1.4, 1.5. https://www.destatis.de/DE/Service/Bibliothek/_publikationen-fachserienliste-18.html?nn=206136 (accessed 18.11.19.).

Hans-Böckler-Stiftung 2019. *Tarifbindung* https://www.boeckler.de/wsi-tarifarchiv_2257.htm (accessed 18.11.19.).

IG BAU, 2018. *Betriebsratswahl: IG BAU zieht erste positive Bilanz*, IG BAU Mediendienst, 17 October 2018, PM 76/2018.

Möller, J., König, M., 2012. The effects of minimum wages in the German construction sector - reconsidering the evidence. EconStor https://www.econstor.eu/bitstream/10419/62064/1/VfS_2012_pid_585.pdf (accessed 12.05.20.).

Müller-Jentsch, W., 2017. *Strukturwandel der Industriellen Beziehungen: 'Industrial Citizenship Zwischen Markt und Regulierung* (second ed.). Springer V, Wiesbaden.

Rattenhuber, P., 2011. Building the Minimum Wage: Germany's First Sectoral Minimum Wage and its Impact on Wages in the Construction Industry, *DIW Discussion Papers*. Deutsches Institut für Wirtschaftsforschung, Berlin.

Syben, G., 2018. *Arbeit 4.0 in Bauunternehmen. Einstellungen technischer Fachkräfte in der Bauwirtschaft zu Industrie 4.0.* Hans-Böckler-Stiftung Working Paper No. 106. Düsseldorf: Hans-Böckler-Stiftung. https://www.boeckler.de/pdf/p_fofoe_WP_106_2018.pdf (accessed 18.11.19.).

6 Formality and Informality in Sub-Saharan Africa and the Ghanaian Construction Industry

Divine Kwaku Ahadzie, Yaw Debrah, and George Ofori

Introduction

Academic and policy dialogs often portray the informal economy as illegal, chaotic and unproductive (Feige 1990; Debrah 2007; Chen 2012). Around two-thirds of non-agricultural employment in African economies is attributed to the so-called 'shadow economy' which accounts for about half of the continent's total gross domestic product (Middleton 2015). The bulk of informal employment generated is artisanal (African Development Bank 2013).

Given this significant contribution, there is now a shift toward embracing this segment of the economy in the formulation of policies and strategies for sustainable development (Middleton 2015). A better appreciation is needed of the informal labor market and its impact on the quality and standards of skills development (Charmes 2012; Akorsu 2013; Aikaeli and Mkenda 2014), and an understanding of initiatives that are being implemented is essential in order to improve the human resource base, especially artisanal capacity, for accelerated development.

Using the construction industry in Ghana as its focus, this chapter considers emerging issues in informal construction and initiatives for upscaling skills and technology and improving labor relationships. The chapter is based on a literature review and interviews. The first section presents an overview of informality in sub-Saharan Africa and in African construction. The second section offers an analysis of the Ghanaian economy and demography and the state of informality and formality. The third section deals with the construction industry in Ghana and the nature of employment relations in construction. We then turn to programs for construction skills training and outline case studies on recent initiatives aimed at improving skills development, workers' welfare and labor relationships. The final section reflects on the way forward in promoting the informal construction sector in sub-Saharan African countries.

Informality in Construction

The construction industry has the highest level of informality in the global economy. Jewell et al. (2005) note that around the world a high percentage of output is produced informally. The reasons for the size of the informal segment (International Labor Organization 2001; Debrah and Ofori 1997) include the low barriers to entry in construction; the large number of distinct activities which require specific skills; labor laws which make it difficult for firms to lay off workers when they are not needed; the small role each trade plays on each project which means that it is expensive for companies to maintain a large pool of workers, given the fixed costs of employment such as holidays and medical coverage, and the convenience and long-standing nature of subcontracting.

The informal sector in construction is not well understood and is difficult to measure, but it is growing both in industrialized and developing countries (Jewell et al. 2005; Wells and Jason 2010). There was a marked increase in informality in many sub-Saharan countries as governments withdrew from investing in construction projects in the era of structural adjustment programs following the 2008 economic crisis (Wells and Jason 2010).

The essence of informality in construction is in the absence of regulation (Wells 2007). Wells highlights four aspects of regulation: regulation of enterprises, the terms and conditions of employment, the process of construction and the product, leading to four interrelated areas of informality – the informal sector of enterprises, informal labor, the informal construction system and informal buildings or settlements. The large number of projects, scattered geographically, makes it difficult to enforce regulations and standards providing a fertile environment for the growth of informality.

Informality in Sub-Saharan Africa

Informality in Africa has been discussed in the literature since the seminal work of Hart (1973) on the urban sub-proletariat in Accra, Ghana (cited in Debrah 2007). The informal sector has been characterized as unregulated, chaotic and unproductive with respect to mainstream economic activities and the sector has been relegated to the background in policy formulation and development programs for several decades (Feige 1990). There is now a paradigm shift toward the integration of the informal segment into the mainstream economy of African countries to engender accelerated development (Middleton 2015). This demonstrates that the informal sector cannot be ignored in the search for a paradigm to drive development in Africa. The United Nations' 2030 Development Agenda and African Union's 2063 Urban Agenda seek to use the informal labor market as a major economic resource for sustainable development and poverty reduction while undertaking the necessary infrastructure development (Middleton 2015).

Close to 50 percent of the GDP of sub-Saharan African countries and 80 percent of employment is driven by the informal sector, with artisans forming the largest proportion of this workforce (Osei-Boateng and Ampratwum 2011; African Development Bank 2013). In Table 6.1 data are presented to demonstrate this phenomenon, focusing on five countries: Ghana, Nigeria, Kenya, Tanzania and South Africa These countries reflect the main regional blocks of sub-Saharan African economies: Western, Eastern and Southern Africa; they are amongst the continent's major players in terms of GDP growth. Table 6.1 indicates that about 70 percent of the active labor force is in employment and about 80 percent of the construction labor force work in the informal sector.

When the data in Table 6.1 are compared with recent literature, it is evident that informality in construction in Africa has stabilized or grown. In 1998 informality in Ghana constituted 80 percent of the active construction workforce (Hormeku 1998) and Table 6.1 shows that the percentage has remained the same. In Kenya, informality constituted 42 percent of construction employment in 2000 (see Mitullah and Wachira 2003), but the table shows that it has witnessed a dramatic increase to 84 percent. The table further reveals that South Africa and Tanzania also have a huge informal presence although South Africa experienced a marginal drop between 1992 and 2002 (QUANTEC 2003; Becker 2004; Saunders 2008) to the current figure of 75 percent. In Nigeria, the largest economy in Africa, close to 90 percent of the construction sector is informal (Table 6.1). Thus, the data show that informality has a huge presence on the continent and governments need to understand and harness its full potential through targeted reforms.

Informality in construction thrives on the African continent because the sector is flexible and self-employed workers are easily able to change their activity (Chen 2012). This includes craftsmanship and artisanal skills. The weaknesses of informal working include income insecurity and lack of protection for the welfare, health and safety of workers (Nyamekye et al. 2009; International Labor Organization 2013). Conditions are unsafe; there are no social benefits such as sick pay, pension and health insurance, or even leave (Aikaeli and Mkenda 2014). Workers are unproductive and uncompetitive as a result of a skills deficit and technological inefficiency (Itasanmi et al. 2019; International Labor Organization 2013).

While in the past informality in Africa could be traced to the low educational level of the workforce, the trend has changed to include a large pool of educated unemployed youths (Nyamekye et al. 2009). It makes economic sense to consider measures to realize the potential of these high caliber skilled workers in the economy and the construction industry.

Table 6.1 Formality and informality in SSA economies and construction industries

Country	Population	Active population	Total employed (%)	GDP (billion)-US$	GDP per capita US$	Informal share on GDP (%)	Formal construction sector (%)	Informal construction sector (%)
Ghana	30,100,849	14,835,313	67.60	66.98	2,202.10	30	20	80
Nigeria	197,405,820	60,000,000	81.20	448.10	2,229.90	65	13	87
Kenya	51,334,456	19,600,000	62.22	95.50	1,816.50	34	16	84
Tanzania	59,639,627	24,890,000	60.82	63.17	1,122.10	42	18	82
South Africa	57,605,562	22,190,000	73.30	351.432	6,001.40	35	25	75
Average			69.03			41.20	18.32	81.68

Sources: World Population Review (2018), Trading Economics (2017), Ghana Data Portal (2017), Kenya Statistical Abstract (2018), Statistics South Africa (2019), National Bureau of Statistics, Tanzania (2018), World Bank (2020) and Business a.m. (2020).

Informality is associated with a burdensome business environment, including lack of clarity in regulations, bureaucratic systems, over-centralization of the administration of businesses such as registration, and high taxes. Chen (2012) advocates four policy directions to counter these factors: creation of more formal jobs, regulation of informal jobs, extension of state protection and increasing productivity of both the enterprise and the worker.

Ghana: Economy and Informality

In Ghana, as elsewhere, the construction industry is of strategic importance. Often described as the engine of growth of the national economy, it is important to other sectors because of its products and its linkage effects (Hillebrandt 2000; Ofori 2012). It is therefore fundamental that the existing support systems are harnessed to drive economic growth and job creation. An ILO study (Ernst and Sarabia 2015) found that total output multipliers in construction were higher than for the whole economy, but total employment multipliers in construction were generally higher in high-income countries than in other economies.

Ghana is located in West Africa. Its total land area is 238,533 square km (Ghana Statistical Service 2013) and Ghana's GDP is estimated at US $ 66.98 billion, while GDP per capita stood at US$ 2,202 in 2019 (World Bank 2020). The provisional GDP estimates for 2017 showed a growth rate of 8.5 percent compared to 3.7 percent in 2016 (Ghana Statistical Service 2018) and the population of Ghana is currently estimated to be 31.1 million (Macrotrends 2020).

The employment generation and multiplier potential of construction was highlighted in a report on housing in Ghana (United Nations Human Settlements Programme 2011) which noted that for every Ghanaian cedi (main Ghanaian currency unit) in construction wages, another cedi is earned as the workers spend the money locally, and for every job created in construction, it is likely that another one is created in industries providing materials, transportation, spare parts and so on. The completed building generates more jobs in internal decoration and fitting out, furnishing and, in future, repair, maintenance, renovation and possible extension. In Ghana, using a projected economic growth rate of three percent, it was estimated that there is a potential for the construction industry to create close to one million jobs in the next 10 years, from the 2013 employment figure of about 400,000 (Ahadzie 2016).

Only a small proportion of the population is qualified: just four percent hold a bachelor's degree and three percent have diplomas such as an HND, teacher or nursing qualifications (Ghana Statistical Service 2017). Of the total working population of 9.2 million, fewer than a million were managers, professionals or technicians and associate professionals

(Ghana Statistical Service 2017). The economy comprises three main sectors: agriculture, industry and services (Ghana Statistical Service 2018), made up of 21 subsectors; five in agriculture, six in industry (which includes construction) and 10 in the services sector (Anaman and Egyir 2019). Construction is the largest subsector.

As shown above, the informal sector in Ghana is a significant proportion of the total (Hormeku 1998; Osei-Boateng and Ampratwum 2011). However, little is understood of the coverage of labor standards and their impact on quality and skills development or on income, productivity and technology (Akorsu 2013). Akorsu and Cooke (2011) draw attention to institutional weaknesses characterized by high levels of income insecurity and the lack of institutional support for the enterprises in the sector (see also Freeman 2009). Lack of understanding of the training and capacity development regime is also a cause for concern although initiatives emanating both from governments and the private sector have created incubators to enhance entrepreneurship and enable competitive skills and technology acquisition (Debrah 2007; Osei-Boateng and Ampratwum 2011). Such support is, nonetheless, limited (International Labor Organization 2013).

The Ghanaian Construction Industry

The construction industry is a major contributor to Ghana's economy, accounting for some 9.1 percent of GDP between 1993 and 2011 (Osei 2013). Whereas Anaman and Egyir (2019) suggest that the industry witnessed a slowdown between 2013 and 2017 resulting from the drop in foreign direct investment and the energy crisis of 2014–2015, data from the Ghana Statistical Service indicate that construction contributed an average 10.4 percent to GDP from 2006 to 2017 (with 13.7 percent in 2016 to 2017) (Ghana Statistical Service 2018; Anaman and Egyir 2019). A construction sector index developed by Osei (2013) showed that the industry has improved significantly in performance and importance over the last two decades and there is a positive relationship between construction activities and the growth of the economy in Ghana. The construction industry has for the last decade been the most consistent contributor to the nation's GDP and arguably has the biggest opportunity for lifting large numbers of Ghanaians out of poverty (International Labor Organization 2013).

Construction works can be classified into residential, other building, civil engineering, heavy engineering and industrial works. Residential construction accounts for about half of the market and other buildings for about a quarter, whereas civil engineering and industrial works together make up the remaining quarter (Ahadzie 2016). Informal work is largely in residential and other building subsectors involving projects ranging from single-family houses to medium-sized blocks of apartments;

from small retail shops to shopping malls; office blocks; educational buildings; and hotels. High-rise apartment blocks and mass housing projects fall outside the activities of the informal segment of the industry because of the size of the projects, the amount of finance required and the nature of technology. Major building works such as government buildings, large hospitals and major educational institutions are executed in the formal sector of the industry using registered contractors. So too are civil, heavy engineering and industrial projects, which are often government financed.

The industry has unique opportunities, drawing from the huge housing requirements which can engender accelerated development. The need for housing in Ghana, to meet a backlog estimated at over 1.7 million units, is worth over US$4 billion, with potential labor earnings in the region of over US$1 billion (Ahadzie 2016). The Public Procurement Act of 2003 (Act 663) requires all public projects to go through a local or international bidding procurement process and construction companies register with the relevant ministries (Ministry of Works and Housing for building works and Ministry of Roads and Highways for roads) in order to be eligible to submit tenders for projects for which they have the capacity and capability.

There is a range of domestic construction companies in Ghana including a number of companies formed by Italian citizens in Ghana soon after the Second World War. Many domestic construction firms in Ghana possess technical expertise but lack other resources such as finance, plant and equipment to undertake major projects (Laryea 2010). Because of the limited local capacity, major projects – such as large hospitals, shopping malls, roads, highways and railways, ports and hydroelectric plants, heavy manufacturing plants and industrial buildings – are often executed by foreign firms (Sutton and Kpentey 2012). To foster capacity building and technology transfer from foreign firms to their local counterparts, there are some restrictions on the number of expatriates who can be engaged and this is dependent on the amount invested by the foreign company which determines the number of working visas permitted (Auffray and Fu 2015).

The Construction Workforce and Working Conditions

The construction sector is dominated by building, mainly residential works and there are minimal barriers to entry. It is labor intensive and, arguably, technologically inefficient. The workforce is young and overwhelmingly male, with a wide range of skills but a low level of education. Employment is informal and the work is transient with no job security. Health and safety hazards result from inadequate regulation and poor enforcement of the laws (Ahadzie 2016; Ofori 2017).

Data from Ghana's labor force survey in 2017 indicate that over 316,000 persons were employed in construction (Ghana Statistical

Service 2017), 3.4 percent of Ghana's total workforce. Only six percent of these workers were female. The survey also showed that of the total employed in construction, 97.7 percent were described as in the 'informal sector'. The professional workforce consists of architects, engineers of various areas of specialization, quantity surveyors and construction and project managers. The second tier includes clerks of works, site foremen and technicians. These professionals and technicians work in the formal sector of the industry. At the artisanal level and below, the construction labor pool comprises tradesmen (masons, carpenters, steel benders, painters, electricians, plumbers, plant and equipment operators and so on) and unskilled workers (who assist tradesmen on sites who work for contractors and subcontractors and are largely 'informal'). Increasingly, main contractors tend to avoid employing permanent workers and rely instead on labor-only subcontractors. The construction workforce also includes workers in building materials (such as aggregates, cement, blocks, steel reinforcement, timber, tiles, paints, electrical and plumbing equipment and fittings, and so on) and those who work for plant hire organizations.

Figure 6.1 shows that since 1992 there has been a steady increase in the hourly rate of earnings, indicating that there is an opportunity to use the construction industry to increase income levels of both skilled and unskilled workers in the sector. The housing sector alone is capable of providing stable jobs and income, although there is a shortage of artisans (Kanyenze et al. 2000; UNECA 2002 cited in Debrah 2007: 1075). The skills gap has been described as the biggest challenge facing the survival and competitiveness of the industry.

The construction industry has a poor reputation in many respects, including the employment practices of the companies, the nature of the work and the working conditions, the rewards and risks and the welfare of the workforce. Construction is referred to as a '4D' industry: dirty, dangerous, demanding and demeaning (Construction 21 Steering Committee 1999). In many countries, construction workers tend to work longer hours and are paid less than in other sectors.

A report in 2015 noted that in Ghana 60 percent of youth aged 15–24 years is economically inactive and 16 percent is unemployed (Evanto Resource Ltd. and the Urban Associates Ltd. 2015). The construction industry therefore offers an important opportunity to develop youth employment. However, the same report noted that careers in the industry are unpopular. Females show little interest in construction work owing to the physical nature of the work and the social stigma faced by women in the industry. Males would prefer further education to be able to work in other sectors while construction work was seen as 'menial' and physically demanding. The reputation of the industry as an unsafe and unhealthy environment also discourages job applicants. The recommendations in the report include provision of training in identified

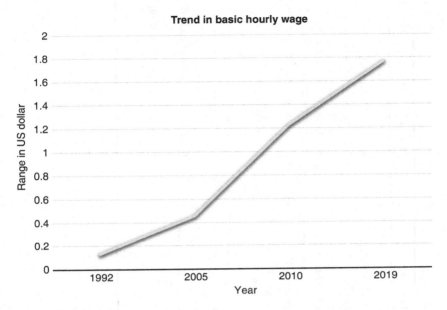

Figure 6.1 Basic hourly wages in construction in Ghana, 1992–2019.
Source: Adapted from Ghana Living Standards Survey 2013 (Ghana Statistical
Service 2013).

trades where the deficit would be greatest; mainstream promotion and
support for gender parity in the industry; establishment of a fund to
provide finance on favorable terms to contractors to acquire equipment
and the funding of projects and training; the introduction of more
streamlined administrative processes and the provision of training in
local languages.

An overview of the potential of the informal segment of the construction industry in Ghana is presented in Table 6.2. The demand for
better workmanship and changing trends toward new systems and materials such as structural steel, curtain walling, plant and crane operations, scaffolding technology, high-quality finishes, special roof systems
and advanced mechanical and electric systems in buildings generate more
demand for high levels of expertise. There is also a strong demand for
specialization even in the traditional skills of bricklaying, plastering,
painting, flooring, tiling, drywall construction, advanced electrical and
plumbing systems, steel framing, architectural sheet metal working and
building maintenance works. Considering these developments, the informal sector of the construction industry is limited and needs to upscale
its technology.

Table 6.2 SWOT analysis of informal labor in the construction industry in Ghana

Strength	Weakness	Opportunities	Threats
• Youthful and vibrant labor force • Multi-skilled workers • Free entry and exit • Highly flexible labor force • Technological ingenuity	• No defined client and employer • Vulnerability to health and safety hazards • Informal terms of employment • Poor organization of workers in the sector • Low level of education • No legal recognition and also protection from labor laws • Tax burdens • Rule of law • Lack of access to credit • Hours of work • Lack of social security	• The emerging housing needs • Diversity into other related trade/skill • National policies to enhance Technical and Vocational Education Training • Potential for new enterprise • Large pool and opportunity for labor union organization	• Skills becoming obsolete • Linguistic and cultural differences • Generational differences • Inappropriate barriers including potential for child labor • Matching with the skills of the predominance of foreign contractors • Changing crafts work environment • Poor occupational hazard and safety • Poor employment relations

Ghanaian Construction Labor Relations

The key actors in construction industry employment relations in Ghana are first, the government as the single major client and its state agents with responsibility for policy direction; second, the labor unions, including the Trades Union Congress (TUC); third professional associations and regulatory bodies and fourth, contractors' and artisans' associations. The following section discusses the contribution of these actors to labor relations and their relationship to informal labor development.

The Government

The main ministries with responsibility for the construction industry in Ghana are the Ministries of Roads and Highways, and Works and Housing. However, many of the aspects of construction lie under the jurisdiction of other ministries.

The Ministry of Education (MoE) is charged with providing relevant education to all Ghanaians to enable them to acquire skills to become literate and productive, to facilitate poverty alleviation and promote socio-economic growth (Ofori 2017). The MoE states that it is committed to establishing an educational system focused on promoting creativity and problem-solving through the development of academic, technical and vocational programs that will assure labour market readiness.

As the number of tertiary institutions grew, both public and private, three organizations were set up under the MoE for the quality management of the educational and training system (Ofori 2017) – first, the National Council for Tertiary Education, a supervisory body of tertiary education responsible for, among others, considering applications for the introduction of new programs in tertiary institutions and advising on their relevance for national development; second, the National Accreditation Board which, as the quality assurance organization, has the authority to accredit tertiary educational institutions and their programs to contribute to the furtherance of better management of tertiary education and third, the National Board for Professional and Technician Examinations (NABPTEX) which is responsible for formulating and administering schemes of examinations and standards for skill and syllabus competencies for non-university accredited public and private tertiary institutions. NABPTEX organizes Higher National Diploma (HND) examinations in Building Technology; Civil Engineering; Construction Engineering and Management; Electrical/Electronic Engineering; Interior Architecture and Furniture Production; Interior Design and Technology; Mechanical Engineering; Procurement and Logistics Management and Surveying and Geoinformatics.

The Ministry of Employment and Labour Relations (MELR) oversees and coordinates employment opportunities and labor-related interventions

(Ofori 2017). It is responsible for the formulation and implementation of policies aimed at creating and promoting decent jobs, and for developing strategies that promote industrial peace and harmony. It resolves labor-related disputes, ensures occupational safety and health and regulates the payment of fair and equitable wages and salaries to employees in all sectors.

The stated policy objectives of the MELR are to promote the goal of full employment and enable all who are willing to work to attain a sustainable livelihood: secure improvement in the productivity of the labor force in order to improve competitiveness and enhance employability so that labor is afforded quality and well-remunerated jobs; provide the fullest possible opportunity to each worker to qualify for and to use skills in a job for which she or he is well-suited; safeguard the basic rights and interests of workers and promote respect for international standards; secure maximum cooperation from, and participation by business, organized labor and other interested parties in decisions on employment policy and stimulate economic growth and development, eradicate poverty and improve the standard of living by minimizing unemployment and under-employment.

Labor Unions

The TUC was formed in Ghana in 1945 and the Industrial Relations Act (Act 299) was enacted in 1965. Regulation of the Ghanaian labor market has improved structurally over time with the Labor Act 663 and Act 665 in 2003 setting up the Labor Commission. The Labor Act provides that any two persons have the right to form a union.

The Construction and Building Materials Workers Union was formed in 1954 (Trades Union Congress and Rosa Luxemburg Stiftung 2012), when the union was recognized as the voice of workers in the construction industry, and its main achievement was the set of binding collective agreements which cover conditions of service and terms of employment. It signed the first national agreement in 1959 and was strong during the era of state involvement in construction with the Public Works Department (PWD), the then Ghana National Construction Corporation and the State Construction Corporation (SCC). The situation changed in the 1980s when the government withdrew from direct participation in construction and the SCC collapsed, eliminating a large part of the formal segment of the construction industry. The union has suffered membership decline ever since, due mainly to the disproportionately large share of informal sector workers within the construction industry. Its current challenges include increasing informalization in construction; the spread of individual employment contracts; increasing use of casual, contract and temporary workers and high levels of instability of companies and labor turnover because of delayed payments to contractors. The union runs seminars and workshops for its leaders and activists and set up the Vocational Leadership Centre, providing young workers with employable skills – as in brick laying, masonry, steel bending and steel fixing.

The General Construction, Manufacturing and Quarries Workers' Union (GCMQWU), formed in 2016, now has over 5,000 members. It has launched campaigns, educational activities and social dialog and is building interest in the union. It cites delays to payments for work done on government projects as a major factor affecting its members. Other concerns are inadequate financial capacity and the need for education and training for its members. It argues that Ghana is facing an acute shortage of workers, with the need being mostly for engineers, plumbers, estimators or quantity surveyors, masons and painters. The union campaigns on occupational health and safety at the workplace and runs events for its members. The GCMQWU, however, organizes workers in businesses which do not necessarily work directly in construction but in allied sectors.

The TUC has traditionally been skeptical of the potential for organization of the informal sector, hoping that it would be phased out if the government focused on increasing formal employment. Informal employment, however, has grown in all sectors of the economy (Osei-Boateng and Ampratwum 2011). The TUC has therefore changed its strategy, introducing initiatives aimed at capacity development in the informal sector. For instance, in 1996 it launched policies to recognize the plight of informal workers and the need for improvement in their working conditions. At its 2012 quadrennial conference, it reaffirmed support for the informal sector by assisting and encouraging the creation of labor unions for these workers.

The TUC has supported the formation of nine unions in the informal sector (albeit none in construction) but the casual and transient nature of employment has been a major challenge. The TUC Secretary General has noted that organizing informal sector workers is not simple; it is expensive and brings little returns (Osei-Boateng and Ampratwum 2011). Some NGOs are also administering initiatives to train and empower informal artisans (some case studies on these are presented below) which compliment these union initiatives.

According to a research officer of the Ghana TUC (interview 2019), improvement in the organization of informal sector workers has become a priority and the Congress is committed to building organization to enable them to benefit from mainstream labor union activities. The TUC pledges that it will continue to do its best to complement the work of its international partners. The research officer stated that

> *The TUC has been able to put in place a three-tier pension scheme with the third tier for informal workers known as the People's Pension Trust and desks have been set up in all regional offices of the TUC for this scheme. There is also a social protection department*

> *with the focus of securing pension arrangements for informal*
> *workers; there is the legal department with a representation on the*
> *National Labor Commission where members and even workers*
> *outside the union can lodge occupational grievances.*

The major problem has been the lack of understanding amongst artisans of how labor unions operate, stemming from the low educational background of most of them, and their lack of trust in the system. Opoku (2018) found that many of the artisans and unskilled workers start their apprenticeship around the age of 15 years. Most of them do not have a high school education and find themselves in construction without any aim to build a sustainable career. Most respondents agreed that construction activity is physically tough and can involve dangerous situations and stress (Opoku 2018), reflecting their occupational challenges.

Professional Institutions and Regulatory Organizations

The professional institutions in Ghana's construction industry include the Ghana Institute of Architects, the Ghana Institution of Surveyors, the Ghana Institution of Engineering and the Ghana Institute of Planners. New institutions for technicians have emerged recently, including the Institution of Engineering and Technology, Ghana. The Ghana Consulting Engineers Association looks after the interests of the consulting firms and professionals.

There have been efforts to strengthen the regulation of some of the professions in Ghana with the introduction of the Architects' Registration Council and the Engineers' Registration Council. Draft Bills for some other professions are also being considered. There has also been a trend of the professional institutions and registration councils to widen their coverage to include technicians and persons with lower-level qualifications.

Contractors' and Artisans' Associations

The two main contractors' associations in Ghana are the Association of Building and Civil Engineering Contractors and the Association of Road Construction Companies. The Ghana Real Estate Developers Association (GREDA) specializes in housing delivery, especially mass housing. The associations focus on the interests of members in their advocacy. For example, the GREDA members operate mainly in house building targeting the upper and middle class with large-scale schemes (Ahadzie 2016). While they rely on artisans to achieve their business goals, they have done little toward capacity building and the enhancement of skills in the informal sector.

There have, however, been recent initiatives aimed at harmonizing the intentions of the stakeholders, combining their efforts toward developing the industry (Ofori 2018). The Built Environment Professionals Association (BEPA) includes the main professional institutions, whereas the Federation of Construction Contractors of Ghana (FCCG) represents the contractors' associations. The Ghana Chamber of Construction Industries (GCCI) brings together BEPA and FCCG. The other notable groupings of industry stakeholders are the Construction Industry Development Forum, which involves representatives of both public and private sector organizations and the Ghana Institute of Construction.

While the professional institutions and trade associations are playing active roles, they focus primarily on the formal sector. For example, whereas the various professional institutions and trade associations have been given formal representation on a number of boards and ad hoc committees geared toward skills development in the country, they have not placed the pressing issues of informal skills development on the national agenda (Real Estate Journal 2016).

There have been several calls for a construction industry development agency to be established (Ofori 2012; Ofori-Kuragu et al. 2016), but despite government declarations of support, so far not much has happened. Without the construction agency, the industry's holistic development cannot be realized, including the development of the informal sector (Ofori 2012).

Occupational Health and Safety

Health and safety is a major concern, but there is currently no specific health and safety legislation. The industry depends on sections of the Labor Act, 663 (2003, part XI); the Factories and Shops Act 328 (1970); the Workmen's Compensation Act 187 (1987); and sections of the Building Regulations, LI 1630 (1996). The recent 2018 National Building Code contains a number of provisions relating to the safe use of materials and practices on site.

From the 2017 labor survey data (Ghana Statistical Service 2017), the construction industry reported a frequency of occupational injury of 65 per million hours worked (the third highest in Ghana) and an injury incidence rate of 86 injuries per thousand workers (fourth highest). Some 346 days were lost in construction (seventh highest) due to accidents with an average of nine days lost per injury (among the lowest). In the previous 12 months, 27,297 construction workers had occupational injuries (this is not proportionally the highest). The construction safety data are significant and more effort is needed if injuries are to be reduced.

Construction Skills

In 1967 the National Manpower Board was established in Ghana to formulate policies for efficient human resource development and utilization. After a study of skills training and manpower needs, it proposed a national vocational training program. This commenced in October 1968 with the ILO as the agency responsible for program execution. A National Vocational Training Institute (NVTI) was established in 1970 with the mandate of coordinating all aspects of vocational training as well as apprenticeships in Ghana.

There have been important initiatives from the Government of Ghana, such as the National Apprenticeship Program and the Ghana Skills and Technology Development Initiative, and also representation of informal labor on the national level tripartite committee to amend and consolidate laws relating to labor and employment. The government's 2001 Skills Training and Employment Program was one of the flagship projects which set in motion the creation of a database in the sector, including opportunities for training.

Institutional Support for Training

The Council for Technical and Vocational Education and Training (COTVET) was established in 2006 to formulate national policies on skills development across pre-tertiary and tertiary education in the formal and informal sectors of the economy and to coordinate and supervise the activities of public and private vocational training and education providers, including informal apprenticeships. COTVET is responsible for reporting on the state of skills development in the country as well as advising the government on all matters relating to the management and improvement of technical and vocational education and training (TVET) in Ghana (Quashie 2018).

Ghana's TVET system is under the purview of the MoE but other ministries providing TVET include the Ministry for Employment and Labour Relations and the Ministries of Youth and Sports, Local Government and Rural Development and Health. The mission in the draft national TVET policy for Ghana is stated as

> improve the productivity and competitiveness of the skilled workforce and raise the income-earning capacities of people, especially women and low-income groups, through the provision of quality-oriented, industry-focused, and competency-based training programs and complementary services

Ghana's country profile on the UNECA (2002) database states that TVET in Ghana aims to contribute to the development of a productive workforce by linking the education system to the needs of the economy. The International Centre for Technical and Vocational Education and Training (2017) also presents an analysis of information on TVET in Ghana.

COTVET notes that pre-tertiary TVET has the dual mission to prepare students both for increasing and widening workplace requirements and also further study. It equips trainees with skills to enhance their employability and livelihoods and provides access to competency-based training (CBT). Policies promote industry-led and demand-driven CBT which is outcome-based and also promotes equitable access, opportunities and career pathways for students and employees to develop their vocational, technical and generic skills; and workplace experience learning which ensures that the theoretical and practical aspects of the CBT model are integrated and prepares students for work. The assessment instruments and learning materials are all developed from industry standards. Certification is through the national TVET framework created by the COTVET.

The introduction of COTVET in 2006 helped to establish TVET as a national priority both in the formal and informal sectors. Institutions seeking to run the curriculum of the CBT program have to be accredited by COTVET and this includes pre-tertiary, tertiary and even informal sector institutions. Both the facilitators and the programs the institution intends to run must be accredited by COTVET and, so far, 20 institutions have been accredited (Quashie 2018). Because the focus has been on formal institutions, however, over 90 percent of craftsmen are unaware of the CBT program. The absence of trade unions in the informal sector makes it difficult for COTVET to reach workers there, especially construction workers (Quashie 2018). For the same reason, it is more difficult to identify training needs in order to establish appropriate interventions. Although there is the potential for CBT to close the skills and competence gaps in the construction industry, more is needed in terms of organization and an enabling environment for artisans in the informal sector to embrace the concept.

The eight-level National TVET Qualifications Framework for Ghana, administered by COTVET, recognizes vocational skills, knowledge and competencies. It classifies qualifications (from Level 1 – traditional apprenticeship – to Level 8 – Doctorate in Technology) according to criteria and standards of learning outcomes.

The framework enables recognition of knowledge and skills to improve employability. Employers benefit from a skilled workforce, with enhanced productivity and quality of products and services; improved employee motivation and assurance of validation of employees' qualifications and capabilities. For the economy there can be improved national competitiveness, a basis for international comparison and opportunities for labor mobility.

There are problems matching the contents of training to industry requirements, improving the quality of instruction, obtaining adequate finance, providing training institutions with up-to-date facilities and equipment and enhancing the perception of technical and vocational training among potential and current students (Darvas and Palmer 2014; Ofori 2017). The system is largely supply driven, facing high costs, low quality of supply and low demand. The curricula tend to be theoretical and it is difficult to attract and retain instructors with marketable and up-to-date skills. The institutes are unable to respond quickly to the changing needs of the market and industry and to target resources effectively. The TVET system also tends to exclude the poor, owing to the direct costs of training. The poorer pupils are also unable to meet the entry requirements of most formal TVET providers. Among the reasons for the lack of support by employers for training is their fear that workers they invest in would be poached by competitors.

Ghana did not have a national body to oversee construction skills training until the inauguration in 2019 of the Sector Skills Council for Construction (SSCC). The SSCC has the aim of developing an understanding of the future skill requirements in the industry in order to reduce skills gaps and shortages and to boost the skills of the construction sector workforce (Ghana Skills Development Initiative undated). The current estimated annual demand for skilled construction workers is between 60,000 and 70,000, but the formal technical institutes in Ghana turn out only 900 per year (Ministry of Education 2010). The informal sector fills the gap but the annual output from that source is unknown. According to COTVET the construction industry needs artisans who understand industry structures, materials and tools, as well as being able to adhere to industry standards (Quashie 2018). Although the NVTI can provide certification of the activities of the artisans in the informal sector, many tradespeople are unaware of the program and those who know about it do not consider it necessary to acquire certification. Apart from the inadequate skills capacity as a result of rapid technological and product development, informal labor in construction also lacks business skills, knowledge about resource use, customer care and financial awareness (Debrah 2007).

Apprenticeship Schemes

According to Osei-Boateng and Ampratwum (2011), the apprenticeship system in Ghana is relatively well developed and effective in providing skills training but, while this may be true of specific vocations such as tailoring, weaving, wood carving and joinery, this is not the case for the construction industry, especially the critical skills of masonry, carpentry, steel bending and placing of reinforcement, tiling, plastering, plumbing and electrical works. To help put this assertion in context, it is important to first have an appreciation of vocational and apprenticeship training for construction in Ghana.

Professionals graduate from undergraduate and postgraduate programs, whereas technicians are educated at diploma level. Currently, some 14 public and private tertiary institutions, including the Kwame Nkrumah University of Science and Technology and the six recently designated technical universities, offer opportunities for professional education. The technicians are educated at technical universities and polytechnics.

Formal Apprenticeships

The history of formal construction skills training in Ghana began in the 1950s with the establishment of the then PWD as an integrated design, construction and maintenance organization to undertake the building and road projects of the government. The major construction firms which were undertaking projects beyond the capability of the PWD at the time were originally 'expatriate' and were incorporated in Ghana in the 1940s. There was a shortage of artisans so the government established trades or crafts training schools in the Western, Ashanti and Volta Regions, products of which would be recruited by the construction and maintenance units of the PWD after a one-year on-the-job training scheme referred to as the 'Fifth Year Apprenticeship' (interview with master craftsman 2019).

The NVTI, which is an agency of the Ministry of Employment and Labor Relations, operates 38 vocational centers in 28 skills areas. Its functions include organizing apprenticeships, in-plant training and training programs for industrial and clerical workers and the training of instructors and training officers; the provision of vocational guidance and career development; the development of training standards and the evolution of effective trade testing and certification policies and programs. It provides an on-going analysis of the country's skilled manpower requirements. The vision is 'to provide the best systems of employable TVET skills' (NVTI 2017: 5). Its mission is 'to provide demand-driven employable skills and enhance the income generating capacities of basic and secondary school leavers, and such other persons through Competency-based Apprenticeship, Master Craftsmanship, Testing and Career Development' (NVTI 2017: 5).

The pilot training institute, the first established by the NVTI in 1970, provided both formal and informal training and retraining for young workers. Today, the Institute offers courses including building construction, building draftsmanship, carpentry and joinery, general electrical installation, welding and fabrication and electronics. The geographical distribution of courses is uneven. Some courses (such as draftsmanship and plumbing) are offered in very few institutes. The data on trainees in construction trades produced by NVTI in 2014–17, show that the largest number took the general electrical skills course, followed by masonry. The numbers for carpentry and plumbing are lower.

Informal Apprenticeships

In Ghana, formal institutional apprenticeship schemes exist side-by-side with traditional, informal apprenticeships run at local level by 'master craftsmen' in trades, such as tailoring, masonry, carpentry and joinery, plumbing and electrical works. Informal apprenticeships account for 80–90 percent of skills training and acquisition in the informal sector (Debrah 2007).

Most artisans and tradespersons in Ghana's construction industry were trained under the traditional informal apprenticeship system. The 2017 labor force survey indicates that of all apprentices engaged in the economy, 13 percent are in the construction industry (Ghana Statistical Service 2017). The Children's Act 1998, part V, outlines a framework for informal apprenticeship training which specifies that the minimum age for such an apprenticeship should be 15 years or after completion of basic education. It outlines the responsibilities of masters or trainers toward apprentices, the apprenticeship agreement, duties and the release of the apprentice (Republic of Ghana 1998). An apprenticeship takes three to four years and starts when the young person and his parents or guardians go to see a Master Tradesman of the family's choice, with a bottle of local gin and a sum of money fixed by the master (United Nations Human Settlements Programme 2011). Each master has a team of trainees who work with him, and they learn the skills on the job. In most cases the apprentice is not paid a wage but receives a daily allowance for meals and transport from the master. The apprentice is expected to learn the main skills of the trade by the end of the third year. Traditionally, the apprentice serves the master for an additional year but this fourth year is not compulsory. After the training, the apprentice must pay the master another token amount and organize a party for his fellow trainees. The apprentice is given a letter of release or testimonial, with details of the training, by the master or the trades association. A few apprentices take NVTI proficiency tests.

The NVTI has an Informal Apprenticeship Department which formulates policies to guide the development and maintenance of the informal infrastructure. It maintains a database of master crafts persons and apprentices, initiates and implements policies to ensure that training equals standards of COTVET and develops policies to ensure that demand-driven competency-based informal apprenticeship takes place nationwide. The department seeks to make informal apprenticeship a centerpiece of its activities and ensures the training of apprentices in the informal subsector is monitored in line with best practices nationwide.

Integrated Community Centres for Employable Skills (ICCES), an agency under the Ministry for Employment and Labour Relations, is responsible for providing vocational, entrepreneurial and skills training at the community level to early school leavers to enable them to establish their own enterprises, generate employment and reduce the rural–urban drift. ICCES's policy objective is to increase the access of young persons to skills acquisition and empowerment for productive employment. Its vision is to be the leader in TVET provision in rural communities in Ghana and its mission is: *'To equip and empower the unemployed, especially the youth, with employable skills through vocational skills training at the community level throughout Ghana'*. Its functions are providing competency-based vocational training and retraining for young persons; providing counseling for trainees and prospective trainees; developing literacy and numeracy skills of trainees and facilitating trainee mobilization for the establishment of micro and small-scale enterprises.

Kwao and Ahadzie (2017) studied skills training in the informal sector in Ghana involving 32 purposely sampled masonry artisans on informal housing construction sites. All the masons confirmed that they had their training through a 'gang master' who determined its content and duration. Many of them wished their training was more structured, systematic and trade specific. Even though the artisans wished for certification to provide evidence of their proficiency, few of them knew about the NVTI, suggesting that the gang masters may not have been NVTI certified. The respondents suggested that the apprenticeship program should be regulated by bringing all master craftsmen under a common platform, that it should be structured and a limit placed on the number of trainees a master craftsman could have at any one time.

This informal apprenticeship system suffers from problems, including a lack of standard content; narrowness of the training and experience provided; the possibility of mistakes being perpetuated; the lack of coordination; the lack of necessary equipment and training facilities and challenges with technological developments. Suggestions for improvement include: formalization and the inclusion of an assessment system; the development of mechanisms to facilitate the articulation of the informal level and standards of skills acquisition with those of the formal TVET system; the encouragement of the formation and recognition of trade associations as a means of delivering training-related assistance to members; the integration of informal apprenticeship training into the formal qualifications framework; and the provision of guidelines for action by government and other stakeholders in informal sector training. For traditional apprentices, the NVTI provides top-up training and proficiency testing and NVTI uses the master craftsmen as a resource when formulating syllabi. Efforts are being made under some schemes, including the Ghana Skills Development Initiative (GSDI), to address the weaknesses of the informal system.

In the next section, we discuss three case studies of skills training initiatives in Ghana.

Case Studies

The case studies included in this chapter describe three initiatives to develop construction skills: World University Services of Canada (WUSC) project; the Global Communities YIEDIE project and the GSDI, which is supported by the German government. The discussion is based on a review of the literature and interviews with senior officers of the organizations conducted by the authors between January and March 2019.

1   *WUSC Project*

The WUSC is a non-profit organization dedicated to providing education, employment and empowerment opportunities for youth around the world (World University Service of Canada (WUSC) 2015). WUSC works with a network of students, volunteers, institutions, governments and businesses to foster youth-centered solutions to overcome inequality and exclusion. While WUSC focuses on empowering and improving the skills of artisans in the informal sector generally, there is a specific focus on involving women and encouraging them to take up livelihoods in construction through market-relevant and gender-inclusive training in relevant skills.

To facilitate gender equality in the residential construction sector and in TVET education and training, WUSC has developed a gender-friendly approach in partnership with the COTVET, and with the support of Uniterra (the name used by WUSC in Ghana) volunteers. This has been pre-tested with selected TVET centers in three cities in Ghana and validated nationally with TVET actors and residential construction sector players to be introduced in TVET institutions. Subsequently, the Residential Construction Mentorship and Coaching Program (RCMCP) for females is being developed in partnership with the Artisans Association of Ghana (AAG). This is a membership-based network of artisans which seeks to train, upgrade and support both master craftsmen and unskilled youth to gain certification. It also assists the empowered artisans to improve their skills using innovative technologies, starts incubator services and identifies projects with economic potential to generate employment.

WUSC works in collaboration with a number of organizations including the ICCES, which, as discussed above, provides community-based vocational, entrepreneurial and skills training to early school dropouts. The WUSC initiative, especially regarding females in the RCMCP, may provide lessons on how to encourage more women to take up careers in the construction industry.

2   *Global Communities – YIEDIE Project*

The Youth Inclusive Entrepreneurial Development Initiative for Employment (YIEDIE) project, which is supported by the

Mastercard Foundation, is designed to create opportunities in the construction industry for economically disadvantaged urban youth in Ghana. A five-year project, implemented by Global Communities, an international NGO, in conjunction with partners, began in February 2015 and ended in March 2020.

The objectives of YIEDIE were to increase employment among young workers (including self-employment) in construction and ensure an enabling environment by construction sector stakeholders. The aim was to train 23,700 youths between 17 and 24 years who have dropped out of school, and live on less than $2 a day, with training in technical, life and entrepreneurship skills leading to employment and higher income. YIEDIE trained young women and men in technical construction skills and helped young workers to start and grow small businesses.

YIEDIE applied an integrated youth-led market-systems model to improve the capacity of youth and service providers. By early 2019, 16,738 workers had been trained. The technical element of the program provided training in 15 construction trades including masonry, carpentry, plaster of Paris design, aluminum fabrication, metal fabrication, tiling, painting, heavy duty machine operation, steel bending, interior design, survey technical assistance, electrical and draftsmanship. The technical training runs for six months and the entrepreneurship training for two months. Successful trainees are then assigned to construction companies and supported to start businesses.

The YIEDIE project was open to candidates who had completed or dropped out of education and who were designated as 'vulnerable.' Potential trainees went through psychosocial counseling and successful applicants were attached to a master craftsperson who provided training based on the curriculum developed with COTVET. Thereafter, the trainee was assessed for the Proficiency One Certificate of the NVTI. Trained artisans could take the test for the Proficiency Two Certificate after some years of experience. YIEDIE focused on the informal sector and liaised with COTVET to ensure that the training fitted with the national qualification framework so that, when a person went through CBT, she or he could gain certification which was unavailable in the informal sector. The program was practice based with assessor standards. The artisans were helped to go through the registration process after which they had also to meet some minimum requirements of procurement systems to be eligible to seek government contracts.

The YIEDIE project became so successful and attractive that it attracted government support, with provisions in the 2017 and 2018 national budgets for the implementation of the CBT TVET program in Ghana. At its close, the program had exceeded its target and trained 25,479 with technical and entrepreneurial skills in the construction sector - 16,020 were trained in technical construction skills while the remaining 9,459 were also trained in entrepreneurship (GhanaWeb

2020). The female enrollment increased from 11 percent in the first year to 30 percent by the end and, while interior decoration had been favorite among them, the majority of the women enrolled in heavy machine operations, painting, tiling, aluminum fabrication, electrical technician and metal fabrication.

From tracer studies, the initiative compiled several success stories of informal artisans who, having received the training, are now executing formal projects. An officer gave some examples (author interview 2019).

For instance, there is a guy who completed YIEDIE, but now he is one of the service providers of the Electricity Company of Ghana. He has won a contract for the wiring of school blocks and several other formal contracts. We have some others in the informal sector who are also doing fantastically well. In fact, three guys who were trained in aluminum fabrication have recently won a contract for themselves for aluminum fabrication works in a mass residential project. We have many of such success case studies. There is also a female tiler in Accra who is doing marvelously well.

YIEDIE made progress in rolling out CBT training so that artisans in the informal sector could gain recognition and have certification. However, there are still challenges relating to the transient interest of young workers and in getting women to embrace careers in the construction industry.

3   *Ghana Skills Development Initiative (GSDI)*

One of the programs for development of informal skills and capacity building is the GSDI which is provided with technical assistance from the German government through the Deutsche *Gesellschaft für Internationale Zusammenarbeit* (GIZ GmbH). GIZ works with COTVET on this initiative. The objectives are

- to provide demand-driven training that targets the youth, apprentices, workers and owners of micro, small and medium-sized enterprises especially in the informal sector
- to support COTVET's CBT program in seeking to combine workplace-based training and school-based training modules at selected TVET providers
- to improve the quality of the traditional apprenticeship system and, therefore, to enhance skills certification and recognition.

Construction skills training has so far been implemented in welding, block laying and tiling, electrical installation and furniture works, and these have been offered in five regions in Ghana.

GSDI I and II were implemented between 2012 and 2016. Phase III of the initiative started in 2016 and ended in September 2019. Generally, GSDI I and II modernized informal vocational training by helping to upgrade traditional apprenticeship training in the selected trades, including those in construction outlined above (GFA Consulting Group 2019). The GSDI model involved cooperative apprenticeship training which constitutes 80 percent of workplace training with master craftspersons and 20 percent training at partner institutions (known as training providers), leading to National Proficiency Levels I and II certificates. Facilitation was based on the CBT, 30 percent of which was theory based with 70 percent based on practice. The initiative had a target of 30 percent of females to enroll to enter more male-dominated fields such as block-laying.

Under GSDI III, the informal construction sector received some modest participation with block-laying and tiling being included. Artisans from the informal construction sector were among the 71 participants in the first national skills competition held in November 2018 (GFA Consulting Group 2019). The regional coordinator of training of GIZ (interview data) anticipated that the program for block laying and tiling would be fully implemented in Phase IV of the initiative. The assessment of the phase shows that the GSDI I to III schemes have been implemented effectively and some useful lessons have been learnt that should help in the development of an appropriate training framework for the construction industry. The challenge rests in the differences in the learning capacity of students which means that they require different teaching methods. How the specific training needs of trainees with diverse skill levels and other differences are being met also forms part of the lessons learnt which will help in development of an appropriate training program for the construction industry.

Conclusion

The informal sector is an important contributor to GDP and employment in sub-Saharan African countries. Artisans constitute the largest percentage of the workforce in most construction industries, and it is therefore necessary to explore and strengthen the linkages between the informal and formal sectors of construction industries and to harness them for sustainable development. The analysis of informal construction activities in Ghana reveals that there are critical gaps in training and skills development, that there is a pressing need to improve working conditions and safety, and that it is necessary to scale up initiatives by the government, the TUC and NGOs. The government has provided the framework and has been seeking to adopt a structured approach to skills development for both formal and informal sector workers. However, insufficient attention is given to the informal sector and to the training needs that it generates.

Informal sector workers have not been able to form trade unions or other organizations to protect their interests although the TUC has, since 1996, encouraged informal artisans to join unions. The TUC has been an advocate for improved working conditions and other benefits such as pensions. Some of the initiatives taken by NGOs and the private sector have the potential to contribute toward the development of skills.

The case studies offer lessons which can contribute to the development of a vibrant informal sector for the construction industry in Ghana. The WUSC has made some headway in encouraging women to participate in its program and there is scope for other skills development programs to learn from it. The YIEDIE project and WUSC project case studies demonstrate that it is possible to bring the artisans together and this is being achieved. There is potential for more collaboration among the stakeholders, including the TUC, to achieve progress. The GSDI model focuses on training as well as empowering artisans to mobilize under unions and/or trade associations. A strength of this model lies in its wide coverage as it operates in many regions and has the potential for expansion across the whole country. The ways in which the needs of trainees with diverse skill levels and backgrounds are being met under GSDI offer lessons which will help in the development of training for construction. The case studies indicate that NGOs are effective in identifying and assessing trainees and in bringing artisans together. The TUC could work with the NGOs to build an effective grouping of workers in the informal sector of construction.

There is potential for a comprehensive and integrated approach to informal sector development. This should go beyond skills and include entrepreneurship, business and project management, assistance with resources, and development of documentation, processes and practices which recognize the needs of the informal sector. A multi-stakeholder approach could be adopted but leadership by the government will be key. The way forward in upscaling the capability of the construction industry in Ghana lies in the holistic development of the industry including the informal sector. A peak construction industry development agency which champions a comprehensive industry development agenda is an urgent necessity.

References

African Development Bank, 2013. Recognizing Africa's informal sector. https://www.afdb.org/en/blogs/afdb-champion-inclusive-growth-acrossafrica/post/recognizing-africas-informal-sector-111645 (accessed 20.02.19.).

Ahadzie, D., 2016. The economic, technological and structural demands of the construction industry in emerging markets south of the Sahara: a case study of Ghana. In: Abdulai, R.T., Obeng-Odoom, F., Ocheing, E., Maliene, V. (eds.), *Real Estate, Construction and Economic Development in Emerging Market Economies*. Routledge, London, pp. 166–193.

Aikaeli, J., Mkenda, B.K., 2014. Determinants of informal employment: a case of Tanzania's construction industry. *Botswana Journal of Economics 12*(2), 51–73.

Akorsu, A.D., Cooke, F.L., 2011. Labor standards application among Chinese and Indian firms in Ghana: typical or atypical? *International Journal of Human Resource Management 22*(13), 2730–2748.

Akorsu, A.D., 2013. Labor standards application in the informal economy of Ghana: the patterns and pressures. *Economic Annals 58*(196), 157–175.

Anaman, K.A., Egyir, I.S., 2019. Economic shocks and the growth of the construction industry in Ghana over the 50-year period from 1968 to 2017. *Research in World Economy 10*(1), 1–16.

Auffray, C., Fu, X., 2015. Chinese MNEs and managerial knowledge transfer in Africa: the case of the construction sector in Ghana. *Journal of Chinese Economic Business Studies 13*(4), 285–310.

Becker, K.F., 2004. *The Informal Economy.* Swedish International Development Agency, Stockholm.

Business a.m. 2020. *Nigeria's informal economy accounts for 65% of GDP – IMF.* Retrieved November 13, 2020 from https://www.businessamlive.com/nigerias-informal-economy-accounts-65-gdp-imf/#:~:text=Unregistered household enterprises comprise a,blog article seen by businessamlive.

Charmes, J., 2012. The informal economy worldwide: trends and characteristics. *Margin: Journal of Applied Economic Research 6*(2), 103–132.

Chen, M.A., 2012. *The Informal Economy: Definitions, Theories and Policies.* WIEGO Working Paper No 1, pp. 90141–90144.

Construction 21 Steering Committee, 1999. *Reinventing Construction.* Ministry of Manpower and Ministry of National Development, Singapore.

Darvas, P., Palmer, R., 2014. *Demand and Supply of Skills in Ghana: How can Training Programs Improve Employment and Productivity?* World Bank, Washington, D.C.

Debrah, Y.A., 2007. Promoting the informal sector as a source of gainful employment in developing countries: insights from Ghana. *International Journal of Human Resource Management 18*(6), 1063–1084.

Debrah, Y.A., Ofori, G., 1997. Flexibility, labour subcontracting and HRM in the construction industry in Singapore: can the system be refined? *International Journal of Human Resource Management 8*(5), 690–709.

Ernst, C., Sarabia, M., 2015. *The Role of Construction as an Employment Provider: A World- wide Input-output Analysis.* ILO Working Paper 994891843402676. Geneva: International Labour Organization.

Evanto Resource Ltd. and the Urban Associates Ltd., 2015. *Youth-Inclusive Value Chain Analysis and Workforce Gap Assessment for the Construction Sector in Ghana.* Global Communities, Accra.

Feige, E.L., 1990. Defining and estimating underground and informal economies: the new institutional economics approach. *World Development 18*(7), 989–1002.

Freeman, L., 2009. Neighborhood diversity, metropolitan segregation and gentrification: what are the links in the US? *Urban Studies 46*(10), 2079–2101.

GFA Consulting Group, 2019. Ghana skills development initiative (GSDI III). https://www.gfagroup.de/projects/Ghana_Skills_Development_Initiative_GSDI_III__3884439 (accessed 3.09.19.).

Ghana Data Portal, 2017. Ghana data at a glance (GDP by major sectors;

population; export and import; poverty; inflation; GNI per capita). https://
ghana.opendataforafrica.org (accessed 25.01.19.).

Ghana Skills Development Initiative, undated. Inauguration of sector skills
bodies and subsequent study tour to India, September. http://ghanaskills.org/
node/159 (accessed 17.05.20.).

Ghana Statistical Service, 2013. *Ghana Living Standards Survey*, report of the
ixth round (GLSS 6), Accra, Ghana Statistical Service.

Ghana Statistical Service, 2017. *Ghana's Labour Force Survey 2017.* Ghana
Statistical Service, Accra.

Ghana Statistical Service, 2018. *Provisional 2017 Annual Gross Domestic
Product. Ghana Statistical Service*: Accra, Statistics for Development and
Progress. 2018 Edition.

GhanaWeb, 2020. YIEDIE project exceeds youth training 23,700 target. Business
News of Monday, 3 February. https://www.ghanaweb.com/GhanaHomePage/
business/YIEDIE-project-exceeds-youth-training-23–700-target-855070 (accessed
17.05.20.).

Hart, K., 1973. Informal income opportunities and urban employment in Ghana.
Journal of Modern African Studies 11(1), 61–89.

Hillebrandt, P.M., 2000. *Economic Theory and the Construction Industry.*
Macmillan, London.

Hormeku, T., 1998. *The Transformation and Development of the Informal
Sector and the Role of Trade Unions*, Paper prepared for an OATUU/ILO/
ETUF Seminar on 'Trade unions and the informal sector', Cairo, Egypt,
4–6 May.

International Centre for Technical and Vocational Education and
Training, 2017. TVETDatabase - Country Profiles: Ghana. http://www.
unevoc.unesco.org/go.php?q=World+TVET+Database&ct=GHA#par0_1.

International Labour Organization, 2001. *The Construction Industry in the
Twenty-first Century: Its Image, Employment Prospects and Skill
Requirements.* ILO, Geneva.

International LabourOrganization, 2013. *Global Employment Trends 2013:
Recovering from a Second Jobs Dip.* ILO, Geneva.

Itasanmi, S.A., Ojedeji, S.O., Adelore, O., 2019. Literacy needs assessment of
artisans in Ibadan metropolis, Oyo state, Nigeria. *International Journal of
Education Literary Studies 7*(2), 57–64.

Jewell, C., Flanagan, R., Cattell, K., 2005. The effects of the informal sector on
construction, *Construction Research Congress 2005: Broadening Perspectives.*
ASCE Library. pp. 1–10. https://ascelibrary.org (accessed 15.05.20.).

Kanyenze, G., Mhone, G.C., Sparreboom, T., 2000. *Strategies to Combat Youth
Unemployment and Marginalization in Anglophone Africa* (vol. 13).
International Labour Office, Southern Africa Multidisciplinary Advisory
Team. ILO, Geneva.

Kenya Statistical Abstract, 2018. https://africacheck.org/wp-content/uploads/
2018/11/Statistical-Abstract-2018.pdf (accessed 25.01.19.).

Kwao, D., Ahadzie, D.K., 2017. Elements of the training of masons in the informal construction industry: an exploratory study. In: Apiah, E., Nortey, R.,
Prempeh, E. (Eds.) Proceedings. *Network of African Designers – Kumasi*

International Design Conference, (4th NAD KIDEC Conference), KNUST, Kumasi Ghana, 11–13th September.

Laryea, S. A., 2010. The Evolution of Indigenous Contractors in Ghana. *WEBAR Conference*, Accra

Macrotrends, 2020. Macrotrends LLC. Ghana Population. 1950–2020 https://www.macrotrends.net/countries/GHA/ghana/population (accessed 15.05.20.).

Middleton, L., 2015. *Working with Informality to Make Informality Work for Africa., Informality Brief 2nd Draft, African Urban Research Initiative (AURI)*, University of Cape Town, South Africa. (*Unpublished Paper*).

Ministry of Education, 2010. *Ghana Skills and Technology Development Project; Construction Sector Analysis Sponsored by The World Bank*. Accra, Ghana. Ministry of Education.

Mitullah, W.V., Wachira, I.N., 2003. *Informal Labor in the Construction Industry in Kenya: A Case Study of Nairobi*. ILO, Geneva.

National Bureau of Statistics, Tanzania, 2018. Statistics for Development https://www.nbs.go.tz/index.php/en/tanzania-in-figures (accessed 25.01.19.).

NVTI, 2017. *NVTI in Perspective*. NVTI, Accra, 5.

Nyamekye, M., Koboré, N., Bonégo, E.R., Kiéma, E., Ndour, B., Jallo, S., 2009. *Organizing Informal Sector workers in West Africa: Focus on Women Workers, Trade Union Strategies. Case Studies from Ghana, Sierra Leone, Senegal and Burkina Faso*. Ghana Trades Union Congress, Accra, Ghana.

Ofori, G., 2012. Developing the Construction Industry in Ghana: The Case for a Central Agency, *A Concept Paper Prepared for Improving the Construction Industry in Ghana*. National University of Singapore, Singapore, 3–18.

Ofori, G., 2017. *Study on Skills and Market Assessment of the Construction Sector in Ghana*. Prepared for State Secretariat for Economic Affairs. Federal Department of Economic Affairs, Education and Research, Switzerland. Accra.

Ofori, G., 2018. *Developing the Construction Industry in Ghana – Importance of the Industry and its Development, Recent Initiatives, Suggestions and a Short-term Strategy: a Short Note 2018*. Mimeo, London.

Ofori-Kuragu, J.K., Owuso-Manu, D., Ayarkwa, J., 2016. The case for a Construction Industry Council in Ghana. *Journal of Construction in Developing Countries* 21(212), 131–149.

Opoku, N.E., 2018. *A Study on Stress Management among Artisans in the Construction Industry in Ghana*, BSc Dissertation, Kwame Nkrumah University of Science and Technology, Kumasi, Ghana. (Unpublished).

Osei, V., 2013. The construction industry and its linkages to the Ghanaian economy-policies to improve the sector's performance. *International Journal of Development and Economic Sustainability* 1(1), 56–72.

Osei-Boateng, C., Ampratwum, E., 2011. *The Informal Sector in Ghana*. Friedrich-Ebert-Stiftung, Ghana Office, Accra.

QUANTEC, 2003. Formal and informal employment annual average estimates, unpublished raw data. www.quantec.co.za (accessed 12.01.19.).

Quashie, R.K., 2018. *An Evaluation of Competency Based Training in the Ghanaian Construction Industry: Emphasis on Craftsmen'*, BSc Dissertation, Kwame Nkrumah University of Science and Technology, Kumasi, Ghana. (Unpublished).

RealEstate Journal, 2016. Official Bi-Annual Newsletter by GREDA for the Housing Industry and the General Public, Issue No. 3, 30 August, pp. 7–8.

Republic of Ghana, 1998. *Children's Act 1998*. UNESCO http://www.unesco.org/ education/edurights/media/docs/f7a7a002205e07fbf119bc00c8bd3208a438b37f. pdf (accessed 17.05.20.).

Saunders, S.G., 2008. *Estimates of the Informal Economy in South Africa: Some Macroeconomic Policy Implications, Doctoral Dissertation*, University of Johannesburg, South Africa. (Unpublished).

Statistics South Africa, 2019. http://www.statssa.gov.za/?m=2019 (accessed 25.01.19.).

Sutton, J., Kpentey, B., 2012. *An Enterprise Map of Ghana* (vol. 2). International Growth Centre in association with the London Publishing Partnership.

Trades Union Congress and Rosa Luxemburg Stiftung, 2012. *Trade Unions and Industrial Relations in Ghana*. Rosa Luxemburg Foundation, Accra.

Trading Economics, 2017. *Ghana Annual GDP Growth at 1-Year High in Q3*. https://tradingeconomics.com/ghana/gdp-growth-annual (accessed 25.01.19).

UNECA, 2002. *Youth and Employment in the ECA Region*, Paper prepared for the ECA Youth Employment Summit, Alexandria: Egypt, 7–11 September.

United Nations Human Settlements Programme, 2011. *Ghana: Housing Profile*. UNHSP, Nairobi.

Wells, J., 2007. Informality in the construction sector in developing countries. *Construction Management and Economics 25*(1), 87–93.

Wells, J., Jason, A., 2010. Employment relationships and organizing strategies in the informal construction sector. *African Studies Quarterly 11*(2 & 3 | Spring 2010), 107–124.

World Bank. 2020. IBRD.IDA. https://data.worldbank.org/indicator/GDP.PCAP.CD.

World Population Review, 2018. GDP by Country 2019. http://worldpopulation review.com/countries/countries-by-gdp/ (accessed 25.01.19.).

World University Service of Canada (WUSC), 2015. *Uniterra 3 – Market Research Findings on the Informal Construction Industry in Ghana*. World Services University of Canada, Canada.

7 Labor Management in the Lebanese Construction Industry

Samar Kleib, Fida Afiouni and Issam Srour

Introduction

The Middle East has been one of the most active construction markets in recent decades. This has reflected the rapid economic development of some countries, such as Saudi Arabia and the Gulf states, but also the requirement to repair damage caused by war and civil conflict. A good example of the latter phenomenon has been Lebanon. With an average of 400 people per square kilometer of land, Lebanon is one of the most densely populated countries in the world, with 90 percent of the population living in urban areas (Abou Jaoude 2015). Its population of 4.5 million has been augmented in recent years due to an influx of refugees from Syria. Recent statistics last updated on May 31, 2020 show that the war in Syria has led to a strong wave of migration to Lebanon with 892,310 registered Syrian refugees (UNHCR 2020), straining Lebanon's substandard infrastructure. Refugees make up at least a quarter of the population (Abou Jaoude 2015).

Lebanon's poor infrastructure results both from decades of civil war and from political and economic instability. The civil war from 1975 to 1990 was a devastating conflict in which around 90,000 people lost their lives and close to a million people experienced displacement (Sune 2011). A new round of conflicts from July 2006 between Hezbollah and Israel saw over a thousand Lebanese deaths, 4,399 injured, and an estimated one million displaced according to Human Rights Watch (2007).

Despite the political instability that the country has witnessed since 1975, including the ongoing wars on its borders (including Syria and the occupied Palestinian territories) and the political uprisings in the region, Lebanon's construction and real estate industry remains the highest contributor to the GDP growth of the country at 21 percent (Lebanon Economic Vision 2018). In fact, in 2016 the overall volume of real estate in Lebanon totaled $8.4 billion, with a volume of 64,248 in property sales transactions, increasing by 1.4 percent from 2015 (BankMED 2017). This increase is due to both Lebanese and foreign investors (Arab and non-Arab) who remain interested in investing in the Lebanese construction and property sector. Overall, both the public and private sectors have played an important role in rebuilding and rehabilitating Lebanon's infrastructure after the 1975–1990 civil war and the 2006 war with Israel (Srour et al. 2011). The investment also, unfortunately, created a very large debt for the Lebanese government, most of which is held by domestic banks (Abou Jaoude 2015).

Three key factors, however, suggest a positive outlook for the construction industry. These relate to, first, the post-conflict reconstruction opportunity in Syria, second, the potential for oil and gas extraction off the Lebanese shores and third the rising popularity of green construction projects. We will detail each in turn.

The post-conflict phase in Syria may be promising for the Lebanese construction industry as it could become one of the most important gateways for reconstruction efforts. According to the World Bank, the rebuilding of Syria represents an industry worth over $200 billion and is expected to generate around 7,000 jobs across a range of sectors (LIBC 2017). Experts predict that potential development and reconstruction of Syria post-war would generate opportunities in the Lebanese construction sector, with a demand for cement that was expected to be around 30 million tons per year in 2014, stimulating demand that will benefit the Lebanese construction materials industry (Awad 2014).

Second, the potential offshore oil and gas activities may stimulate development. The US Geological Survey in 2010 estimated that in the Levantine Basin area, which is shared by Lebanon, Syria, Israel, Gaza and Cyprus, there are 1.7 billion barrels of oil and 122 trillion cubic feet of gas (Knell 2013). The consortium of Italy's Eni, Russia's Novatek and France's Total planned to start drilling exploratory wells (Lebanon Gas and Oil 2019) and these activities are expected to benefit many sectors, especially the construction industry (Ifpinfo 2014). As Lebanon gears up to explore its offshore oil and gas resources it is critical that environmental protection is a high priority. Oil and gas development activities have significant environmental risks which could impact Lebanon's marine ecology, air quality, sea water quality, underwater archaeological sites and human health, and have negative climate change impacts. While Lebanese citizens at large would be directly impacted, specific communities most at risk include those along the Lebanese coast, businesses working in the fisheries, tourism and shipping sectors and in environmental management (LOGI 2017). Despite these environmental risks, the oil and gas activities would have a positive impact on the construction industry with jobs created for technicians and field workers to enable the expected construction and installation activities (Arthur D. Little Consultancy 2018).

A further opportunity for the construction industry in Lebanon is through the implementation of 'green construction concepts' (Srour et al. 2011). According to the United Nations Environment Program (UNEP), green buildings are energy-efficient buildings that drastically reduce emissions, material, and water use and have the potential to reduce energy usage by up to 80 percent (UNEP 2011). A sustainable approach to building will not only have a significant impact on the work of design engineers, but will also create new jobs such as energy auditors, green assessors, green construction coordinators and suppliers of green materials and systems (Srour et al. 2011). The estimated number of jobs created because of these green projects varies between 690 and 1,380 per year. Furthermore, according to local manufacturers and suppliers, 3,300 jobs were anticipated by 2020 to cover the demand exclusively for solar water heaters (Srour et al. 2011).

Against this backdrop, this chapter highlights the high degree of informality in employment in the construction industry in Lebanon. It documents current labor market practices and points out key priorities, given the context of the local workforce and the changing institutional landscape. It draws on available secondary data on the construction industry in Lebanon and supplements this with additional research in order to analyze the workforce experience. The research uses a mixed method approach, drawing on a survey of site workers and on interviews with foremen and HR managers in a sample of 10 construction organizations.

Overview of the Construction Industry

As detailed above, the construction and property industries are key to the Lebanese economy, with construction companies having gained experience not only from their domestic market, but also from projects in the rest of the Arab world (Ifpinfo 2014). Construction loans went up by 12.8 percent year-on-year to $9.18 billion by the end of 2013 (Mikhael et al. 2014). This increase was mainly the direct consequence of Banque du Liban and the financial sector's stimuli to boost demand.

The construction industry is commonly divided into three major segments – building, heavy/civil engineering and industrial construction. Building projects include residential, commercial and institutional buildings. Heavy/civil engineering projects include dams, tunnels, roads, highways and bridges – typically entailing the use of heavy machinery. Industrial projects include manufacturing plants, power plants, refineries and petro-chemical facilities. In Lebanon, building construction has the largest market share followed by the heavy construction sector and then the industrial construction sector (Srour et al. 2011).

As in other parts of the world, the construction industry in Lebanon is fragmented and relies heavily on subcontracting (Bosch and Philips 2002). This is particularly the case for medium- and large-scale projects, which are typically led by a local general or main contractor. This main contractor executes part of the project, usually concrete works, and hires a host of specialty subcontractors for electrical, mechanical and glazing works among others. Enabling or preparatory work is usually handled by one or two other firms: a geotechnical consultant and an excavation contractor. For government projects the same approach is applied, whereby a leading contractor wins the tender from the government, and then selects subcontractors to perform the work in some regions and/or during some specific parts of the construction phase. Usually, the subcontractors are the small companies or family business companies that are not able to win the bids on substantive projects, so they end up working as subcontractors for larger firms. This, for example, was a common practice during the installation of fiber optic cable in Lebanon, according to anecdotal evidence from industry experts.

In terms of personnel, small scale building projects are typically led by one person, referred to as the project manager or engineer. The site is managed by a general foreman, or site superintendent, who supervises the work of the various crews. The typical crews in a building project cover the following trades: concrete, carpentry, steel, mechanical, electrical, tiling and painting. Each crew includes a skilled or experienced worker along with at least one junior worker. The organizational structure for a large building project is much more complex. In addition to the project manager, there is usually a construction manager who supervises the work in the various disciplines: architecture, civil, electrical and mechanical. Each of these disciplines includes one (or more) engineer and architect. There will normally be at least three foremen covering civil, electrical and mechanical work. Each foreman supervises one or more crews comprising both skilled and junior workers.

The Workforce in the Construction Industry

Unfortunately, as one writer has commented, labor market statistics for Lebanon are 'scant, incomplete, outdated and in some cases contradictory' (Abou Jaoude 2015: 6). This makes estimates of the size and composition of the workforce difficult. The working population was estimated at 1.2 million in 2007, while the inactive population (people not seeking a job or enrolled in education) was 1.6 million (Yaacoub and Badre 2011). An important feature of the Lebanese labor market is the large size of the informal sector, which in 2011 the World Bank estimated as over 36 percent of the total workforce while some 67 percent of the workforce did not contribute to any social insurance system (World Bank 2011 cited in Abou Jaoude 2015). The majority of migrant workers work in domestic service, construction, car repair and gas stations. While there is no clear delineation between the formal and informal economies in Lebanon, in terms of individual workers the law requires all employees to be registered in the national insurance fund (ILO and FES 2016). In reality, however, many workers are not registered, not just in the informal sector but including some of those in formal enterprises.

Unemployment in Lebanon is high, especially among young people, and the female workforce participation rate is very low, despite educational levels being higher than for males. One of the other key features of the Lebanese economy is the recent major influx of unskilled immigrant labor while, at the same time, younger and educated Lebanese workers are emigrating to other countries (Abou Jaoude 2015).

The Lebanese workforce is distributed across a wide range of sectors ranging from the service sector, financial intermediation and insurance sectors, trade, manufacturing, transport, telecommunications and agriculture. In 2009, nine percent of the workforce was formally employed in the construction sector (Yaacoub and Badre 2011).

Most of the construction workforce is composed of migrants who are informally hired. Before the Syrian crisis in 2010, Syrians represented 55 percent of unskilled workers and 30 percent of skilled workers. By 2012, Syrian workers comprised 70 percent of both unskilled and skilled workers (ILO 2017). However, almost all professional level positions (such as engineers and architects) continue to be filled by Lebanese workers (95 percent in 2010 and 93 percent in 2012) (ILO 2017). Most of the foreign workforce is undocumented, often working in unsafe conditions with low wages, estimated to be 25–50 percent lower than those of the Lebanese workforce, and with no benefits, apart from sleeping quarters and food provided by their employers (ACTED: Agency for Technical Cooperation and Development 2014). They lack health and accident insurance coverage, which is particularly serious given the high-risk nature of construction activities. Even before the war in Syria started, construction jobs in Lebanon were the main source of employment available to Syrian youth (even those who are under-aged), with the majority of Syrian migrants finding work in the Lebanese construction sector, with agriculture taking second place (ACTED: Agency for Technical Cooperation and Development 2014).

The challenge of managing such a diverse workforce is augmented by the diversity in the quality, quantity and composition of developer firms in the construction sector in Lebanon (Srour et al. 2011) and the industry is characterized by complex project-based environments and changing conditions (Maloney 1997; Raja et al. 2013). For instance, as in other countries, companies in the Lebanese construction industry rely heavily on subcontracting with a short-term focus that comes at the expense of longer-term employment stability (Raja et al. 2013). On one hand, the high-end building developments are managed by a limited number of firms that have reputable consultants and contractors, primarily operating in Beirut and featuring high standards in design and workmanship. On the other hand, small- and medium-scale developers, most often family businesses, deliver low-to-medium quality finishing work and often rely on subcontractors that engage migrant workers informally and are operating at lower costs (Srour et al. 2011). This in turn affects the way that human resources are managed and thus the fragmentation of HR policies (Marchington et al. 2010).

Construction Labor Practices

Private sector employment is regulated by laws that govern Lebanese employers, most notably the Lebanese Labor Law of 1946, the Social Security Law established in 1963 and the Trade Union Law that was established in 1952 (LEADERS 2019). The Labor Law, which was modeled on French Labor Law, provides economic protection for workers, the weaker party in the employer–employee contractual relationship, as well as protecting them from any condition or restriction that might affect their rights (LEADERS 2019). According to article 624 of the Labor Law, the contract between employer and employee must contain clauses that discuss work, wages and economic subordination. The Ministry of Labor is responsible for labor inspections but is understaffed and lacking in technical expertise (Abou Jaoude 2015).

It is important, moreover, to mention that the Lebanese labor market is currently stagnant and is greatly affected by the ongoing flows of migration of workers from neighboring countries. The number of informal and self-employed workers is growing but these workers do not generally join unions (ILO and FES 2016). Informal working in the private sector may be as high as 50 percent and it is highly concentrated in the fields of agriculture, commerce and construction (ILO and FES 2016).

Union rights are not guaranteed. Although the law recognizes the rights of workers, a trade union requires an authorization granted from the Ministry of Labor. The Ministry is responsible for governing elections in the union as well as oversight of the results. The law also prohibits the participation of the union in any political activity in the country, as well as setting rules regarding rights of members to protest (International Trade Union Confederation 2012). The law distinguishes between private and public sector workers on the one hand, and between Lebanese and non-Lebanese workers on the other, when it comes to the rights associated with the establishment of a union (International Trade Union Confederation 2012). Moreover, there is a major constraint on the establishment of unions because the Labor Law does not specify the deadline for the Ministry of Labor to approve or disapprove the authorization of the union. This means that the establishment of the union is dependent on the ministers in charge – who may be politically affiliated – and whose deferral of approval may mean that the union is never formally initiated (Bou Khater 2019). The Ministry of Labor, which holds the details of trade unions and federations, does not publish official statistics on the number of trade unions, their members or geographical distribution (ILO and FES 2016). The main union confederation in Lebanon (the General Confederation of Lebanese Unions) claims 58,000 members but this is only 2.5 percent of its potential membership (Abou Jaoude 2015). A report by the ILO-FES in 2016 concluded that 'the trade union structure in Lebanon is lacking in terms of democratic characteristics, including the absence of leadership elections based on unity and continuity and in connection to a clear national set of demands' (ILO and FES 2016: 48). The construction workforce is largely informal and composed of migrant workers so unions face a particularly difficult task in organizing them. Even though there are labor unions in the Lebanon, none is tailored to construction work and there is very limited participation by construction workers in any of these unions.

Rather than relying on union support, construction workers in Lebanon rely on their peers and supervisors to protect their interests. Workers are hired by foremen, site engineers, construction managers and project managers and their pay, benefits and working conditions are at the mercy of these individuals (Srour et al. 2017). This fragmentation makes it hard to apply any standardized employment policies and practices, due to the multi-layered and dynamic nature of the industry (Marchington et al. 2010), and due to the diversity of the nationalities working in this industry (Awwad et al. 2014). Most of the workers are engaged on a daily basis and are paid by the day and it is rare to find any formal contractual relationship between these workers and their employers. These semi- and un-skilled workers have no tertiary education but are usually employed because they possess basic skills in construction and they are able to perform the tasks allocated to them on site. As for foremen and quality control operators, they are in a less precarious position as they receive a monthly wage (United Nations Development Program, UNDP 2016). Typically, the positions of site manager and site engineer are granted to Lebanese nationals, while non-nationals constitute around 55 percent of the site workers. Those who have accumulated years of experience can become group leaders or site foremen (Srour et al. 2017).

Health and Safety

Occupational Health and Safety standards at the workplace are critical in the construction industry. Many hazards threaten the lives of workers on site, such as the risk of falling from heights, trench collapse, scaffold collapse, electric shock and blast, due to the absence of safe working systems and the failure to use proper personal protective equipment (Liy et al. 2016). In Lebanon the starting point for construction safety laws and regulations was Decree no. 136 of 1983: work related to injuries and emergencies, and Decree no. 11958 of 2004: safety and protection in construction. The 1983 decree stipulates the employers' responsibilities in cases of occupational injuries and corresponding compensation and the workers' entitlements. Decree no. 136 also stipulates what the sanctions are in the case of violations.

If we compare the Lebanese safety, Decree no. 11958 of 2004 with the US OSHA 126 regulation, for example, we find that the Lebanese decree requires that the materials used on the construction site be of 'good quality,' but without defining any strength requirements for scaffolds and planks, and does not specify wall slope measurements relevant to the soil type for excavations. Essentially, the Lebanese regulations, unlike OSHA, are vague and leave the decision on implementation of safety regulations up to the contractors or companies involved (Awwad et al. 2014). There is a lack of awareness among small- and medium-size contractors about developing and applying safety training programs on site, although large contractors exhibit a stronger commitment to safety issues (Awwad et al. 2014).

These risks are prevalent not only in Lebanon, but also in other neighboring Middle Eastern countries. For example, as part of its preparation for the FIFA World Cup 2022, Qatar has embarked on major construction efforts, which have, tragically, resulted in high numbers of fatalities and serious accidents. A total of 1,200 workers was reported to have lost their lives by 2014 and the number was estimated to reach 4,000 before 2020 according to a report published by the International Trade Union Confederation (ITUC 2014: 15) in March 2014.

Due to the absence of effective health and safety regulations in Lebanon and the lack of attention given to health and safety, construction companies are at the top of the list when it comes to workplace accidents and fatality rates. While Lebanese occupational safety law requires that accidents must be reported within 24 hours, there are no official statistics on accidents and fatality rates in the workplace. This neglect in reporting is due to the inadequate and insufficient number of inspectors, making the process of controlling the incidence of accidents and injuries in the worksite much harder (Obeid 2015). The Order of Engineers and Architects in Lebanon is the only party that checks the technical aspects of construction projects, but there is no formal institution to monitor construction sites during the execution phase. A few companies hire technical controllers to perform safety reviews and audit, but these efforts remain limited and are not standardized. The absence of standardized systems or procedures for safety management in Lebanon, and the limited number of inspectors to monitor hazards and protect workers from the accidents that may occur at the site, is associated with numerous yet often undocumented tragedies (Chahine 2005).

We turn now to the results of our own research project.

Our Research

Our research examines the workforce management practices of the Lebanese construction industry. To extend the accounts in the secondary literature, we focused particularly on the experience of foremen and of workers. We adopted a mixed method approach (Kettles et al. 2011) integrating quantitative survey results with qualitative research derived from interviews. Such an approach allows for a wider and clearer understanding of the management practices implemented in the construction industry in Lebanon. Quantitative methods allowed us to gain an overview of the perception of management practices by construction workers, whereas qualitative methods gave us access to managers in order to develop further explanations about such practices (Pasick et al. 2009).

Participants and Procedures

Initially we conducted an online search to obtain a list of construction companies in Lebanon that have a formal HR department and identified 30 such companies. We contacted them via email and secured the consent of ten companies to participate in this study. We interviewed foremen and held informal conversations with HR managers, one in each company, and conducted a survey of 263 construction workers subcontracted to work on the sites of these ten companies. This number comprised construction workers of different nationalities (Lebanese, Syrians, Egyptians and Palestinians). All of our sample participants were male. We started the study by visiting the construction sites and distributing a questionnaire to construction workers during their working hours. A research assistant supported respondents, some of whom were illiterate, to complete the questionnaire and to check their answers. The survey was administered in Arabic to match the workers' language skills and to ensure their complete understanding and cooperation.

Ten interviews were conducted with Lebanese and Syrian foremen and the questions focused on the respondents' backgrounds, experience, contracting arrangements and management functions in their daily work.

Informal discussions were held with HR managers regarding the evolution, role and structure of the HR department and most importantly the challenges faced. The HR department was usually located in the company's headquarters, the majority in Beirut, the capital of Lebanon, and often far from the actual construction sites. Although informal, these conversations were useful in outlining a distinctive and different perspective and in enabling triangulation (Heale and Forbes 2013).

Data Analysis

To generate descriptive statistics and explore significant correlations, we analyzed the data collected from the 263 workers using the t-test and ANOVA test in SPSS version 24. The interviews were transcribed in Arabic to capture the original language and then translated into English by the first author who is bilingual. The transcripts were later checked and edited by a specialized linguist. The first and second authors then read the transcripts several times to familiarize themselves with the data and engaged in an inductive thematic analysis to identify common themes and categories.

In the next section, we present the management perceptions of their roles and of the HR function, followed by the employee survey findings. Where relevant, we present findings from both the survey and interviews to contrast the perceptions of management and construction workers.

Management Perceptions

This section presents the findings of the qualitative interviews conducted with the foremen. Three main themes were identified: (1) the invisibility of HR, (2) the responsibilities and challenges of foremen and (3) health and safety management. We present the first two themes in order to understand the organizational context in which workers operate. We present the findings of health and safety management along with our employee findings to provide a more comprehensive view of safety management perceptions by both management and employees, as this point generated most controversy and dissonance between management and employees.

The Invisibility of HR

All the foremen interviewed agreed that the HR function was largely invisible in terms of providing the support to recruit, select, train, reward and manage performance. Both the survey and interview results show a high level of informality in how management tasks are conducted, and those fall mainly under the responsibility of the foreman, with other decisions being made on a need basis:

> 'No official work for HR.' (Foreman 2)
> 'HR is only an image in these companies - we do all their work.' (Foreman 3)
> 'HR is just a façade!' (Foreman 4)
> 'HR is not involved in the process because simply there is no process.' (Foreman 5)
> 'HR is involved to a limited extent.' (Foreman 7)

Our informal discussions with the HR managers validated the above statements:

> 'It is so hard to control the flow of workers in this unstable industry, and most of the workers are illegal coming from Syria.' (Company F)
> 'We left this responsibility to the managers on the worksites, we rarely recruit a Lebanese foreman officially.' (Company A)
> 'How can we recruit a worker of unknown origin without legal

papers?' (Company B)

These quotes emphasize the distance between the HR function and the workers on site. Because the construction industry is project based and the work location shifts from project to project, it is almost impossible for corporate HR personnel to have any impact at site level. This high level of informality in management practices is later corroborated in our survey findings, with regard to the recruitment of construction workers.

Responsibilities and Challenges of Foremen

The foreman is the key person in the operational system on site. He is the liaison between the management and the workforce and faces numerous responsibilities and challenges. We interviewed 10 foremen (seven Syrians and three Lebanese). We found that the responsibilities of a foreman include translating policies for the workers, communicating management information, maintaining a good quality of output while respecting deadlines, correcting poor work and minimizing waste.

> *'The first responsibility as a foreman is to deliver the work on time and to use efficiently the resources that we have. I supervise 20 to 30 workers.' (Foreman 1)*
> *'We ensure that everyone is doing his job in the right efficient way and our aim is to deliver all the projects on time.' (Foreman 2)*

In Lebanon, a foreman's job is complicated, due to the national diversity of the workforce and low literacy rates that inhibit the foreman in achieving the project goals.

> *'I control the work of the Syrian workers to ensure we deliver good work'. (Foreman 3)*
> *'I monitor the work while and after they are doing it.' (Foreman 8)*
> *'Dealing with the unskilled labor makes the work very difficult and sometimes the main reason for the projects' delays.' (Foreman 5)*

There are many unexpected challenges that occur on a daily basis that require the foreman to stay alert in order to attend to challenges and mishaps:

> *'We have a problem if we don't have the needed resources and the workers hardly understand the instructions of the foreman. Also, with the hard work conditions they tend to take a lot of breaks.' (Foreman 1)*
> *'Everything is hard on the site from the workers to the work*

conditions in addition to the expectations of the management; there is a lot of pressure.' (Foreman 10)

Workforce Perceptions

The workforce sample comprised 263 male participants, 94 percent of whom were Syrian while only five percent were Lebanese and the remaining one percent from other nationalities. The age profile of the workforce says much about the workforce experience. Approximately nine percent of the participants were under 18 years old, the youngest being a 14-year-old boy working with his 16-year-old brother on the same site; 65 percent were between 18 and 30 years old; 23 percent were between 31 and 50 years and three percent were 51 years old and above. Almost two-thirds (65 percent) of the participants were married. Nine out of ten participants held no educational qualification, while just three percent had a technical degree and one percent had obtained degrees in other fields. Finally, regarding years of experience, 22 percent of the participants had less than one year of experience, 49 percent had one to ten years of experience, 25 percent had 11 to 20 years of experience and four percent had 21 years experience and above.

Informal Recruitment

In keeping with the general informality of labor market institutions in the Lebanon, our survey confirmed that recruitment and selection of Lebanese construction workers is extremely informal. Workers are hired on a word-of-mouth basis and the foreman (or skilled worker) typically recruits workers who are related to him or are from the same town, or otherwise recruited on a walk-in basis as needed. Recruitment through social networks, known as 'wasta' in Arabic, is one of the most important factors that emerge from the literature on recruitment in Lebanon, and in the Arab world more generally. Wasta, similar to other social networks such as Guanxi in China and Blat in Russia, is a common, almost required, way of doing business in regions and cultures where each practice prevails (Hutchings and Weir 2006; Ali and Weir forthcoming). As such, it could be argued that wasta is not just favoritism or corruption, but rather a part of the culture that creates cohesion in countries of the Arab Middle East (Ali and Weir forthcoming). The importance of wasta in Lebanon is almost unparalleled, with 90 percent of respondents to a Gallup poll agreeing that 'knowing people in a high position is critical to getting a job,' which is 30 percent higher than the average for Middle Eastern and North African countries (Hutchings and Weir 2006; Sultana 2017).

Inevitably, there is therefore no written job description for the majority of roles. Over half of the participants (59 percent) agreed/ strongly agreed that the recruitment process is informal with an introduction to the job through discussions with the foreman or skilled workers but with no documented records. During our observations and informal talks with workers and foremen, they all emphasized the fact that recruiting was mostly based on the referrals from their social networks. When asked if applicants are hired on the basis of their skills and abilities, more than three quarters were neutral. This reflects the informality of hiring processes and the reliance on foreign labor that is usually recruited through personal social networks, without any formal qualifications but rather based on their experience in the construction industry. This view was confirmed by the fact that 63 percent of survey participants claimed that the nationality of the applicant plays a major role in recruitment, with priority given to foreign labor, and of course migrant workers might be expected to accept lower wages, no social security and an absence of effective safety measures. The vast majority of the participants indicated that they had not gone through a medical test before being hired.

Interestingly, the interview results with management confirmed the informality of recruitment and its reliance on wasta, and the only selection criterion for workers is for them to be legal:

> 'A worker bring his relatives and so on. Others came to the site and ask for work.' (Foreman 3)
> 'No selection criteria, for a Syrian he should be legal only.' (Foreman 6)
> 'They should be legal and we have connections with some people who let Syrian people work in Lebanon in the construction so we contact them whenever we need workers.' (Foreman 10)

Training and Development

While recruitment and selection is informal, there seems to be some attention given to basic training to ensure that workers have the basic knowledge needed to perform the job adequately. Around half of the participants stated that their employer conducts some training for employees, but almost nine in ten said that training was not a company priority, although a large majority stated that the training program has improved their productivity and their knowledge, for example, how to operate machines. Because employees come from diverse backgrounds with various levels of qualifications, training seems to be adopted to ensure that all workers have a basic understanding regarding operating machines and handling equipment.

The foremen were also skeptical about the importance of training, which relies mostly on the notion of learning by doing.

> 'We train them at the beginning and then they learn everything by themselves.' (Foreman 2)
> 'They usually know their work; we train them sometimes on some complicated machines but it is rare to happen.' (Foreman 6)
> 'They learn by trying everything; we offer them the guidelines.' (Foreman 9)

Given our findings on training and development, we can conclude that employees appreciate the little training they receive, given the absence of prior qualifications, and training was perceived as much needed to help them improve their performance. The management highlighted the scope for improvement. Organizations could benefit in terms of productivity, safety and efficiency if training was given a higher priority.

Low Pay

A minority of participants (around 30 percent) said that they were not paid regularly and on time. Their responses shed light on the serious human rights abuse in this sector with workers forced to work long hours, being denied rest days, having their pay withheld or having deductions made. Some 71 percent felt that that their pay was unfair, 85 percent reported not having access to company provided health services and almost none had a pension or end of job indemnities. Furthermore, 78 percent did not feel that their pay related to their performance and over half – 53 percent – felt that their supervisors and management did not appreciate their efforts.

The workforce survey results reflect the significant power imbalance in this sector between contractors and their workers. Abuses occur because construction workers are perceived as 'a dispensable resource to be dismissed and reemployed in response to the cyclical nature of the construction market' (Loosemore and Lim 2016: 428). This highlights the disparity in power between workers and contractors, and in particular the injustice and exploitation of migrant labor in a subcontracting system that leaves them devoid of support.

The management findings confirm this power imbalance. When asked how to keep workers motivated, despite low pay, the answers demonstrated a harsh management style:

> 'They should stay motivated alone (laughing).' (Foreman 2)
> 'It's their problem they should be motivated or they lose their job.' (Foreman 3)
> 'They are obliged to stay motivated or we fire them.' (Foreman 6)
> 'I can't care less' (Foreman 8)

Employee Voice

The majority of participants (87 percent) said that they have the right to express their opinions at work and almost three-quarters (72 percent) indicated that negotiations between individual employees and management take place. There was, however, no indication of any formal methods for consultation. There is no trade union support and there are no alternative formal mechanisms in place to allow employee voice. Some 60 percent believed that management takes no notice of their suggestions and complaints, so that even when views were put forward they were often unheard due to the absence of mechanisms for consultation and due to the power imbalance between employers and workers. The vast majority of participants (99 percent) stated, however, that prayer breaks are allowed, which means employees are able to practice their religious beliefs while at work.

Health and Safety

Health and safety was the topic that generated the most dissonance between the survey results and the interview findings. According to the foremen, there is a growing awareness of safety rules and regulations, with foremen trying to implement safety measures, often in reaction to a fatal incident, but struggling to make workers comply. The following statements illustrate this view:

> 'We offer the workers helmets and belts; they have to wear this equipment.' (Foreman 1)
> 'At our company we had an accident a worker fell from 10 metres and he died and since that time safety became a priority to us and we have a safety person who regularly passes every week to check if the safety measures are applied.' (Foreman 2)

Comparing this to the survey results, we note that the perceptions of construction workers of safety measures were barely positive, with only half of workers perceiving that safety was receiving sufficient attention although 69 percent of employees stated that accidents on site are promptly investigated.

Interestingly, the foremen stated that management make a lot of effort to promote safety in the workplace but, rather than focusing on systemic issues, they blame the workers for carelessness. The following quotes illustrate the negative perceptions that management has of foreign construction workers.

> 'Our workers came from a war generation where a helmet and a belt are more than enough.' (Foreman 3)

> 'We do our best to make them comply with safety rules but some workers don't believe in it; they are the generation of war coming from Syria.' (Foreman 5)
>
> 'Workers don't know the importance of the safety rules – they think they can protect themselves without the safety equipment but we oblige them to wear the helmets and safety boots and belts.' (Foreman 6)
>
> 'They are stubborn! They fear nothing.' (Foreman 8)
>
> 'If we leave the workers without any control they will not wear any safety equipment - they don't know the importance of the safety in the site.' (Foreman 10)

Workers, when surveyed, took a different view, indicating that safety clothing and equipment was often unavailable and only one in ten stated that they receive the required workplace health and safety training at the start of the job. Similarly, only 12 percent confirmed that safety wear and apparatus was made available to them when operating machines and only 44 percent stated that their company provided them with durable and safe hard hats and belts when working at an elevation of ten meters or more. Only 12 percent stated that the construction company provided them with hearing protection and only 12 percent agreed that maintenance on machines was conducted regularly.

Another alarming finding pertains to safety training. While such training is crucial to prevent accidents from happening and to reduce the fatality rate on sites, few of the foremen stated that they provide effective safety training:

> 'We provide safety training and training on the machines for the beginners.' (Foreman 1)
>
> 'We train them on the safety regulations and how to wear the equipment.' (Foreman 2)

While some others acknowledged the lack of safety training in their company, and expected workers to learn on the job:

> 'They learn by trying everything we offer them the guidelines.' (Foreman 9)
>
> 'Training? Forget about it with these workers.' (Foreman 7)

There was a significant inconsistency in the survey answers with employees first saying that safety measures are implemented, but when asked for more detail, acknowledging that safety equipment is not always provided. One explanation could be that construction workers were afraid to give a negative answer or, if we take into account management views of employees, another explanation would be that their standards of safety are so low that they perceive that the current measures appear sufficient. Given the high numbers of fatalities on site, based on anecdotal evidence, we tend to believe that the former explanation is more likely, with low skilled and precarious foreign labor being afraid to disclose low safety standards for fear of losing their jobs or being subject to disciplinary measures.

Given the vagueness of the official health and safety laws in Lebanon, these results are not surprising. The regulations leave the decision on implementation of safety regulations up to the contractors or companies involved (Awwad et al. 2014) and our findings indicate the need to work on national level policies to promote safety, because employers are often not concerned about health and safety issues.

In conclusion, our research highlights the inadequate nature of management practices in the construction industry, with key concerns pertaining to recruitment, safety and training. The recruitment process is informal and ad hoc, with a strong preference given to the recruitment of foreign unskilled labor with little investigation of a worker's skill levels.

Relationship Between Nationality and Worker Perceptions

Seven t-tests were conducted to investigate how Lebanese and Syrian participants evaluate and rate the management functions of their organizations. The results of the t-tests revealed that Lebanese participants rated their organizations as having higher levels of positive recruitment and selection strategies and lower levels of safety compared to the Syrian participants. This is interesting because Lebanese workers are paid higher wages than their Syrian counterparts while Lebanese workers' level of dissatisfaction with the standards of safety, compared to Syrian participants, is most likely to be a reflection of disparity in the level of awareness of safety measures across the two groups, or perhaps due to differential treatment between local and foreign labor.

Relationship Between Age and Worker Perceptions

Age was also an important factor in determining the attitudes of participants toward management processes at the workplace. Our research revealed that there was a significant correlation between age and training and development with participants who were 51 years old or older rating their organization as having higher levels of training and development compared to participants who were between 18 and 30 years old. This result may be explained by the fact that older workers are typically more established or hold senior positions in their organizations. Another potential explanation for this finding is that younger workers tend to be more demanding than older, rendering them more dissatisfied with their current work conditions.

Discussion and Conclusions

The results of our research presented in this chapter depict a negative picture of management practices and working conditions in the construction industry in Lebanon. Even though construction is a major contributor to the Lebanese economy, its management practices are predominantly informal and left to the discretion of the foremen, who often lack expertise in managing people. It was clear from our findings that HR departments in Lebanese construction companies have little impact on site behavior for many reasons: the unstable nature of the industry, the unsteady nature of the contractual environment, the diverse nationalities of workers on site and the difficulty in controlling the flow of illegal foreign workers amidst the unstable political situation in Lebanon and the ongoing war in Syria.

Nationality plays an important role in the recruitment process of construction workers due to the fact that migrant workers accept lower wages than their Lebanese counterparts (ILO 2014). Due to the current political instability in Syria, most of the Syrian workers enter Lebanon as undocumented workers and in an unofficial way. Considering that the recruitment process of these Syrian workers is informal, construction companies and their representatives feel free to bypass the rules and regulations of the Lebanese Labor Law and, additionally, not conduct required medical tests for the workers (Ajluni and Kawar 2015). The lack of functional workplace inspection means that there is no external pressure to observe regulations.

Health and safety at work has been receiving increased attention in Lebanon in recent years and the focus has been on supervising progress in construction activities and ensuring the compliance of workers with the safety regulations (Serpell and Ferrada 2007). While there is legislation setting out employers' responsibilities for health and safety and penalties for violations, several challenges remain. These include the absence of regulatory bodies to update and implement rules on safety management, the lack of enforcement of existing rules and regulations and the general dearth of safety education, awareness and commitment. All these factors, coupled with the transient and undocumented nature of construction work, lead to the breach of workers' rights for proper compensation, working in a safe environment and for job security and associated benefits.

Perhaps a common thread underpinning our findings is the significant power imbalance between contractors and construction workers that, coupled with the informality of working practices, and the prevalence of subcontracting, leads to abuse, to sub-optimal work conditions and to diluted accountability. This subcontracting system has been shown to undermine the rights of construction workers who are poorly organized and highly exploited (Ngai and Huilin 2010). There is thus a large gap between the formal regulations and the actions in practice (An and

Watanabe 2010). This informality and insecurity in employment practices, and the exclusion of construction workers from labor protection systems, have rendered them prone to precarious work with excessive working hours, low pay and high risk of occupational accidents (Yun 2009). This pattern is clearly evident in Lebanon.

The improvement of construction labor conditions in Lebanon requires a coordinated effort by various stakeholders, along with greater accountability. This includes policy makers such as government departments (for example, the Ministry of Labor), trade unions and other construction regulatory and professional bodies (for example, the Order of Engineers and Architects). The effort should also comprise key construction project players, including clients, real estate developers, designers, consultants, technical controllers, project management professionals, contractors and suppliers. Finally, third party entities such as insurance companies should be involved in the reform of health and safety. The absence of any formal apprenticeship or training systems for construction work also suggests that there is considerable scope for productivity improvements.

Perhaps contractors and clients have the most important role to play in requiring decent work conditions from their subcontractors, including adherence to sustainable development goals. Major clients can require the presence of a clear safety policy to protect the health and lives of the workers, decent work conditions and a risk management strategy as well as an emergency response system, as a binding condition in the bidding process, and as part of their socially responsible strategies.

References

Abou Jaoude, H., 2015. *Labour Market and Employment Policy in Lebanon*. European Training Foundation. https://www.etf.europa.eu/en/publications-and-resources/publications/labour-market-and-employment-policy-lebanon (accessed 03.06.20.).

ACTED: Agency for Technical Cooperation and Development, 2014. *Labor Market in Beirut and Mount Lebanon* 22 January. https://www.acted.org/en/ (accessed 03.06.20.).

Ajluni, S., and Kawar, M., 2015. *Towards Decent Work in Lebanon*: International Labour Organization, ILO Regional Office for Arab States– Beirut 10 June 2015. https://www.ilo.org/wcmsp5/groups/public/---arabstates/---ro-beirut/documents/publication/wcms_374826.pdf (accessed 03.06.20.).

Ali, S., Weir, D., Forthcoming. Wasta: Advancing a holistic model to bridge the micro-macro divide. *Management and Organization Review*.

An, T., Watanabe, T., 2010. Research on labour-service subcontracting management in Chinese construction industry. *Japan Society of Civil Engineers* 66(1), 329–340.

Arthur D. Little (Consultancy), 2018. *Building the Lebanese Oil Sector: Strategic Thoughts for a Successful National Experience* October 2018. http://www.adlittle.com/sites/default/files/viewpoints/adl_building_the_lebanese_oil_sector_-min.pdf (accessed 03.06.20).

Awad, K., 2014. 'Future Concrete Lebanon 2014 to Tackle Technological Advancements Amid Positive Trend in the Industry' 9 June 2014. https://www.zawya.com/mena/en/press-releases/story/Future_Concrete_Lebanon_2014_to_tackle_technological_advancements_amid_positive_trend_in_the_industry-ZAWYA20140609090117/ (accessed 03.06.20.).

Awwad, R., Jabbour, M., El Souki, O., 2014. Safety practices in the Lebanese construction market: contractors' perspective in *ISARC*, In: Proceedings of the *International Symposium on Automation and Robotics in Construction, 31(1)* January 2014. Vilnius Gediminas Technical University, Department of Construction Economics & Property.

BankMED, 2017. *Analysis of Lebanon's Real Estate Sector* Bankmed - Market & Economic Research Division- Beirut-Lebanon. https://www.bankmed.com.lb/BOMedia/subservices/categories/News/20170531091923395.pdf (accessed 03.06.20.).

Bosch, G., Philips, P. (Eds.), 2002. *Building Chaos: an International Comparison of Deregulation in the Construction Industry*. Routledge, London.

Bou Khater, L., 2019. *Understanding State Incorporation of the Workers' Movement in Early Post-War Lebanon and its Backlash on Civil Society*. Civil Society Knowledge Centre, Lebanon Support. https://civilsociety-centre.org/paper/understanding-state-incorporation-workers-movement-early-post-war-lebanon-and-its-backlash (accessed 05.11.19.).

Chahine, J., 2005. Lack of safety measures in construction claims another life. *The Daily Star Newspaper- Lebanon* 17 August. https://www.dailystar.com.lb/News/Lebanon-News/2005/Aug-17/7835-lack-of-safety-measures-in-construction-claims-another-life.ashx (accessed 03.06.20.).

Heale, R., Forbes, D., 2013. Understanding triangulation in research. *Evidence-Based Nursing 16(4)*. 98–98.

Human Rights Watch, 2007. *Why They Died: Civilian Casualties in Lebanon During the 2006 War* 19 (5E), 5 September 2007. https://www.hrw.org/report/2007/09/05/why-they-died/civilian-casualties-lebanon-during-2006-war (accessed 03.06.07.).

Hutchings, K., Weir, D., 2006. Guanxi and Wasta: A comparison. *Thunderbird International Business Review 48* (1), 141–156.

Ifpinfo, 2014. Construction in Lebanon remains one of the most attractive sectors 1 June 2014. IFP Info News. https://www.ifpinfo.com/construction-in-lebanon-remains-one-of-the-most-attractive-sectors/ (accessed 03.06.20.).

ILO, 2014. *Syrian Refugees in Lebanon Face Harsh Working Conditions*. ILO Newsroom, ILO Regional Office for Arab States, 4 April 2014.

ILO and FES, 2016. *Characteristics and Structure of the Union Movement in Lebanon*. The Consultation and Research Institute, 17 November 2016. ILO Publications, International Labour Office, Geneva https://www.ilo.org/wcmsp5/groups/public/---arabstates/---ro-beirut/documents/publication/wcms_535107.pdf (accessed 17.11.20).

ILO, 2017. *Matching Skills and Jobs in Lebanon: Main Features of the Labour Market – Challenges, Opportunities and Recommendations*. International Labor Organization, Geneva. https://www.ilo.org/beirut/information-resources/factsheets/WCMS_559673/lang--en/index.htm (accessed 22.06.20.).

International Trade Union Confederation, 2012. *Annual Survey of Violations of Trade Union Rights – Lebanon.* https://www.refworld.org/docid/4fd8893fc. html (accessed 03.06.20).

International Trade Union Confederation (ITUC), 2014. *The Case Against Qatar; Host of the FIFA 2022 World Cup. ITUC Special Report March 2014.* ITUC, Brussels.

Investment Development Authority of Lebanon (IDAL), 2009. *Active Labor Force Breakdown by Economic Activity.* Central Administration of Statistics, Beirut-Lebanon. https://investinlebanon.gov.lb/Content/uploads/CorporatePageRubric/180403022602645~IDAL-LEBANESE%20LABOR%20FORCE.pdf (accessed 03.06.20.).

Kettles, A.M., Creswell, J.W., Zhang, W., 2011. Mixed methods research in mental health nursing. *Journal of Psychiatric and Mental Health Nursing* 18(6), 535–542.

Knell, Y., 2013. Gas finds in East Mediterranean may change strategic balance. *BBC News,* 13 May 2013. https://www.bbc.com/news/world-middle-east-22509295 (accessed on 03.06.20.).

LEADERS, 2019. *The Labor Sector in Lebanon: Legal Frameworks, Challenges, and Opportunities* Relief Web international – UNHCR, 31 May 2019. https://reliefweb.int/sites/reliefweb.int/files/resources/69776.pdf (accessed 03.06.20).

Lebanon Economic Vision, 2018. *McKinsey Report* October 22, 2018 https://www.economy.gov.lb/media/11893/20181022-1228full-report-en.pdf (accessed 03.06.20.).

Lebanon Gas and Oil, 2019. *Lebanon Oil and Gas Sector Ready for the Next Level* 8 May. http://www.lebanongasandoil.com/index.php/news-details/181 (accessed 03.06.20.).

LIBC, 2017. *Lebanon Positions itself as Hub for Syrian Reconstruction* The Lebanese International Business Council – Beirut, Lebanon, 25 May 2017. http://www.libc.net/2017/05/25/lebanon-positions-itself-as-hub-for-syrian-reconstruction/ (Accessed 03.06.20.).

Liy, C.H., Ibrahim, S.H., Affandi, R., Rosli, N.A., Nawi, M.N., 2016. Causes of fall hazards in construction site management. *International Review of Management and Marketing* 6 (8S), 256–263.

LOGI, 2017. *Environmental Impact of Petroleum Activities in Lebanon – Review of the Strategic Environmental Assessment (SEA) Lebanon Oil and Gaz Initiative, May 2017* https://logi-lebanon.org/uploaded/2017/10/5ODZQNGL_SEA%20Report%20final.pdf (accessed 03.06.20.).

Loosemore, M., Lim, B.T.H., 2016. Intra-organisational injustice in the construction industry. *Engineering, Construction and Architectural Management* 23(4), 428–447.

Maloney, W.F., 1997. Strategic planning for human resource management in construction. *Journal of Management in Engineering* 13(3), 49–56.

Marchington, M., Cooke, F.L., Hebson, G., 2010. Human Resource management across organizational boundaries, *Sage Handbook of Human Resource Management: 460–474.* SAGE Publications Ltd.

Mikhael, M., Chami, M., Daou, R., 2014. *Lebanon Economic Performance Annual Report 2013.* Blominvest Bank. https://blog.blominvestbank.com/wp-content/uploads/2014/12/Lebanon-Annual-Report-2013-.pdf (accessed 19.06.20.).

Ngai, P., Huilin, L., 2010. A culture of violence: The labor subcontracting system and collective action by construction workers in post-socialist China. *The China Journal*, (64): 143–158.

Obeid, A.R., 2015. *Health and Safety in Construction Industry of Cyprus.* Eastern Mediterranean University. Özay Oral Library, Famagusta, North Cyprus via Mersin 10 Turkey.

Pasick, R.J., Burke, N.J., Barker, J.C., Joseph, G., Bird, J.A., Otero-Sabogal, R., Tuason, N., Stewart, S.L., Rakowski, W., Clark, M., Washington, P.K., Guerra, C., 2009. Behavioral theory in a diverse society: like a compass on Mars. *Health Education and Behavior 36*(Issue 5 Supplement), 11S–35S.

Raja, J.Z., Green, S.D., Leiringer, R., Dainty, A., Johnstone, S., 2013. Managing multiple forms of employment in the construction sector: implications of HRM. *Human Resource Management Journal 23*(3), 313–328.

Serpell, A., Ferrada, X., 2007. A competency-based model for construction supervisors in developing countries. *Personnel Review 36*(4), 585–602.

Srour, F.J., Srour, I., Lattouf, M.G., 2017. A survey of absenteeism on construction sites. *International Journal of Manpower 38*(4), 533–547.

Srour, I., Chehab, G., Matt, J., 2011. *Green Jobs in the Construction Sector in Lebanon.* ILO report, Geneva. https://www.ilo.org/wcmsp5/groups/public/---ed_emp/---emp_ent/documents/publication/wcms_168091.pdf (accessed 03.06.20.).

Sultana, R., 2017. *Career Guidance and Livelihood Planning across the Mediterranean Challenging Transitions in South Europe and the MENA region.* Sense Publishers, Rotterdam.

Sune, H., 2011. The historiography and the memory of the Lebanese civil war, *Online Encyclopedia of Mass Violence*, 25: 1–14. Sciences Po, France.

UNEP, 2011. *Towards a Green Economy: Pathways to Sustainable Development and Poverty Eradication – A Synthesis for Policy Makers.* www.unep.org/greeneconomy (accessed 03.06.20.).

UNHCR, 2020. *Operational Portal – Refugee Situations, 31 January 2020* United Nations High Commission for Refugees. https://data2.unhcr.org/en/situations/syria/location/71 (accessed 03.06.20.).

United Nations Development Program (UNDP), 2016. *Mind the Gap: A Labour Needs Assessment for Lebanon* Beirut, Lebanon, 13 March 2017. https://data2.unhcr.org/en/documents/details/54480 (accessed 03.06.20.).

World Bank, 2011. *The Challenge of Informality in the Middle East and North Africa.* World Bank, Washington DC.

Yaacoub, N., and Badre, L., 2011. *The Labour Market in Lebanon. Statistics In Focus (SIF)*, Central Administration of Statistics, Lebanon. Issue number 1, October 2011. http://www.cas.gov.lb/images/PDFs/SIF/CAS_Labour_Market_In_Lebanon_SIF1.pdf (accessed 03.06.20.).

Yun, A., 2009. Regulating multi-layer subcontracting to improve labour protection. In: *Regulating for Decent Work (RDW) Conference. International Labour Organization.* July 2009: 8–9.

8 The Russian Construction Sector

Informality, Labor Mobility and Socialist Legacies

Ekaterina Serezhkina, Claudio Morrison and Olga Cretu

Introduction

This chapter analyzes current trends, main institutional features and employment practices in the Russian construction sector. Based on ethnographic research in Russia and Moldova, the study adopts a bottom-up approach privileging the point of view of migrant labor which dominates site level trades in the sector. The chapter focuses on recruitment, employment relations and work organization to understand their impact on the quality of the labor process and workers' well-being.

The post-Soviet labor process possesses a high degree of informality: institutions often stand as 'hollow shells' and large gaps exist between formal procedures and actual practices. In this text, the worker's voice is employed to fill these gaps and assess crucial changes and lasting continuities relative to the Soviet past.

The Soviet workplace was characterized by a distinctive labor process. Skilled workers and line managers were forced to bend rules in order to achieve strict targets set by all-powerful but distant planning officials. This gave rise to individualized bargaining, sustaining an autonomous and apparently chaotic labor process. Workers' accounts show how the restoration of private property and capitalist management has evolved rather than replaced such practices to the detriment of workers' interests.

The Russian construction sector, like construction elsewhere, employs a high proportion of migrant labor and employment arrangements follow stratification along ethno-national lines. However, the status of internal and international migrants, mostly from the former Soviet Union (FSU), sets it apart from its western equivalents. Studying labor mobility from a 'sending' country allows full appreciation of the transnational processes associated with the recruitment and management of a multinational workforce.

The first section of this chapter considers change in work and employment in Russia. This is followed by discussion of the construction industry, including its formal institutions, training and safety systems.

The empirical section of the chapter contains a case study capturing the diversity in working conditions, pay, skills and occupational safety experienced by workers in a highly informal and segmented labor market. Conclusions reconnect actual experiences with major trends at industry level to suggest likely future scenarios.

Country Background: Russia's Employment and Industrial Relations

Following the collapse of the FSU, the Russian economy has undergone major upheavals. In 2010, the World Bank declared transition to capitalism accomplished (Mitra et al. 2010) but both western and Russian analysts continue detecting post-socialist legacies distorting the rule of law and efficient market mechanisms. The country's political economy, including industrial relations, has seen marked changes – from 1990s President Yeltsin's liberal approach to Putin's paternalistic and autocratic rule. However, continued state commitment to neo-liberal reforms and employers' 'low road' HRM policies have further degraded labor standards. Increased labor mobility and casualization of the employment relationship have resulted.

Under Putin the state attempts social regulation employing tripartite social dialog (Vinogradova et al. 2015). Formally, regulations on working time, pay and dismissal remain fairly strict relative to Brazil, India or China (Krzywdzinski 2018). Flexible pay, agency work and mass redundancies are severely constrained by legislation, corporatist relations and direct political pressure (Danilova et al. 2012). However, such restrictions are more than compensated by tolerance of employers' non-compliance with labor legislation, particularly in the areas of working time and wage payments (Vinogradova et al. 2015). This new 'social market contract' envisages an exchange between social protection and the state's forcible demand for workers' passivity and political support. State-sponsored corporatism favors collaborative unions at the expense of independent labor representation. Despite obvious limitations, 'at the level of the enterprise the union fulfills its social function' (Vinogradova et al. 2015: 200) insofar as workers appreciate a Soviet-type 'social wage' provided by a 'just enterprise' (Morris and Hinz 2017: 12). After the 2008 global financial crisis, a de-facto strike ban has not prevented unofficial acts of protests by workers and militant unions (Christensen 2017). The latter, however, have been subjected to systematic pressure from above, preventing the consolidation of genuine collective bargaining (Bizyukov 2018). Foreign firms have been the only sites where union organizing has taken hold (Krzywdzinski 2018; Sippola 2016). This notwithstanding, western employers have failed to display a 'home-country' effect in enterprise-level industrial relations (Sippola 2016).

The 'emerging dominant Russian HRM approach' is characterized by high wage differentiation, limited employee involvement and a corporate view of employees as cost rather than as resource (Andreeva et al. 2014). Compensation systems remain focused on performance-based remuneration, narrow task fulfillment and low-trust relations, often relying on Soviet-era bonus systems (Krzywdzinski 2018: 181). Nowadays, however, the discretionary distribution of benefits is employed in a punitive manner (Krzywdzinski 2018: 180–181). Managers also display hostility toward collective bargaining, resisting compromise with trade unions (Morris and Hinz 2017: 3). These practices extend to foreign-owned green-field establishments. The resulting climate among ordinary workers is one of fear and mistrust, which affects their willingness to comply with even basic performance standards. These arrangements breed employer-driven informality and labor mobility (Barsukova 2015).

The precarization of labor is happening via 'informal and semi-formal jobs, a lack of development of legal and social rights of workers, arbitrary wage …' (Morris and Hinz 2017: 3). Galenkova finds that 'informal employment is spreading among the most vulnerable sections of the labor force including migrants, the rural youth and the disabled' (Morrison and Bizyukov 2017: 555). According to Gimpelson and Kapeljushnikov (2014), since the 1990s the informally employed have grown to a quarter of the total labor force. Furthermore, from 2000 a sizable wage gap of 15–20 percent has emerged between the formal and the informal sectors. Informal employment in Russia has an industry distribution typical for developing countries with employment rates in the non-service sector being twice as high for both genders. A distinctive Russian feature, however, is the prevalence of males in the informal sector; The construction industry share in informal employment grew from 26.2 percent in 2010 to 28.6 percent in 2015 (Karabchuk and Zabirova 2018: 747).

Lacking any effective means for bargaining, workers have opted for mobility, generating consistently high levels of turnover, approximately ten million people annually during the last 15 years (Morris and Hinz 2017: 6). Long-distance mobility has become a key survival strategy for working class families (White 2009). Turnover highlights the dualist character of the labor market: 'wastage of low-skilled workers, on the one hand, and mobility for high-skilled workers, on the other' (Morris and Hinz 2017: 6). Adding to internal mobility, the post-2000 period has seen a substantial growth in short-term work-oriented migration, predominantly from the FSU countries (Mukomel 2014). In 2015, there were over 11 million international migrants (Chudinovskikh and Denisenko 2017) while irregular migrants averaged 5–6 million in 2011 (IOM 2017). Most migrants are young males from FSU countries using the visa-waiving system which allows a three-month stay, extendable to one year upon purchase of self-employment permits. A job rotation system builds on this scheme, whereas individual workers or whole gangs (or 'brigades') have to leave the country once their permits expire to be replaced by friends or relatives. These breaks, lasting up to several months, also allow workers to physically recuperate and seek better alternative employment. This system, however, delays career progression and re-settlement. Migrants' coping strategies rely mainly on informal networks and on living transnationally (Mukomel 2014: 138–161). In the last decade, migrants' ethnic and socio-cultural composition changed rapidly. Migrants currently tend to be younger, less educated and from rural areas in Muslim Central Asian republics as opposed to earlier skilled workers of European origin. FSU migrants are largely employed informally through intermediaries (Morrison et al. 2013). Russian sources estimate the distribution of migrant employment by sector at 33 percent for trade and repair services, 27 percent for construction and 17 percent for personal, social and housing services (Mukomel 2014). The construction sector however retains the highest concentration of migrant workers. Here, Russians holding compulsory resident cards can enjoy formal wages and working conditions while Russian internal migrants, Slavic and Asian migrants are subjected to a downwardly graduated set of employment provisions (Morrison et al. 2013). Segmentation does not mean rigid segregation: informality equally affects local and incoming workers, while skilled 'illegal' migrants can earn more than officially employed Russians.

Workers' agency is sustained by an 'unbalanced' labor market. In highly industrialized areas analysts report a depleted labor market (Danilova et al. 2012; Krzywdzinski 2018). In addition to poor vocational training and regional imbalances, this owes much to the mismatch between workers' expectations and the quality of jobs on offer. Skilled workers can reject better paid formal jobs characterized by heavy workloads, increased monitoring and intensification, thanks to the availability of low-paid employment in traditional ex-Soviet factories where slack is allowed by complacent managers. They then rely on informal jobs to supplement their income (Morris and Hinz 2017). Labor shortages and informality are historically interrelated, sustaining recruitment and promotion practices which rely less on merit and performance than on personal loyalty and connections.

In summary, capitalist transition has built on casualization and segregation by gender, nationality, and place of residence, as opposed to skills growth and social cooperation, fueling workers' dissatisfaction. Lacking bargaining tools, labor employs individual mobility to improve their position, though collective struggles are increasingly visible. Employers and the state respond by alternating paternalistic and autocratic policies.

Industry Overview: Russian Construction in Figures

Official statistical indicators, despite their limitations, clearly outline the resurgence of the industry from the transition years and highlight significant changes in structure, product orientation and internal relationships relative to the Soviet period (RossStat, 2017: 268–283).

Most recent data by the Russian Federal State Statistics Service indicate that the Russian construction industry employs 5.5 million people. Employees are distributed across approximately half a million enterprises or 10 percent of all registered businesses, almost all of which are in private hands (RossStat 2017). Second-quarter 2018 data recorded 489,000 enterprises, down by 11 thousand units from the same period in 2017 (RossStat 2018). Small enterprises accounted for 262,000 units or 11.8 percent of the total in the economy, employing 1.2 million workers. Among them 234,000 micro-enterprises had in total 486,000 employees (RossStat 2017). Data by gender were not available.

In 2016, the total construction volume of residential premises reached approximately 80 million square meters, meeting government housing targets in volume terms. However, financial indicators failed analysts' expectations. The sector Gross Value Added (GVA) amounted to 5,246 billion roubles or approximately 5.7 percent of total GVA. The total value of works in the first half of 2018 was 2,922 billion roubles (99 percent relative to the first half of 2017). Sector output and gross domestic product (GDP) relative to the whole economy in 2016 were respectively at 6.6 percent and six percent after a steady year-on-year decline from 7.9 and 7.4 percent in 2012 (RossStat 2017).

Activity indicators display performance trends consistent with the well-known dynamics of the Russian economy as a whole. The industry suffered serious decline in the 1990s followed by steady recovery during the Putin years, and particularly between 2005 and 2010. Geographical and territorial distribution unsurprisingly favored large urban areas in European Russia: the central and Volga federal districts totaled, respectively, 24 and 16 million, while others ranged between eight and five million. Moscow city and region, with 3.4 and 8.9 million, respectively, made up half of the central district output. The financial crisis took its toll, but was effectively countered, only to fall back again after 2014 when western sanctions, lower oil revenues and weak demand precipitated a new downturn.

In 1992, with the economy in free fall and social housing at a standstill, the share of residential housing for the general population had fallen to a meager 12 percent of total overall building construction. A decade later it had climbed up to 40 percent, a proportion which remained roughly unaltered despite volumes doubling in the following decade. The growth appears to be sustained by the category 'by population at own expense and credits,' signaling the shift from state funded social housing to a market-driven housing boom (RossStat 2017).

The shift from public investments to private consumption as the main driver in the sector is confirmed by data on the final use of completed buildings. Among non-residential buildings, the most significant change is represented by the share of commercial properties, amounting to 35 percent of overall non-residential space completed in 2017 (RossStat 2018), despite recent decline. This is consistent with the rise of the retail sector, reflected in shopping malls replacing factories in the suburban landscape. Within this category, the only segment countering the downward trend is agriculture. Evidently, this sector bounced back thanks to Russian counter-sanctions (following the annexation of Crimea in 2014) which curtailed imports of foodstuff from Western countries.

Data about the typology of funding agents confirm the growth of private actors at the expense of public ones. The growth of the 'private,' that is, developers, first at the expense of the state then of individual funding is indicative of the growing strength of private enterprise. After the 2009–2011 crisis and even more after the 2014 shock they became the main driver of the construction industry's growth as Figure 8.1 demonstrates. Data for mid-2018 record 119,300 delivered buildings, improving on the 96,700 completed in mid-2017.

Data on wages and employment require the most careful consideration, given the high level of total and partial informality in the sector. Employment, as shown in Figures 8.2 and 8.3, has experienced sustained growth in both relative and absolute terms during the boom years. Construction has been the only non-service sector to do

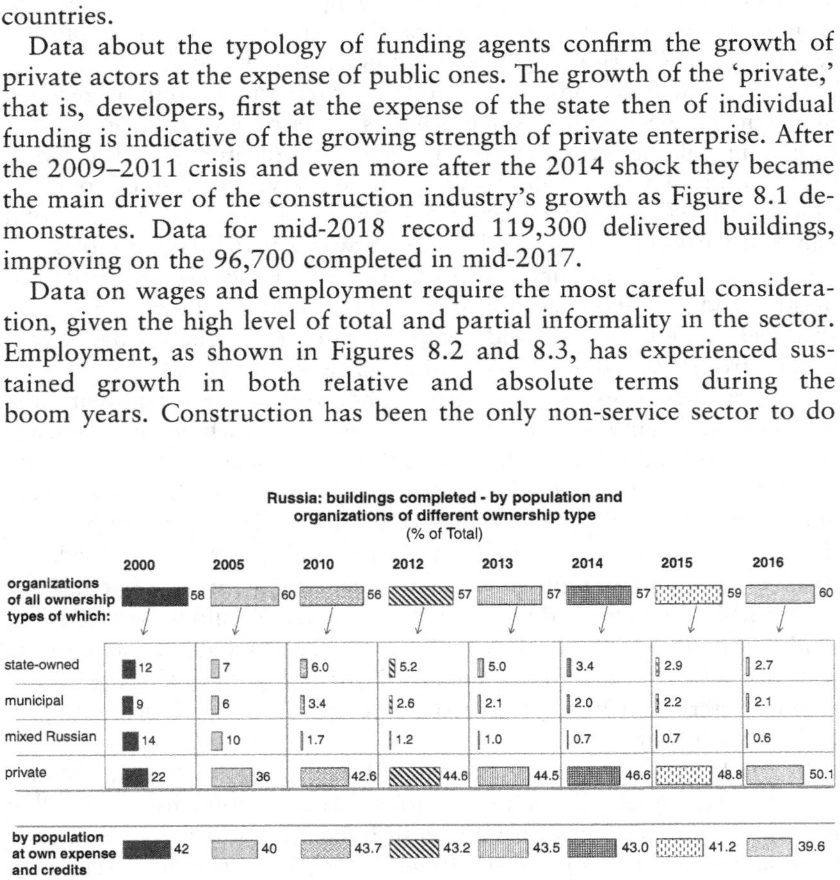

Figure 8.1 Russia: buildings completed – by population and organizations of different ownership type.

Source: Authors' own calculation.

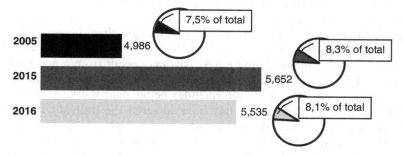

Figure 8.2 Russia: average annual number employed in construction.

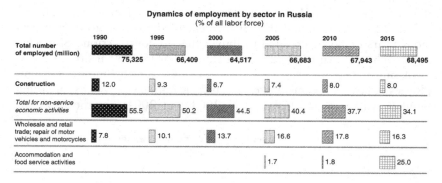

Figure 8.3 Dynamics of employment by sector in Russia.
Source: Authors' own calculation.

so, despite the well-known high levels of informality. On the other hand, fluctuations in employment levels in both directions may be greater than formally acknowledged.

Estimates for informal employment by sector indicate that construction holds the highest levels of informally employed and self-employed, respectively at 14 and five percent in 2015, twice as many as in trade or agriculture (Karabchuk and Zabirova 2018: 747). Informal employees have grown in number since 2010 with self-employment doubling. These data suggest that increasing reliance on casual labor is one of the responses to the crisis. The shift to self-employment is another strategy for increasing flexibility and cutting costs, a move explicitly favored by authorities' increasing reliance on *patent* (self-employed working visa) for FSU migrants.

A relative decline in average earnings is another feature of the period starting in 2012. The officially recorded Average Monthly Nominal Wage for 2018 stood at 33,678 roubles, slightly up from 32,188 in 2016. Real, that is informal wages, as we will see in the case study, vary considerably but are generally higher than the above-mentioned figure for qualified Slavic workers. Historical series show that, from 2012, construction wages have been trailing behind the total country average. The position is illustrated in Figure 8.4. This may result from a number of factors. A growing reliance on informal workers may have a statistically negative effect as this group includes better paid workers. Also, competition from new migrants may have lowered the individual and collective bargaining power of established workers. Both informality and competition in a segmented market facilitates employers' cost-cutting.

To understand these dynamics and make sense of these figures, we must turn to the analysis of experts and practitioners. In the first instance, we look into the boom years up to the 2009–2011 crisis period. In an interview on the causes and possible responses to the crisis, the then president of the Russian Federation of the Construction industry, Nikolay Koshman, noted that 80 percent of the sector growth in previous years could be credited to 'buyer-funded construction' (Shmeleva 2009). This in turn resulted from a state-sponsored expansion of credit availability. Government initiatives included direct funding for employees of law enforcement agencies and the military as well as for young families. Changes in legislation in 2003 and 2004 laid the basis for

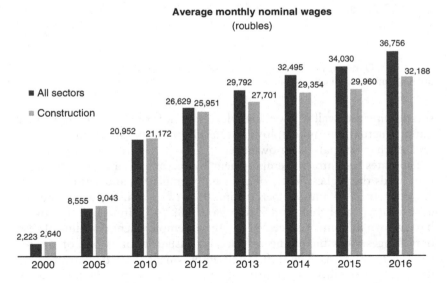

Figure 8.4 Average monthly nominal wages in Russia (roubles).
Source: Authors' own calculation.

growth. The 214th law, in 2004, opened the door to shared-equity construction whereas individual citizens were put in a position to access credit on a par with builders and developers provided the development plans were registered and properly licensed. This way buyers would directly fund the building and developers could avoid having to sell flats in bulk afterwards. Putin intervened directly to force a reduction in interest rates and an extension of repayment periods. Banks found this proposition interesting and started to support even small builders (Shmeleva 2009).

Growth also had unpalatable side effects. The risk of fraud through pyramid schemes or overselling increased as did the risk of poor quality output as 'rough' businesses took advantage of those opportunities (Shmeleva 2009). The decline in quality was also blamed on key changes in regulation: in 2003, Federal Law no. 184 essentially abrogated key construction standards previously set under Soviet legislation. Migrant labor did not escape the blame:

> *Let's take concrete, you need to mix its components carefully, produce a sample and gain certification. Migrants will do with spades and a vat, mix it all up, get paid and leave. So you cannot be surprised if two years ago an overpass collapsed.*
>
> (Shmeleva 2009: 3)

The Russian economy, and construction within it, did not escape the consequences of the 2008 global financial crisis. The banking sector simply stopped funding for developers and equity buyers 'advising clients to await a fall in prices' (Naumov and Sergeev 2011: 1). Early assessments foresaw an impending collapse whatever the stimulus put together by the authorities. Output in 2009 recorded a relatively minor decline. Experts pointed out though that a major decline would appear only in 2012 because of the one and a half to two years' gap between planning and completion (Bashkatova 2010). However, already in the summer of 2011 major consulting agencies were hotly debating the surprise resurgence of the sector. Year-on-year output jumped by 17 percent. This unexpected outcome was at odds with both investment and intermediate output, leading some to suggest that official statistics may be 'optimistic'. Others concluded that the only explanation for this statistical anomaly is that 'builders are now in receipt of state funding and have rushed into completing earlier frozen projects' (Butrin and Shapovalov 2011).

State funding and lower labor costs therefore have helped the industry out of the crisis. The shift toward cheaper locations and different types of output contributed to recovery in 2013–2016. State preference for 'economclass' (Russian equivalent of affordable housing) coincided with a move out of expensive central locations (Voskresenskij 2011). The discrepancy between surface output and values at current prices, the decline of average flat dimensions and the increase in rural buildings seemed to confirm this trend.

The crisis, following a period of expansion and radical transformation, has brought up a host of structural problems that exceed issues of growth. Experts lament the heavy reliance on unskilled labor, the absence of educational and labor market infrastructures (Privalov 2014) and a lack of implementation of safety and technical regulation (Ivanova et al. 2011). These flaws contribute to poor output quality and high workplace accident rates. This host of issues is investigated by analyzing industry institutions and engagements between all actors in the building community.

Russian Construction Governance: Institutions, Vocational Education and Occupational Safety

Over the last decade the industry has struggled with poor regulation, personnel shortages and lack of effective institutional arrangements, resulting in poor quality, widespread illegality and heavy reliance on the informal employment of unskilled migrants. We turn now to the evolution of the industry's governance structures focusing on legal and institutional reforms aimed at improving safety and professional training. There is a multiplicity of governmental and non-governmental bodies charged with the construction sector governance. Their prerogatives and corresponding legislation have undergone continuous changes over the last decade. Major failures in personnel training and safety standards have inspired an ongoing overhaul of their structures and legal foundations.

The key governmental bodies are the Ministry of Construction and the Ministry of Labor, the latter in charge of health and safety. Two inspectorates operate in the sector, one covering building regulations (excluding atomic power), the other overseeing workplace safety, respectively: the *Gosnadzor*, part of the federal environmental, industrial and nuclear supervision service (Gosnadzor 2019), and the federal labor inspectorate (Labor Inspection, RosTrud 2019), part of the labor and employment federal service or RosTrud. Experts point out the duplication of norms and overlapping responsibilities between them.

The main non-governmental bodies on the employer side are the National Union of Building Companies or NOSTROY (NOSTROY 2019) and the Russian Federation of Building Companies, in short RSS (Russian Federation of Builders 2019). The latter, established in 1991, is the largest employers' representative body. Members include 260 regional federations and other collective institutions totaling 41,000 individual organizations. Its leaders and constituent members cooperate with governmental and legislative bodies in drafting new legislation and take part in the tripartite commission on the employers' side. Its structure includes up to 20 separate expert committees, devoted to discussing and generating recommendations to other social partners on specialist subjects. None, however, is dedicated to health and safety. NOSTROY instead was established in 2009, completing the state-sponsored process of moving the industry toward self-regulation. Key legislation included President Putin's decree in 2003 on the reduction of state interference in the economy, the 315 Federal Law on 'self-regulated organizations' and the 148 Federal Law on changes to the construction code as well as other legislation, later modified in 2016. Self-regulated organizations (SROs) are federations of individual enterprises tasked with 'preventing damages caused by faulty construction work, improving the quality of works and ensuring observance of contractual obligations' (NOSTROY 2019). Self-regulation replaced the licensing system. NOSTROY is the SRO central body and unlike the RSS enjoys real powers under the authority of the construction ministry. It is entrusted with ensuring observance of relevant sector legislation by members, setting up new standards and contributing to reforms on quality, health and safety and professional qualifications. Membership in these organizations is a key requisite for doing business and taking part in public tenders. Small companies, however, find it difficult to join up as it requires multiple certifications and compulsory contributions to insurance funds to cover civil and contractual liabilities. Membership amounts to just below one hundred thousand enterprises.

The main trade union in the construction sector is the Federation of Building and Building Materials' Workers (in short, Builders' Federation of Russia or BF), affiliated to the successor of the official Soviet trade union confederation. An NGO-type migrant workers' union is also registered in Moscow, alongside the powerful BF territorial branch (Ivanova et al. 2011). The BF union has retained its traditional welfare functions and actively participates in social partnership at national level and in the workplace (Ilchenko 2001) but membership has dwindled to approximately 200,000 (Builders' Federation of Russia 2019a). These developments can be explained by the union's reaction to 1990s restructuring when the union staked its survival on retaining collaborative relations with state institutions (Ilchenko 2001). Moscow authorities granted inspection powers and insisted on contractors accepting unionization. Conversely, the union has displayed continued support for state and municipal policies, from Crimea's annexation to the current 'law and order' response to the 2019 opposition marches (Moscow Builders' Trade Union 2019). The union's main areas of activity focus on welfare management, safety inspections (only where union members exist) and social dialog. However, experts maintain that the range of benefits currently provided to workers can hardly compare with the material and moral incentives available under Soviet rule (Ivanova et al. 2011: 45). Crucially, the union has stayed away from mobilizing, and specifically organizing the now predominantly migrant workforce. Historically the union was known for its combativeness from when it was led by and stood up for workers (Ilchenko 2001). Now, the union officially declares solidarity but openly lobbies for reducing migrant presence in favor of 'Russians' (Builders' Federation of Russia 2019b). In 2010, interviews with union officials revealed that

> *the powerful Moscow branch of the construction union officially opposes illegal immigration; in reality, it is hostile to migrant workers as such.*
>
> (Morrison et al. 2013)

The independent migrants' union helps migrants with residence documentation and deals with their grievances regarding authorities' abuses and employers' discrimination (Ivanova et al. 2011: 135–136). The official union by contrast has little or no support from its putative constituency and is suspended from the reality of workers' experience, requiring management support as a necessary condition for its survival (Croucher and Morrison 2012).

Industry Structure and Corporate Practices

The structural features of the industry and its flaws originate from privatization and the ensuing private sector development in the 1992–2002 period (Hanin 2012). The Soviet construction industry consisted of very large, highly integrated structures with territorial or technical specialization capable of independently planning and completing large projects. Contrary to general belief, this was consistent with international practice where a few main contractors dominate the industry while small businesses feature normally as subcontractors. However, these Soviet structures were wasteful, slow and poorly mechanized. Privatization led to the disintegration of most of these entities with a significant loss of capacity, know-how and qualified personnel. These holdings numbered just 2,056, averaging 4,128 employees each, working in 22,000 sub-units. By 2002 there were already 137,156 enterprises (employing just 5,094), of which 130,000 had fewer than 100 employees. New structures have their advantages: they are lean, extremely flexible and well suited to exploit the advantages offered to small–medium enterprises for surviving the hardship of transition economics. However, they are also averse to any control or cooperation. The process of disintegration was also highly uneven. The Moscow house-building trust survived almost intact and in civil engineering both the oil and transport ministries transferred into private entities. A process of concentration occurred over the decade.

However, the winners were not efficient market competitors but economic agents with serious political backing or connections with corrupt officials (Hanin 2012: 116). Government attempts at preventing corruption through public tender faced resistance. Foreign companies took advantage of the vacuum, raising fierce complaints by local firms. The long-term effects of reforms were a serious loss of capacity in civil engineering and heavy construction and the growth of an 'uncivilized' type of entrepreneurship.

The introduction of self-regulation in 2009 and its recent amendments have radically reshaped the normative framework aiming at increasing integration and accountability within the industry. Moving away from licensing, the state has transferred to SROs responsibility for verifying companies' compliance with state regulation in areas such as compulsory employees' certification and health and safety (Biryuleva 2010). The state has retained regulative and inspection powers. The power transfer was meant to deliver both higher quality of built environment and greater safety of building processes. The 2016 reform introduced regionalization, asking individual companies and architectural practices to join SROs at their headquarters' location, resubmission of their certification and, crucially, transfer of insurance funds into secure accounts. Since then, the number of SROs declined by a third, a fact that experts explain by the disappearance of 'empty shells' (Privalov 2017). Equally, half of the expected insurance funds are unaccounted for, apparently a result of bad investments during the crisis. Experts further lament SRO's lack of verifiable results and the ease of acquiring membership. Opinions remain divided as to whether reforms should be allowed to run their course or whether self-regulation should be scrapped in favor of reinstating direct state licensing.

Professional Education and Employee Qualifications

Relevant qualifications and life-long training are legally sanctioned requirements for skilled workers, managers and specialists, a Soviet classification including engineers and technical personnel (Biryuleva 2010). The industry is strictly regulated and SROs are expected to play a key role in introducing new standards, innovating within the curriculum and verifying compliance. Specifically, where companies are seeking SRO membership employees must possess the relevant qualification and they are forbidden to work unless their employer obtains appropriate certification. Employees ranging from the company director to skilled workers must undergo re-qualification courses every five years. In addition, certification of companies by SROs for dangerous, complex and exceptional projects requires additional training. Since 2017, it is compulsory for building contractors that their chief engineer and architect are included in the National Register of Construction Specialists.

Registration is subject to relevant qualifications, ten years of experience on the job and three years of seniority in their current position. Only then are professionals allowed to sign off documentation, for which they are personally liable to their clients, and their companies can receive the 'go ahead' for a project by TehNadzor (Chindyaskina 2018: 92). SROs are required to develop sector-specific further education through co-operation with specialist Higher Education institutions, contributing to curriculum innovation, the introduction of life-long learning and re-qualification courses. Relevant educational institutions fall into two general categories: specialist technical schools (PTU – *professional'noe tehnicheskoe uchilish'e*) and higher educational institutions (VUZ – *vysshoe uchebnoe zavedenie*).

Experts maintain, however, that state regulation has failed to establish an effective system of responsibility attribution equivalent to those operating in the West that the educational system does not satisfy industry demands (Privalov 2014) and that labor market trends display continued shortages of qualified personnel (Chindyaskina 2018). Various structural and contingent causes explain these failures. First, since the 1990s vocational education declined as Soviet ministries were dismantled and public interest moved away from low-yielding professions. By 2010 the industry suffered from excessive reliance on unqualified personnel. Job offers outstripped demand because the shortage of graduates was worsened by unappealing pay and conditions and resulting high turn-over. Further education fell short of employers' expectations and the sale of qualifications became widespread practice as the risk of exposure was low (Biryuleva 2010). Historically, Soviet enterprises responded to poor cooperation between education and industry by establishing direct links with individual institutions. However, during the 2008–2010 crisis this practice declined: enterprises supporting re-training and further education of workers fell from 56 to 46 percent (Bondarenko 2010). Higher education decline and market shortages have prompted a diversification of strategies: large holdings set up their own training centers; high-end developers turn to specialist recruiters (Zyryanova 2012); while design work can be outsourced to consulting (Privalov 2018). However, preference for experienced candidates rather than young graduates persists, highlighting how few companies take the long-term view and invest in training the next generation. Segmentation in the industry and labor market means that attention remains fixed on improving education for high-end professions demanded by luxury developers in capital cities (Privalov 2018).

Labor market dynamics, reflecting the general trends outlined in the previous section, confirm that most enterprises have little appetite for local skilled workers. In the 2005–2010 period the percentage of enterprises requiring formal qualifications rose or remained stable for managers but fell for skilled workers, from 49 to 39 percent. The indicator for job-seekers' personal characteristics was at 50 percent for managers and 30 percent for workers, an absolute low across sectors (Bondarenko 2010: 80–81). A developer explains:

> *Unlike in China where only formally trained workers are allowed into the industry, here [in Russia] learning partly happens on the job.*
> (Privalov 2018: 24; see Krzywdzinski 2018)

The proportion of migrants on sites currently reaches 75–80 percent, a recruitment manager maintains, because

> *migrants are employed as general labourers and finishers on projects for the mass-market segment.*
> (Privalov 2018: 24)

Qualitative research findings indicate that employers resent demands from local qualified labor for formal employment contracts, decent wages and legal entitlements such as lunch breaks, paid sick leave and holidays (Morrison et al. 2020; Rudenko 2011). They resort to FSU intermediaries activating long chains of recruitment. Intermediaries play a crucial role in regulating employment but are blamed for abuses (Human Rights Watch 2009). They can be simple recruiters or be involved in the actual work on site and the size of collectives can vary from a dozen people to a few hundred. Some point out their contribution to stable employment:

> *Nowadays it is not that common to deceive workers, they are interested in a stable market. They try to obtain residentship and work permits. This is in the interest of the employers as well: the intermediary takes responsibility for workers' behaviour. This is a decent form of employment relations yet exist as part of the 'shadow economy'.*
> (interview with Russian Academy of Science academic, Moscow 2010)

European workers enter individually through transnational networks organized in gangs or 'brigades' (nationally based teams headed by 'brigadiers') based on Soviet 'labor collectives', informally defined work groups normally encompassing all workers in a workplace (see Schwartz 2004). Younger, less educated Asian workers initially enter the market through more regimented networks (see Rudenko 2011). Experts refer to the 'Moscow system,' an arrangement whereby large shipments of Asian workers are organized by agencies circumventing quota restrictions. The 'brigade leader' recruits people, oversees their work on site and is responsible for meeting targets and paying wages, cash in hand (Morrison et al. 2020). Intermediaries play a crucial role in regulating employment but are blamed for abuses (Human Rights Watch 2009).

Occupational Safety Regulation and Outcomes

The subject of occupational health and safety represents the most dramatic and controversial aspect in the regulation and management of Russian construction. Safety principles and rights are enshrined in the Constitution, the Labor Code and other legislation (Ivanova et al. 2011). Presently, there exist more than two million safety-related norms for businesses (Fedorets 2017: 17). Yet, according to official statistics, construction displays the highest level of fatalities by sector and occupies second place for work-related injuries (RossStat 2019).

The key term for occupational safety in Russian law and enterprise operations is *ohrana truda* (OT), literally labor protection: 'the system [aimed at] preserving the life and health of workers in the production process consisting of legal, socio-economic, techno-organizational, sanitary, rehabilitative and other measures' (NOSTROY 2019: 4). The term *bezopasnost' truda* (BT), literally work safety, is also in use. Occupational safety rules for construction are found in labor law, but also in urban planning legislation, among rules for the design, renovation and use of buildings. Collective bargaining is also an important tool to ensure that appropriate safety measures are adopted and implemented (Kalsin 2010: 145). Norms establishing safety-related obligations can also be found in the technical regulations issued by the Construction Ministry (Sto Nostroy 2019: 10). The latest acts of legislation on occupational safety, called 'Standard systems of work safety and management systems of work protection', were issued in 2015. More recently the government launched the 2018–2025 'Safe Work' program aimed at raising employers' self-interest in observing safety regulations and increasing effectiveness in incident prevention and safety inspection (MinTrud 2018). No implementation act had been passed at the time of writing but some were under scrutiny by legislators. Current legal requirements are now detailed in a normative compendium released by NOSTROY to guide businesses through implementation (NOSTROY 2019). According to this source, all construction enterprises are required to set up a labor protection management system (SUOT) – the set of interrelated measures defining the policy and objectives of the employer, and the specific procedures for their achievement. Enterprises employing more than 15 people must employ a safety manager, and a separate safety department is required above 50 employees. NOSTROY holds an online register which should automatically check members' compliance with safety standards. At enterprise level, workers and (or) their union representatives should be allowed in the dedicated commission managing safety. Unions hold rights to inspection (whenever their members are present) and are consulted when the site safety management plan is drafted.

Over the years, experts have pointed out the limitations of state regulation and business practices in explaining obvious failures. The very notion of occupational safety in Russian law is contested. According to the director of the Moscow Institute of Occupational Safety, the terms currently in use are often employed as synonyms but their meanings and implications are contradictory (Fedorets 2017). BT, akin to its international equivalents, pertains to the assumption of reasonable risk in their activities by employers; OT – originating in Soviet legislation – demands a system and set of measures dictated by the state (Fedorets 2017: 15). The overlap between these opposing conceptions results in a number of fallacies. First, there is the excessive normative burden derived from state attempts at preventing every potential hazard. State interventionism interferes with entrepreneurial freedom and ultimately discourages employers from autonomously and conscientiously performing risk assessment. Secondly, there is the overlap between construction and labor ministries' functions. Paradoxically, as they legislate in areas where their inspectorates lack powers, gaps are created. Furthermore, the obligation to incorporate safe systems at design stage means that both inspectors and developers uniquely focus on paperwork while inspectorates do not intervene on site. OT is also said to focus excessively on technical aspects rather than on attitudes, also failing the objectives of International Labour Organization conventions to change local actors' behavior (Ivanova et al. 2011). As for unions, their presence coincides with lower incident rates but their disregard for migrants, the most likely victims of OT failures, undermines their achievements. The greatest obstacle to a safety culture and broader quality improvements derives from informality in the employment relationship, largely tolerated and exploited by all institutional actors (Altman and Morrison 2015). This is the issue to which we now turn our attention.

Case Study: Workers' Accounts of Informal Employment in the Moscow Region

This section explores informal recruitment, employment and work organization, employing key informants' and workers' first-hand accounts. The relationship between institutional failures and poor labor outcomes are well exemplified by the case of Moscow. For 20 years Mayor Yury Luzhkov was the driving force behind the city expansion, guiding Moscow's transformation from gloomy communist capital to glittering center of wealth and restored Russian traditions. However, the inefficiencies generated by his management included devastation of architectural and natural resources and escalating corruption (Vasilyeva, 2009). His removal in 2010, amidst scandals surrounding the transport system collapse, pharaonic building plans and alleged funds embezzlement partially recognize these inefficiencies (Sputniknews 2011). The new Moscow administration has doubled its budget and diverted most of it toward urban renewal, attracting praise for its ambitions, but also criticism for top-down decision-making and lack of transparency (Gershkovich 2018). Its latest project, arguably aimed at better housing politically loyal residents, encompasses the demolition of 10 percent of the old Soviet housing stock and the relocation of approximately 1.5 million people (Smyth 2018). Migrant workers are central to urban development in more ways than one, as the highbrow *Kommersant* reports:

> *the Moscow mayor Sergej Sobjanin has demanded tougher migration policies in the capital; attics and cellars must be searched for illegal migrants. Genuine Muscovites should receive priority access to jobs.*

This is not to say that locals will queue for poorly paid jobs on construction sites. What is clear is where migrants will go if expelled from the city – the suburbs. There, at least there is no talk of squeezing them out. Furthermore, there will always be jobs for them.

> *Even when the builds are completed someone will be needed to clean the streets and mow the lawn.*
>
> (Voskresenskij 2011: 3)

Russian analysts often associate industry flaws with migrant labor. The following section is written from migrant workers' points of view to investigate the relationship between inefficiencies, informality and labor outcomes.

Informal Recruitment and Intermediaries

Most migrants conceptualize their experience as *zarabotka* – leaving one's place of residence temporarily to make a living. They have no specific commitment to the sector or place of work. Research participants were brought to construction by friends or relatives, but all recognize the crucial role played by intermediaries in deciding migrants' employment:

> *To work in another sector you need contacts: everything goes through intermediaries. This is the way it works: there is a brigadier who has long worked in the field. And people know that if you turn to him there's a job awaiting you. It is up to his intelligence and his ability to bargain, whether people go to work with him or not. Wages are also his responsibility.*
>
> (Author interview with Victorio, Kishinev 2012)

Intermediaries can be simple recruiters or be involved in the actual work on site and the size of collectives can vary from a dozen people to a few hundred. Some point out their contribution to stable employment relationships:

> *they are all interested in retaining good relations. Nowadays it is not that common to deceive workers, they are interested in a stable market. They try to obtain residency and work permits. This is in the interest of the employers as well: the intermediary takes responsibility for workers' behavior. This is a decent form of employment relations yet exist as part of the 'shadow' economy.*
>
> (interview with Russian Academy of Science academic, Moscow 2010)

However, the informal nature of these relationships means that they are always open to abuses from above and contestation from below:

> *I have my share of experience with intermediaries! a lot of work to do and no one wants to pay for it!*
>
> (Author interview with Sergei, Transdnistria 2010)

Workers have learned to defend their interests by relying on the solidarity of the collective:

> *One morning we stopped working because of unpaid wages. The brigade leader: 'come on, let's get to work.' Once he failed to pay again, people started to quit.*
>
> (Author interview with Slavic, Moscow 2010)

The lack of institutional bargaining tools means that disputes can rarely be sustained over time and extended beyond small collectives, leaving workers to opt for exit strategies.

Informal Employment: Ethno-national Segregation, Pay and Working Conditions

Migrant workers universally report irregularities in their employment relationship. They appreciate the immediate advantages of working irregularly but denounce employers' insistence on it.

> *In Russia I work without a contract. Even if I had a work permit they employ without contract. the employer finds it inconvenient because of the 30 per cent tax [higher contribution rate for migrant workers]. Those who get citizenship they are on a contract.*
>
> (Author interview with Stas, Moldova 2010)

The more experienced declare their skepticism of formal integration. Dyma, on the scaffolding since he was sixteen, points out:

> *I do not think that a passport makes a difference: Russians too work informally – The firm has no interest having many [employees] formally employed.*
>
> (interviewee, Moldova 2010)

Russians employed by a main contractor voice equally skeptical remarks:

> *I am officially employed, yes, but it's a fraud! We never get holidays and as for sick leave they only allow it in serious cases, which are normally their fault anyway.*
>
> (Author interview with Viktor, Moscow 2010)

Informality allows employers to casualize labor but also forces them into collusion with authorities to avoid hefty fines. Worker respondents confirm the need for protection to avoid migration police raids:

> *When we worked for the administration, they [police] did not bother us. the management would complain to the governor.*
>
> (Author interview with Roman, Moldova 2010)

Pay and working conditions are regulated by custom rather than law and, to an extent, are subject to informal bargaining:

> *we do not get paid holidays: it's the fault of the brigade leader – he could do much more for his brigade.*
>
> (Author interview with Andrei, Moldova 2010)

Conditions vary by size, trade and financial position of each company. Trades are segregated along ethno-national lines and there is an understanding that different jobs belong to specific nationalities.

> *We build multi-storey housing for the army. We take care of the internal finishing; houses are built by a brigade from Chuvashia. The company employs brigades of different nationalities: Byelorussians, Moldovans, and Uzbeks. We [in our brigade] are all Moldovans.*
>
> (Author interview with Viorel, Moldova 2012)

Discrimination in pay and conditions exists according to citizenship, nationality and place of residence. Respondents often report that Russians enjoy a privileged position including higher pay, formal employment, holidays and welfare entitlements:

The Russians I work with get higher wages; they are specialists with seniority records.

(Author interview with Fedor, Moldova 2012)

Slavic migrants depend on piece-rates and skills progression in order to improve their earnings, but they normally struggle to gain formal employment and therefore are always exposed to wage non-payments and summary dismissal:

Qualified workers leave – why is that? Wage arrears: you can't even get what you earned!

(Author interview with Slavik, Moscow 2011)

Asian workers earn a fraction of the standard wage:

Asians work with Asians. I saw it myself that they are paid less. They work less effectively. Sometimes they do not lack skills just documents. It is their own compatriots that cheat them.

(Author interview with Vitya, Moscow 2010)

This is not to say that networks are conveyor belts leaving workers with no choice. Individual strategies can aim at either advancing toward better employers or progressing in the recruitment chain. Career paths have proved fluid as new waves of different nationalities join the labor market. Migrants seek higher qualifications and on-the-job skills enhancement to raise their job-market prospects. Workers' accounts record high demand for qualified and conscientious workers but no reference to employers' training and retention policies. Segregation, the lack of job security and seniority progression stimulate high turnover, affecting skills retention and productivity gains.

The Informal Workplace: Labor Collective, Informal Bargaining and Absent Unions

Individualized relations, based on personal loyalty and experience, extend to work organization. Management retains typical Soviet characteristics such as worker's relative autonomy and paternalistic control. A Russian brigade leader explains:

The brigade leader is on site but the site manager is another job. The construction firm has its own manager and (down the hierarchy) a superintendent, a foreman. They have their own functions. The foreman checks the work and reports back to the brigade leader about the whole site. The foreman (also) orders supplies – I tell him if something is needed. The superintendent deals with the supply of concrete, he checks the quality of the concrete. The brigade leader seeks work (for team members). In each brigade there are several teams. I answer for the casing. We have like communism or socialism: we come together and decide everything collectively. The brigade leader pays off wages. The enterprise documentation shows something else.

(Vitya, Moscow 2010)

This organization reflects state-dependent enterprises' tendency to retain or revive Soviet practices (Kosals and Izyumov 2011). Other accounts detail its key features (casual supervision, rush to deadlines, informal bargaining) and confirm their popularity:

The job is always the same there is nothing to control. They come and check once a week. The brigade leader is one of us [Moldovan] the superintendent is local. The BL organize the work: he is not too strict but he pressures us. If we fall behind with the plan he shouts: "faster! Let's finish this month!" We do not get paid holidays: it's the fault of the brigade leader – he could do much more for his brigade.

(Andrei, Moldova 2010)

Segregated national teams rely on cultural homogeneity and brigadier' management skills to sustain cooperation and boost performance. Less common multinational collectives can fare equally well, among qualified and motivated workers, relying on Soviet-time commonalities and working class camaraderie. In both cases, there is clear evidence of competitive pressure on local workers.

Workplace relations are governed by informal, individualized practices. Unions remain absent and hostile toward migrants. In 2019, they advised the Ministry of Labor to introduce a 60 percent quota for enterprise-level migrant employment *'to make room for Russians'* (Builders' Federation of Russia 2019b). Participants display a wide range of views on collective struggles, but significantly none embraces an ideological rejection of unions as socialist institutions. Nonetheless, they are conscious of unions' unwillingness or inability to represent them.

Unions should defend workers' rights but I've never seen that. Strikes are more realistic propositions.

(Author interview with Victorio, Moldova 2011)

At the old factory I joined the union to get children holidays vouchers. Now why? Everybody knows they don't work. If employers don't pay the brigade will stop working. I am against protests. They may work abroad, not here. Legal channels don't work either.

(Vitya, Moscow 2010)

The older workers associate unions with traditional socialist service functions while the youngest participants have hardly heard of them. Experienced migrants denounce official unions' poor performance in the FSU and in some cases contrast them with western European counterparts. Workers' accounts also highlight the limitations of the labor collective as a bargaining tool. Once its potential is exhausted, migrants resort to individual actions which generally result in further mobility.

Occupational Safety

In Soviet-times workers' relative autonomy implied responsibility for achieving targets with poor materials and equipment to strict deadlines. This encouraged managers and workers to violate procedures and technical specifications leading to hazardous work practices. Lengthy shifts and disregard for health and safety are still universally reported by respondents.

> *Yes, it is heavy and dangerous work, when we work at height. [Safety equipment] gets in the way of working; there were [fatal incidents], people fell off; here they do not check: you have drunks at work; in four years two died: a guy just arrived, no induction, fell and crashed to the ground. Minor injuries are more frequent: often something falls on your head, leg or hand; [the protection helmet] is uncomfortable, falls down all the time.*
>
> (Viktor, Moscow 2010)

The segregation of the workforce has worsened this predicament. If Russian internal migrants are subjected to hazardous work, other groups fare worse.

> *Moldovans are in charge of removing asperities from reinforced concrete structures once we cast them. It is a dirty and unhealthy job because of the dust. They use no protection but it's their problem, they don't value their health as we do.*
>
> (Vitya, Moscow 2010)

> *We heard that Russians hate Tajiks and Kirgiz, not Moldovans. They work as slaves in Moscow. They work twelve/thirteen hours a day – we could not keep up with them despite the equipment and they had just shovels – still they hate them.*
>
> (Author interview with Gregory, Moldova 2010)

Disregard for safety prevailed in the Soviet-type labor process; casualization and segregation has reinforced this behavior. The declining educational and sector-specific background of most migrants, alongside the rapid change in product and equipment typology has exacerbated safety risks. Well-structured collectives and individual skill-enhancement strategies do counter these risks but workers' experience is squandered by high turnover and lack of managerial support.

Summary and Conclusions

The Russian construction industry has endured multiple economic crises and restructuring during the last three decades, emerging as a major employer with a dynamic private sector. Post-transition recovery has been followed by sustained growth in the first decade of the 21st century. The industry has weathered well through the 2008 global financial crisis, partly thanks to state support, less so after 2014/2015 when hit by the unfavorable conjuncture which followed the Ukrainian conflict and Western sanctions. Small- to medium-sized companies aimed at the residential market have proliferated thanks to liberalization in the 1990s. More recently, an institutional framework has developed around state-sponsored self-regulated business federations and tripartite social dialog. High employment levels have provided migrant workers with a relatively high source of income and, to an extent, with skills-enhancement and career-progression opportunities.

This notwithstanding, the industry has developed structural imbalances and suffers from the general shortcomings of Russian political economy. Privatization has depleted its civil engineering capacity and pool of qualified personnel. Self-regulation has bypassed at least half of small- to medium-sized firms with serious consequences for the quality and safety of their operations. Most employers focus on short-term objectives and operate under the aegis of informality. There is little appetite for HRM strategies aimed at training and retaining qualified staff and, as a result, vocational education has languished. The government's traditional approach to regulation has reduced safety and responsibility to a bureaucratic procedure. It is only lately that government policy has been re-oriented toward creating a positive environment to stimulate corporate innovation.

Labor, specifically migrant workers, has borne the brunt of these flaws, enduring abuse at the hand of managers and intermediaries, informal employment and with appalling safety records. The labor market is effectively segmented, enforcing differential treatment according to ethno-national and skills characteristics. Official trade unions, for their part, remain unwilling or unable to act beyond the narrow confines of government-designated activities in large companies. Workers as a result are left to their own devices to carry out collective bargaining and design individual career trajectories. While industry leaders and experts question the informal employment of unskilled migrants, the general attitude of institutional actors suggests that no autonomous interventions should be expected in this area other than minimizing the ill effects of informality. Workers' protests and the diminished assistance from migrant recruitment pools are the most likely factors which may force medium-term policy changes.

References

Altman, Y., Morrison, C., 2015. Informal economic relations and organisations: everyday organisational life in Soviet and post-Soviet economies. *Journal of Organizational Change Management 28* (5), 749–769.

Andreeva, T., Festing, M., Minbaeva, D. B., Muratbekova-Touron, M., 2014. The Janus Faces of IHRM in Russian MNEs. *Human Resource Management 53* (6), 967–986.

Barsukova, S. (Ed.), 2015. *Esse o Neformal'noj Jekonomike, ili 16 Ottenkov Serogo* [Essay on the informal economy, or 16 Shades of Grey]. Higher School of Economics, Moscow.

Bashkatova, A., 2010. 'Stroitel'stvo spolzaet k kollapsu' [Construction draws near collapse], *Nezavisimaya Gazeta*, 08.02.2010.

Biryuleva, D. K., 2010. Podgotovka kadrov kak osnova samoregulirovaniya v stroitelnoj otrasli [cadre training as basis for self-regulation in construction]. *Upravlenie Ekomicheskimi Sistemami 3* (12).

Bizyukov P., 2018. Labor Protests in Post-Soviet Russia. *Conference Paper, BUIRA 2018: The return of politics to employment relations*, London: Middlesex University, 27–29 June.

Bondarenko, N., 2010. Osobennosti kadrovoj politiki "krizisnogo perioda. 2008–2010' [specificities Train. policy crisis years], *Vestn. Obshestvennogo Mneniya 4* (106), 73–90.

Builders' Federation of Russia, 2019a. *Our History.* STROP, Moscow.

Builders' Federation of Russia, 2019b. [quota of foreign labor force reduced to 80%], *'Dolya inostrannoj rabochej sily snizhena do 80%'.* STROP, Moscow.

Butrin, D., Shapovalov, A., 2011. *Stroiteli pokazali nematerial'nyj rost* [construction gave signs of intangible growth], *Kommersant*, 18/08/2011.

Chindyaskina, Y. U, 2018. 'U stroitelej razygralsya kadrovyj golod' [developers feel skill shortages], *Kommersant. Ekonomicheskij Forum*, 24.05.2018.

Christensen, P. T., 2017. 'Labor under Putin: the state of the Russian working class. *New Labor. Forum 26* (1), 64–73.

Chudinovskikh, O., Denisenko, M., 2017. *Russia: a Migration System with Soviet Roots.* Migration Policy Institute, Moscow.

Croucher, R., Morrison, C., 2012. Management, worker responses and an enterprise trade union in transition. *Industrial relations: a Journal of Economy and Society 51* (S1), 583–604.

Danilova, E., Jadov, V. A., Davjej, P. (Eds.), 2012. *Rossijane i Kitajcy v Epohu Peremen: Sravnitel'noe Issledovanie v Sankt-Peterburge i Shanhae Nachala XXI Veka* [Russians and the Chinese in an Epoch of Change: A Comparative Study in St Petersburg and Shanghai at the Beginning of the 21st Century]. Logos, Moscow.

Fedorets, A., 2017. 'Aktualnye problemy pravavogo regulirovaniya. "Ohrana Truda" protiv "bezopasnosti stroitelnogo proizvodsta" [current problems in

legal regulation. Labor protection versus occupational safety in construction].
Zhurnal Glavnogo Inzhenera 12 (December), 11–18.

Gershkovich, E., 2018. Sergei Sobyanin, Moscow's high priest of urban renewal, is biding his time. *The Moscow Times*: 06/09/2018.

Gimpelson, V., Kapeljushnikov, R. (Eds.), 2014. *V Teni Regulirovanija. Neformalnost na Rossijskom Rynke Truda* [In the Shade of Regulation. Informality in the Russian Labor Market]. Higher School of Economics, Moscow.

Gosnadzor, 2019. *Gosudarstvennyj Stroitelnyj Nadzor* [State construction inspectorate]. Gosnadzor, Moscow.

Hanin, G. I., 2012. *Ekonomicheskaya Istoriya Rossii v Novejshee Vremya. Tom 3* [Contemporary history of Russia. Vol. 3]. NGTU, Novosibirsk.

Human Rights Watch, 2009. *'Are You Happy to Cheat Us?' – Exploitation of Migrant Construction Workers in Russia*. HRW, New York.

IOM, 2017. *World Migration Report 2018*. IOM, Geneva.

Ilchenko, N., 2001. 'Sozdanie i vossozdanie profsoyuznyh organizacij v stroitelnom komplekse Moskvy' [formation and re-constritution of trade union organizations in the Moscow construction complex]. In: Borisov, V., Clarke, S. (Eds.), *Profsoyuznoe Prostranstvo Sovremennoj Rossii* [Trade Unions Landscape in Contemporary Russia]. ISITO, Moscow, pp. 281–300.

Ivanova, Z. I., Kofanov, A. V., Druzhinin, A. M., 2011. *Socialnye Problemy Stroitelnogo Kompleksa* [Social problems of the construction industry]. RF Education Ministry/Moscow Construction University, Moscow.

Kalsin, A., 2010. 'Kollektivnyj dogovor i lokalnye normativnye akty ob ohrane truda v stroitelstve' [collective agreement and local norms concerning labor protection in construction]. *Tr. i Socialnye Otnosheniya 8*, 145–150.

Karabchuk, T., Zabirova, A., 2018. Informal employment in service industries: estimations from nationally representative Labor Force Survey data of Russian Federation. *Service Industries Journal 38* (11/12), 742–771.

Kosals, L., Izyumov, A., 2011. The Russian defence industry confronts the market: findings of a longitudinal study. *Europe-Asia Studies 63* (5), 733–756.

Krzywdzinski, M., 2018. *Consent and Control in the Authoritarian Workplace: Russia and China Compared*. Oxford University Press, Oxford.

MinTrud, 2018. *Gosudarstvennaya programma Rossijskoj Federacii 'Bezopasnyj Trud' na 2018–2025* [Russian Federation state programme 'Safe Work'], RF Government Act n. 363: 30.03.2018.

Mitra, P., Selowsky, M., Zalduendo, J., 2010. *Turmoil at Twenty: recession, recovery, and reform in Central and Eastern Europe and the former Soviet Union*. World Bank, Washington DC.

Morris, J., Hinz, S., 2017. Free automotive unions, industrial work and precariousness in provincial Russia. *Post-Communist Economies 29* (3), 282–296.

Morrison, C., Bizyukov, P., 2017. Informal and uncertain: employment relations though the broken mirror of Russian social sciences. *Work, Employment and Society 31* (3), 553–559.

Morrison, C., Sacchetto, D., Cretu, O., 2013. International migration and labor turnover: worker's agency in the construction sector in Russia and Italy. *Studies of Transitional. Societies 5* (2), 7–20.

Morrison, C., Sacchetto, D., Croucher, R., 2020. Migration, ethnicity and solidarity: 'multinational workers' in the former Soviet Union, *British Journal of Industrial Relations*, 1–24: doi:10.1111/bjir.12518.

Moscow Builders' Trade Union, 2019. *The Union Supports Law and Order*. PSM: 06.08.2019.

Mukomel, V. (Ed.), 2014. *Migranty, Migrantofobii i Migracionnaja Politika* [Migrants, Migrantophobia and Migration Policies]. Academia, Moscow.

Naumov, I., Sergeev, M., 2011. 'Stroitel'nyj krizis ne otpuskaet Rossiyu' [The construction crisis does not spare Russia], *Nezavisimaya Gazeta*, 16.06.2011.

NOSTROY, 2019. *About the Union*. NOSTROY, Moscow.

Privalov, O., 2014. 'Vechnaya borba' [Endless struggle], *Kommersant "Stroitel"*, 07.08.2014.

Privalov, O., 2017. 'Beskonechnaya istoriya. Samoregulirovanie' [never-ending story. Self-regulation], *Kommersant 'Stroitel'*, 10.08.2017.

Privalov, O., 2018. 'Utolit legkij kadrovyj golod' [quenching skills shortages], *Kommersant 'Stroitel'*, 09.08.2018.

RossStat, 2017. *Russia in Figures*. RossStat, Moscow.

RossStat, 2018. *Statistical Review* (vol. 2). RossStat, Moscow, (101).

RossStat, 2019. *Proizvodstvennyj Travmatizm v Rossii v 2018* [Occupational incidents in Russia in 2018]. RossStat, Moscow.

RosTrud, 2019. *Open labor inspection*, Moscow: RosTrud.

Rudenko, A., 2011. 'Socialnaya adaptaziya trudovyh migrantov v stroitelnoj otrasli Sankt-Peterburga [social adaptation of labor migrants in St. Petersburg construction sector]. *Zhurnal Soziologii i Sozialnoj Antropologii* 14 (4), 86–104.

Russian Federation of Builders, 2019. *About the Federation*. OMOR/RSS, Moscow.

Schwartz, G., 2004. Core periphery of the 'collective': labour segmentation in the Russian industrial enterprise. *Industrial Relations Journal* 35 (3), 271–285.

Shmeleva, E., 2009. 'Stroiteli zhdut deneg. Gosudarstvennaya pomosh' idet slishkom medlenno, [builders expect money. State support is coming in too slowly], *Rossijskaya Gazeta*, 29.05.09.

Sippola, M., 2016. Dancing to the tune of the employer? Union-management relationships at Nordic subsidiaries in Russia. *Economic and Industrial Democracy*, 40 (4), 913–931.

Smyth, R., 2018. How the Kremlin is using the Moscow renovation project to reward and punish voters. *PONARS Eurasia 513*, 1–5.

Sputniknews, 2011. *Rampant corruption among reasons for firing Luzhkov, presidential administration says, Sputnik Russia*, 26.10.11.

Sto Nostroy, 2019. *Sistemy Upravleniya Ohrany Truda v Stroitelnyh Organicaziyah* [Labor Protection Management systems for construction organizations]. Nostroy, Moscow.

Vasilyeva, N., 2009. Russia: Roads Perfect Example of Moscow Corruption, *The Associated Press*: 9/09/2009.

Vinogradova, E., Kozina, I., Cook, L. J., 2015. Labor relations in Russia: moving to a "MarketSocial Contract"?. *Problems of Post-Communism* 62 (4), 193–203.

Voskresenskij, A., 2011. 'Strojki mchatsya iz Moskvy. Pochemu developery pereezzhayut za MKAD' [Building moves out of Moscow. Why developers move beyond the Moscow Ring Road], *Kommersant 'Dengi'*, 14.03.2011.

White, A., 2009. Internal migration, identity and livelihood strategies in contemporary Russia. *Journal of Ethnic and Migration Studies 35* (4), 555–573.

Zyryanova, M., 2012. 'Kadrovyj vopros reshat samostayatelno' [self-made solution to skills shortages], *Kommersant 'Stroitel'*, 09.08.2012.

9 Sustaining 'High Road' Employment Relations in the Swedish and Danish Construction Industries

Jens Arnholtz and Christian Lyhne Ibsen

Introduction

The construction sectors in Denmark and Sweden have historically followed the Nordic 'high road' of coordinated market economies by combining high educational levels, high-quality production, high productivity and high wage levels at par or even higher than the economy in general (Druker et al. 1996). Undergirding this 'high road' approach has been the presence of strong trade unions and employers' associations that bargain collective agreements for most of construction. In Sweden, trade union density in construction was around 65 percent in 2016 (LO/Sweden 2015), whereas in Denmark it was around 70 percent in 2010 (Toubøl et al. 2015).

We depart from Wolfgang Streeck's arguments about 'beneficial constraints' (Sorge and Streeck 1988; Streeck 1991) to understand how the 'high road' was made possible. The idea behind 'beneficial constraints' is essentially that companies are forced to become more productive and/or quality focused due to regulatory constraints. This is because constraints increase factor input costs and companies therefore need to improve their products and services – to increase prices and/or improve productivity – to offset labor cost increases to achieve the same level of profitability. But following such a high road has been more of a balancing act than a stable equilibrium and this involves a constant negotiation and coordination of flexibility, skill development, productivity and decent labor standards among the social partners. Although this negotiated coordination is based on a mutual recognition between social partners, it also involves real dilemmas. How can productivity development be maintained at a level that will allow wages to progress in parallel to those of the exporting manufacturing sector? How can the stable supply of skilled labor be secured? What is the right balance between the flexibility employers want to accommodate market fluctuations and the labor standards that workers want to protect themselves from the very same fluctuations? Despite these dilemmas, the sheltered nature of the sector has implied that the social partners have predominantly had to solve these dilemmas among themselves. With high collective agreement coverage, high organizational density and an institutionalized system of pattern bargaining, there have been few exit options for employers who are dissatisfied.

In recent years, however, an alternative to the 'high road' negotiated coordination has emerged, offering different options to employers in both countries. With the eastwards enlargement of the European Union (EU) in 2004, an increasing number of mobile workers and companies from the new member states have entered both countries' construction sectors (Arnholtz and Andersen 2016). Labor cost differences allow eastern European subcontractors to employ business strategies based on lower labor costs, whereas Danish and Swedish employers have gained the option of hiring unorganized workers with lower expectations regarding wages and labor standards. Although employers in both the countries have been hesitant about taking up these new options, their very existence has put trade unions on high alert. Not least because of the Laval ruling in 2007 by the European Court of Justice (ECJ), which made industrial action against foreign contractors much more cumbersome for trade unions in Denmark and Sweden (Arnholtz 2014).

As such, subcontractors and labor migration from the newer EU member states have constituted the main challenge in both the countries' construction sectors – and this to an extent where the debates about 'social dumping' overshadow the need for continuous negotiated coordination. In other words, the classical problems addressed by negotiated coordination have been replaced by more contentious conflicts about which road to follow and how to govern the sector in general. Owing to different bargaining systems and strategies, construction social partners in the two countries have chosen different ways of dealing with migrant labor and social dumping (Ibsen and Thelen 2017).

This chapter compares and discusses how the specific bargaining relations in the two countries have produced these differences and how these differences might affect the future ability of social partners to sustain a 'high road' approach to employment relations in construction. We conclude that the 'high road' balance still exists and and – while approaches differ – is relatively robust in both countries owing to the continued efforts of social partners to retain a highly regulated sector, a relatively generous welfare state that keeps reservation wages high, and the current economic recovery, which has increased demand for labor.

Construction in Denmark and Sweden

The construction sectors in Denmark and Sweden continue to be important, accounting for around six percent of both total employment and total economic output in 2014 (OECD 2017). The sector is divided between large contractors and a myriad of smaller subcontractors. The Swedish industry used to be concentrated in larger companies than were found in Denmark, but this difference has gradually become negligible in recent decades. In Sweden, employment has seen an almost continuous growth for two decades. Over the last 20 years, employment has increased by more than 60 percent. In Denmark, employment in construction increased by close to 35 percent for 1994–2007, but then declined again as the economic crisis hit. At present, employment in Danish construction has grown once again, but the employment expansion is still far behind that of Sweden.

In both countries, construction work is still highly male dominated. Around ten percent of the construction workforce are women, and this share has been stable during recent decades (Statistics Denmark 2019; Statistics Sweden 2019). This general share, however, conceals important occupational differences. For example, in Denmark 30 percent of painters are women compared to only four percent of masons (Statistics Denmark 2019).

The share of reported self-employment has been slightly decreasing in recent years in both countries. Just under ten percent are self-employed in Denmark, whereas the share is under eight percent in Sweden. Although information on the share of bogus self-employment is not available in national accounts, anecdotal evidence suggests that this is still not as major an issue in Denmark and Sweden as it is in Anglo-Saxon countries (see chapters 10 and 11 in this volume). One reason for the low incidence of misclassification is the union presence on construction sites, with unions making sure that employers are identified when appropriate. However, as we show below, the use of posted and migrant workers in residential construction constitutes a challenge that has parallels with the issue of bogus self-employment.

In both Sweden and Denmark, the construction sector is divided between construction, civil engineering and specialized construction work. The last category is by far the largest in terms of both employment and turnover, with approximately 70 percent of employment and 50 percent of turnover in the sector coming from specialized construction. In both countries this is the labor-intensive part of the sector, where a majority of the workers have a vocational and technical education, whereas construction and civil engineering are more capital intensive and often rely on a combination of high-skilled engineers and unskilled labor. Specialized construction work is mostly – but not exclusively – residential, whereas civil engineering is mostly non-residential.

In terms of value added per hour, the Swedish and Danish construction industries are among the most productive in Europe (see Figure 9.1). Despite the economic slump since 2008, labor costs have increased steadily in both countries over the last two decades. However, the productivity level is far from stable. In Sweden, value added per hour has dropped substantially in the period after 2006, whereas there is an increase in Denmark.

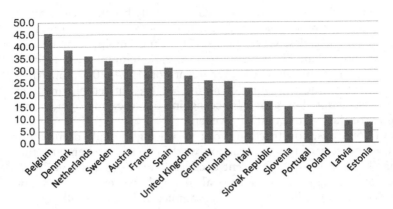

Figure 9.1 Added value per hour in construction (Euro, 2015).
Source: Authors' calculation based on OECD STAN data.

Although the construction sectors of both Denmark and Sweden are subject to the same structural conditions as in other countries – such as a high share of small companies with a high turnover rate, a strong reliance on subcontractors and volatile demand – the overall performance of the sector is more stable. In the following section, some of the institutional foundations of this stability are explained. We then go on to consider the particular challenges that labor migration and subcontracting are posing for the Nordic 'high road' in construction.

Danish and Swedish Construction – Cases of the Nordic 'High Road'

In many countries fragmentation, bogus self-employment, unskilled workers and low wages mark the construction sector (see Chapter 1, in this volume). By contrast, the Nordic countries boast highly organized construction sectors, with well-educated and highly organized workforces, multi-employer collective bargaining and relatively high wages. It might be assumed that substantial state regulation was the cause of this well-regulated situation, but Danish and Swedish labor markets are in fact mainly regulated through collective agreements rather than statutory laws. These collective agreements are negotiated between trade unions and employers' associations on behalf of their respective members. The basic premise of these agreements is that workers respect employers' right to manage and refrain from engaging in strikes for as long as the collective agreement lasts. In exchange, employers abide by the labor standards set out in the agreements. These include wage levels and working time but also standards set on other issues. In the absence of a collective agreement, trade unions have the right to take collective action to force employers to sign one. In both countries trade unions can even engage in collective action against companies in which they have no members. Furthermore, they can call on the sympathy action of other trade unions to make the industrial action more effective. In other words, trade unions have substantial power resources and can use them if there is no collective agreement. During conflicts, both parties can suffer considerable losses and for this very reason both parties have strong economic interests in maintaining industrial peace.

Moreover, the well-regulated nature of the Swedish and Danish construction sectors rests on an institutionalization of this balance of power between workers and employers which promotes cooperation and compromise. First, as the social partners are directly involved in shaping labor market regulation through collective bargaining and tripartite negotiations, they will seldom challenge or disavow these rules. This implies that both workers and employers will typically support the legitimacy of the rules and take on responsibility for their enforcement on a day-to-day basis. If they are unhappy with specific rules, they will bring this issue to the negotiation table rather than circumventing the rules. Second, the collective agreements always have an inbuilt temporal limit (typically two to three years), which implies that the partners know that they will have to find new compromises in the future. Unlike the political arena, where labor regulation can be subjected to 'winner-takes-all' politics, the Swedish and Danish models are based on an acknowledgment that compromises are continuously required. Third, as the models partially serve to take wages out of competition through high collective agreement coverage rates, the system promotes cooperation between workers and employers when it comes to productivity development.

Although the systems have many benefits, they are also based on self-governance and, to deliver results that are acceptable to both workers and employers, the systems need to be based on a balance of power. In particular, trade unions have to be very strong to uphold these systems by forcing individual companies to sign collective agreements. If trade unions are unable to do so, employers will start to defect in applying the terms of the collective agreement or covered companies will lose out in competition with companies not covered by these agreements. Collective agreement coverage has never been 100 percent in either country, but the standards set by collective agreements typically set the pattern for companies that are not covered. What is important, however, is that trade unions represent a creditable threat to companies that stray too far from the standards set by the collective agreements. Thus, the threat of industrial action is crucial for upholding the extent of bargaining coverage and attempts to limit the scope for industrial action is accordingly 'poison' for Danish and Swedish construction unions – a theme we will return to in the sections below.

The Role of the Unemployment Benefit System

There are several institutions that underpin the 'high road' in construction of the two Nordic construction sectors. One is the unemployment benefit system in Denmark and Sweden, which has traditionally helped support workers' bargaining strength. First, both countries have union-led, state-supported unemployment funds, usually labeled as Ghent systems (Kjellberg and Ibsen 2016). In countries with non-mandatory union membership, unionization is subject to free-rider problems when the public goods produced by trade unions – for example, collective agreements – can be enjoyed at no extra cost and with no exclusivity by non-members. The Ghent system ameliorates this problem by providing a selective incentive (a benefit only members get) in the form of unemployment insurance when union and unemployment fund membership are considered as a package deal (Due and Madsen 2006). In construction, employment is seasonal and subject to repeated short spells of unemployment. Having the Ghent-system therefore provides an additional benefit for unions in construction. For decades it sustained high union density during economic cycles and structural changes in the labor market. Second, both countries historically had relatively high net replacement rates for the unemployed. Among the provisions of the Scandinavian welfare state are generous unemployment benefits which tend to ward off the creation of a low-wage sector by pushing up reservation wages (i.e. the wage level under which workers will not accept a job). Thus, employers not only confront strong trade unions in wage setting but also an unemployment benefit system that precludes certain wage levels.

As Kjellberg and Ibsen (2016) have indicated, recent changes to the unemployment benefit system have challenged construction unions, both on the recruitment and retention of union members and the reservation wage. In Sweden, the attack on union organizing involved an increase in unemployment insurance costs whereby fund fees were raised considerably in January 2007 and from July 2008 were more tightly aligned with the risk of unemployment. The introduction of differentiated fund fees then caused a very dissimilar development of union density among blue-collar workers compared to white-collar workers due to the considerably higher rate of unemployment among the former. By reducing the incentive to join unemployment insurance funds, the incentive to join unions also diminished and union densities fell dramatically. Between 2006 and 2010, union density in construction fell from 79 to 70 percent. This decline has continued and construction union density was down to 61.8 percent in 2018 (Kjellberg 2019).

In Denmark, the attack came in a different way. In 2002, the government abolished the traditional requirement for employees to join unemployment insurance funds within their occupations. By allowing cross-occupational funds to tap into the hitherto occupational mono-polies of the traditional unemployment insurance funds, a new market for unemployment insurance – and thus, an alternative to union-administered funds – was created. Consequently, cross-occupational un-employment funds offered membership of wage-earner organizations that are not party to collective agreements and therefore can offer low-cost memberships. These organizations are often called 'yellow unions' because they often do not support the use of industrial action. The blue-collar unions, related to *Landsorganisationen i Danmark* (LO), the Danish Confederation of Trade unions, were hit especially hard by the competi-tion, worsening the existing decline resulting from structural changes in the labor market. In 1995 LO-related construction unions organized between 77 and 81 percent of construction workers. By 2012, this share was down to 61 percent. By contrast, the alternative 'yellow' unions went from es-sentially having no members in construction to organizing 10 percent of construction workers (Toubøl et al. 2015: 68). To make matters worse, young workers are more prone to choose yellow unions.

Similarly, the generosity of unemployment benefits has been under attack, while still being far above Anglo-Saxon countries (see Figure 9.2). In Sweden, net replacement rates declined from 2002 through until 2014 when the Social Democratic government took office and provided more

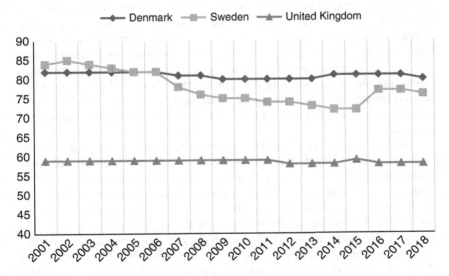

Figure 9.2 Net replacement rates in unemployment. Denmark, Sweden and United Kingdom 2001–2018.
Source: Authors' calculation based on OECD.
Notes: Rates for couple with two children and partners earning average wage. Duration of unemployment two months and previous in-work earning was average wage. Does not include housing benefits.

generous benefits. The Danish replacement rate also dropped slightly, which has to do with a specific regulation that entails a small deduction in the yearly benefit increase if wages increase more than two percent. This deduction can be a maximum of 0.3 percent. The deducted increase goes to labor market policy initiatives. However, in Denmark, the maximum duration of unemployment benefits was halved to two years in 2010, which threatened thousands of long-term unemployed with losing unemployment benefits altogether. In both the countries the reforms had the effect of decreasing the attractiveness of unemployment insurance and weakening income protection, the latter most likely having a depressing effect on reservation wages.

The Role of Apprenticeships for High Road Construction Work

A second important institution underpinning the Nordic 'high road' is the vocational education and training (VET) system. In both Denmark and Sweden, vocational training takes place at the upper secondary level of the educational system. The systems generally differ with Denmark having a much stronger involvement of employers through apprenticeships, whereas Sweden opted for a school-based model that dates from the 1960s. In Sweden VET students obtain allowances from the state for the entire duration of their education, whereas Danish VET students are hired and paid as apprentices. However, in Sweden there is a strong apprenticeship component in construction VET systems specifically. In both countries social partners are heavily involved in education and training standards, approving companies for training and attracting young people to the building and construction trades. This inclusion of employers and trade unions generally supports a smooth transition from education into employment, but also secures a recruitment channel for trade unions.

The first year in Swedish VET is almost exclusively spent at the vocational school within the specific program. In the second and third years, students choose a specialism and alternate between two to three days a week at school attending theoretical classes, and two to three days at the company. The main route to becoming a construction worker in Sweden with a professional certificate is through upper secondary vocational education in the profession followed by a mandatory apprenticeship, as a paid employee. Together, it requires 6,800 hours, including 2,800 hours credited by finishing upper secondary school. The 2,800 hours is noted in an education e-book that is provided by the Swedish Construction Industry Training Board (SCITB) and describes eight categories of main tasks in the construction industry. Another important document details goals specified by the SCITB, which comprises 64 competencies that a worker with a professional certificate should possess. Thus, the pathway to become a construction worker is based on 'serving time' as an apprentice and the development of vocational competences follows a five-stage system, with pay increasing as the amount of time served increases and experience grows (with presumed increase in competence). By spending time at a workplace and documenting the hours in an education book, they finally reach the 6,800 hours required for a professional certificate. Consequently, the opportunities to develop competences depend on the workplaces' ability to educate (i.e. provide tasks that foster development of the 64 competences described by the SCITB), subject to an agreement between the construction companies and the Swedish Building Workers' Union. Each apprentice receives wages based on his/her productivity (rate of work) and five incremental increases with time served, from 50 to 88 percent of the wages of a fully paid worker with a professional certificate.

Denmark has a dual-track upper secondary education system. It is divided into a track for education that qualifies students for access to higher education and a track for vocational or technical education that qualifies students for entrance to the professional labor market (Helms Jørgensen 2013). Education for most construction specialties normally takes four years to complete. The first 20–40 weeks consists of a basic course, although it is possible for adult learners (aged 25 years and above) to be exempted from this basic level. Upon completion of the basic course, the students are obliged to secure employment as an apprentice with a training company or, if they are not able to do so, apply for a limited number of school-based training programs. For about three and a half years education alternates between periods at school and more extensive periods of on-the-job training in a company. During the main part of the education, the student/apprentice works with a company as an employee and receives a salary, which they are also paid while they attend school. Upon completion of vocational education, success in the final examinations results in the issuing of a vocational work certificate and the student is thereafter a certified tradesperson. In construction, the Advisory Board for Education and Training for the Building and Construction Industry coordinates nine trade committees with parity representation from employers' associations and trade unions. The different specialties are constantly being revised and updated in the light of changes to skills demand.

Although more reliant on company-level training than the Swedish system, the Danish VET system does receive support from the State. The training companies are economically compensated for the school-based periods through the Employers' Reimbursement System. In recent years, getting apprenticeship placements has become a problem, albeit less so in construction than in other areas. Sometimes, apprenticeships are 'patchwork' solutions between multiple companies that together fulfil the requirements. In response, the social partners and the state have reformed the employers' reimbursement system to incentivize more firms to take apprentices.

Denmark is praised for the way in which the VET system provides opportunities for working class labor market entrants and ensures a very smooth school-to-work transition, as reflected for example in the very low youth unemployment rates in the country. However, the system has also been criticized for stratifying educational opportunities (and with that, subsequent employment prospects) along class lines, as students are sorted early on into either a vocational or an academic track with low permeability between the two. The Swedish emphasis on uniform educational opportunities is often credited for internationally low levels of educational inequality and for providing high-quality general education at the upper secondary level to all students regardless of class background. Moreover, the porous line between academic and vocational tracks has produced relatively high levels of tertiary education – another potential plus in the future economy. Yet Sweden's more school-based training has also been criticized, above all, for the lack of a tight connection between the content of training and the needs of firms, making for an overall more difficult school-to-work transition. Thus, youth unemployment has been a persistent problem in the Swedish labor market. To some extent, Swedish construction is an outlier in Sweden with its traditional use of workplace-based learning and tighter connection to employers through apprenticeships. However, compared to the Danish system, the Swedish construction programs use less workplace-based training through apprenticeships.

Collective Bargaining and Wages

A third institutional pillar of the Nordic 'high road' is, as already mentioned, the collective bargaining system. The 1980s and 1990s were times of major changes to collective bargaining in Denmark and Sweden. Before the 1980s, the bargaining of wage increases and general terms and conditions took place at the national level between peak level confederations of labor and employers, ensuring a high degree of wage compression and wage moderation. In the 1970s and 1980s, employers (and some skilled workers' unions) responded to the economic crises and increased international competition with calls for more flexibility. These calls led to a dismantling of peak-level bargaining, which was replaced with industry-level bargaining and framework agreements on wages that allowed substantial wage differentiation at the company level (Due et al. 1994; Kjellberg 2009). Some commentators proposed that industry-level bargaining entailed a risk of spiraling wages if unions and employers in sheltered sectors, like construction, agreed on higher wages than manufacturing because they could pass on costs to consumers. Other commentators proposed that coordination across industries could be achieved through pattern-bargaining around agreement in manufacturing. Finally, some commentators feared that decentralization of wage bargaining to the company level would increase wage inequality because employers would differentiate on skills and productivity levels or even discriminate against workers based on personal preferences (Ibsen and Stamhus 1993; Iversen and Wren 1998). A tighter relation between wage increases and productivity developments might also spur increasing inequality because industries differ widely in the latter.

The collective bargaining systems that ensued in both countries from the 1980s to 1990s managed to strike a balance between wage flexibility, wage moderation and wage inequality (Ibsen 2016). Multi-employer agreements allow substantial wage differentiation at the company level, but local shop stewards negotiate with management to ensure constraints on differentiation. Multi-employer agreements establish minimum wage levels under which local bargaining levels cannot fall. This ensures that wages are still relatively compressed. Finally, across industries labor cost increases are more or less in line with increases in manufacturing which sets the pattern (Ibsen 2016). This ensures that other industries either hold the line or keep up with manufacturing. In the case of construction, the fear was that construction workers would achieve wage levels that were too high because of the industry's sheltered nature.

The concerns about construction workers' wages outpacing manufacturing wages due to its sheltered nature have, however, proven unfounded. Indeed, Danish manufacturing wage increases have outpaced those in construction. In Sweden, the ratio is very stable, testament to the very tight coordination of wages across sectors in this country (Ibsen 2016).

One of the key rationales for wage moderation and a tight coordination of wages around the key bargaining sector of manufacturing is that it provides for steady real wage increases and high levels of employment. Figure 9.3 shows the real hourly wage increase of construction workers in the two countries. Indeed, in most years since 1993 construction workers have enjoyed good real wage increases in the period, but we also see that Danish construction workers incurred real wage losses or stagnation more often than their Swedish colleagues. This might be an indication of a higher degree of wage moderation in Denmark than in Sweden.

Besides tight coordination, there are two other potential explanations for the lack of wage inflation in construction since decentralization. First, high unemployment kept wage demands in check in the 1990s and after the financial crisis. Second, the increasing influx of migrant workers in the sectors since the mid-2000s may have dampened wage increases despite economic booms. It is to this latter question that we now turn.

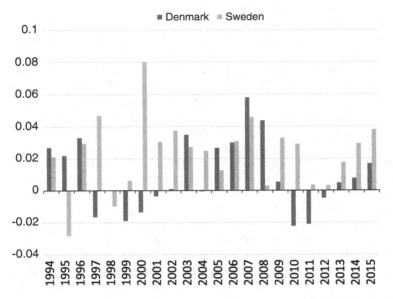

Figure 9.3 Real hourly wage movement of construction workers in Denmark and Sweden, 1994–2015.

Source: Authors' calculation based on EU KLEMS (2019). KLEMS stands for capital (K), labor (L), energy (E), materials (M) and service inputs (S).

EU Enlargement and Company Strategies

Rather than a static equilibrium, the compromise-based 'high road' that marks these two construction sectors rests on a balance of power that can change over time and this has gradually happened after the enlargement of the EU in 2004. Welcoming eight Eastern European countries as new member states was an event of significant political importance – a victory for democracy and the European integration project. At the same time, however, it caused both political and economic transformations that may prove to have had negative long-term consequences in some areas. In relation to this chapter, the major process of transformation that is of interest was the unprecedented flow of labor within Europe. Millions of Eastern European workers used their new won right to free movement to seek work in the old, Western European member states, and companies from the new member states found new business opportunities by sending their workers to perform jobs abroad. Underlying this flow of labor were the socio-economic differences between old and new member states. In a major sender country like Poland, unemployment was 18 percent at the time of accession and average wages were one-fifth of those found in Sweden and Denmark. For Polish and Baltic workers, taking even low-paying jobs in the Nordic countries was economically attractive and companies from the new member states could use wage differences as a major competitive advantage.

Consequently, both countries have experienced a doubling of the number of migrants in their labor markets during the last 15 years. In Denmark, available statistics suggests that the number of migrant workers has increased substantially in the construction sector. In 2005, around 500 East Europeans were registered as working in the Danish construction sector but by 2017 the number was around 21,000. While no comparable statistics exists for Sweden, it is safe to assume that a substantial part of the general inflow of foreign workers in the same period has also gone into the construction sector. Although some of these workers are regular labor migrants, others are posted workers sent by employers in their home countries to perform specific tasks. As explained later, the latter group is covered by special EU regulations, which challenge the functioning of the Danish and Swedish regulatory systems. However, this inflow of labor migrants has in general exposed weaknesses of the systems.

Maintaining the balance of power between workers and employers has been difficult when faced with a sustained inflow of poorly organized workers, with low wage expectations and no tradition of worker militancy. More specifically, this new group of workers has tipped the balance of power in the employers' favor for three reasons. First, domestic companies have hired labor migrants directly. Doing so, employers can exploit these workers' low wage expectations and lack of trade union membership during local wage negotiations. In both Sweden and Denmark, collective agreements in the construction sector prescribe local wage negotiations and these local negotiations typically account for a substantial part of the wages paid. Average wages are therefore around 30 percent higher than the minimum wages stipulated by collective agreements. Negotiating with foreign employees, employers can typically get away with paying the minimum wage alone. At the same time, however, this direct employment of labor migrants is not unproblematic for companies. Being based on high-skill/high-productivity production processes, Danish and Swedish companies will often find it difficult to integrate workers whose skill profile is different and who come from countries where low productivity and low wages provide the dominant model in the construction sector. In some cases, companies re-organize their labor process to fit their new employees (Haakestad and Friberg 2017) or companies are established around a workforce of labor migrants. In other cases, however, companies opt for other strategies.

A second strategy is to use foreign subcontractors. To many of the bigger construction companies this is an attractive strategy, which allows them to reap the advantages of lower labor costs while avoiding the challenge of reorganizing their own production. The foreign subcontractors will often rely on a low-productivity/low-wage strategy but will still be able to make competitive offers on specific tasks. Not only do their workers have lower wage expectations but also there are specific EU regulations which set limits on what trade unions can do to increase the wages of these workers. Furthermore, although labor migrants employed in a domestic firm will typically interact with the organized domestic workers, shop stewards and trade union representatives, the posted workers sent by foreign subcontractors are often kept in complete isolation from domestic workers who might inform them about their labor rights (Caro et al. 2015). Obviously, for the domestic main contractor hiring foreign subcontractors can entail problems. Although they may not need to re-organize their own production process, they will need to coordinate it with subcontractors who use different production strategies. Furthermore, main contractors may experience more problems with trade unions when using low-paying subcontractors and they will also need to share some of the profit with these subcontractors. This raises the question why these companies do not simply stick to a strategy of high-productivity production and then dump additional costs on their clients.

To answer this question, we need to realize that major clients have become much more focused on cost efficiency during the last 15 years. This goes both for public authorities concerned with maximizing efficiency under tight budgets, but also major companies that want to lower their investment costs to stay competitive in international markets (Arnholtz et al. 2018). For these big clients there is a third strategy, namely that of hiring foreign main contractors. A good case in point is the expansion of the Copenhagen Metro, a ten-year construction project run by an Italian main contractor with a huge number of foreign subcontractors (Arnholtz and Refslund 2019). Using foreign companies as main contractors is becoming increasingly common, not just on major projects but also on smaller ones. This implies that domestic entrepreneurs need to find new ways of staying competitive and one such strategy is to use foreign subcontractors, as mentioned above. In other words, the formerly sheltered construction sectors of Denmark and Sweden have become increasingly internationalized since the EU enlargement and this internationalization has put pressure on wages and other labor costs just as it has made it harder for trade unions to secure collective agreement coverage and enforcement.

Coordination, Collective Actor Responses and Institutional Changes

While the inflow of foreign workers has put pressure on labor standards, institutional changes have been a major consequence. To understand this, we need to change focus from the strategies of individual companies to the responses of collective actors – trade unions and employers' associations. Even though the Swedish and Danish systems are very similar, and the pressure from migrant labor comparable, responses and institutional changes have been very different. In both countries, construction trade unions have been very aggressive in their attempts to ensure that collective agreements cover foreign companies, but the extent to which employer associations have played along with this has been very different. If we want to understand the underlying reasons for this, we need to look at how collective bargaining in the construction sectors is coordinated with collective bargaining in other sectors.

As already mentioned, there is an acceptance in both countries of the principle that exposed sectors should set the pace of wage development. However, in Denmark this principle is enforceable to a much larger extent than in Sweden. The reason is that in Denmark every sector-specific collective agreement is required to be approved by the board of the Danish Confederation of Employers (Dansk Arbejdsgiverforening – DA) (DA) in which Danish Industry, which represents the manufacturing sector, has a majority vote. Also, the vote for approval of the collective agreements on the trade union side is coordinated in the sense that all agreements are voted on jointly. What this implies is that a sector like construction is strongly embedded into the overall bargaining system. Construction employers cannot agree to things that other employers' associations will not agree and construction workers cannot cause an industrial conflict without the support of other trade unions. Under contract, Swedish construction workers can cause an industrial dispute by rejecting the collective agreement and, when doing so, they can hope to get their employer counterpart in construction to accommodate their demands (Ibsen 2016). Although the Swedish and Danish construction unions are of somewhat similar strength in terms of trade union density and industrial dispute possibilities, this institutional difference has made big differences in how the issue of foreign workers have been tackled.

In 2003 and 2004, the electricians' union in Sweden made demands for new rules relating to working time. They argued that workers should be compensated when employers' poor planning caused the work to become stressful. Employers refused, objecting that poor planning was a collective problem for which both workers and employers should take responsibility. Furthermore, they argued that stressful work was already regulated by statutory law and to put it in the collective agreement would imply that employers would suffer a double penalty. Nonetheless, trade unions insisted on their demands and they gave notice of a strike. In a Danish context, such a dispute would never come to pass as the electricians' union is too small to vote through a strike on their own. In Sweden, however, the strike threat was real and the electrical contracting employers started to give in, despite the objections of the employers' confederation. Although this dispute had nothing to do with labor migrants, it nonetheless formed part of the background for Swedish employers' actions after the EU enlargement. Being frustrated with what they perceived as a disproportional use of force by their trade union counterparts, they sought to use the new situation to promote institutional change.

This strategy became clear during the now famous Laval conflict, where a small Latvian construction company renovating a school in the Stockholm area was met with demands for the application of collective agreements by the main construction union – *Byggnads*. The company made various attempts to avoid signing the agreement and the conflict eventually proceeded to the Swedish labor court. At this point, Swedish employers decided to support Laval financially in an effort to have the case referred to the European Court of Justice (ECJ) (Woolfson and Sommers 2006). Although the case was referred to the ECJ because of concerns about discrimination and obstruction of the free movement of services, the aim of the Swedish employers was to gain some general limitations to the trade unions' actions (author interview 2010). The union eventually lost the case, which implied that restrictions were placed on trade unions' possibility of taking collective action against foreign construction companies. After the ECJ ruling came in late 2007, a Commission in Sweden conducted a comprehensive legal inquiry to determine the legal adjustments needed to make the Swedish system compatible with the EU law. The Commission delivered its report in December 2008 and its proposal formed the basis for a legislative proposal presented in 2009. After a contentious debate, in April 2010 the Swedish parliament adopted a reform which put strict limitations on trade unions' right to collective actions against foreign companies. In response, trade unions complained to the International Labour Organization about the restrictions on their rights to collective action. Further legislative initiatives followed in 2012 and 2016. What is noteworthy, however, is that despite the long tradition of regulating new labor market developments through collective bargaining, in the period from 2004 to 2014 the issue of foreign workers and foreign companies was never a subject of collective agreement change in the Swedish construction sector. Instead, the forum for institutional change was the parliamentary arena.

We can contrast this with developments in Denmark. When the inflow of foreign workers started to increase around 2006, relations between employers and trade unions in Danish construction were quite co-operative. In 2004, these co-operative relations had proven their worth when construction had been instrumental in securing a private-sector-wide parental leave reform (Due and Madsen 2006). In 2007, they proved their worth once more when employers and trade unions found new, joint solutions to the problems arising around labor migration and posted workers. A new clause was introduced into the collective agreement concerning so-called 'adopting negotiations.' If the union could establish a probable cause for believing that the collective agreement was violated, a meeting would be held in which the employers' association and its member firms had to prove that the collective agreement was not violated. This reversed burden of proof was very important to trade unions because they faced a challenge in controlling the application of the collective agreements in companies that mainly employed labor migrants. Furthermore, a clause encouraging companies covered by the collective agreement to promote coverage among their subcontractors was also introduced. Although the clause did not make subcontractor coverage mandatory, it did send a signal about the employers' willingness to promote collective agreements (Arnholtz and Andersen 2018). Finally, a reform of the pension clauses was made to ensure that migrant workers would also be entitled to a pension under the collective agreement.

When the Laval ruling came at the end of 2007, it was clear that it had implications for the Danish system as well because of the clear similarities with the Swedish system. However, the Danish way of tackling it was very different to that of the Swedish. A tripartite commission of trade union, employer and state representatives was swiftly assembled, and a short report on the ruling, its implications and how they should be tackled was quickly produced. Rather than being based on a lengthy legal investigation, the report was based on a common understanding among the three parties and a common will to preserve the Danish system as effectively as possible. Because of the trade union moderation induced by the Danish system of coordination, Danish employers were not as dissatisfied with the status quo as their Swedish counterparts and for that reason they did not try to use the ruling to promote institutional change. Rather than putting strict limits on trade union action, the Danish reform went a long way toward preserving the system as it was (Blauberger 2011).

This is not to say that there was no contention over the issue of migrant labor. Because of the financial crisis, every fourth job in the Danish construction sector disappeared between 2008 and 2010, but the number of migrant workers kept on rising. Leading up to the 2010 bargaining round, migrant workers and fear of 'social dumping' became the primary bargaining issues for trade union members. Trade unions made several demands, such as a substantial rise in the minimum wage rate, the introduction of chain liability whereby main contractors took responsibility for the employment failures of subcontractors, and a requirement for making collective agreement coverage of subcontractors mandatory. However, employers refused these demands outright. Instead, the 'adopting negotiations' were transformed into so-called '48-hour meetings' that could be called on the basis of only a suspicion of violations of the collective agreement. These meetings had to be held within 48 hours in an effort to avoid foreign companies stalling and then disappearing. Additionally, new procedures were added which required foreign companies to make a gradual payment of pension and holiday contributions rather than the once-a-year system used for Danish firms. This was a response to an increasing number of cases in which foreign companies neglected to pay these contributions before leaving the country. Both 48-hour meetings and these new payment procedures have become a central tool for the trade unions in enforcing the collective agreements and their introduction testifies to the prevailing willingness of the social partners to find common solutions (Arnholtz and Andersen 2018).

The Limits of Beneficial Constraints and Different Forms of Trade Union Strength

The first period after the EU enlargement suggests that the strong co-ordination of the Danish bargaining system has acted as a 'beneficial constraint' for Danish construction unions, who were able to gain gradual improvements of their capabilities vis-à-vis the issues of labor migrants through collective bargaining. In contrast, the less-coordinated nature of the Swedish system caused strong antagonisms between employers and trade unions, which led employers to exploit the EU enlargement to promote institutional change.

From 2012 and onwards, however, the picture started to change. In Denmark, trade unions were growing increasingly dissatisfied with the situation. Although they had gained some new tools via collective bargaining, they were fighting an up-hill battle to contain the problems caused by the diverse employer strategies described above. Therefore, they still wanted new and more powerful tools, such as the main contractors to take overall responsibility in relation to employment issues within the supply chain (referred to as chain liability) and mandatory collective agreement coverage of subcontractors. Employers, however, were unaccommodating – especially because manufacturing employers very clearly expressed their opposition toward such initiatives. Even if construction employers had wanted to accommodate trade union demands, they would not be allowed to and, on the trade union side, metal workers and service workers were not willing to throw the whole private sector into conflict for issues that mainly pertained to construction. During the bargaining rounds of 2012, 2014 and 2017, trade unions and employers in construction failed to reach compromises but their differences were absorbed by the coordination mechanisms, which implied that no conflict arose. Consequently, co-operative relations fundamentally deteriorated and trade unions started to seek new ways to promote institutional change. Most importantly, they started to lobby for public authorities to put mandatory collective agreement coverage and chain liability into their construction tenders (Arnholtz and Andersen 2018).

By contrast, Swedish construction unions started to use their power to push through changes in the collective agreements. In the 2013 collective bargaining round, the unions demanded a so-called 'main contractor responsibility,' which would make the main contractors responsible for the whole contract chain in a construction project. Although employers initially declined, they eventually agreed to establish a working group on the issue. The group presented a proposal in February 2014 which called for increasing transparency in the subcontracting chain but without any economic liability on the part of the main contractor. Although employers were satisfied with these results, the main union was not and called for an annulment of the 2013 agreement (which should have lasted until 2016). A new bargaining round therefore started in March 2014, and the main issue was the main contractor responsibility. Strikes were called, mediators stepped in to develop a working group proposal and, in the end, a compromise was found. This compromise entails the main contractors being required to maintain an up-to-date list of all subcontractors available for the union and that the main contractor must assist in identifying and resolving disputes between subcontractors and the union. If the dispute cannot be resolved, the union has the right to refer the dispute to a special arbitration board. The board decides whether a payment obligation exists and, if so, determines the amount. The money is paid from a special fund financed by employers and the fund is entitled to claim back payment from the subcontractor who has violated the agreement. The compromise ensures that the union and its members get paid if a subcontractor is in violation of the collective agreement but it alleviates the risk for the individual main contractor of having to pay for such a subcontractor. Two years later, a very similar arrangement was adopted in the Danish construction sector. Where Swedish unions had been able to get this by themselves, however, the Danish reform was the result of the implementation of the 2014 Enforcement Directive concerning the posting of workers. Had it not been for this piece of EU legislation, it is very unlikely that Danish construction unions would have been able to push through such a reform.

That said, trade union strength consists not only in being able to force organized employers to accommodate bargaining demands, but also in enforcing the agreements made. In this respect, Danish construction unions still achieve much better results than their Swedish counterparts – in part, because they have better tools. Through their 48-hour meetings, they have managed to make collective agreement coverage among foreign companies much higher and more effective (Arnholtz 2019).

Conclusion: End of the 'High Road' or Still a Model?

In an international comparison, Danish and Swedish construction sectors stand out as extremely well organized in terms of trade union density, collective agreement coverage and a host of other parameters. Construction workers are well educated and most companies opt for a high-productivity, high-wage production strategy. For this reason, it would be tempting to recall Wolfgang Streeck's arguments about 'beneficial constraints' (Sorge and Streeck 1988; Streeck 1991) to understand how this was made possible. As indicated in the introduction, this argument suggests that regulatory constraints increase input costs and force companies to become more productive and/or quality focused to achieve the same level of profitability. In employment relations, this leads to a 'high road' approach to manage workers. However, following Streeck's own reflections on these concepts (Streeck 2009; Sorge and Streeck 2018), we should acknowledge that rather than a static equilibrium, upheld by functional complementarities, the 'high road' approach that has marked these two countries' construction sectors is a historical phenomenon which has also depended on institutions like unemployment insurance and VET system, a certain balance of power between trade unions and employers, as well as a willingness to compromise between parties. In both countries, we have seen joint efforts between workers and employers to promote productivity, and thereby secure that basis for high wages. However, underpinning this co-operation is also the knowledge among employers that trade unions can pose a credible threat to companies that try to go for a 'low road' strategy.

This 'high road' balance has, however, been challenged by the increasing inflow of migrant labor with lower wage expectations and no tradition of union organizing. Especially in Sweden, trade unions have been challenged to secure the collective agreement coverage of migrant workers and have had little success in ensuring the effective enforcement of the few agreements they have signed with foreign companies. At the same time, OECD data (OECD 2017) show that the Swedish construction sector has experienced a substantial fall in productivity. Although both productivity and labor standards are still high in the Swedish industry, the close correlation in the number of migrant workers and the decline in productivity could indicate that the sector is in a process of shifting from a high to a low strategy of production. By contrast, the Danish construction sector has retained and even improved its productivity while at the same time Danish trade unions have fared better at securing collective agreement coverage – and especially in the enforcement of these agreements.

References

Arnholtz, J., 2014. *A 'Legal Revolution' in the European Field of Posting?: Narratives of Uncertainty, Politics and Extraordinary Events*, Department of Sociology. University of Copenhagen, Copenhagen.

Arnholtz, J., 2019 Posted work, enforcement capacity and firm variation: evidence from the Danish construction sector *Economic & Industrial Democracy. Online first.*

Arnholtz, J., Andersen, S. K., 2016. *Udenlandske virksomheder og udstationerede arbejdstagere i bygge- og anlægsbranchen.* FAOS, University of Copenhagen, *Copenhagen.*

Arnholtz, J., Andersen, S. K., 2018. Extra-institutional changes under pressure from posting. *British Journal of Industrial Relations* 56, 395–417.

Arnholtz, J., Meardi, G., Oldervoll, J., 2018. Collective wage bargaining under strain in northern European construction: Resisting institutional drift? *European Journal of Industrial Relations* 24, 341–356.

Arnholtz, J., Refslund, B. 2019. Active enactment and virtuous circles of employment relations: How Danish unions organised the transnationalised Copenhagen Metro construction project. *Work, Employment and Society.* 33(4), 682–699.

Blauberger, M., 2011. With Luxembourg in mind ... the remaking of national policies in the face of ECJ jurisprudence. *Journal of European Public Policy* 19, 109–126.

Caro, E., Berntsen, L., Lillie, N., Wagner, I., 2015. Posted migration and segregation in the European construction sector. *Journal of Ethnic Migration Studies* 41 (10), 1600–1620.

Druker, J., White, G., Hegewisch, A., Mayne, L., 1996. Between hard and soft HRM: human resource management in the construction industry. *Construction Management and Economics.* 14, 405–416.

Due, J., Madsen, J. S., 2006. *Fra Storkonflikt til Barselsfond - Den danske model under afvikling eller fornyelse.* Jurist- og Økonomforbundets Forlag, København.

Due, J., Madsen, J. S., Jensen, C. S., Petersen, L. K., 1994. *The Survival of the Danish Model. A Historical Sociological Analysis of the Danish System of Collective Bargaining.* DJØF Publishing, Copenhagen.

Haakestad, H., Friberg, J. H., 2017. Deskilling revisited: Labour migration, neo-Taylorism and the degradation of craft work in the Norwegian construction industry. *Economic and Industrial Democracy* 41 (3), 630–651.

Helms Jørgensen, C., 2013. The role and meaning of vocations in the transition from education to work. *International Journal of Training Research* 11 (2), 166–183. 10.5172/ijtr.2013.11.2.166.

Ibsen, C. L., 2016. The Role of Mediation Institutions in Sweden and Denmark after Centralized Bargaining. *British Journal of Industrial Relations* 54, 285–310.

Ibsen, C. L., Thelen, K., 2017. Diverging solidarity: labor strategies in the new knowledge economy. *World Politics* 69, 409–447.

Ibsen, F., Stamhus, J., 1993. *Fra Central til Decentral Lønfastsættelse.* Jurist- og Økonomforbundets Forlag, Copenhagen.

Iversen, T., Wren, A., 1998. Equality, employment, and budgetary restraint: the trilemma of the service economy. *World Politics* 50 (4), 507–546. 10.1017/S0043887100007358.

Kjellberg, A., 2009. The Swedish model of industrial relations: self-regulation and combined centralisation-decentralisation. In: Phelan, C. Ed., *Trade Unionism since 1945: Towards a Global History.* Peter Lang, Oxford.

Kjellberg, A., 2019 *Kollektivavtalens täckningsgrad samt organisationsgraden hos arbetsgivarförbund och fackförbund. (Studies in Social Policy, Industrial Relations, Working Life and Mobility* (Vol. 2019). Department of Sociology, Lund University, Lund, No. 1.

Kjellberg, A., Ibsen, C. L., 2016. Attacks on union organizing – reversible and irreversible changes to the Ghent-systems in Sweden and Denmark. In: Larsen, T. P. Ed., *Den Danske Model set udefra* (Vol. 12). Jurist- og Økonomforbundets Forlag, Copenhagen, pp. 279–302.

LO/Sweden, 2015. *Facklig anslutning år 2015 – Facklig anslutning bland anställda efter klass och kön år 1990–2015.* LO/Sweden, Stockhom.

OECD, 2017. *STAN STructural ANalysis Database.* OECD, Paris.

Sorge, A., Streeck, W., 1988. Industrial relations and technical change- the case for an extended perspective. In: Hyman, R., Streeck, W. (eds), *New Technology and Industrial Relations.* Basil Blackwell, Oxford, pp. 19–47.

Sorge, A., Streeck, W., 2018. Diversified quality production revisited: its contribution to German socio-economic performance over time. *Socio-Economic Review* 16, 587–612.

Statistics Denmark, 2019. *Beskæftigede efter branche (DB07) og køn (RAS309).* https://www.statbank.dk/statbank5a/SelectVarVal/Define.asp?Maintable= RAS309&PLanguage=0. Accessed on October 19, 2019.

Statistics Sweden, 2019. *Arbetskraftsundersökningarna (AKU).* http://www. statistikdatabasen.scb.se/pxweb/sv/ssd/START__AM__AM0401__AM0401I/ NAKUSysselSNI07Ar/ . Accessed on October 19, 2020.

Streeck, W., 1991. On the institutional conditions of diversified quality production. In: Matzner, E., Streeck, W. (eds), *Beyond Keynesianism. The Socio-Economics of Production and Full Employment.* Edward Elgar, Aldershot.

Streeck, W., 2009. *Re-Forming Capitalism: Institutional Change in the German Political Economy.* Oxford University Press, Oxford.

Toubøl, J., Ibsen, C. L., Jensen, D. S., et al., 2015. Det mobile danske arbejdsmarked og organisering af lønmodtagere. *LO-dokumentation.* LO, København.

Woolfson, C., Sommers, J., 2006. Labour mobility in construction: European Implications of the Laval un Partneri Dispute with Swedish Labour. *European Journal of Industrial Relations* 12(1), 49–68.

10 Self-employment and Labor Relations in the UK Construction Industry

Janet Druker and Geoffrey White

Introduction

Labor relations in the UK construction industry are set within a turbulent environment, subject to a competitive contractual framework, a cyclical economy and fluctuating client preferences. In pursuit of clients and contracts, contractors squeeze costs and in doing so undermine employment standards. The price of a fractured, subcontracted industry has largely been paid by the UK's construction workforce – predominantly self-employed and male. The effects are felt in an instability that is inherent in labor management and labor relations. Yet in some parts of the industry and on particular contracts, different patterns are discernible.

This chapter outlines differing perspectives on labor relations, considering the contrast between a market-driven approach to management in which employees have little voice and one in which employees have some opportunity for representation, typically through trade unions. It points to a conflict of interest in work relationships that has shaped current arrangements. The first section considers the structure of the UK construction industry, exploring the effects of subcontracting on the form of labor engagement and the prevalence of false self-employment. It identifies differences within and across the sector. It then points to the challenges inherent in contractual pressures and to some of the consequences and contradictions resulting from these arrangements – in skill shortages and reliance on a migrant workforce and in damaging consequences for workers' health and safety. In the second section of the chapter, we identify areas where management initiatives have been more consultative or collaborative and we ask why these have emerged. In the final, concluding section, we point to the coexistence of contrasting – indeed conflicting – standards as an inherent feature of contractor strategy.

The work is based both on published sources, including collective agreements, and on interviews with key participants in industrial relations in construction, including industry, employer and union representatives.

The Construction Industry and Self-employment

In the introduction to this book, we outlined fundamental differences in employer approaches to employment relations. This chapter points to the dominance of market focused and unitarist traditions in the UK construction industry. It highlights the underlying conflict between the major parties in the industry and the occasional appearance of pluralist practices, where alternative approaches to management are visible. Far from being mutually exclusive perspectives, this chapter points to distinctive management styles that co-exist, varying pragmatically by project, client and context.

The UK construction industry is a pressurized, insecure and too often a dysfunctional working environment. The inherent discontinuities associated with the intensive, competitive contracting environment render coordination and planning profoundly difficult, and successive reports intended to modernize the industry and to improve performance have failed to have the hoped-for impact (Green 2016). The first section of this chapter describes the industry's modus operandi in terms of employment standards, training and health and safety.

In order to understand how labor is engaged and managed, we have first, to consider the way in which the industry operates. UK construction is part of a globally competitive market and some of the biggest firms are subsidiaries of American (e.g. Bectel), Australian (e.g. Lendlease) or European (e.g. Skanska) parent organizations. Asian contractors, for example the China General Nuclear Power group, are increasingly visible.

Work is divided between the private and the public sectors, with the private sector taking the larger share. The limited size of the public sector constrains the potential reach and impact of government and of modernization initiatives.

Each of the component parts of the industry fluctuates in terms of the level of activity but, in periods of peak activity, industrial and commercial buildings, schools and hospitals, housing, civil engineering and infrastructure may be competing for labor. Fluctuations in the economic cycle, in interest rates and in public expenditure have a huge impact on the level of activity. The insecurity within the sector is reflected in the structural changes of recent years and some of the family businesses and well-known companies of the last century have disappeared. The collapse of Carillion plc, one of the largest UK contractors, in 2018 led to shock waves as projects were halted, workers and subcontractors remained unpaid and the burden fell on taxpayers (Plimmer 2018). Insolvencies have risen in recent years with 3,106 in construction in England and Wales in the third quarter of 2019 – up from 2,792 insolvent construction firms just two years earlier (The Gazette 2020).

Work is predominantly project based and each project involves the creation of a team to co-ordinate and deliver the work required. Unless a client has a long-term program of work, with an established procurement process, each project team must be created from scratch, bringing together contractors and subcontractors. Processes and procedures are initiated afresh. The client is often more interested in results and cost and less in the process or in how the project is undertaken. Project teams are working across organizational boundaries and tend to recreate the patterns of work and the culture that have gone before, inhibiting innovation.

Only a small number of firms are significant employers, with the industry comprising many small firms. The growth in subcontracting and the fragmentation of the industry has led to a rise in the number of firms overall – from 202,407 to 325,736 (over 60 percent) between 2008 and 2018, with smaller firms (below 115 employees) making up over 99 percent of that number (ONS 2019: Table 3.1a Great Britain). The smallest firms – those with seven or fewer employees – constitute over 90 percent of the total. Firm registrations and contracts are concentrated especially in London and the south-east of England.

With notable exceptions, larger contractors have abandoned direct employment of the operative workforce. They define their role in terms of management of the contract, a responsibility which involves subcontracting, with subcontractors subcontracting in their turn, the process being repeated through a contractual chain which leads, ultimately to self-employed workers (Farmer 2016). This subcontracting process fragments employment and means that management of the supply chain is a critical issue for labor standards. From the contractors' perspective, this may appear to facilitate flexibility and encourage a downloading of risk but the counter effect rests in the challenges to co-ordination and, on occasion, an absence of control at the locus of productive activity. It is a model which has been adopted by other employers in the so-called 'gig' economy where workers are designated – sometimes wrongly – as 'self-employed' and in this way deprived of their employment rights.

The workforce is predominantly male and although women sometimes find a place in professional and managerial roles, they are rarely engaged as operatives. Of the 2,310,000 workers in the industry between October and December 2019, 2,027,000 million were male and only 283,000 female (ONS 2020), a proportion (12 percent) that has remained broadly consistent over the last ten years. The culture of the industry inhibits female employment (Clarke and Gribling 2008), and women in construction encounter pay gaps that are worse than in other sectors. The UK construction industry is similar to that in other countries in that it employs seven to eight percent of the total workforce – a figure that has diminished slightly as the UK workforce has grown in size.

Self-employment is common throughout UK industry and has grown significantly in other sectors but is highest within the construction sector. The number of self-employed construction operatives fluctuates according to the state of the industry but with a long-term tendency to increase – rising from 633,000 in September 2001 to 806,000 in September 2019 (ONS, 2019 – Table Jobs 2 December). The use of self-employed labor has a lengthy history within the industry and was resisted by trade unions for decades. Its use increased notably following the national building industry strike of 1972 when construction employers sought to break union influence, a process further encouraged by the Thatcher government after 1979.

The use of self-employed labor is not inevitable – it is not used to the same extent in some other European countries, for example, in Sweden which has a stronger regulatory regime (MacKenzie et al 2010; see Chapter 9, in this volume) – and is very much a matter of choice for the contractor or subcontractor. Self-employed workers have fewer employment rights and the work is less secure and more difficult to organize collectively. It offers a preferred form of engagement for contractors and subcontractors, who choose to outsource the management process thereby containing labor costs, offloading risks and avoiding union militancy.

The dispersal of self-employed workers is not uniform. Although the figures above suggest that around one-third of the workforce was self-employed in 2019, the proportion of site operatives who are self-employed is much higher. Professional and management staff are generally employed on permanent, open-ended contracts but there are parts of the industry, especially in London and the south east, where self-employment for operatives is the norm and where almost everyone is self-employed. In housebuilding, for example, the vast majority of work is done by subcontractors. The house builder acts as management contractor but then subcontracts all the work, which is largely undertaken by self-employed workers (interview: professional association representative). In repair, renovation and maintenance, self-employment is commonplace, whereas in engineering construction and in electrical contracting the proportion of operatives who are self-employed may be lower.

A special 'Construction Industry Scheme' (CIS) carries a tax status that offers the appearance of legitimacy to self-employed construction workers although in terms of their employment position and employment rights this self-employed status may not be substantiated. 'False' self-employment is common (Seely 2019). In legal terms, the distinction between employment and self-employment is opaque and although successive governments have discussed the potential for clearer tests to distinguish between these different forms of engagement, to date there are no specific proposals (Seely 2019). It is the employer who selects the form of engagement and while there can be benefits to both sides if self-employed status is used, there are also disadvantages for self-employed workers. The employer saves on National Insurance Contributions and offloads the risks of employment. Self-employed workers may benefit in the short term, because their payments for social benefits are lower than for employees and their taxation liabilities may be lower too, but in the medium to longer term they may lose benefits and state pension entitlement. Clearly there is a cost advantage for businesses that work in this way and firms that bear the proper costs of employment are at a competitive disadvantage. Although the loss of taxation income might seem, potentially, to be an area for government concern, governments have been reluctant to intervene, perhaps because in the existing industry (CIS) scheme they have something that is partially successful. It raises some income and this may be preferable, from the government's perspective, to changes that could potentially be unpopular and which might be subject to new forms of tax avoidance and evasion.

The complex web of relationships involved in the deployment of workers on site is further complicated by the use of intermediaries to facilitate false self-employment and to arrange for payment to the worker. Agencies are used for all types of labor – including professionals and managers – but their use is especially common for self-employed operatives and it is often agencies that take the responsibility of placing workers with a subcontractor. In this way, the subcontractor offloads the risk of engaging workers on a self-employed basis when they should in fact be directly employed. The relationships are further complicated by the use of payroll or 'umbrella' companies that undertake to make wage payments – often charging the worker a fee. The payroll company pays the workers and when the subcontractor gets paid – maybe three or six months later – he settles with the payroll or umbrella company. The worker who receives payment in this way pays for the privilege, being charged to have their earnings paid into their bank account. These intermediary companies often avoid taxation through offshore locations (Seely 2019).

It follows then, from the perspective of the worker, that construction work is precarious and income insecurity a fundamental problem. Underpayment and late payments are common complaints and when work is interrupted, for example because of bad weather, there are few entitlements to benefit or to compensation.

The construction industry is segmented, with professionals and managers more likely to be retained on open-ended employment contracts. Other workers may be engaged through subcontractors, through agencies or other intermediaries and the ways in which workers are engaged and paid have important implications for training, and for health and safety on site and it is to these issues that we now turn.

Skill Shortages

The fragmentation of the industry has led to a failure over many years, to provide appropriately for the training and skills development needed for the next generation of the industry's workers. This is an acute problem because the UK construction workforce is aging and it is estimated that there could be a 20–25 percent decline in the available labor force within the next ten years (Farmer 2016). The mobility of the industry and the short-term nature of projects require the planning and organization of training on a national basis, yet the system set up to do this is diminishingly effective in the face of the fragmentation of the industry.

The Construction Industry Training Board (CITB) was founded as a statutory body in 1964 and, following a government review of its activities in 2017 (Department for Education (DfE) 2017), continues to carry the responsibility for upgrading the industry's skills base. Nonetheless, skill needs – both current and future – far outweigh the current level of training provision (CITB 2017). Funded by a levy, calculated on the use of directly employed workers and the engagement of self-employed operatives, it is applicable to employers with a pay bill over a specified threshold level (McGurk and Allen 2016). The levy is used to fund training grants and to support trainees, but in recent years grant money paid out has not equaled levy funding coming in and so CITB funds cumulate while training needs grow.

In a cross-sectoral analysis of skill shortages undertaken in 2017, the construction industry was reported as being the sector with the highest density of skill-shortage vacancies (DfE 2018). Two in every five vacancies were identified as hard to fill because of a shortage of applicants with the appropriate skills and qualifications (DfE 2018: 41). New entrant training, typically offered to young people, is provided both through apprenticeships (currently attracting financial support by government) and through full-time training schemes in colleges, with the expectation that the college-trained person will go on to work in the industry. Based on its survey, the CITB reported that the number of first-year trainees in Great Britain's construction industry stood at 15,800 in 2016/2017 – just about one-third of the level of 2005. This shocking situation is compounded by the fact that the majority of trainees undertake lower level qualifications and progression rates from college to site level working are poor (CITB 2017).

The UK's training system has been compared unfavorably with other European countries in terms of the quality of training, in its rigid and narrow focus and in its failure to provide more thoroughly for occupational skills (Brockmann et al. 2010). The fact that the construction industry fails to attract a sufficient number of high-quality entrants is perhaps because of its poor reputation as an employer and the inherent insecurity of employment, but also because construction employers are less likely to publicize the opportunities and encourage school leavers to join them (DfE 2018). This is compounded by an inhospitable culture, which makes it less receptive to female entrants and to those from the black and minority ethnic (BAME) communities so that effectively it is recruiting from under half of the potential new entrants (Clarke and Gribling 2008).

The scale of the problem is widely acknowledged but is compounded by the structure of the industry – with many small firms – and by the fact that so many workers are self-employed. Firms are unlikely to provide training for workers provided by subcontractors, or those who are self-employed or engaged through agencies (Forde et al. 2008). The use of subcontract labor, agencies and self-employed workers leads to skill shortages – but skill shortages may, in turn, increase demand for these workers (Forde and MacKenzie 2007). The shortfall in construction training has been described as a 'ticking time-bomb' that is exacerbated by the demographic change already mentioned, by low productivity and, potentially, by the loss of migrant labor following the UK exit from the European Union (EU; Farmer 2016: 8). We now examine these last two points.

Skills shortages are blamed for poor-quality work and for the absence of innovation and improvements to productivity (interview – convener steward, 2019: Farmer 2016) and construction productivity in the UK is below that of the US (Dromey et al. 2017: 8). An emphasis on pre-site manufacture as a solution to productivity problems has been projected and examples include Laing O'Rourke, a major contractor with a manufacturing facility which tackles those aspects of the construction process that can be undertaken off-site, providing components that can be assembled in situ by crane. Off-site manufacture offers a means through which processes can be standardized and the impact of the skills gap minimized, but paradoxically it does not change the record for productivity because in measuring output, pre-site manufacture becomes part of the manufacturing sector rather than being counted within the construction figures. At site level traditional skills retain their importance. The Federation of Master Builders (FMB) reported, on the basis of a membership survey, that 60 percent of small construction firms were having a difficulty in finding bricklayers and 54 percent had difficulties in finding carpenters and joiners (FMB 2015: 6). If there is a shift in terms of skills, it is taking place through a period of transition as opposed to an overnight eradication of traditional skills but small employers remain concerned by bureaucracy in the training bodies and by the quality of the candidates as well as by the uncertainty of workloads.

Migrant Workers

UK construction employers have, historically, turned to migrant workers as a solution to the skills challenge. Ireland and the British Commonwealth provided a steady flow of entrants to the UK industry for much of the 20th century and with the expansion of the EU, the labor market opened up, from around 2004, to workers from the EU accession countries. Workers from central and eastern Europe were then more readily able to access opportunities in the UK, either through conventional labor migration or because they had been 'posted' by construction companies or manpower agencies (Arnholtz et al. 2018). Migrant workers provide a response to the need for flexibility with the advantage – from the point of view of employers – that they may return to their country of origin in the event that work is not available (Meardi 2012). Their numbers are higher in house building than in other parts of the industry. In the home building workforce census undertaken by the Home Builders' Federation in 2017, 19.7 percent of respondents were from overseas – the majority from the EU, which represented 17.7 percent. Romania, Poland, Lithuania and Ireland were the most common countries of origin (Home Builders' Federation 2017:7). Government statistics suggest lower figures for the industry as a whole – for example, in August 2018 non-UK nationals accounted for 13 percent of workers in building; eight percent of all workers in the construction activities subsector and seven percent in civil engineering. However, there is an ongoing challenge of obtaining accurate statistical information in an industry with high levels of informal working. Workers from outside the EU, whose immigration status may be questionable, may nonetheless find a place in the industry (Vershinina et al. 2018).

Crossborder migration provides a 'hyper-flexible buffer' to the construction workforce, with migrants seen as adaptable, mobile and willing to tolerate long hours of work, especially where their UK experience contrasts favorably with employment standards in their home country (Meardi 2012). They are particularly vulnerable to exploitation, especially where they have little or no spoken English and are reliant on site on someone who may or may not be a gang master for their work and security (interview: convener steward). Self-employment is the usual option, but workers are vulnerable to underpayment and wage theft (Vershinina et al. 2018). The opportunity to engage migrants may change following the UK's departure from the EU and, while the UK government is planning for a skills-based immigration system (UK Home Department 2018) at the time of writing, it is unclear how such changes will impact on construction.

We turn now to the question of health and safety, which is, inevitably, affected by work insecurity, limited training and an absence of worker representation.

The Challenge to Health and Safety

Successive reports have pointed to the need for 'decent and safe working conditions' in the construction industry (Construction Task Force 1998: 4; Donaghy 2009) and yet it remains an intrinsically high-risk employment sector. The fatal injury rate in UK construction, at 1.6 per 100,000 workers, is around four times the all industries rate, although the long-term trend has been downward since the 1980s. Government statistics show that around 2.6 percent of workers in construction suffered an injury, which is 50 percent above the all industries rate and is statistically significantly higher (Health and Safety Executive (HSE) 2018). In addition to the risk of death or injury, the health risks have been identified not only as musculoskeletal and work-related disorders but also mental health issues. Construction workers in the UK are covered by both general health and safety at work legislation and specific legislation covering the construction industry. The economic impact of health and safety failings in the industry has been estimated as £1,062 million in 2016/2017 (seven percent of the total cost for all industries) and some 2.4 million working days were lost each year between 2015/2016 and 2017/2018 due to workplace injuries or work-related illness (HSE 2018).

All UK workers are covered by the Health and Safety at Work Act 1974 and associated Regulations (e.g. on personal protective equipment or manual handling). In addition, there is general legislation on health and safety consultation with employees and the reporting of injuries, diseases and dangerous occurrences. There is also specific legislation covering the construction industry, including the Building Act 1984, which is supported by a series of Building Regulations, and the 1994 Construction (Design and Management) or CDM Regulations. The CDM Regulations originated in an EU directive requiring specific health and safety procedures at temporary or mobile construction sites. There have been three separate enactments of the CDM regulations, the last one in 2015, to ensure they meet the requirements of the EU Directive.

According to statistics for Great Britain (HSE 2018), there were 38 fatal injuries on construction sites in 2017/2018, around the average for the period from 2013/2014 to 2016/2017. Almost half of the fatal injuries were due to falls from height but other causes were collapsing structures, being hit by an object, being struck by a moving vehicle or contact with electricity. These statistics also show that there were 58,000 non-fatal injuries in 2017/18, around 50 percent higher than the all industries rate, but the trend has been downwards since 2000/2001.

Additionally, the HSE figures indicate that in 2018, 82,000 construction workers were suffering from work-related ill health, of which 62 percent were musculoskeletal disorders and 25 percent were related to mental health issues such as stress, depression or anxiety (HSE 2018).

The trend in total self-reported work-related ill-health has, however, remained flat in recent years and the rate is not significantly different to the figures for all workers. The rate of reporting of musculoskeletal disorders was, nonetheless, significantly higher than for other workers. The rate of ill health is significantly higher among carpenters/joiners and construction/building trades than workers across all occupations, whereas for plumbers, heating and ventilating engineers and electricians it is not.

Mental health is also an issue. In research by the UK statistical agency (ONS 2017), around six in a thousand construction workers reported suffering from stress, depression or anxiety. The research also indicated that the risk of suicide among low-skilled male laborers was three times higher than the national male average, especially in construction (ONS 2017).

To conclude this discussion, we note that there are disadvantages for employers as well as employees in the prevailing approach because poor training standards and high-risk health and safety are coupled with reputational damage to the industry, making it more difficult to attract and retain effective teams. These challenges are reinforced by a tradition of conflictual labor relations and it is to this issue that we now turn.

Labor Relations and Management Style

Employment relations in UK construction can be characterized by an approach known as 'double-breasting' (Dundon et al. 2015; Druker 2016). This is a dual-track approach wherein employers – or in this case large contractors – adopt pragmatic and bifurcated routes to labor management depending on the context of work, on the client and on the contract. On one hand, contractors are hostile to trade unions and seek to prevent union activists having an influence on site. This management ideology (Fox 1966) is essentially unitarist. On the other hand, where the client or circumstances suggest that there are advantages in doing so, the same contractors may take steps toward a pluralist approach, endorsing direct employment, committing to training arrangements and higher standards of health and safety and making concessions (or at least the appearance of concessions) to trade unions.

In the context of essentially conflictual relations between capital and labor, anti-union strategies represent the default position because union militancy and industrial action have the potential to derail projects that are of finite duration, where cost and delivery date are targets which, when missed, carry financial penalties. There is little time on short-term contracts to build constructive and pluralistic relations with trade unions and in the majority of cases contractors seek to work through the subcontracting process, avoiding or bypassing trade union influence. Although industrial action is relatively uncommon, contractors are aware of the potential implications should project planning be derailed with resulting delays.

The use of self-employment encourages a fear of job loss and permits the appearance of modest personal advantage through self-employed status. Short-term, project-based work means that the self-employed worker is always vulnerable to unemployment or dismissal. The relative security of direct employment and the employment rights that go with it are lost. Management style is harsher as there is a fear factor in being self-employed and those who are in the most precarious positions are unlikely to speak up about working conditions or health and safety (interview: industrial relations officer). Relationships are changed and managing the performance of a self-employed workforce – the aggression that may be used – is very different for a supervisor or manager to dealing more carefully with the directly employed.

> *It's not just the hard management – it's the daily dynamic between a supervisor and their workforce.*
> (Interview: Industrial Relations Officer)

Historically, resistance to unions was coordinated through employer blacklisting, with an employers' association designated for this purpose, bringing together information about trade unions and union activists from the companies that subscribed to its organization (Druker 2016). This practice continued even in the early years of the 21st century and, while it was poorly executed, it nonetheless jeopardized the livelihood of those who were identified and whose names were listed (Smith and Chamberlain 2015). Implicitly, this approach acknowledged the inherent antagonism in workplace relations but sought to resolve it by avoiding unionization. Following enquiries, court cases and settlements on behalf of the victimized workers, it appears that this type of blacklisting has been brought to a close, but the underlying low-trust relations have not disappeared (Druker 2016).

The creation of personal advantage for the worker is the second factor to consider, but it is integrally related to the first. Self-employed status brings tax advantages and workers, who may be falsely defined as self-employed, and those who engage them may share a financial incentive in claiming that their employment income is in fact income from self-employment. As we noted above, this means that workers can reduce their tax liabilities and increase their take-home pay. The individual worker may not always be clear that the engagement is made on a self-employed basis and may only find this out when seeking to claim holiday pay, sick pay or redundancy pay (Seely 2019). In fact, in the longer term, the worker may lose significant state benefits – for example, state pension and jobseekers' allowance (Seely 2019). Although self-employed workers receive a modest enhancement to pay because of their tax status, this may not in fact compensate for the benefits lost. It is sometimes claimed that it is the operatives who insist on self-employed status but of course in an industry where self-employment is the norm, the worker has little choice but to accept that form of engagement as it is often the only way to find work

Despite – and in contrast to – the comments above regarding the anti-union stance by employers, unions still play some part in the construction industry, both through national collective bargaining and also, in a few cases, through a site-level presence.

Unusually within UK industry, the construction industry still has national collective bargaining agreements, which have survived in name but in practice may be bypassed. Historically, national bargaining enabled employers to standardize wages, taking them out of competition. In reality though, for the construction agreement at least, while there may be an appearance of standardization, the rates paid at site level are not those specified in the agreement and contractors seek savings through the use of self-employed labor engaged on variable day rates. From the employers' perspective, the agreements offer a framework for dispute resolution and a mechanism for containing risks in the event of industrial action. The agreements range from the Construction Industry Joint Council (CIJC) – the largest, covering building and civil engineering – to smaller and more specialized settlements, for example, for heating and ventilating engineers and for plumbers (for England and Wales). The agreements for Electrical Contracting (for England, Wales and Northern Ireland) and for the Engineering Construction Industry set national guaranteed rates of pay and are more regularly observed but in these areas too collective bargaining is challenged. There is no longer a national employers' association for the construction industry and although Build UK, an 'umbrella' organization, was created in 2015 to bring together different strands of activity, it is the national contractors' group which shapes construction negotiations. The trade union side is led by Unite the Union. Successive surveys have underscored the low level of trade union density in construction as compared with other industries (Cully et al. 1999) and of course smaller sites or workplaces are least likely to be organized. The UK official statistics, from the 2019 Labour Force Survey, indicate that union membership density in construction was 11.7 percent, down from 30.4 percent in 1995 (DBEIS 2020). It was highest in civil engineering at 17.7 percent with building at 10.1 percent and specialized construction activities at 9.8 percent. The proportion of construction workers indicating that they were covered by a collective agreement in 2019 was 15.2 percent (DBEIS 2020).

There are nonetheless some sites where trade union representatives are in place, typically in situations where the client has specific requirements or where the contractor seeks an open and on-going relationship with the union. Wright and Brown (2013) suggest that there are new forms of 'joint regulation' where employers and unions are coordinating action on labor standards across the supply chain of firms but our research suggests that this is an optimistic view of developments. Outside of major projects, which we will discuss below, there are currently only a few, largely London-based, sites with full-time convener stewards in place and, typically, they are in situations where the contractors' risk and reputation are at a premium.

This raises the question, is it possible for the construction industry to work in a different way and it is this question that we seek to address in the section that follows.

What Does Better Practice Look Like?

Bigger projects and high-profile clients are more likely to generate better labor standards (Eldred 2018), although this is by no means uniformly the case. It is clear though that, where on a large site employment and labor relations are inadequately managed, the consequences can be costly. This point was illustrated on the London Underground Jubilee Line Extension in the 1990s when industrial action threatened timely project completion.

There are good reasons why larger projects may invoke a different and more positive approach. First, they are of high value, with a commensurate high risk of financial loss for the lead businesses involved – both for the client and for major contractors. A pluralistic perspective – acknowledging worker interests and the role of trade unions in addressing site problems – offers greater potential for minimizing and containing workplace conflict. Second, such projects are longer term, offering a target for trade union activists who have a better opportunity to recruit members and establish a real presence on site. Third, they attract public interest and overt and damaging conflict carries a risk of reputational damage for those involved. Fourth, they are able to employ more informed and specialist staff who are interested in project success and the potential for a 'legacy' within the industry.

The importance of the client's role in setting a tone and culture for construction projects was acknowledged more than 25 years ago (Latham 1994: pp 3–5) and has been a recurring theme in subsequent reports (Construction Task Force 1998, Farmer 2016). Clients such as British Airports Authority plc and their successor organizations creating Heathrow Terminal Five (T5; 2002–08); the Olympic Development Authority, as client for the London 2012 Olympic Park (2007–11); Crossrail (2011–18), the new London rail link; Electricite de France Energy for Hinkley Point C (HPC) nuclear power station (2016–30); the Thames Tideway new sewage disposal project for London and High Speed Two (HS2), the new north–south rail link, have all established values and commitments which are intended to inform management decision-taking and encourage pluralistic procedures. There is a degree of isomorphism as key players look to the legacy of previous initiatives but the difference in context – in the purpose and value, funding, geographical location, political context and parties involved – means that each project is distinctive. Where the client is wholly or partially publically funded, there may be political pressures to avoid risk and some of the traditions of public sector employment may come into play – where community interests and factors such as diversity and inclusion in employment are given greater weight. The recognition of political interest is accompanied by the realization that over the duration of long-term projects, such as HPC or HS2, political control may shift and that risk and reputation management require attention not just to today's priorities but to the shape that they may take in the future.

The first challenge is the question of the underpinning philosophy or rationale. Are employee representatives – normally trade unions – to have a role? Is there to be, in the words of one site agreement, a 'close social partnership' (Hinkley Point C 2017). Is it clear that differences will be resolved at the lowest level practicable? Is there recognition of the diversity on site, of the potential contribution of non-traditional construction recruits, for example in the BAME community? Is this approach communicated clearly to all participants?

A key test of approach rests in the use of direct employment, which is more likely to be preferred where it is perceived to encourage long-term employment relationships that enable employers to be confident about the benefits of investment both in training and in health and safety so that productivity and safety can be maximized (Eldred 2018: 16). The commitment to direct employment may be shaped in different ways.

On one hand, there may be some creative ambiguity, so that individual contractors or subcontractors can bypass the requirement. On the other hand, there may be an explicit commitment to direct employment which leaves little scope for evasion. Much depends on the way in which such commitments are formulated and operationalized. On the London 2012 Olympic Park, the 2007 commitment was to the 'ethos of a directly employed workforce' (Olympic Delivery Authority 2007: principles (e)), a form of words that created the expectation among subcontractors that it might not be applied in practice and that market-led practices would predominate. The use of self-employed labor in the early stages was challenged and greater consistency was subsequently asserted in management practice (Druker and White 2013). At HPC, where there is a resonance of the stronger traditions of collective regulation exerted through the engineering construction agreement, there is a clear formal commitment to an 'engaged social partnership' (Hinkley Point C 2017) and operatives must be 'directly employed by a Tier One contractor or subcontractor under a contract of employment' (Hinkley Point C 2018a:

clause 17). Until such commitments are tested, they may appear to echo the laissez faire approach of other commercial contracts which refer to direct employment and to the application of collective agreements but without any substantial backing for the rhetoric. Provisions may be ignored in practice and there may be a wide gap between the contract provision and the site experience as subcontractors turn to the self-employed. Effective trade union organization can react and challenge abuses and their position is stronger if they work within the ambit of a clear social partnership.

Contractors differ of course in the approach that they take to employment. Some, a minority, prefer to employ a larger proportion of their workforce directly, whereas others retain a stronger commitment to the flexibility and cost containment of self-employment. A willingness to employ directly, however, cannot be equated with a commitment to acknowledge the right to worker representation. At least one of the UK's national contractors with a high commitment to direct employment (the approach preferred by union policies) and to training, is more resistant to union organization. In a further paradox, the acknowledgment of trade union representation does not mean that contractors will require direct employment. Contractors with full-time union conveners at site level may still engage self-employed workers. This dichotomy might be interpreted as evidence of variations in the unitarist position. Even where union representatives are in place, they may be limited in their freedom of maneuver.

Given these ambiguities, because self-employment for operatives is the norm and as collective agreements are routinely neglected, it requires a confident and strategic commitment from the client and Tier One contractors to give full effect to the application of direct employment and pluralistic processes that differ fundamentally from the long-standing experience of many project participants. Moreover, commitments to prevent false self-employment do not automatically resolve a tendency to the default, that is self-employed practice. Where Tier One contractors are themselves engaging trade contractors or subcontractors, they must, in turn, repeat the requirement for direct employment in contracts with their subcontractors. Running alongside the contractual provision is the need to monitor or audit practice – a process that must be initiated and sustained by the client or their delivery partner if their contractual provision is to be effective.

At an early stage, decisions are taken on the ways in which the project will relate to national collective bargaining arrangements. Once again, this involves choices – either for a bespoke site agreement or agreements or for reference to national collective agreements. A bespoke arrangement may be more robust. In the cases of both Heathrow T5 (2002–08) and HPC, currently in progress, decision takers opted for bespoke, project-related agreements. At T5, a Major Projects Agreement was initiated with general application and supported by a Supplementary Projects Agreement (Deakin and Koukiadaki 2009). At HPC, where adherence to the national Engineering Construction Industry Agreement was initially anticipated both by employers and unions, a project-based approach is preferred. A Common Framework Agreement, signed by the client, the Tier One contractors and the trade unions is supported by separate, sector-based agreements for engineering construction, civil engineering, site operations and supervisors. Initially referred to by some participants as 'Engineering Construction plus,' it may also have been influenced by the example of T5. The agreements include commitments on direct employment and collective bargaining, as well as health and safety and training. Projects of this scale provide a showcase for local recruitment, skills development, inclusion and diversity and community commitment. The possibility of escalating costs (a major concern, for example, on HS2) is a significant threat and behind these initiatives lies the risk that, in a multi-party project, individual contractors and subcontractors will each adopt different approaches to employment and different rates of pay with a consequent de-stabilization of labor relations. From the contractors' point of view, there are obvious advantages in avoiding this situation. At the same time, the client is not the employer but can take advantage of the opportunity to influence the approach to employee relations through commercial contracts with Tier One contractors and the requirements that they may stipulate with Tier Two and other subcontractors.

A critical question for the credibility of this approach rests in the underlying philosophy. To what extent are trade unions to be recognized and given scope to organize effectively? The HPC agreements point to a provision that is inherently pluralistic, distinctive in its stated intention to create processes that are 'fair and socially just.'

> *It is the intention of all parties that workers will be: managed in a fair and socially just manner; treated with dignity and respect; and provided with the highest possible level of reward. In return, workers will be expected to positively contribute to the project's success by: respecting managers, supervisors and project facilities; and working in accordance with the project ethos of high standards of safety (zero-harm), quality and productivity.*
>
> (Hinkley Point C 2018b: clause 21)

The agreements preclude self-employment and provide clearly for benefits that would never apply to a self-employed worker. They specify a grading structure and payment arrangements, provision for pay reviews, working hours, holidays, rest breaks, pensions, additional allowances and milestone schemes. They also require a commitment to the project and productivity.

Across the construction industry, the recognition of trade unions remains problematic. As mentioned above, union density within the private sector of the construction industry remains low. Unite the Union, the largest organization representing construction workers, is faced with the challenge of organizing a mobile and largely self-employed workforce and, while membership remains higher than average among electricians and workers in mechanical and engineering construction, it remains low in building and civil engineering.

A test of the extent of pluralism rests on the extent to which trade union officers have access to the workforce for union recruitment and the extent to which trade union membership and representation become the norm. This was the case at T5. At HPC, blacklisting is specifically precluded and unions have established an integral role, with officers liaising with the client and Tier One contractors in a 'Top Table' Forum, with oversight of the application of collective agreements. Nominated full-time officials are entitled, with advance notice, to visit the site and unions are able to claim 'all appropriate facilities' to carry out their functions. Union membership is encouraged and union representatives take a role in employee induction, with union-accredited shop stewards working through individual contractors and suppliers.

A bespoke agreement is by no means the only route to a more pluralistic approach to employment relations in construction. An alternative perspective is the endorsement of standards set out in national collective agreements. This poses problems for trade unions because low pay rates in the national agreement for the construction industry do not match the expectations of workers on mega-projects (interview: union officer). Although a couple of agreements (engineering construction and electrical contracting) reflect greater union influence, the CIJC sets rates of pay that are low, so commitment to observing them may have little real effect. Both Crossrail and the London 2012 Olympic Park projects used national collective agreements as a benchmark but on the London 2012 Olympic Park, an early Memorandum of Agreement, cross-referring to national collective agreements was accompanied by an Industrial Relations Code of Practice. A similar, but rather weaker route has been taken by High Speed Two, where an Initial Framework Agreement has bound contractors to 'industry benchmarks' without specifically referring to collective agreements. The bespoke agreement on the HPC model provides a stronger commitment because it endorses a direct relationship with trade unions both at project level, through individual contractors, and by setting pay rates that are above national agreements.

The early stages of a project are critical in establishing the credibility of these provisions and shaping the future for effective and pluralistic employment relations on the project. This is a defining moment because early commercial contracts may have been let before employment relations priorities were formulated and before specialist industrial relations staff are appointed. Key provisions, such as direct employment, may not have been included and subcontractors may, legitimately, be able to argue that their costs have not been formulated to encompass such provisions. The role of the project leader or Chief Executive and the degree of support and the capability of senior colleagues are important in giving effect to espoused commitments (Druker and White 2013). Until appropriate regulation and a culture of compliance is established, there is a risk that the values and commitments that have been written into agreements will be lost in daily practice with an escalation in project risks around employment relations that are both financial and reputational at a later stage.

At an operational level, the challenges within the subcontract organization derive from the credibility of the commitments and the specificity of their implementation. Once the significance of those commitments is understood by subcontractors, there remains the question of implementation – of the recruitment and management of a directly employed workforce. One industrial relations officer (interview) noted that many supervisors lack the skills and experience associated with managing directly employed people. In normal circumstances, if someone who is self-employed as a carpenter or steel fixer is perceived to be unsuitable, their contract can very easily be terminated. There is no question of following a disciplinary procedure, managing performance, listening to complaints, legislating for taxation, sick pay or benefits. Managing the performance of a directly employed workforce requires skills that are different to managing the self-employed CIS worker.

> *The aggression that you may use – because there's a certain fear factor in being self-employed because of that type of thing – could be a lot harsher than maybe with an employee who can strike back with a set of rights. So that goes back onto what the unions are saying quite rightly that also impacts on how the employee may argue about the work environment or the health and safety. Because they're on a very loose foundation, a very wobbly foundation, they are less likely to speak up than they would if they're a fully-fledged employee.*

(interview: industrial relations officer)

Significantly, collective agreements – whether they are bespoke or draw from national provision – provide for the management of conflict. Disputes procedures acknowledge the potential for disagreement and specify the ways in which it should be contained.

In summary then, while major projects may throw up formal policies and procedures that suggest a pluralist perspective with opportunities for workforce engagement, it is up to clients, major contractors or most of all trade unionists, to challenge the inherent market-based philosophies within the default traditions of management in UK construction. In an industry where there has been so much discussion about routes to enhance productivity, it is hard to resist the view that direct employment, coupled with a perspective that is rooted in collaborative pluralism, could strengthen the potential for productivity gains on many larger sites, tackling skill shortages, improving health and safety standards and enhancing the industry's reputation.

Conclusion

From the account above, it is clear that approaches to work and labor relations in the UK construction industry must be understood at three distinct but inter-related levels. First, there is a historical legacy that is embodied in multi-employer national collective agreements which have survived many changes in the industry and yet in their specifics no longer correspond to the reality of working practices. Although some agreements – notably engineering construction and electrical contracting – continue to be relevant to site behaviors, this is not the case in building and civil engineering, where there is little knowledge or understanding, either among project and site managers or among the majority of the workforce, of the content or the potential implications of these agreements for practices on their sites. Yet, it is these agreements that may come in to play in the event that a major client requires an approach that is different from the norm.

Second, contracting organizations have their own traditions and philosophies, influenced in a few cases by the culture of parent companies outside of the UK. Trade union representatives in firms that operate in more than one European country may access opportunities to attend European Works Councils and yet may find that it is difficult to challenge entrenched self-employment practices in their own organization or on their own UK site. In some cases, businesses are influenced by strong leaders, personalities who have grown the business and impacted on its management style. Their personal choices may lean toward a unitarist perspective which is likely to predominate but, with the flexibility required in a contracting environment, they may adapt to a modified pluralist practice when the need arises.

Third, because construction projects bring together a number of players and organizations, each with their own culture and preferences, there remains the question of management of the multi-organizational project. There is no necessary or automatic co-ordination between the different contractors' on-site employment relations and the absence of industrial action in recent years has encouraged a degree of complacency about the need to plan for this eventuality. Yet, in many cases, there is the potential for union organization and for co-ordination across organizational boundaries, the potential for problems to escalate and for challenges to management authority to deflect from the planned project logistics. Larger projects such as HPC have an interest in fostering a different management ideology, emphasizing an approach that rests in a social covenant between employer and worker.

Different levels of analysis then, but also different ideologies of management, are deployed in order to sustain the diverse range of activities that come under the heading of 'construction.' The major reports intended to re-purpose construction activity have yet to acknowledge the importance of the construction workforce as central to that process of change. Although individual contractors have sought to tackle some of the key 'people' problems besetting the industry, for example, in the fields of inclusion and diversity, training and health and safety, none of them has been fully prepared at the strategic level to tackle the underpinning challenge of direct employment and the accompanying issues of employee representation and voice. The distinction made by Fox (1966) in the 1960s remains relevant here – between the unitarist perspective that predominates within much of the industry and the pluralist view of the world that shapes the approach on the most significant mega projects. The unitarist view is essentially short term – focused exclusively on completion of the project on time and to cost. No other interest is acknowledged and there is no opportunity for employees – either individually or collectively – to impact significantly on their own work situation. Any alternative is currently contingent on project context, usually within a longer timeline. Where a major client sets out specific requirements, project leaders, Tier One contractors and subcontractors have the capacity to adapt and modify the conventional stance, working with employment standards that may be ignored in other locations. Ultimately though, the industry is currently defined by the way in which these two distinct management ideologies co-exist, with an approach that is essentially context based – with the same organization adopting contrasting and distinct perspectives in different locations.

References

Arnholtz, J., Meardi, G, Oldervoll, J., 2018. Collective wage bargaining under strain in European construction. *European Journal of Industrial Relations* 24 (4), 341–356.

Brockmann, M., Clarke, L., Winch, C., 2010. The apprenticeship framework in England: a new beginning or a continuing sham?. *Journal of Education and Work* 23 (2), 111–127.

CITB, 2017. *Training and the Built Environment, 2017*. CITB, Bircham Newton, UK.

Clarke, L., Gribling, M., 2008. Obstacles to diversity in construction: the example of Heathrow Terminal 5. *Construction Management and Economics* 26, 1055–1065.

Construction Task Force (Chaired by Sir John Egan), 1998. *Rethinking Construction: Report of the Construction Task Force to the Deputy Prime Minister, John Prescott, on the scope for improving the quality and efficiency of UK construction*. Department of Trade and industry, London.

Cully, M., Woodland, S., O'Reilly, A., Dix, G., 1999. *Britain at Work as Depicted by the 1998 Workplace Employee Relations Survey*. Routledge, London.

DBEIS, 2020. *Trade Union Membership, UK 1995-2019*. Statistical Bulletin. Tables A14, 1.8 and 1.11. Department for Business, Energy and Industrial Strategy, London. https://www.gov.uk/government/statistics/trade-union-statistics-2019 (accessed 30.06.20.).

Deakin, S., Koukiadaki, A., 2009. Governance processes, labor–management partnership and employee voice in the construction of Heathrow Terminal 5. *Industrial Law Journal 38* (4), 365–389.

Department for Education, 2017. *Building Support: the Review of the Industry Training Boards*. DfE, London.

Department for Education, 2018. *Employer Skills Survey, 2017*. IFF Research, London.

Donaghy, R., 2009 *Report to the Secretary of State for Work and Pensions: One death is too many. Inquiry into the underlying causes of construction fatal accidents*. London, Presented to Parliament by Secretary of State for Work and Pensions, July 2009 Command 7657.

Dromey, J., Morris, M., Murphy, L., 2017. *Building Britain's Future: The Construction Industry after Brexit*. Institute for Public Policy Research, London.

Druker, J., 2016. Blacklisting and its legacy in the UK construction industry: employment relations in the aftermath of exposure of the Consulting Association. *Industrial Relations Journal 147* (3), 220–237.

Druker, J., White, G., 2013. Employment relations on major construction projects: the London 2012 Olympic construction site. *Industrial Relations Journal 44* (5–6), 566–583.

Dundon, T., Cullinane, N., Donaghey, J., Dobbins, T., Wilkinson, A., Hickland, E., 2015. Double breasting employee voice: an assessment of motives, arrangements and durability. *Human Relations 68* (3), 489–513.

Eldred, A., 2018. *Employment relations on a major construction project*. Crossrail Learning Legacy https://learninglegacy.crossrail.co.uk/documents/employment-relations-on-a-major-construction-project/ (accessed 27.03.19.).

Farmer, M., 2016. *Modernize or Die: Time to Decide the Industry's Future*: Construction Leadership Council, London.

Federation of Master Builders, 2015. *Defusing the Skills Time Bomb: Boosting Apprenticeship Training Through Construction SMEs*. FMB, London.

Forde, C., MacKenzie, R., 2007. Getting the mix right? The use of labor contract alternatives in UK construction. *Personnel Review 36* (4), 549–563.

Forde, C., MacKenzie, R., Robinson, A., 2008. Firm foundations? Contingent labor and employers' provision of training in the UK construction sector. *Industrial Relations Journal 39* (5), 370–391.

Fox, A., 1966. Managerial ideology and labour relations. *British Journal of Industrial Relations* 4, 1–3.

Green, S., 2016. *Modernize...or not.* Construction Research and Innovation (4), 24–27.

HSE, 2018 *Construction statistics in Great Britain 2018.* Health and Safety Executive. 31 October www.hse.gov.uk/statistics/industry/construction/pdf (accessed 30.09.19.).

Hinkley Point C, 2017. *Construction project industrial relations common framework agreement.* Signed December 2017, unpublished.

Hinkley Point C, 2018a. *Engineering construction sector agreement,* unpublished.

Hinkley Point C, 2018b. *Civil engineering agreement,* unpublished.

Home Builders Federation, 2017. *Home building workforce census, 2017.* HBF, London.

Latham, M., 1994. *Constructing the Team: Final Report of the Government/ Industry Review of Procurement and Contractual Arrangements in the United Kingdom Construction Industry.* HMSO, London.

Loosemore, M., Dainty, A., Lingard, H., 2003. *Human Resource Management in Construction Projects: Strategic and Operational Approaches.* Spon Press, London and NY.

MacKenzie, R., Forde, C., Robinson, A., Cook, H., Eriksson, B., Larrson, P., Bergman, A., 2010. Contingent work in the UK and Sweden: evidence from the construction industry. *Industrial Relations Journal* 41 (6), 603–621.

McGurk, P., Allen, M., 2016. *Apprenticeships in England: Impoverished but Laddered.* Institute for Construction Economic Research, Michigan State University, East Lancing.

Meardi, G., 2012. Constructing uncertainty: unions and migrant labor in construction in Spain and the UK. *Journal of Industrial Relations* 54 (1), 5–21.

Olympic Delivery Authority, 2007. *Memorandum of Agreement.* Olympic Development Authority, unpublished, London.

ONS, 2017. *Suicide by Occupation, England: 2011 to 2015: Analysis of Deaths from Suicide in Different Occupational Groups for People Aged 20 to 64 Years, Based on Deaths Registered in England between 2011 and 2015.* Office for National Statistics. https://www.ons.gov.uk/peoplepopulationandcommunity/ birthsdeathsandmarriages/deaths/articles/suicidebyoccupation/england2011to2015#main-points (accessed 30.09. 19.).

ONS, 2019. *Annual Construction Statistics.* Office for National Statistics. https://www.ons.gov.uk/businessindustryandtrade/constructionindustry/ datasets/constructionstatisticsannualtables (accessed 18.02.20.).

ONS, 2020. *Labor Market Statistics:Time series: all employment by industry,* February.

Plimmer, G., 2018. Carillion collapse set to cost tax payer at least £148 million. *Financial Times* 7 June 2018.

Seely, A., 2019. *Self-employment in the construction industry.* House of Commons Library Briefing Paper number 196 23 August 2019. UK Parliament, London.

Smith, D., Chamberlain, P., 2015. *Blacklisted: the Secret War between Big Business and Union Activists.* New Internationalist Publications, Oxford.

The Gazette, 2020. https://www.thegazette.co.uk/insolvency/content/103422: (accessed 18.02.20.).

UK Commission for Employment and Skills, 2018 *Employer skills survey, 2017. Research report August 2018.* London, IFF Research.

UK Home Department, 2018. *The UK's future skills-based immigration system.* Cm9722 Presented to Parliament by the Secretary of State for the Home Department, London.

Vershinina, N. A., Rodgers, P., Ram, M., Theodorakopoulos, N., Rodionova, Y., 2018. False self-employment: the case of Ukrainian migrants in London's construction sector. *Industrial Relations Journal 49* (1), 2–18.

Wright, C. F., Brown, W., 2013. The effectiveness of socially sustainable sourcing mechanisms: assessing the prospects of a new form of joint regulation. *Industrial Relations Journal 44* (1), 20–37.

11 Creating a Sustainable Industry and Workforce in the US Construction Industry

Dale Belman and Russell Ormiston

Introduction

The construction sector of the US confronts most of the issues of employment quality addressed in this volume. Industry stakeholders – owners, employers and labor – have some notable successes in creating the institutions that promote long-term sustainability of worker skills and 'good' employment practices in the sector. These practices include well-developed training programs, good wages and benefits, and an emphasis on worker safety and health. However, these are hardly uniform in the American construction industry. These best practices characterize the employment relationship in the signatory (unionized) sector. But union contractors and workers do not operate in every construction market; their impact is predominantly in non-residential construction. In other corners of the construction industry – namely certain trades in the residential sector – labor practices are informal and include low wages, wage theft, no training, racial and gender discrimination, unsafe working conditions, and payroll and tax fraud. These practices threaten the long-term sustainability of workers and firms.

The bifurcation of labor practices in the industry has not gone unnoticed, as industry stakeholders have publicly grappled with developing necessary government policies and establishing an industry response. In addition to promoting 'good' employment practices, addressing workplace exploitation in these dark corners of the industry is critical to developing the capacity of the construction sector to complete projects in a timely and efficient manner at predictable costs. Although common employment concerns are widely recognized, the deep fragmentation of the industry has been an obstacle to coordinated action to address issues that affect capacity, efficiency and profitability.

This chapter provides an overview of the employment relationship in the American construction industry. It will start by offering a broad perspective of the sector, including its size, structure and overall working conditions. To illuminate the wide variability of labor practices within the industry, we then compare and contrast the two extremes: the 'high road' practices of the signatory, non-residential sector against the exploitative, 'low road' practices in many trades of the residential construction industry. We contrast labor–management relations in each sector while highlighting critical differences in the issues central to this volume: training systems, working conditions, pay and provision of benefits and diversity. Through this approach, this chapter also identifies the structural causes of the bifurcation of the American construction industry and how these represent considerable challenges for industry stakeholders interested in promoting 'best' practices.

Construction in the US

Industry Structure

Construction represents one of the largest industries in the US. Accounting for 4.2 percent of the country's gross domestic product, the industry put $1.2 trillion of value in place in 2016. According to the Construction Chart Book (CCB), there were 10.6 million workers in the sectoral workforce in 2015, including 7.5 million employees, 2.4 million 'independent contractors' and 700,000 unemployed (Center for Construction Research and Training (CCRT) 2018). The construction sector is composed of many distinct sub-industries. While the most important distinction is between residential and non-residential, the latter can be further divided into industrial, heavy and highway, institutional and commercial. The non-residential sector is bigger than residential, with the former accounting for 59 percent of the industry's value put in place in March 2020 according to the authors' analysis of US Census Data (2020).

While there are marked differences between residential and non-residential construction, there are some common characteristics. Employers and workers in both sectors are structured around trades and projects. Most work is completed by specialist firms that focus entirely on specific parts of construction such as carpentry or electrical work. A firm's work on a typical project is of limited duration and employers need to continually bid and obtain new projects to maintain consistent work for themselves and their employees.

A firm's success in obtaining new work is constrained by a US construction market that is highly competitive and, perhaps more than any other industry in the country, characterized by small firms. As of the first quarter of 2018, there were 797,287 construction companies in the US, not including the additional two-plus million individuals working as independent contractors. Of firms with at least one employee, 91 percent employ fewer than 20 workers, and 66 percent have fewer than five workers (Bureau of Labor Statistics 2020a). While there are large national and international construction firms, only 0.23 percent of construction employers have 250 or more employees on their payroll.[1]

Another constraint on long-term firm viability is the volatility of American construction markets. Construction projects create consumer and producer durables that are costly, easily deferred, and sensitive to broad economic trends. Residential and industrial projects are also sensitive to interest rates and increases quickly reduce the demand. Expectations about the near and mid-term performance of the economy also factor into demand. Firms typically seek to take advantage of favorable economic times by increasing capacity during the expansion phase of the business cycle. Declining expectations can quickly reduce demand and activity in construction.

The sensitivity of the construction industry to broader economic trends has been demonstrated over the last two decades. As demonstrated in Figure 11.1, the economic expansion that occurred in the US through 2008 featured growth rates in construction that far outpaced the rate of growth in the broader economy. A strong economy featuring rising consumer and investor confidence are ripe conditions for starting new construction projects and, predictably, the American construction economy soared through the economic expansion. But those tailwinds can quickly turn to headwinds when the economy sours. The housing collapse in 2008 led to one of the worst economic downturns in modern American history. The construction industry, however, featured some of the worst losses of any sector in the economy and the after-effects of the sector-wide slowdown continued to reverberate through the industry 10 years later.

These characteristics of the American construction industry – small firms lacking in regular work and volatile industry demand – have

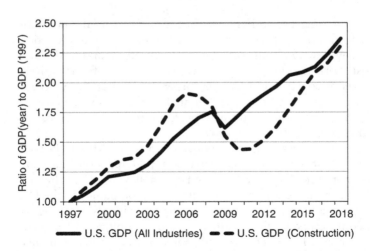

Figure 11.1 Ratio of nominal GDP (year) to nominal GDP (1997), US, all industries and construction, 1997–2018.
Source: US Bureau of Economic Analysis,www.bea.gov.

consequences for the sustainability of the sector's labor force. Because many firms struggle to maintain enough work to keep employees consistently employed, workers move from firm to firm to maintain a regular paycheck. This deters firms from providing training for their workers, as employers may be subsidizing training costs for workers who will join a competitor. This is exacerbated by the volatility of construction demand. When construction markets start to decline, the drop in labor demand causes workers to exit the industry in search of work in other sectors of the economy. Individual workers also recognize this volatility and are similarly dissuaded from making training investments themselves given concerns about immediate and long-term employment. Given the basic structure of the industry – and the absence of government involvement – the US construction sector features significant challenges in motivating the training and development investments that are necessary for the reproduction of labor.

Volatility and uncertainty permeate all levels of the construction industry. Just as firms are reluctant to invest in firm training, the uncertainty surrounding future demand can make companies more hesitant to invest in capital and new technologies. By limiting investment in both physical and human capital, the volatility of construction markets inhibits productivity growth.

American construction is reliant on extensive use of subcontractors. Projects, large and small, are overseen by a general contractor (GC) or a construction manager (CM). GCs are active participants in projects: bidding, having their own craft workers on the project, and partaking in monetary risks. CMs are hired by owners to oversee projects: to solicit bids and manage subcontractors. They do not have craftworkers, are typically paid a percentage of the cost and do not participate in project risk. The move from GC to CM has decentralized authority for projects, opening opportunities for costly errors associated with poor coordination. Both types of supervision involve the farming out of most – if not all – of the work to specialist trade subcontractors (e.g. carpentry, electrical) and these firms often subcontract further to other construction entities. Project success therefore depends on tight coordination of subcontractors and their workers but the enormity of subcontracting makes this a challenge. The shift from GCs to CMs has shifted risk down to subcontractors. Efficiency requires that subcontractors coordinate their work and move on and off the project according to a fixed schedule. Delays in starts and completions will push back the timing of future project work, as many trades cannot start until those working on the earlier stages are finished. Further, these delays can easily compound because full crews may not be available for the revised schedule, particularly during tight construction markets.

The coordination of construction work faces another challenge: as workers regularly move between employers – and into and out of the industry altogether – it can be difficult to efficiently identify, recruit and deploy a sufficient number of craft workers to a particular project. This is less of a concern on small projects, as it can typically be addressed by workers in the 'local' labor market. That said, a 'local' labor market can be as wide as 250 kilometers and often requires construction workers to undertake long commutes from their residence to a job site. But co-ordination issues become exponentially more problematic for large projects, where labor demand far exceeds local supply. These large projects – such as urban infrastructure, nuclear power plants or even large office projects – not only stress local markets, but their requirement for supplemental out-of-market workers (or 'travelers') creates challenges that can lead to substantial increases in cost, delays in the start or completion of a project, or both.

Construction Employment

As stated earlier, there were almost 10.6 million workers in the construction industry workforce in 2015 (Center for Construction Research and Training (CCRT) 2018). Most of these individuals worked in the private sector and public employees comprised just under four percent of the construction workforce in 2015. While most workers are employed in a skilled trade, industry employment includes managers, first-line supervisors, sales and administrative personnel. An occupational breakdown of the US construction industry is featured in Table 11.1. The largest trades are laborers, carpenters and electricians, each with more than 500,000 workers nationally.

The American construction industry is racially and ethnically diverse, and employs large numbers of immigrant workers. According to the CCB, slightly more than 20 percent of the construction workforce comprises members of racial minorities and more than one-quarter of the labor force identifies as Hispanic (Table 11.2) (Center for Construction Research and Training (CCRT) 2018). Both are overrepresented in less-skilled trades such as drywall and roofing. The proportion of the workforce that identifies as Hispanic increased from 9.0 percent in 1990 to 28.6 percent in 2015, and a significant proportion of Hispanic workers are immigrants. This is unsurprising, given construction's longtime role as a port of entry to labor markets for those new to the US.[2]

Women comprised 9.2 percent of total industry employment in 2015, but 2.4 percent of the skilled trades according to the Construction Chart Book (Table 11.2) (Center for Construction Research and Training (CCRT) 2018). Although there has been progress in bringing racial and ethnic minorities into the labor force, the participation of women in the trades has not progressed as rapidly. When considering the employment of racial and ethnic minorities among male workers, gauging diversity involves a natural metric: the proportion of men from each demographic

Table 11.1 US construction workers: occupation, union density and earnings (2015)

Occupation	Number (in thousands)	Percent of industry	Percent union members	Average annual earnings ($)
Construction laborer	1,611	16.2	12	37,100
Carpenter	1,134	11.4	14	46,910
Manager (except construction manager)	906	9.1		119,270
Construction manager	709	7.1	8	96,290
First line supervisor	625	6.3	15	65,620
Electrician	560	5.6	32	54,800
Painter/paperhanger	524	5.3	7	39,570
Administrative support	485	4.9	2	36,280
Pipelayer, plumber, pipefitter and steamfitter	462	4.7	28	54,300
Professional	390	3.9		*
Heating, ventilation and air conditioning	301	3.0	16	45,950
Operating engineer and other equipment ops	252	2.5	22	51,380
Installation, maintenance and repair	232	2.3	19	46,910
Roofer	213	2.1	12	40,590
Driver/sales worker and truck driver	165	1.7	12	*
Brick, block and stone masons	162	1.6	15	50,590
Service/sales	155	1.6		*
Drywall and ceiling tile installer	154	1.6	12	46,890
Carpet, floor and tile installer	131	1.3	7	43,900

Note: Occupations accounting for less than 1 percent of the construction labor force have been omitted (e.g. iron workers, welders, material moving, sheet metal workers, inspectors, glaziers). Data on employment and unionization are derived from the 2018 Construction Chart Book. Data on average annual earnings by occupation are taken from the 2015 Occupational Employment Statistics program via the Bureau of Labor Statistics (https://www.bls.gov/oes/tables.htm). *indicates aggregate occupation for which there is no compatible earnings estimate.

Table 11.2 The demographic composition of the construction workforce, US, 2015

	Racial minority (%)	Hispanic (%)	Female (%)
All industries	23.9	16.4	46.8
Construction industry	20.3	28.6	9.2 (2.4 craft occupations)
Construction occupations			
Painters	27.7	51.7	
Laborers	27.3	45.7	
Drywall	26.9	61.2	
Roofers	26.4	54.4	
Cement/concrete	24.3	49.7	
Carpet and tile	20.9	44.7	
Truck drivers	20.8	NA	
Ironworkers	19.1	NA	
Carpenters	18.9	30.8	
Sheet metal workers	18.4	NA	
Welders	17.7	21.4	
HVAC	16.8	17.9	
Plumbers	16.7	22.3	
Repairers	16.7	19.6	
Electricians	15.3	18.8	
Operating engineers	NA	16.7	

Notes: Racial minority categories include all non-white workers (African—American, Native American, Asian and Pacific Islanders). The Hispanic column includes all persons who identified themselves in the enumeration or survey process as being Spanish, Hispanic or Latino; this can include anyone of any race.Source: 2018 Construction Chart Book.

group should be comparable between the construction industry and the balance of the labor force. This is less clear with women, as work requirements and institutional structures may make the work less attractive. There is a need to distinguish between institutional barriers to women's participation – such as long commutes and regular movement of job sites that may make it more difficult for women situated in a more traditional gender role – and the potential barriers presented by a historically male-dominated industry culture. Recent changes in the equal opportunity requirements of apprenticeship programs will establish goals for bringing underrepresented groups into the workforce and compel greater participation by women in the future (Cornell Law School 2020).

Consistent with broader patterns in the national labor force, the average age of construction workers rose from 36.5 to 41.2 years between 1985 and 2015. The average age of union and non-union workers is 42.3 and 39.2 years, respectively. Older workers comprise a larger proportion of independent contractors (Center for Construction Research and Training (CCRT) 2018). The graying of the American construction workforce poses challenges; industry stakeholders are concerned about identifying, training and maintaining a sufficient number of younger workers. The failure to do so will increase construction costs and lead to delays in the timeliness of projects (Littlehale 2018: 49).

Wages and Working Conditions

Inclusive of craft workers, managers, sales, professionals and administrative support, the average employee earned an hourly wage of $30.62 in April 2019 according to the Bureau of Labor Statistics (Bureau of Labor Statistics 2020a), that is $2.76 more than the average US private sector wage. In 2018, 49.1 percent of wage and salary workers in construction participated in an employer-sponsored health insurance plan, a rate significantly lower than the labor market as a whole. Only 33.7 percent of workers were eligible to participate in an employer-sponsored retirement plan Center for Construction Research and Training (CCRT) 2018(Center for Construction Research and Training (CCRT) 2018). These numbers inflate the incidence of benefits in the construction industry, as they only account for those who are legally 'employees' of a construction company and do not include the millions of independent contractors who work in construction. Most importantly, these numbers do not include the most vulnerable workers in the industry: those who work entirely 'off-the-books.'

The industry-aggregated numbers also mask the differences in benefits by union status. Union construction workers are typically more skilled, earn higher wages and operate in better – and safer – working conditions than their non-union counterparts. Encapsulating hourly wages and benefits – including those legally required of the employer – the total hourly cost of a union construction worker in the US in March 2016 was $56.71; in contrast, non-union total compensation was $31.82 per hour (Center for Construction Research and Training (CCRT) 2018). This is partially attributable to differences in wages, but there are also sizable disparities in benefits coverage. Nearly all workers in the unionized sector have access to health and pension benefits. In contrast, non-union workers – and especially independent contractors – feature substantially lower rates in both categories.

In addition to union status, wage disparities also exist by trade. There are considerable earnings differences between the most populous trades in the US (see Table 11.1). The trades with the highest wages and earnings (electrical, plumbing, operating engineers) involve greater skills and require more training; in the union sector, this manifests itself in longer apprenticeship programs. The trades with the lowest wages and earnings (laborers, painters, roofers) require less skill and serve as a port of entry into the construction industry. Workers in these trades are also particularly vulnerable to being undercut by individuals working 'off-the-books.' The statistics in Table 11.1 – which rely on official government statistics and measure legal employment – likely underrepresent wage and earnings disparities between the trades on job sites across the country.

Health and Safety

Although there have been improvements in safety and health performance over the last decade, construction remains a dangerous industry. It features considerable risk of fatal and non-fatal accidents along with exposure to silica, lead, nanomaterials, microwave radiation and other hazardous substances. US construction had 9.7 fatalities per 100,000 workers in 2015, and featured more deaths on the aggregate than any other industry in the country. US fatality rates are higher than those of most other developed countries (Center for Construction Research and Training (CCRT) 2018). Fatalities are more common among small employers: those with fewer than 20 employees account for 37.5 percent of employment but 57.0 percent of fatalities. In contrast, those with 100 or more employees account for 28.9 percent of employment but 16.7 percent of fatalities (Center for Construction Research and Training (CCRT) 2018).

Non-fatal injury rates declined sharply from 2003 to 2015, from 270 to less than 140 per 10,000 full-time equivalent workers according to the Construction Chart Book (Center for Construction Research and Training(CCRT) 2018). However, construction remains riskier than all major industries except transportation and agriculture. Modest fines and the small number of state and federal inspectors dampen the effectiveness of regulation. Workers' compensation requirements – that employers maintain insurance to remunerate employees when they miss time due to a workplace injury – offers a second policy lever to compel employers to maintain safe workplaces. Insurance premiums are 'experience rated,' tied to the safety history of the employer and attached to the type of construction the firm performs. Reflecting the high rate of injuries and fatalities in construction, on average, workers' compensation accounted for 3.6 percent of total compensation in construction in 2015; this percentage was more than twice as high as manufacturing (1.5 percent) and the national average (1.4 percent).

An Industry Divided

The previous section outlined the structure of the American construction industry, but the idea of a singular industry is misleading. The sector is fragmented by building type (residential/non-residential) and trade (electrical, carpentry, etc.). In some corners of the construction industry, labor and management collaborate to resolve common problems (including worker training), ensure workplace safety, and promote 'high road' workplace practices. The cooperation of organized labor groups and management associations in these areas of construction is unique among American workplaces and is responsible for fostering some of the best workplace practices in the US, especially within blue-collar industries. These best practices include fully and privately funded apprenticeships, high wages and employee benefits, and a shared commitment to worker safety and health that is critical given the inherent dangers of construction work.

These 'high road' workplace practices are typically limited to the signatory sector of the industry. In other parts, construction employers engage in systematic and exploitative labor practices. Contractors pay poverty-level wages, routinely violate labor and employment laws, engage in wage theft, disregard safety and health regulations, and commit tax and payroll fraud. These actions have one goal: to reduce labor costs. As a result, construction is considered an industry of last resort for many, with weak (if any) attachment between employers and employees and a constant churn of workers in and out of the industry that make it difficult to develop and maintain a sustainable and skilled workforce.

The divergence of workplace practices within the industry can largely, but not exclusively, be defined by the *type* of construction in question. The presence of organized labor and 'high road' labor practices are distinguishing characteristics of a sizable portion of the non-residential construction sector. In contrast, the violation of labor and employment laws and other means of worker exploitation have emerged as the defining feature within most residential (and light commercial) trades. It was not always this way. The divergence in labor practices between the residential and non-residential sectors of the American construction industry is largely the result of institutional, legal and economic changes over decades. The next two parts of this chapter will highlight the differences between the residential and non-residential sectors, and what can be learned from the structures of each about cultivating the environment necessary to promote high road labor practices.

Residential Construction

Residential construction starts with homebuilders. These firms are responsible for acquiring land, obtaining permits, designing and constructing new residences, and marketing and selling these homes. The American home building market is fragmented by region and is populated by many small firms. A survey by the National Association of Home Builders indicates that the median homebuilder started just six homes in 2016; 66 percent of its members started ten or fewer (Ford 2017). However, the home building market has consolidated over the last 25 years. Following the approach adopted by Abernathy et al. (2012), we calculate that in 1994 the ten largest homebuilders (by number of homes) accounted for 9.7 percent of new homes sold in the US; in 2017, the ten largest companies were responsible for 27.5 per cent. Some of these large companies have grown by expanding their footprint nationally and, correspondingly, their practices have increasingly influenced the market.

The expansion of large homebuilders has influenced the residential construction market. First, 90 percent of large homebuilders rely on CMs rather than GCs, with some firms developing their own in-house CM units (Abernathy et al. 2012). Second, large homebuilders have amplified the amount of contracting and subcontracting in residential construction. This has enormous implications for labor practices: under federal and most state laws, homebuilders and CMs are not liable for illegal labor practices committed by subcontractors.

The amount of subcontracting in residential construction is staggering. Seventy percent of homebuilders use between eleven and thirty subcontractors to build an average single-family home; larger homebuilders often hire up to forty subcontractors to complete 100–150 separate activities at the home site (Walsh et al. 2013). Beyond the legal ramifications, the decomposition of work into an increasing number of distinct activities – thereby deskilling the work – has been attributable, in part, to the response of homebuilders and contractors to a persistent shortage of skilled labor in the residential sector. This has also led homebuilders to deskill work by increasingly relying on prefabricated housing (Walsh et al. 2013). While some components of homebuilding still require some capital and high-skill components – preparing a site and installing utilities, for example – other areas of residential construction (e.g. drywall, roofing, framing) require far fewer resources and less skilled labor.

The deskilling of work has lowered the barriers to industry entry for both firms and workers. The result is that the residential construction industry is dominated by small employers. Of the more than 511,295 residential construction contractors, the Bureau of Labor Statistics identified in the first quarter of 2017, 88.4 percent had fewer than ten employees; less than one percent had more than fifty workers (Bureau of Labor Statistics 2020b).[3] Low barriers to entry lead to many employers being significantly undercapitalized and struggling to cover operating costs. The competitive pressures on these small firms to win project bids and stay afloat underlies an industry-wide spiral of declining profitability and worsening labor practices. As profit margins are squeezed, contractors have increasingly emphasized finishing jobs quickly – sacrificing craftsmanship – to maximize profits through volume. This has led to a decline in construction quality (Juravich et al. 2015).

The deskilling of work has also lowered barriers to entry for workers. While proven, dependable workers may become crew foremen, the limited skill requirements in some trades make workers quickly replaceable. The replaceability of workers – and the thin profit margins in the residential industry – cause firms not to retain employees during lean times, exacerbating the loose attachment between employers and employees.

These issues shape the residential construction industry. As discussed earlier, the transient nature of the employment relationship causes firms to be reluctant to make training investments lest they subsidize a future worker for their competition. Workers continually search for available opportunities, and are typically unemployed for intervals during the year. Income instability leaves them incapable of funding their own training, but many workers exit the industry altogether when offered more stable employment. Given the lack of training and regular departure of experienced employees, the residential construction sector suffers from a persistent shortage of skilled laborers that has enormous implications for the cost and timeliness of housing construction (Littlehale 2018: 49).

The loose attachment between employers and employees has been exacerbated by declining union presence in the residential industry. Unions represented 50 percent of the residential craft workers in 1950. The post-World War II construction boom and a shortage of skilled craft workers provided a hospitable environment for unions, giving them leverage at the bargaining table. Union influence in residential construction, however, was short lived. Union representation fell below 20 percent in the 1970s and has been declining ever since. Presently, with union density in single digits, the residential sector operates virtually union-free in many locations. The decline in union influence is the result of many factors, including decades-long differences in the economic conditions of the residential and non-residential sectors.

The decline of organized labor in residential construction has put downward pressure on workers' earnings and reduced the viability of multi-employer training opportunities. It has also removed a critical institutional check against exploitative labor practices in the residential sector. While some workers' claims of unfair labor practices are still addressed with the help of local unions, much of this work falls on the shoulders of community social justice organizations. Worker centers and interfaith groups often help aggrieved workers file formal complaints with the US Department of Labor, investigate and pursue adjudication of illegal labor practices, and engage in outreach to raise public awareness of worker exploitation.

To be clear, the residential construction industry in the US is not monolithic. Labor practices vary by trade, with primary differentiating factors being the barriers to worker and firm entry. For example, contractors engaging in site preparation, utility installation or custom home remodeling often have some form of barrier to entry (capital, skill, licensing, etc.) that provides insulation against the downward price pressure of competition and allows for the sustainability of respectable labor practices. But this is a relatively small proportion of the market. In the larger trades that have limited or no barriers to worker or firm entry – such as framing, drywall, roofing – workplace practices are among the very worst in the US.

Reviewing the worst practices of the American residential construction industry may seem out of place in this volume. Their contrast against the *best* practices that have sustained for decades in portions of the non-residential sector – despite operating in the same legal and economic environment – reflects the importance of private sector and public sector institutions in shaping workplace practices in the US. It also reveals how barriers to entry and the economics and legal structures of the American market constrain efforts to promote best practices to all areas of the construction industry.

In the most competitive corners of the residential sector in the US, the ability to win bids – by completing the work at lowest costs – is the deciding factor in a firm's economic survival. As a result, a clear modus operandi has evolved among contractors: reduce labor costs through whatever means necessary. This approach has its economic advantages, as contractors are able to cut corners on labor and save upwards of 30 percent (Ormiston et al. 2019). Given the competitive pressures within some trades, this has made it all but impossible for many 'good' employers to continue to operate in the residential sector.

In order to reduce labor costs, firms in the residential sector follow a standard playbook, incorporating both legal and illegal practices. Among legal avenues, employers keep wages low and fail to offer their workers any supplementary benefits (e.g. health insurance). How low are wages? This answer is elusive. First, most surveys of American workers do not distinguish between those employed in the residential sector vs. the higher-paying non-residential sector. While determining an exact average wage in residential construction is difficult, a survey of 1,194 construction workers on various job sites (not limited to residential) across Texas estimated that 52 percent had wages below the federal poverty line (Worker's Defense Project 2013). Nationally, surveys indicated that eight to 11 percent of all blue-collar construction workers live in poverty (Ormiston et al. 2017). Considering the well-accepted wage differential between sectors, it is reasonable to assume that most of the working poor in the industry work in the residential sector.

While worker surveys do not distinguish between residential and non-residential construction, some surveys of employers do offer this distinction. But results of these surveys are misleading since a substantial portion of the industry operates within the 'underground economy'. Firms operate 'underground' as a means of concealing illegal labor practices that allow them to reduce labor costs to the minimum. A main employer motivation is to avoid legally required taxes and benefits. When a firm hires an 'employee' in the US, companies are taxed as a proportion of the employee's earnings. Those 'contributions' are used to fund state and federal social programs including unemployment insurance, workers' compensation and the employer share of Social Security and Medicare. But these contributions are expensive, and the competitive pressure on labor costs has compelled many contractors to evade these expenses.

An established method of evading employer contributions is to not hire people as employees but rather as independent contractors. Under US labor law, companies are neither required to pay public contributions on payments made to independent contractors, nor are firms required to pay these workers overtime which, under the US law, is 1.5 times the worker's hourly rate. Hiring independent contractors is legal. State and Federal laws, however, differentiate an employee from an independent contractor, and misclassifying workers to evade payroll contributions represents payroll and tax fraud.

The residential construction industry is awash in employee misclassification. Using federally required random audits of state unemployment insurance programs, studies have estimated that misclassification in the broader construction industry – including both residential and non-residential employees – is from 14.8 to 30 percent of the industry's workforce, depending on the state (Donahue et al. 2007; Joint Legislative Audit and Review Commission 2012). These estimates may significantly underrepresent the amount of misclassification. For example, researchers at Local 525 of the Michigan Regional Council of Carpenters conducted a census of drywall installers in southwest Michigan, visiting job sites and talking to workers and crew foremen over the period of several years. They determined that 66 of 71 drywall contractors – 93 percent – misclassified at least half of their workforce (Ormiston et al. 2020). Of the 1,840 workers identified, local 525 estimated that 1,345, or 73 percent, were misclassified. Interestingly though, whereas 93 percent of contractors were deemed to misclassify workers, the percentage of total workers misclassified at 73 percent was substantially less because the region's largest drywall contractor – by a wide margin – was deemed to be operating above board, designating all 200 of its workers as employees.

Misclassification is rampant because it reduces labor costs for contractors, but this amounts to wage theft and its impact is widespread. In one of the few large-sample surveys of residential construction workers in the US, Bernhardt et al. (2009) found that 70.5 percent of workers reported instances where they were not paid overtime. Workers misclassified as independent contractors or 'off-the-books' are also denied access to social programs – such as Social Security, worker's compensation and unemployment insurance – because their employer is not contributing their share of the funds.

Wage theft in the residential construction sector is often more direct. Hiring someone as an independent contractor involves *some* regulatory filings, such as issuing an IRS Form 1099 to the worker. Increasing numbers of contractors avoid government oversight by hiring workers via cash-only, under-the-table payments. This puts workers in a precarious legal position. Contractors, often second- or third-level subcontractors, fail to pay their workers upon completion of a job (Juravich et al. 2015). Many of these subcontractors are informal, transient operations and simply disappear from the local market, leaving workers with no redress. But even when contractors are more established, wage theft and other illegal practices continue unabated as workers are unwilling to file complaints with government authorities. Unauthorized immigrant laborers, a sizable portion of the residential workforce, are especially reluctant for fear that filing a report would alert authorities and put them at risk of deportation.

Reducing labor costs in residential construction goes beyond minimizing contractors' payroll and tax costs. Cost-conscious contractors often do not provide safety training or observe job-site safety regulations. When paired with work crews with limited experience on a construction site, the result is a combination that significantly exacerbates what is already inherently dangerous work. While comprehensive data in the residential subsector of construction are rare, Chapman (2013) has estimated that residential construction had the highest rate of non-fatal injuries of any sector of the US economy. Studies have also demonstrated that union contractors – who operate almost exclusively in the highest risk areas of non-residential construction (factories, highways) – have better safety ratings than non-union contractors, who operate in both residential and non-residential markets.

To appreciate how the desire to minimize labor costs has become embedded into the culture of residential construction, there is one additional, criminal lever that some employers pull: insurance fraud. As stated earlier, employers in most states are required to purchase a workers' compensation insurance policy in the event that one of their workers gets hurt on the site. Policies can be expensive, depending on the injury rates of the trade in question, it can cost a firm anywhere from five to 25 percent of their payroll. Most GCs or CMs will require that all subcontractors working on a job site present a valid certificate of insurance before they can win a project bid and begin work.

Because workers' compensation can represent a substantial part of employers' labor costs, minimizing those costs becomes paramount. A small number of contractors work without a license, while others may present a fraudulent or expired certificate. But the most egregious means of minimizing workers' compensation costs is through the use of shell companies. An individual will create a shell company and purchase a 'bare-bones' workers' compensation policy, representing themselves to an insurance agent as a small company (two to four employees) in a relatively safe construction trade (e.g. drywall installation). That individual will then 'rent' out copies of their certificate of insurance to any interested contractor for a fee below the cost of a legitimate policy, allowing both parties to realize profits. There is a workers' compensation policy in place in case a worker gets hurt on the job, but the insurance ends up paying a worker for whom no premium was collected. A Florida state taskforce, a state particularly hard hit by such schemes, estimated that it cost the State $1 billion in lost workers' compensation premiums annually.

In sum, the development of sustainable labor practices in the American residential construction industry faces two critical challenges for industry stakeholders and government policymakers. First, volatility in demand at the firm level has led to a loose attachment between workers and employers; volatility at the market level has similarly led to a loose attachment between workers and the industry as a whole. This makes training investments unattractive, leaving a perpetual shortage of skilled, experienced laborers. Second, to ensure economic viability in an industry without adequate economic barriers to entry, competition among firms for bids has compelled employers to try and minimize labor costs by any means necessary. Over time and without adequate government intervention, exploitative and illegal labor practices have become embedded in the culture of the industry. This requires a comprehensive overhaul of the employment relationship in the industry.

Signatory Sector

Stakeholders in the construction industry face challenges differentiating them from other sectors in the American economy. The volatility of firm demand necessitates worker movement between employers. Uncertainty about firm and market demand can inhibit employers' and workers' investments in training. Given competitive markets without adequate government involvement, one potential outcome is that of residential construction: a 'race to the bottom' where construction work is often seen as employment of last resort, a series of dead-end jobs that leaves workers vulnerable to illegal and exploitative labor practices.

It does not have to be that way. The volatility of firm and market demand is an inherent characteristic of *all* construction, not just residential. In some corners of the American construction industry – namely non-residential construction – these issues are addressed through the use of collective bargaining. Under a collective bargaining agreement (CBA), a labor union agrees with a contractor organization on the terms and conditions of employment for its members while working for any 'signatory' employer (a firm that signs the contract). This agreement serves as the foundation for the creation of joint labor–management institutions that address collective workplace, functional and strategic issues.

The institutions developed by the CBA help to resolve some of the fundamental issues. For example, the labor problems associated with volatility in demand for an individual firm are mitigated by the use of a 'hiring hall'. In administering the contract, the union plays an active role in coordinating the movement of its members between signatory employers. This minimizes the time and effort for a tradesperson who is unemployed and looking for work, increasing the odds of a regular paycheck and increasing industry attachment. Joint labor–management committees also increase this attachment by administering group health insurance and pension benefits. While these benefits are tied to *individual* employers in nearly every other industry in the US, these programs are funded across all signatory employers via a collectively bargained per-hour contribution for each worker hour on the job. This allows workers to move between firms without disruption in their benefits.

Perhaps the most notable joint labor–management institutions in the signatory sector are the registered apprenticeship programs. Registered apprenticeship programs adhere to government requirements, but are funded through a per-hour deduction shared by employees and employers at a rate determined in the contract. By making training investments a shared, collectively bargained contribution, both firms and workers resolve their respective stumbling blocks to skill development. The primary employer disincentive to fund training in the non-union sector (including residential) is concern that any training investment would be lost if the worker moved to a competing firm. But while workers may still move between firms, an employer can be assured that their portion of the training investment will be recouped because any individual working for them will have participated in the apprenticeship program. Workers, meanwhile, implicitly 'pay' for training by contributing a few cents per hour worked to the apprenticeship program; this absolves them of having to come up with the money upfront.

The signatory sector is composed of 15 international unions, the companies that employ their members, and the array of committees and organizations that carry out the joint labor–management activities. The degree of union membership varies by trade, with higher rates typically among trades requiring higher skill levels or occupational licensing, as well as among workers operating in certain subsectors of the industry and in different regions of the country.[4] As an example, the Construction Chart Book (Center for Construction Research and Training 2018) highlights that 34 to 44 percent of workers operating in the heavy civil/ industrial construction sector were unionized in 2012, far surpassing other subsectors such as residential and light commercial. Further, unionization is typically much stronger within states in the Northeast and Midwest regions of the country.

The counterpart of the international unions are construction employer associations, including the Associated General Contractors (AGC), the National Electrical Contractors Association (NECA), the Mechanical Contractors Association, the Sheet Metal Contractors Association and other smaller associations. The national associations developed from local associations of trade contractors that banded together to bargain more effectively and prevent 'whip-sawing.'[5] Although some associations, such as the AGC, have both signatory and non-signatory members, most only allow signatory contractors to remain members. For the most part, non-union contractors do not belong to employer associations because they do not have to bargain. Where this does happen, employers' associations represent only a small proportion of open shop contractors.

Starting at the local level and moving up to the national organizations, unions and employer associations are surrounded by joint labor– management committees that oversee apprenticeship programs, health insurance programs and pensions programs, and address issues such as safety. At the national level, there are also joint committees for specific industries such as pharmaceuticals and nuclear power. These typically have representation by unions, employers and construction owners, and are intended to discuss broad industry issues and develop industry-specific agreements. There are also jointly administered national agreements, which supersede some parts of local agreements to provide standardized work rules and conditions for large owners, such as industrial firms. The General Presidents' Maintenance Agreement bans work stoppages during the period of a project, aligns holidays across trades, requires the use of union labor, and provides an orderly means of resolving jurisdictional disputes but otherwise adopts local standards for wages and benefits.

Bargaining in construction is, mostly, local by trade. Bargaining involves the local union representing a craft and the counterpart local employer association. Most employer associations bargain with a single craft; local associated general contractors typically bargain separately with the local architectural trades (carpenters, laborers, ironworkers, operating engineers, cement masons and bricklayers). The outcome of bargaining depends on local labor market conditions and the demand for construction services with settlements. The tenor of bargaining depends on local union leaders, who need to balance the demands of their membership against the effect of realizing those demands on the economic position of their signatory companies. Local unions have some control over the availability of union labor by allowing union members from outside the local to work as 'travelers' (i.e. members working away from their home local's jurisdiction). Travelers are an important element in moving craft labor to locations where there are shortages. Once hired for a job, health insurance and pension contributions are credited to their home local.

Bargaining in construction differs from most US bargaining in that contracts are settled over total compensation: wages, healthcare and pensions, as well as the expense of apprenticeship programs and industry funds. These are used to advance signatory industry concerns such as recapturing market share for the signatory sector. They are based on craft hours worked. Once settled, the labor–management committees that oversee each program determine the amount required per craft hour for the program from employer and employees. The final wage rate is the residual after these subtractions. Each of these labor–management committees has equal representation of labor and management; it is only through joint decisions, typically with expert advice for pension and health care, that the amounts needed are determined. What is unique within the US about the structure of bargaining in construction is the centrality of local multi-employer organizations and the explicit joint role of management and labor in making decisions about training, benefits and other functions central to the employment system.

Although larger than residential contractors, non-residential contractors are typically small; craft workers need to move regularly to new projects, often with a new employer. Firms likewise need to regularly recruit craft workers for their current project. Both firms and craft workers face information and public goods problems. The information problem is the lack of knowledge of the skills and professionalism of workers hired onto the project, or the quality of employment offered by the firm. The public goods problem is that as the firm is unable to provide continuous employment: it shares its craft workforce with other contractors. If firms operate entirely on their own, they are unlikely to invest in improving productivity through training when they are not likely to benefit from that improved productivity. Craft workers are also unlikely to have the time or monetary resources to pursue training to improve their productivity and earnings. Similarly, the mobility of craft workers discourages individual firms from providing retirement benefits or healthcare (in the non-signatory sector, firms typically provide neither healthcare nor pension benefits and on those occasions where they do so it results in a commensurate reduction in pay). The development of shared training, healthcare and pension programs within the signatory industry enables employers and unions to share the benefits and costs of these programs as well as establish shared standards and expectations. The sharing of the costs and the returns among signatory employers also supports movement of the craft labor force to areas where it is needed.

The distinction between employee, manager and owner is more fluid in construction than in other industries. The small size of firms provides craft workers with a wide range of responsibilities on the job, allowing them to develop the skills necessary to manage construction projects or even open their own firm. Construction remains one of the few industries in which the foremen are chosen from and remain union members while serving in a management role. It is common for national construction GCs to have current union members among their operative managers to the level of vice president. Many union apprenticeship programs incorporate training to help journeymen start their own firm; senior journeymen often have a sophisticated understanding of the employer side of the business and some pension funds allow for continued participation by small employers. The permeability of the barriers between craft workers and employers has oriented unions toward direct engagement with the decision making and the business of construction than more traditionally class-conscious unions.

The joint labor–management relationship in construction is also strengthened through the use of Taft-Hartley trusts to oversee apprenticeship and benefit programs. The Taft-Hartley Act of 1947 allowed the establishment of joint labor–management trusts to provide health insurance, retirement, training and other purposes of joint concern.[6] The joint trusts mitigate the public goods problem for training and benefits by sharing the costs and gains among the signatory employers. The availability of multi-employer health and pension funds provides for benefits and facilitates ready movement of craft workers between projects and employers. The amounts employers pay to the trusts are determined by craft hours worked for the employer. Large firms with many employed craftworkers pay more than small firms, but make greater use of the shared resource. Management and union trustees, who oversee these trusts, are aware of current conditions in the industry, recognize the capacity of firms to support current programs, and weigh the trade-offs needed to keep the funds solvent and the benefits at sustainable levels.

Joint labor–management relationships are not only contractually mandated; they are fostered and strengthened by the recognition of a common opponent: non-union contractors, often referred to as the 'open shop.' Open shop contractors have provided direct competition to union contractors and workers and have engaged in decades-long efforts to weaken the institutional underpinnings of the signatory sector. At the height of union power in the industry, the strength of construction labor allowed the negotiation of generous collective agreements; when compared to the highly unionized manufacturing industry, average hourly earnings in construction rose from 120 percent of manufacturing earnings in 1960 to 153 percent in 1973.

Unions maintained their dominant role in non-residential construction through the recession of 1979–1982, but the labor movement subsequently declined, partly because of the efforts of the open shop and the broader business community. In response to cost increases, large industrial users undertook a systematic campaign to develop a non-union alternative through the Business Round Table (BRT). Part of the BRT's effort was to encourage its industrial owners to use non-union firms, even if those firms were initially less capable than their union counter- parts (Linder 2000). Areas historically dominated by craft unions, such as the petroleum industry along the Gulf Coast, developed non-union alternatives, particularly for maintenance. Alternatives to union ap- prenticeship programs were also supported, to further reduce industrial users' dependence on craft unions. The effort to reduce the role of the building trades unions was notably successful in the oil and gas regions of Louisiana, where state-wide union membership in construction fell from 29.8 percent in 1983 to 3.9 percent in 2019 (Hirsch and MacPherson 2020).

Union density in construction was also weakened by a series of court decisions in the 1970s, notably *Peter Kiewit Sons' Co., 231 N.L.R.B. 76* (1977). These decisions weakened unions by allowing firms to operate signatory and open shop subsidiaries that maintained an arm's length relationship with union subsidiaries. Given slack construction labor markets from the late 1970s into the mid-1980s, the open-shop side of double-breasted firms was able to recruit substantial numbers of craft workers from the signatory side. As one commentator noted (Flint 1977):

> *By the thousands, union workers* are *putting their cards in their pockets or in their shoes and go to work non-union because that is the only way they can find a job.*

Union density in US construction fell from 39.5 percent in 1973 to 27.5 percent just ten years later. This rate has continued to decline, dropping to 20 percent in 1993 and to 12.6 percent in 2019 (Hirsch and Macpherson 2020).

The member internationals of the North American Building Trades Unions (NABTU) tried to reverse the growth of the open shop with limited success. What emerged in the late 1990s was the 'Value Proposition': unions would work directly not only with employers but also owners to make union construction more attractive than open shop work. This can be summarized in a quote from Sean McGarvey, President of NABTU:

> *Our value proposition is unlike anything that can be found any- where, It is a value proposition that is predicated upon one unpretentious idea: that we can, and do, provide a wide range of services, resources, and manpower that results in bottom-line monetary value for those owners and end-users who choose the path of partnership over the 'low road' path of wage stagnation, exploitation and sub-standard quality outcomes.*

(McGarvey 2013)

This emphasis on value creation has moved the signatory industry toward extensive use of project labor agreements (PLAs), codes of professional conduct for union members, and unions' strategic use of their pension funds to promote union construction, and greater integration between unions and signatory employers.[7] For unions, survival has become directly linked to more effective and deeper-reaching labor–management cooperation.

Training is central to a high productivity industry that provides careers and family-supporting incomes, profits to employers and good quality work to owners. The current US apprenticeship system, overseen and regulated by the Office of Apprenticeship Training of the US Department of Labor, is the source of most skilled craft labor for the signatory sector and, indirectly, much of the open shop. The system, established by the Fitzgerald Act of 1937, has three components: on-the-job training supplemented with substantial formal classroom training, the use of formal indentures (contracts) which codify employment standards for each apprentice, and third-party approval and oversight of the agreement. Other sources for construction training are the US military, community colleges and privately sponsored programs. The military is an important source of craft workers and the signatory and open shop sectors compete for those leaving the military. Community colleges graduate relatively few completely trained workers, many entering apprenticeship programs on graduation. The indenture establishes a wage scale over the course of the apprenticeship, sets the length of apprenticeship, specifies the branch of the trade should the apprentice attain competency, and spells out whether the apprentice is to be paid for 'school time'. The signatory sector has about 250,000 apprentices enrolled at any one time and accounts for approximately 90 percent of the enrollment in registered construction apprenticeships (interview with representative from the US Department of Labor, Bureau of Apprenticeship Training).

Apprenticeship programs are central to maintenance of the skilled workforce of the signatory sector.[8] They are structured to improve the skills of new workers, upgrade the training of journey workers, and introduce craft workers to new technologies. The programs are overseen by national committees with staffs that monitor the training provided by local programs and update their materials and methods regularly. National apprenticeship conferences are used by trades to provide training in teaching and updated methods to instructors who bring these to apprentices and journey workers. There is considerable emphasis on developing instructor skills; a fully qualified apprenticeship trainer in the plumbing and pipe-fitting industry will have completed 200 hours of professional and technical courses over five years. The more sophisticated programs use university faculty to train instructors. The incorporation of digital technologies into construction has necessitated considerable updating of curriculum and training methods over the last two decades.

In addition to training workers on codes of conduct, apprenticeship programs are being used to provide skills needed by workforces involved with project development and site management. For example, the United Association provides 'three-day look ahead' training through which craft workers determine whether they have the supplies, tools and plans required for the next three days of work. Similarly, apprentices and particularly journey workers receive training in managing work crews, skills such as estimating and in establishing their own firm. National apprenticeship conferences increasingly provide forums for discussions between employers and top-level union officials to address shared issues.

In addition to training, compensation is an essential dimension of maintaining a family-supporting lifestyle and economically robust signatory firms. This requires a balance between the generosity of compensation and meeting the competitive pressures from the open shop. The thirty-year decline of the signatory sector has reflected a disjuncture between the rise of open shop construction and the consequent emerging competitive conditions, bargained outcomes and the economic position of firms, both labor and management have become more aware of this balance and bargain with this in mind.

Concern with the economic position of firms is not distant from union and management bargaining agents in construction. Unlike many organized industries, the centrality of projects makes the signatory sector particularly vulnerable to unrealistic settlements. Excessive settlements are quickly translated into fewer winning bids and a loss of market share and employment, particularly in those markets where there is a vigorous open shop. The loss of market share from the 1970s to the 1990s was due to the change in the competitive environment of the signatory sector. Both parties in bargaining tend to be aware of this competitive threat.

This concern has been institutionalized by labor and management. Several international unions and employer associations use the Construction Labor Research Council, a private research organization funded by employer associations, to assess signatory market share and other competitive factors and provide this to labor and management bargainers. This compels the parties to understand their position in the market and set their demands accordingly. Another factor affecting signatory market share are strikes, and their potential effects on owners' views of using signatory contractors. Strikes potentially delay construction and affect costs. The International Brotherhood of Electrical Workers and National Electrical Contractors' Association (NECA) have largely avoided strikes over contract bargaining through the Industry Council of the Electrical Industry. This council, made up of equal numbers of management and union representatives, meets four times annually to hear unresolved bargaining disputes. Locals and employers who participate in the council briefly present their position and information to the council in a semi-public forum. At the end of the day, council members meet and issue a binding decision. There are few strikes in the electrical industry and the reputation of signatory electrical work is excellent. Other internationals, such as the United Association, have adopted similar institutions.

The use of joint labor–management committees to oversee benefit programs advantages the signatory sector in supporting ready movement of labor to potentially distant projects while maintaining benefit coverage. In addition to allowing union members working for multiple employers within a local jurisdiction to accumulate pensions and continue healthcare coverage, union members can travel to projects outside of their local's jurisdiction, find work and receive payments into their home pension and health plans. This enhances the flow of skilled labor nationally and works to the advantage of both workers and employers. Signatory employers are better insured against labor shortages than non-signatory employers.

In order to make signatory construction the preferred method of construction, unions have followed a course of greater engagement with owners, the community and the public sector. One dimension of this has been the negotiation of project labor agreements (PLAs) directly with owners. Both PLAs and community benefit agreements may include terms such as priority access to admission to pre-apprenticeship and apprenticeship programs and other benefits to residents of a community or stakeholders in a school district. Community benefit agreements are more often signed with public bodies such as school boards and place great emphasis on the community benefits. These agreements provide terms which the end users value in return for an agreement to use either union labor or, if open shop firms participate, employ labor under union conditions. PLAs universally provide assurances of adequate craft labor for projects. They may additionally provide favorable changes in union work rules such as flexible starting times, greater freedom in the use of second shifts, or other project-specific advantages. Local labor–management committees often monitor PLA projects and establish informal dispute resolution procedures to address jurisdictional disputes and other matters that might interfere with a project. Ideally, such disputes are resolved without the owner's awareness.

The Boston Harbor Decision of the US Supreme Court (*Building & Construction Trades Council v Associated Builders & Contractors of Mass./R.I. Inc., 1993*) allowed public bodies to sign PLAs in their role as construction owners. Cities, school boards, port authorities and other public authorities have used public construction to provide favored access to apprenticeship programs for the residents of disadvantaged areas.

The Port of San Francisco PLA explicitly provided extensive community oversight of selection into apprenticeships (Garland and Saufi 2002). PLAs have also been used to establish pre-apprenticeship programs for individuals whose skills are insufficient for admission to apprenticeships. School construction PLAs have similarly been used to engage local signatory employers and unions in vocational training programs and provide hands-on experience with craft work. There is considerable enthusiasm in the signatory sector for these programs, as they recruit from a younger labor force and serve to screen those who are recruited.

The signatory sector continues to face serious challenges. Some multi-employer pension funds are underfunded and require Congressional action to allow them to put their fiscal houses in order. The open-shop sector is a fierce competitor that uses its ability to evade labor and employment law to realize substantial cost advantages. While their incidence is less, some of the illegal labor practices described earlier in this paper are not limited to residential construction. In addition, because the open-shop sector lacks an effective training program for construction workers, it poaches a significant number of trained workers from the signatory sector. Many of these workers go on to become crew leaders for the less-skilled open-shop labor force. Likewise, the political and legal arenas remain fraught: lobbying by the open shop has found sympathetic ears among policy makers who seek to dismantle regulations and limit the influence of organized labor. This has resulted in the repeals of several states' prevailing wage laws, reductions in state licensing requirements and limitations placed on the ability of government bodies to use PLAs. Each negatively affects the market position of the signatory sector.

In the terms of the values espoused in this volume, the signatory sector of construction is the dynamic segment of the industry. It is providing the better rewarded jobs that attract the best workers. It has developed the training infrastructure and resources needed to keep up with the rapid change in technology and methods. It offers superior productivity that is sufficient to provide signatory firms reasonable returns to their investment. It features a strong alliance between craft workers, their unions and their employers. This combination of factors has proven sufficiently strong that there are now active efforts by firms and owners in the historically anti-union South and Southwest to involve the signatory sector in the building of that region. Given the broad human resource challenges facing the industry as a whole – an aging labor force, trouble attracting younger workers, issues with pay and compensation, the need to incorporate new technologies, the need to train and then to continuously upgrade employee training, ongoing issues with work hazards and long-term threats to health – the signatory sector provides a clear path to family- and firm-supporting work and a model for firms to adopt in their efforts to survive and prosper. Whether the signatory sector can overcome both the internal and external economic and political forces that work against it remains an open question.

Notes

1 Many of the larger construction firms do not directly hire craft workers, but partner with local firms on projects who handle hiring.
2 Construction Chart Book 2018 Section 15, Chart 15a. Foreign-born workers comprise 24.7 percent of the construction labor force; this includes 15–20 percent who are unauthorized workers. The influx of Hispanic workers may have displaced African-Americans from the construction labor force.
3 Data based on analysis of 'Quarterly Census of Employment and Wages'. Bureau of Labor Statistics, http://www.bls.gov/cew
4 In the US, licensing requirements are established by states. Although most states require licensing for electricians and the pipe trades, this is not universal.
5 Whip-sawing occurs when a single large trade union has contracts with a number of small employers in a locality. The union can then pick a target, threaten a strike against that one employer, get a contract and go on to pick off each successive employer individually. Employer associations guard against this by bargaining together. Their right to lock out employees when unions attempt to whip-saw individual association members has been upheld by the Supreme Court.
6 Taft-Hartley Trust Funds are established through collective bargaining, under Section 302 of the Taft-Hartley Act of 1947. They are administered by boards with equal labor and management representation and are common when a group of employers, usually in the same industry, join with the unions with whom they have bargaining agreements, to establish a multi-employer trust. The trustees of the plans are charged with determining what types of benefits will be included. Payments of these benefits are made from a trust which is funded by employer contributions established through negotiations and through investments (http://www.macoalthtf.org/taft-hartley-trust-funds.html).
7 Pension funds are jointly overseen by labor and management through Taft-Hartley joint funds. The building trades have been moving to strategic use of large pension funds to promote signatory construction through organizations such as the Housing Investment Trust. Investment is regulated by the US Department of Labor, Office of Retirement Security.
8 There are registered construction apprenticeship programs outside of the signatory sector. Some, such as those sponsored by the independent electrical contractors' association are well structured and successful. Others allow employers to pay substandard wages on federal construction projects (Bilginsoy 2005).

References

Abernathy, F., Baker, K., Colton, K., Weil, D., 2012. *Bigger Isn't Necessarily Better: Lessons from the Harvard Home Builder Study*. Lexington Books, Lanham, MD.

Bernhardt, A., Milkman, R., Theodore, N., Heckathorn, D., Auer, M., DeFillipis, J., et al., 2009. *Broken Laws, Unprotected Workers: Violations of Employment and Labor Laws in America's Cities*. Center for Urban Economic Development, University of Illinois Chicago; National Law Employment Law Project; UCLA Institute for Research on Labor and Employment, Los Angeles.

https://cloudfront.escholarship.org/dist/prd/content/qt1vn389nh/qt1vn389nh.pdf?t=nya8ll (accessed 10.02.18.).

Bilginsoy, C., 2005. Wage regulation and training: the impact of state prevailing wage laws on apprenticeship. In: Azari-Rad, H., Philips, P., Prus, M.J. (Eds.), *The Economics of Prevailing Wage Laws*. Ashgate, Aldershot, UK, pp. 149–168.

Building & Construction Trades Council v Associated Builders & Contractors of Mass./R.I. Inc., 507 U.S. 218 1993. https://supreme.justia.com/cases/federal/us/507/218 (accessed 01.05.20.).

Bureau of Economic Analysis 2020. *Industry Economic Accounts Data: GDP by Industry*. https://apps.bea.gov/iTable/iTable.cfm?reqid=56&step=2&isuri=1#reqid=56&step=2&isuri=1 (accessed 16.05.20.).

Bureau of Labor Statistics 2020a. *Quarterly Census of Employment and Wages* www.bls.gov/cew (accessed 16.05.20.).

Bureau of Labor Statistics 2020b. *Current Employment Statistics* www.bls.gov/ces (accessed 16.05.20.).

Center for Construction Research and Training (CCRT), 2018. *The Construction Chart Book: The U.S. Construction Industry and its Workers* (sixth ed.). Center for Construction Research and Training. Washington D.C. https://www.cpwr.com/sites/default/files/publications/The_6th_Edition_Construction_eChart_Book.pdf (accessed 16.05.20.).

Chapman, L. J., 2013. *Literature Review and Environmental Scan for Better Translation of Research to Practice in Residential Construction*. Center to Protect Workers Rights, Silver Spring. https://www.cpwr.com/sites/default/files/publications/residential_construction_r2p_literature_review_chapman.pdf (accessed 15.03.18.).

Cornell Law School Legal Information Institute 2020. 29 CFR part 30 - *Equal Employment Opportunities in Apprenticeship* https://www.law.cornell.edu/cfr/text/29/part-30 (accessed 01.05.20.).

Donahue, L. H., Lamare, J. R., Kotler, F. B., 2007. *The Cost of Worker Misclassification in New York State*. Digital Commons at Cornell University, School of Industrial and Labor Relations, Ithaca, N.Y. http://digitalcommons.ilr.cornell.edu/reports/9 (accessed 16.05.20.).

Flint, J., 1977. Trade unions losing grip on construction *New York Times*, 12 December 1977, page 73, https://www.nytimes.com/1977/12/12/archives/trade-unions-losing-grip-on-construction.html (accessed 16.05.20.).

Ford, C., 2017. *Who are NAHB's builder members?* National Association of Home Builders, 1 May 2017, http://www.nahbclassic.org/generic.aspx?sectionID=734&genericContentID=256985&channelID=311 (accessed 15.09.18.).

Garland, L., Saufi, S., 2002. *Port of Oakland, A Project Labor Agreement Primer*. National Economic Development and Law Center, Oakland.

Hirsch, B.T., MacPherson, D.A., 2020. *Unionstats.com Cambridge*; (accessed 16.05..20).

Joint Legislative Audit and Review Commission, 2012. *Review of Employee Misclassification in Virginia*. http://jlarc.virginia.gov/pdfs/reports/Rpt427.pdf (accessed 15.10.18.).

Juravich, T., Ablavsky, E., Williams, J., 2015. *The Epidemic of Wage Theft in Residential Construction* UMass-Amherst Labor Center Working Paper Series, https://www.umass.edu/lrrc/research/working-papers-series/wage-theft (accessed 10.09.18.).

Linder, M., 2000. *Wars of Attrition, Vietnam, the Business Roundtable and the Decline of Construction Unions.* Fanpihua Press, Iowa City.

Littlehale, S., 2018. *Rebuilding California: The Golden State's Housing Workforce Reckoning.* Smart Cities Prevail, Oakland.

McGarvey, S., 2013. Building trades need to leverage assets, push union value, chief says. Michigan Building and Construction Trades Council The *Building Tradesman Newspaper* http://www.michiganbuildingtrades.org/newspaper/building-trades-need-to-leverage-assets-push-union-value-chief-says (accessed 01.05.20.).

NLRB Peter Kiewit Sons' Co., 231 N.L.R.B. 76, 1977. National Labor Relations Board. https://www.nlrb.gov/cases-decisions/decisions/board-decisions (accessed 16.05.20.).

Ormiston, R., Belman, D., Hinkel, M., 2017. *New York's Prevailing Wage Law: A Cost- Benefit Analysis.* Economic Policy Institute, Washington, D.C. https://www.epi.org/publication/new-yorks-prevailing-wage-law-a-cost-benefit-analysis (accessed 15.05.20.).

Ormiston, R., Belman, D., Brockman, J., Hinkel, M., 2020. Rebuilding residential construction. In: Osterman, P. Ed., *Shifting to the High Road: Job Quality in Low-Wage Industries.* MIT Press.

United States Census Bureau, 2020. *Construction Spending* https://www.census.gov/construction/c30/c30index.html (accessed 14.05.20.).

Walsh, K.D., Sawhney, A., and Bashford, H.H., 2013. *Cycle-Time Contributions of Hyper-Specialization and Time-Gating Strategies in US Residential Construction* http://citeseerx.ist.psu.edu/viewdoc/summary?doi=10.1.1.452.3725 (accessed 15.05.20.).

Workers Defense Project, 2013. *Building a Better Texas: Construction Conditions in the Lone Star State.* http://www.workersdefense.org/Build%20a%20Better%20Texas_FINAL.pdf (accessed 08.11.18.).

12 Conclusion

Geoffrey White, Janet Druker and Dale Belman

This book highlights the contrasts between the more regulated 'high road' approach to labor relations and the informality and challenges that are so often visible. There are marked differences between countries in terms of labor market structure; skills formation and training, the composition of the workforce and the experiences of migrant workers; health and safety and innovation and productivity. Yet international comparisons should not be allowed to disguise the fact that contrasts or tensions are evident within countries as well as between them, shaped by the contextual climate, including prevailing economic pressures.

Subcontracting is universal across all of the countries reviewed and its proliferation has challenged governments as well as workers, trade unions and employers' associations. This volume indicates that for the future, more could be done to regulate and regularize performance, especially by lead businesses – key clients and main contractors – who have a significant role to play in bringing about change.

We conclude by offering a brief summary on key areas.

Skills

In many locations, the construction industry faces problems in recruiting and training adequate numbers of skilled workers and in challenging male-dominated recruitment practices. In general, training opportunities are only available to the formally employed workforce or those progressing into it and outside these arrangements the absence of an effective system of skills formation is clearly problematic.

At its most positive, strong craft traditions with traditional apprenticeships in particular skills (bricklaying, carpentry and joinery, plumbing, electrical work, masonry and painting) have sustained traditional methods of skill formation in conjunction with formal structures for worker representation and collective bargaining. In northern European examples, there are well-established routes for young people into construction work. For instance, in Germany (see Chapter 5) there is a staged process that provides for 19 skill pathways managed via a uniform approach. Each year of training takes the trainee to a higher stage of skill development while a ratio of one trainee to nine skilled workers is seen as the target on site. Some contractors run their own training schemes to ensure a supply of skilled workers. Yet many larger German contractors no longer provide skills training and most training is undertaken by mid-sized firms. In the Scandinavian countries, the system of vocational education and training is an important feature of the 'high road' approach to employment relations. In both Sweden and Denmark, vocational training takes place at the upper secondary level of education, and in both countries the social partners (employers and unions) are heavily involved in education and training standards. Yet the challenge of a widening European Union (EU) labor market has required adaptation from the key industry players.

In the US, there is also a national approach to training, overseen by the Office of Apprenticeship Training of the US Department of Labor. The system has three components: on-the-job training supplemented with substantial formal classroom training, the use of formal indentures (contracts) which codify employment standards for each apprentice and third-party approval and oversight of the agreement. The national apprenticeship system provides a system for standardizing skills and training by occupation and so improving worker mobility. In the unionized or 'signatory' part of the industry, apprenticeship programs must adhere to government regulations and they are funded through a deduction based on an employee's pay at a rate determined in the contract. By making training investments a collectively bargained contribution, both firms and workers resolve their biggest respective stumbling blocks to skill development. The disincentive for employers to fund training is avoided if an employer can be assured that a contribution to the training investment will be recouped because any individual working for them will have participated in the apprenticeship program. The US training system, like the German, emphasizes continuous professional development so that workers' skills are regularly updated to take account of new technologies and working methods. Within the unionized part of the US industry, the construction unions provide a major contribution to skills training and hence trainees are inducted into union codes of conduct. Yet the increasing role of the non-signatory sector undermines training arrangements as well as unionization. In Argentina there is a similar contradiction. Although the main construction trade union, UOCRA, plays a significant role in the training system, the non-registered sector relies on an informal and untrained workforce – or on those who have been trained through the registration system.

In Chapter 6, Ahadzie, Debrah and Ofori offer two interesting exemplars of training for women in Ghana, where the World University Services of Canada supports skills development for young people. They have a specific focus on young women with mentoring and coaching programs for the residential sector. Another project, the Youth Inclusive

Entrepreneurial Development Initiative for Employment, has succeeded in raising the number of young women entrants – as well as young men – to the industry. Yet, in general, training provision in Ghana confronts the challenge that most of the construction workforce is in informal and casual employment. The Council for Technical and Vocational Education and Training, established in 2006, formulates national policies on skills development in both the formal and informal sectors but because of the focus on formal institutions 90 percent of craftsmen – the majority of whom work in the informal economy – are unaware of these programs. Currently the demand for skilled construction workers in Ghana is between 60,000 and 70,000 a year, but the formal technical institutions only produce 900 a year, the shortfall being met by traditional informal systems of apprenticeship.

In other locations there may be little provision for formalized training for site workers and no permanent or ongoing location where skills can be formed. The consequences are illustrated in Brazil (Chapter 4) where employers are reluctant to invest in training, but rely instead on unskilled migrant workers. This fundamental problem has been exacerbated by the fragmentation of the industry through increasing subcontracting and sub-subcontracting. Many of our contributors note that the small size of most subcontracting firms means that they often fail to train, while the main contractors, in absolving themselves from the responsibility for employment on site, have little interest in skill formation and development. In Lebanon, skills needs are met through a migrant workforce so there is little incentive to train construction workers.

Construction may be viewed as an unattractive career option and hence demand for apprenticeships has fallen in many countries, leading to an aging workforce. Within the UK, the growing informality and the breakdown in collective bargaining has been accompanied by the unraveling of construction training and workforce development. A national Construction Industry Training Board, created in 1964, has the responsibility for reproducing and upgrading the industry's workforce. The Board is funded through a levy on employers, calculated on the use of directly employed workers and the engagement of self-employed operatives, to pay for training grants and support trainees (McGurk and Allen 2016). The system has been eroded over time and a major skill shortage is emerging as the workforce ages. Yet there is a commitment by lead businesses to training arrangements and inclusivity on distinctive major projects. A similar fall is found in Australia (see Chapter 3) and for similar reasons to the UK – a decline in the role of large contractors as employers and the inability to train among small- and medium-sized subcontractors. There has also been a decline in the role of the public sector in skills training and instead the use of migrant labor has been seen by employers as the preferred solution.

Elsewhere, training systems vary. In Russia, relevant skills accreditation and a requirement for life-long learning are legally required. The construction industry is highly regulated by law and employers are expected to play a key role in introducing new standards and updating skills. Employees are forbidden to work unless they possess a relevant qualification and all workers, from management down to skilled level, must undergo re-qualification every five years. However, there are continued shortages of skilled labor. Part of this problem results from the decline of labor force planning after the collapse of the old Soviet systems, and employers have relied increasingly on unskilled and unqualified labor. Some employers have sought to remedy this situation by establishing their own training centers but, overall, few companies are interested in investing in training for the future. Again, migrant labor is the cheaper alternative.

Migration

Migrant workers make a key contribution to construction activities in all the countries that are considered in this book. Although circumstances vary significantly between countries, migrants provide the numerical flexibility and the additional skills that sustain bursts of economic activity, at a relatively low cost and with considerable advantages to the receiving economy. Migration takes different forms and the diversity of experience was summed up in a report by the Building and Wood Workers' International stating:

> [t]here are many different types of migrant workers. They can be internal or international, temporary, 'circular' or permanent. They can be posted workers sent abroad for a temporary period by their home employer. They can be workers with valid work permits or workers without the required permits, known as undocumented or irregular migrants Most are economic migrants. Some migrant workers and their families have fled persecution and war, although they may not have official status as political refugees. There are also environmental migrants, who have left areas because of drought and famine Building and Wood Workers' International (BWI) (2013: 3; cited in Buckley et al. 2016: 2).

Insecurity and informality are the defining characteristics of the migrant experience in construction. In Brazil, migrants move from rural to urban areas within the country, finding work in the informal economy, with low pay and insecure conditions. In other cases, migrants cross borders. Kleib, Afiouni and Srour (Chapter 7) point to the numerical importance of migrants from other countries and in particular from Syria – representing as much as three quarters of the construction workforce.

Many are undocumented, poorly paid and vulnerable to employer abuse. The authors highlight the segmented nature of the construction workforce, with Syrian workers, escaping conflict in their own country, paid between a quarter and a half of the equivalent Lebanese worker's wage. Informal working is the norm, safety standards are neglected and union rights exist solely on paper. Insecurity is the defining feature of the experience of migrant workers in Argentina too, but moderated by individual contacts because family and friends from the country of origin are a key resource in opening up job opportunities and the trade union, UOCRA, seeks to provide support. Insecurity is characteristic of Russian construction and here too migrant workers encounter a stratified and segmented labor market in which problems such as absence of holiday pay and non-payment of wages are recurrent problems.

In the cases above, migrant workers operate in the informal economy outside of the scope and influence of the formal structures of collective bargaining, working sometimes as refugees and often as undocumented workers. The situation is rather different for posted workers. In the EU the right to freedom of movement and freedom to work across borders has been accompanied by tensions between those freedoms and the rights of EU member states to create their own national regulation (Arnholtz and Andersen 2018). The arrival of employers and workers who are outside of established institutional arrangements in the host environment may lead to lower pay and poorer conditions for those who are posted, and this calls into question the mutual recognition of national standards of labor regulation. Following European legislation in the form of the Posting of Workers Directive in September 1996, the issue has continued to be a controversial one when workers in the home country have found negotiated terms and conditions undermined by posted workers, as they were in the Lindsey Oil refinery dispute in the UK in 2009 (Barnard 2009). This challenge exists in 'high road' locations too, depending on the nature and type of regulation in place and the responses of social actors. In Chapter 9, Arnholtz and Ibsen show how this has challenged but not fundamentally undermined the Danish 'high road' approach to labor relations, with no discernible impacts on productivity. In Sweden, by contrast, the trade union has had limited success in collective bargaining coverage in its dealings with foreign companies with one consequence being a fall in productivity.

Health and Safety

Workers in the construction industry face an unsafe and unhealthy working environment. Data from industrialized countries, where statistical series are more likely to be compiled, indicate that construction workers are three to four times more likely to die from accidents at work compared to workers in other sectors (Comaru and Werna 2013). Many more suffer from occupational health problems such as musculoskeletal complaints, noise-induced hearing loss, respiratory diseases, the effects of vibration and skin problems from working with hazardous material. In many countries there is also a continuing long-term impact for those working with asbestos. In the developing world, moreover, the risks associated with construction work are three to six times greater than in the developed world, where health and safety laws provide some regulation of the workplace (Comaru and Werna 2013). Endemic subcontracting and fragmentation of work, generating pressures to complete tasks quickly through piecework reward systems, leads to a cavalier disregard for safety. This is borne out by the fact that the most serious accidents have been found to occur among subcontractors (Comaru and Werna 2013). Casual workers are less likely to receive safety training or to have the confidence to challenge unsafe working conditions, compared to directly employed workers.

Some 30 years ago the International Labour Organization published a code of practice (International Labour Office 1992) covering the duties of the various parties to the labor process, including government authorities, employers, self-employed persons, workers, designers and architects/engineers and clients. It is still relevant because it spans a wide range of working conditions on construction sites including risk avoidance, welfare issues, safety training and the reporting of accidents and diseases. Improvements in health and safety are particularly found where there are strong trade unions. As Ladbury et al. (2003: 2) argue, the fundamental issue is not the presence of legal or codified constraints on employers, but rather the need for effective mechanisms to ensure that laws are applied and monitored. Trade unions have a significant role to play in this respect. Government agencies and trade unions typically have limited resources to enforce the law and health and safety standards are higher where there is training, effective monitoring and prevention, rather than simply retribution after the event.

Not surprisingly, the regulation of health and safety is stronger in developed countries and the contrast between the US, Germany, the UK, Denmark/Sweden and Australia with other countries in this volume is clear. Even so, construction workers suffer more than most others from dangerous and unhealthy working conditions. Mortality rates in US construction are higher, at 9.7 fatalities per 100,000 workers, than all other industries except agriculture and mining (see Chapter 11). In contrast, the rate of fatal injuries in manufacturing was less than five per 100,000. Fatalities in construction are also more likely to occur among small employers. In the UK, the fatal injury rate in construction, at 1.6 per 100,000 workers, is around four times the all-industries rate and around 2.6 per cent of workers in construction suffered an injury, which is 50 percent above the all industries rate (Health and Safety Executive 2018). In addition to the risk of death or injury, the health risks have been identified as not just musculoskeletal and work-related disorders, but also mental health issues.

Legislation provides an important mechanism to enforce safe and healthy working environments (Loosemore et al. 2003). The US, for example, has extensive health and safety legislation (The Occupational Safety and Health Act, 1970) and workers can enforce requirements, especially where unions are present. There is an advisory committee on construction safety in the US Department of Labor and specific guidelines for construction site hazards. In the UK, construction workers are covered by both general health and safety at work legislation and specific legislation covering the industry (see Chapter 10) but, even so, despite recent improvement, the industry continues to have the highest number of fatalities and injuries at work of any sector. Trade unions can impact on safety standards, through collective bargaining, through lobbying for improvements to legal standards and through site level organization to ensure that standards are upheld. 'high road' labor practices are closely associated with better standards of health and safety.

An additional policy lever is through workers' compensation insurance. In the US, it is a requirement that employers pay workers' compensation insurance to remunerate employees should they miss time at work due to a workplace injury. This offers an additional pressure on employers to maintain safe workplaces because insurance premiums are 'experience rated' or tied to the safety history of the employer, as well as attached to the type of construction the firm performs (see Chapter 11). In Germany, there is also a dual structure of state safety and health provision on one hand and autonomous accident insurance institutions' requirements on the other. The government (at both Federal and State levels) enacts legislation and provides regulations and the rules of state boards. After examination of these regulations and rules, and with government approval, the accident insurance institutions release their own safety and health prevention rules (EU-OSHA 2019). In Denmark, the Danish Working Environment Authority is responsible for ensuring compliance with occupational health and safety law and has various sanctions which it can use to ensure compliance by employers. In Australia, Safe Work Australia is the national work health and safety policy agency, but workplace health and safety is regulated by States and territories rather than at Federal level. Each State and territory has its own regulatory body and laws.

Looking at the other countries in this book, there are strong variations in health and safety performance, depending on the historical and political context and the level of economic development. In Argentina, the continuing influence of past Peronist corporatist policies has ensured that health and safety laws are in place but the nature of the industry, with many small companies and many informal workers, has made enforcement difficult. The trade union role is fundamental in campaigning for a safer working environment.

In Russia, safety principles and rights are enshrined in the Constitution, the Labor Code and other legislation and there currently exist some two million health and safety requirements for businesses (Chapter 8). Despite this, the official safety statistics indicate that construction has the highest number of fatalities of any industry and the second-highest number of work-related injuries. Occupational safety rules are found in labor law and also in urban planning legislation and among rules on the design, renovation and use of buildings. Norms establishing safety-related obligations can also be found in the technical regulations issued by the Construction Ministry and current legal requirements are detailed in a compendium to guide businesses through implementation. According to this source, all construction enterprises are required to set up a labor protection management system – defining the policy and objectives of the employer and the specific procedures for their achievement. Enterprises employing more than 15 people must employ a safety manager, and a separate safety department is required above 50 employees. Unions hold rights to inspection (whenever their members are present) and are consulted when the site safety management plan is drafted. A union presence coincides with lower accident rates, but disregard for migrants, the most likely victims of safety failures, undermines their achievements. The most significant obstacle to a safety culture in Russia, however, derives from informality in the employment relationship, largely tolerated and exploited by all institutional actors.

The less formalized the working arrangements, the greater the risks in the work environment. In Ghana (Chapter 6), while health and safety on construction sites remains a major concern, it is currently not covered by industry-wide legislation. The high degree of informal working and the absence of worker organization on site make regulation and recording of injuries difficult and many deaths and injuries on these informal sites go unrecorded.

Finally, in common with other Middle Eastern countries, Lebanon (Chapter 7) has little in the way of state regulation of health and safety and the high incidence of informal working by a largely migrant workforce poses huge problems. Trade union organization is weak and hazards threaten the lives of workers on site. There are no specific laws or regulations that mandate companies to follow safe practices, yet the need for them is clear. Lebanese regulations are vague and leave the decision on implementation of safety regulations up to the contractors or the companies involved. Small and medium-size contractors lack the awareness and capacity to develop and apply safety training programs on site, although there is some evidence that larger contractors exhibit a stronger understanding of safety issues.

Innovation

Construction is sometimes characterized as lacking the capacity to innovate through the adoption of new methods or techniques and the complexity and lack of repetition in construction projects makes innovation challenging. This has to be a major cause for concern as the world confronts the challenges of climate emergency. More than 90 per cent of the world's infrastructure projects are either late or over-budget and the industry has the lowest productivity gains of any industry (Economist 2017). Investment is limited both by the small size of firms and by the limits to the leadership that any one firm can exert on the industry. Traditional methods often dominate in both technology and the organization of work, even in the presence of available improvements.

Chapters 3 and 4 point to areas of innovation, including the use of building information modeling (BIM), building design and scheduling, the use of pre-fabrication, task automation and robotization, the use of driver-less machines and combined worker–robotic machines. In other chapters we see that the use of prefabrication at off-site locations continues to grow. Paradoxically though, off-site manufacture transfers part of the building process into the manufacturing sector, so that the gains in overall construction productivity – the time that it takes for a building to be completed – are not reflected in the construction statistics (Chartered Institute of Building 2016). A major global issue is the huge variation in building regulations between countries, so that prefabricated parts may only be usable within a certain jurisdiction. Improvements such as BIM have provided a step in the right direction by supporting digitized staging of the work process and a few firms are mass producing homes through prefabrication, such as BoKlok (a subsidiary of IKEA, the flat pack furniture retailer) in Sweden and Katerra in the US. Interestingly, though, both of these companies use their own labor to erect their buildings and do not subcontract (Economist 2017).

The adoption of these new techniques progresses unevenly, but with more evidence of change within countries with 'high road' labor practices. An educated and skilled workforce has the potential to assimilate changes in technology and in working practices and labor–management partnerships ease workforce concerns. This reflects both the larger gains from improved productivity in these industries and the greater ability to train and further develop the workforce in the needed skills. Where it is not easy to obtain low-cost labor, the substitution of technology and technique is a clear path to improving industry performance and returns. Where low-cost labor is available, by contrast, the gains from investment are less certain and may deter even secure firms from undertaking the needed steps. The reliance on low-skilled labor in Brazil (Chapter 4), for example, undermines the impetus for innovation and constrains improvements in productivity. Indeed, in some developing countries, the potential for job creation generated by labor-intensive work processes may be welcome because of the potential for poverty alleviation.

Advanced training systems in the 'high road' countries facilitate the introduction of technology, techniques and new work organization. Apprenticeship programs and continuous professional development provide a shared means for vendors of technologies to disseminate their advances and be assured that they are used correctly. Changes in methods can be taught systematically and adopted relatively quickly. These same advantages are not available to industries which depend on informal employment relations with little-to-no formal training.

The Role of Clients and Main Contractors

This book carries many accounts of fragmentation and cost imperatives within the construction industry. The ethos of subcontracting is culturally embedded. Yet there are examples of lead businesses – main contractors typically working in close conjunction both with clients and with subcontractors – taking significant responsibility for the working conditions, training arrangements and health and safety standards that are established on their sites.

The client sector is of course segmented, but clients – and especially larger clients – have significant potential to impact on industry standards. Public sector and infrastructure clients such as water or energy companies or airports have the capacity to manage work on a portfolio basis with repeat business facilitating relations with the main or management contractors. Long-term relationships based on mutual trust can be reinforced through continued association and, in this way, partnerships encourage the delivery of best value for the client together with a more regulated approach to employment, to training and to team building. Within complex contractual arrangements, effective lead businesses manage relationships and working practices, ensuring that their initiatives are replicated at every level of the contractual chain, meeting commitments on time and on budget but, in doing so, taking account of the employment practices and social costs of the construction process.

The framework and standards set in the recruitment and management of subcontractors are critical. Clients for projects of international importance may be influenced by the reputational importance and public visibility of their projects and set examples that reflect best practice. This was the case at the 2012 London Olympics (Chapter 10) where standards were set for main contractors and cascaded to subcontractors. Project success in these circumstances is supported by recognition of trade unions, with collective bargaining setting standards on wages and working conditions, health and safety and commitments on diversity and equality of opportunity. Consistent with this approach is the attention given to the community as well as to project success. In the US an emphasis on value within the signatory sector has encouraged the use of project labor agreements. Similarly, community benefit agreements signed with public bodies such as school boards enhance working conditions and union representation at the same time as placing greater emphasis on community benefits. In the real world, exemplar projects will never be perfect – but the standards set enable the industry to move forward. In Brazil, the joint liability accorded by law to main contractors encourages closer attention to both the financial and employment responsibilities of their subcontractors.

The Final Word

The evidence in this volume suggests that skills shortages, limits to productivity gains and poor standards of health and safety should be neither necessary nor inevitable features of the construction sector. Governments, clients of the industry and leading businesses are in strong positions to tackle them. Employee voice is underrepresented and trade unions have a legitimate and important role to play in effecting improvements.

In an international industry of such importance, it is neither an unrealistic proposition to suggest that investment could provide a way forward to revive economic fortunes, nor is it unreasonable to expect that values should be questioned or that working conditions should be improved. The role and responsibilities of all of the parties to the construction process should be in question. Alternative approaches are possible and desirable – to de-risk the industry and to overcome the many disadvantages of current, often dysfunctional, arrangements. Apart from the limitations associated with skill shortages coupled with a gender and racial imbalance in recruitment, low productivity and high levels of health and safety risk, current arrangements entail impediments to team working and high transactional costs associated with extensive subcontracting. Importantly, they are wasteful and inhibit skill-based innovations that encourage sustainability or innovation.

As we confront both climate emergency and economic turbulence it is possible – indeed we would argue it is essential – to seek change in the industry, but it is not possible to unpick what has gone before. The legacies of the past require critical evaluation, and this book goes to press at a time when there is a unique opportunity to scrutinize traditional approaches and to seek alternatives.

References

Arnholtz, J., Andersen, S. K., 2018. Extra-institutional changes under pressure from posting. *British Journal of Industrial Relations* 56 (2) 395–417.

Barnard, C., 2009. British jobs for British workers: The Lindsey Oil Refinery Dispute and the future of local labour clauses in an integrated EU market. *Industrial Law Journal 38* (3). 245–27.

Buckley, M., Zendel, A., Biggar, J., Frederiksen, L., Wells, J., 2016. *Migrant Work and Employment in the Construction Sector.* Sectoral Policies Department, Conditions of Work and Equality Department, Geneva, ILO.

Building and Wood Workers International (BWI), 2013. *Rights Without Frontiers: Organising Migrant Workers in the Global Economy.* BWI. Cited in Buckley et al. 2016:2, Geneva.

Chartered Institute of Building, 2016. *Productivity in Construction: Creating a Framework for the Industry to Thrive.* CIOB, London.

Comaru, F., Werna, E., 2013. *The Health of Workers in Selected Sectors of the Urban Economy: Challenges and Perspectives: Multi Sectoral Approach.* Working Paper WP288 Geneva, International Labour Office, Sectoral Activities Department.

Economist, 2017. Efficiency eludes the construction industry. *The Economist*: 17 August https://www.economist.com/business/2017/08/17/efficiency-eludes-the-construction-industry (accessed 12.04.20.).

EU-OSHA, 2019. *The German System for Safety, the Rules of State Boards.* European Agency for Safety and Health, Bilbao, Spain. https://osha.europa.eu/en/about-eu-osha/national-focal-points/germany#:~:text (accessed 12.04.20.).

Health and Safety Executive, 2018. *Construction Statistics in Great Britain, 2018,* https://www.ons.gov.uk/businessindustryandtrade/constructionindustry/articles/constructionstatistics/2018 (accessed 20.05.19.).

International Labour Office, 1992. *Safety and Health in Construction: a Code of Practice.* ILO, Geneva.

Ladbury, S., Cotton, A., Jennings, M., 2003. *Implementing Labour Standards in Construction: A Sourcebook.* Water, Engineering and Development Centre, Loughborough University, Loughborough.

Loosemore, M., Dainty, A., Lingard, H., 2003. *Human Resource Management in Construction Projects: Strategic and Operational Approaches.* Spon Press, London and New York.

McGurk, P., Allen, M., 2016. *Apprenticeships in England: Impoverished but Laddered.* Institute for Construction Economic Research, Michigan State University, East Lansing.

Index

274 *Index*

Labor Law 138; labor unions
138–9; population 133; real estate
volume 133; unemployment 137
Lendlease 206
literacy and literacy rate (Argentina)
20; Ghana 123
Lithuania 212
London 2012 Olympic Park 217–18,
221, 265
London Underground Jubilee Line
Extension 217
Lula da Silva, Luíz Inácio 23, 66
Luzhkov, Y. 171–2

Macri, Mauricio 18, 23
main contractor responsibility 70,
201, 265
Major Projects Agreement (UK) 220
manslaughter laws (Australia) 42
marginal employment 12
Maritime Union of Australia 41
Master Builders Association (MBA)
(Australia) 40, 42
McGarvey, S. 248
McGrath-Champ, S. 47
Mechanical Contractors Association
(USA) 245
medium-sized establishments 94–5
Meister (master craftsman)
(Germany) 98
Melbourne 36
Menem, Carlos 22
mental health 214
Mercosur 17, 28
micro-enterprises 18
Middle East 8, 133
migrant workers 259–60; Argentina
20–1, 23, 27–8; in Australian
construction industry 47–8; in
Brazilian construction industry 72;
in Danish construction industry
195; in Lebanese construction
industry 137; in Russia 157–8; in
Russian construction industry 169,
173–5; support for 27–9; in
Swedish construction industry 195;
in United Kingdom construction
industry 212
minimum wage 12, 99; Germany 84
Minimum Wage Act (Germany) 91
Ministry of Employment and Labour
Relations (Ghana) 113–14
mortality rates 261

Moscow Institute of Occupational
Safety 171
Moscow system 169
MRV, (Brazil) 60

National Accreditation Board
(Ghana) 113
National Agreement for the
Engineering Construction Industry
(UK) 216, 220
National Apprenticeship Program
(Ghana) 118
National Association of Home
Builders (USA) 237
National Board for Professional and
Technician Examinations
(Ghana) 113
National Building Code (Ghana) 117
National Classification of Economic
Activities (CNAE) (Brazil) 71;
subcontracting 71
National Council for Tertiary
Education (Ghana) 113
National Decent Work Agenda
(*Agência Nacional do Trabalho
Descente*) (Brazil) 66
National Electrical Contractors
Association (NECA) 42, (Australia);
245, 250 (USA)
National Labor Forum (Brazil) 66
National Register of Construction
Specialists (Russia) 168
National TVET Qualifications
Framework for Ghana 119
National Union of Building companies
(NOSTROY) (Russia) 164–5
National Vocational Training Institute
(NVTI) (Ghana) 118, 121–3
neo-liberalism/ neo-liberal
governments 23, 43
New South Wales 35
New Zealand, migrant workers
from 48
Nigeria 105
North American Building Trades
Unions (NABTU) (USA) 248
NOSTROY (Russia) 164–5, 170–1
Novatek 134

occupational health and safety 117,
260–3; in Argentinian construction
industry 26–7; in Lebanese
construction industry 139–40,

Printed in the United States
by Baker & Taylor Publisher Services

Printed in the United States
by Baker & Taylor Publisher Services